Contents

Acknowledgments

We would like to acknowledge and express our appreciation to those people who have assisted us in the production of this book and say thank you very much to editor Dave Cella and his colleagues Lisa Gordon and Maro Asadoorian for their encouragement and support. You are highly valued for your helpful suggestions and friendship.

The contents of the text material for each profession were largely obtained from government sources, especially *Occupational Outlook*, 2007–2008, the Department of Labor. We also obtained information from the organizations representing each profession, as well as various documents through the Internet and selected reports in current journals, magazines, and newspapers. We used some literature from college catalogs and other professional literature.

We do appreciate the contributions of myriad groups of scientists, organizations, and others whose combined efforts provided us with national health objectives for the next 10 years (*Healthy People 2010: Understanding and Improving Health*, Department of Health and Human Services). It reflects the scientific advances of the past 20 years and provides insight into trends and opportunities for improvement in the coming decades.

Last, but certainly not least, we thank the teachers and students whose expressed wishes for this kind of information has propelled us to the *Fifth Edition*. We truly hope that it will satisfy your need for information regarding the various health professions available to you and the challenges that await you.

Please let us know your thoughts and wishes so that we can serve you even better with the next edition.

P. S. Stanfield, Twin Falls, ID
N. A. Cross, Chicago, IL
Y. H. Hui, West Sacramento, CA

Preface

We are pleased to provide you with this expanded and revised *Fifth Edition* of *Introduction to the Health Professions*. We'd like to thank the teachers for their continued use of the book and hope that this edition continues to meet their needs. As you have seen, the health field is very fluid, and in this edition we have tried to include as much new information as space would permit.

We kept the existing two major categories in place with the necessary upgrades and we have made changes as follows.

The first category contains updated information on the following:

- Increased number of individuals who are uninsured and grass roots efforts—cities and states—initiating universal health care for their citizens.
- Policy recommendations by healthcare organizations and consumer groups to expand federally supported healthcare coverage of children.
- Increased demand for healthcare workers because of the change in demographics of the population with a shift to greater numbers above 85 years and fewer numbers in younger age groups resulting in a shortage of healthcare workers.
- Expanded options for supportive living for the aging population including assisted living, community-based and consumer-directed programs.
- Current thinking on Medicare coverage including preventive care and prescription drug coverage.
- Higher costs of health care.

As presented in the previous editions, the changes that have occurred in each profession are modified from the latest *Occupational Outlook* (U.S. Department of Labor, 2007–2008). A brief analysis of the changes in the chapters on health professions is as follows:

The chapters on clinical laboratory technology, dentistry, dietetics, health-related professions, medicine, occupational therapy, optometry, pharmacy, physician assistants, psychology, and respiratory care practitioners (7–8, 10–13, 18–19, 21, 24, and 30) are revised and updated, especially sections on work description, education and legal requirements, employment trends, and earnings. Information has been deleted from some of these chapters because it is no longer applicable.

The chapters on communication impairments, emergency medical services, imaging modalities, miscellaneous technologists and technicians, miscellaneous therapists and assistants, nursing, physical therapy, social workers, and veterinary medicine (9, 14–17, 20, 22–23, 29) have been completely rewritten including the deletion or addition of some para-health professions.

All the chapters pertaining to health information personnel, health services administration, federal and state regulators, and health education (25–28) have been updated according to the latest *Occupational Outlook*, especially information regarding educational and certification requirements, salaries, and anticipated job growth. Other revisions cover the changes in roles and responsibilities in health careers in accordance with changes in healthcare delivery systems. An example is the use of electronic medical records.

The progress of technology and demands of the population reflect the need for more health services and additional training of health workers in many fields. Students will need to upgrade their own education to meet the requirements of the changing scene.

THE HEALTHCARE SYSTEM IN THE UNITED STATES

U.S. HEALH CARE

Key Terms

- Acute infectious disease
- World Health Organization (WHO)
- Socioeconomic status (SES)
- Chronic illness
- Prevention
- Effects of expanded technology

Objectives

After studying this chapter the student should be able to:

1. Discuss the changes in health problems among the U.S. population during this century.

2. Identify expected future developments in the health of the population that will influence the healthcare professional.

3. Name five new medical technology advances in the United States.

4. Identify the role of the government in the expansion of health care.

This fifth edition differs in several respects from the first four editions because of the unfolding events stemming from the attacks on the World Trade Center in New York on September 11, 2001. This event not only altered our personal lives, but also changed our priorities in ways that we could never have anticipated.

Protecting U.S. citizens against physical, biochemical, and nuclear attacks and supporting U.S. military forces has become the number one priority. The United States will need to confront the complex issues regarding healthcare reform as soon as possible. With that premise, we begin the first chapter with a look back at healthcare issues and protocols developed in the last decade of the twentieth century. Much of the material from the fourth edition is still relevant. Updates to the succeeding chapters reflect changes and demographics anticipated for the twenty-first century, including changes in health care and health practitioner career choices.

A Look Back

Since the dawn of recorded history (and undoubtedly before), human beings have suffered sudden and devastating epidemics and diseases. In the United States in the second half of the nineteenth century, the most critical health problems were related to contaminated food and water, inadequate housing, and sewage disposal. A countrywide cholera epidemic and a yellow fever epidemic killed more than 30,000 Americans between 1853 and 1858.

By 1900, improving environmental conditions had brought infectious disease epidemics under control. Cities developed systems for safeguarding the milk, food, and water supply, and health departments began to expand, applying case findings and quarantines with good results. The pendulum of disease had swung away from acute infectious diseases and toward chronic conditions. Pneumonia, tuberculosis, heart disease, enteritis, diarrhea, and accidents were the major conditions requiring treatment in the 1900s.

The most important factor in the decline in mortality during the twentieth century was essential hygiene, supported by home and workplace improvements and attempts to improve the environment. Better hygiene accounts for approximately one-fifth of the reduction in mortality.

Improved nutrition also contributed to the falling death rate by increasing resistance to diseases. Lack of proper food and the resulting malnutrition had been largely responsible for the predominance of infectious diseases. Nutritional status remains a critical factor in a person's response to infectious diseases, especially in young children. According to the World Health Organization (WHO), the best "vaccine" against common diseases is an adequate diet.

With epidemics behind them, the scientific community began working on better surgical techniques, new treatment methods, new tests to facilitate accurate diagnoses, and better treatment of individual diseases. The number of hospitals grew rapidly, and medical schools flourished.

Within a few years, medical care and patterns of disease had totally changed. The arrival of antibiotics in the 1940s signaled the end of the dominance of acute infectious disease and the ascendancy of chronic illnesses such as heart disease, stroke, and cancer as the conditions that account for two-thirds of the deaths in this country. Other conditions that significantly affect the quality of life are arthritis, arteriosclerosis, and blindness.

Medicine must now confront diseases and health problems that are to a large extent the result of environmental influences. Beginning in the 1980s, it became obvious that changed patterns of disease now threaten humanity. For example, acquired immune deficiency syndrome (AIDS), a combination of immune system defect, viral disease, and cancer, is one of the new chronic diseases challenging the medical community. Globalization and international travel increase the risk of exposure to infectious diseases such as avian flu and severe acute respiratory syndrome (SARS). For example, SARS, first reported in 2003 in Asia, spread to North and South America and other parts of Asia within a few months.

A Look Forward

Most diseases we confront today, whether physical or mental, are associated with personal lifestyle choices. Individuals can take responsibility for most of these, such as physical activity, eating habits, smoking, drinking alcoholic beverages, using illicit drugs, practicing personal hygiene, and so forth. Addressing these personal choices is more important for individual health than any measures society as a whole might take to protect itself from hazards and provide safe and essential foods.

The predominance of chronic illness as the major threat to health raises many issues for the future. Chronic illnesses related to genetics, lifestyle, and the environment will require a reexamination of methods of intervention. It is generally accepted that the chronic disease process begins long before the appearance of symptoms. This fact changes the approach to the planning and financing of health care. Since the exact date of the onset of a chronic disease cannot be pinpointed, the focus of treatment should be prevention. Prevention, directly related to major changes in lifestyle and personal habits, cannot be accomplished on a short-term basis. Many habits that accompany disease, such as heavy smoking, overeating, and excessive stress, are behavior patterns that cannot be changed with one-time activities, technology, or lectures.

The role of medical care in preventing sickness and premature death is secondary to that of other influences; yet healthcare funding is based on the premise that medical care plays the major role. The public concept of health is that intervention by the doctor and early discovery of disease will prevent or cure disease, when in fact health is determined mainly by the lifestyles people choose to follow.

Optimal treatment for chronic illness requires health care that is long-term and continuous—at present, health care in the United States is primarily short-term and intermittent. The funding of health care is a major reason for this. Although behavioral and environmental influences are the greatest contributors to poor health, healthcare funding regards surgery and drugs as core responses . Health insurance pays for treatment of acute diseases and for hospitalization, but the current method of financing health services emphasizes payment for specialized services, such as surgery or cardiac care, which reinforces the reliance on short-term, intermittent health care. Improved health care requires a redistribution of resources toward prevention of disease, care of the acutely ill who require immediate treatment, and ongoing care for those with chronic diseases.

It appears likely that disease patterns within the population will undergo other changes, creating new conditions that will require further alterations in service and intervention. Next, we consider the effects of expanded technology on the healthcare field.

Today, organ transplants, laser beam surgery, gene splicing, magnetic resonance imaging (MRI), and computerized axial tomography (CAT) are commonplace procedures. The continuing surge of technological advances is not without problems. Excessive cost remains a factor, one that affects the financial structure of the entire healthcare system. Salaries for the highly specialized personnel who operate the often costly equipment and interpret results can be overwhelming. These increased costs are visible in the form of higher health insurance premiums, costlier hospital stays, higher government payments to the system, and increases in total medical bills. This advanced technology has not only increased medical costs, but also created a social and ethical problem. Funding limits make advanced treatments unavailable to some people. The poor, who may need such treatments desperately, have no access to them.

This incredible growth of technology has affected all health professions. Students entering the health field today recognize that they must excel academically and master technical skills. Less time is spent learning personal, nontechnical aspects of care. This value system is reinforced by professionals, peers, administrators and by the general public. Excellent technical performance has become the standard, at the cost of the personal human touch.

The federal government plays an increasingly influential role in the direction of health care. It dominates the healthcare system by virtue of its expanding monetary support of technology and services, and because it sets the policies for provision of health care. As health services enter the twenty-first century, it becomes apparent that the social philosophy of the twentieth century is obsolete and we are moving toward a philosophy that holds society, through government, responsible for organizing and maintaining adequate health care for all people. Once considered an individual responsibility, health care is now considered a right to which everyone should have access.

In the next chapter, the various categories of health services now provided and maintained by public and private funding are explored. Because there is no single "U.S. Health care System," the many ways in which health care is delivered may prove puzzling. This should not be surprising, given the historical perspective on health services, the diverse subsystems in operation in the United States, and the dynamics of social and technological change.

Summary

HEALTH TRENDS

1. Leading causes of death in the United States in 2005 were heart disease, cancer, cerebrovascular accidents (CVA), chronic obstructive pulmonary disease (COPD), accidents, diabetes mellitus, Alzheimer's disease, pneumonia and flu, chronic kidney disease, and septicemia.

2. Mortality rates in the twentieth century showed a remarkable change: Death rates from infectious diseases declined significantly. Deaths from stroke and heart disease rose to epidemic proportions in the first half of the century but declined dramatically after 1950. Rates of lung and stomach cancer also decreased. Infectious diseases such as

tuberculosis and smallpox, also declined, along with infant and maternal mortality, presumably due to improved hygiene and immunization.

3. By 2005, life expectancy reached its highest level ever. The decline in death rates was especially notable among the young and old. The significant decrease in death rates among the elderly was presumably due to collaboration between medicine and public health in efforts to educate the public, especially about lifestyle changes, including personal hygiene, vaccinations, and social and environmental changes.

4. Approximately one-half of all deaths in the United States in 2005 occurred in people younger than age 75.

5. Over 50% of deaths in the United States are now related to behavior: diet and lifestyle, physical activity, tobacco and alcohol use, illicit use of drugs, motor vehicle accidents, toxic agents, and microbial agents.

6. Role of socioeconomic status (SES) on health: poverty, unemployment, homelessness, lack of education, race, ethnicity, social class, lack of access to care, and women's issues.

7. Regarding homelessness: alcohol and substance abuse problems, lack of education and job skills, unemployment, mental and physical disabilities including chronic mental illness, lack of institutional support for those with severe mental illness, incarceration, and lack of low-cost housing.

8. The most prevalent mental illnesses are anxiety disorders and clinical depression. Direct costs related to medical care and indirect costs in loss of productivity total nearly 200 billion dollars a year in the United States.

Some Health Strategies for the Twenty-First Century

1. In the twenty-first century, strategies to improve health and healthcare access to everyone include the following: (1) create alliances across political boundaries/partnerships; (2) improve data sources to monitor the health of the patient population; (3) create task forces to monitor, report, and design interventions to address SES differences in health; and (4) reduce health disparities between rich and poor.

2. The *Healthy People 2010* initiative (U.S. Department of Health and Human Services) has set objectives to address the issues of the twenty-first century: (1) implement advances in preventive therapies, vaccines, drugs, assistive technologies, and computerized systems; (2) change how medicine is practiced; (3) broaden prevention and the science base. These broad approaches should increase the healthy lifespan and afford health protection, promotion, and prevention.

These objectives will affect all health professionals and change the practice of medicine as we know it.

CATEGORIES OF HEALTH SERVICES

2

Key Terms

- Department of Health and Human Services (DHHS)
- Public Health Service (PHS)
- Health promotion and illness prevention services
- Diagnosis and treatment
- Rehabilitation
- Healthcare facilities
- Managed care organization (MCO)
- Health maintenance organization (HMO)
- Preferred provider organization (PPO)
- Medicare and Medicaid
- Diagnosis related groups (DRGs)
- Informed consent
- Health teams
- Public hospital
- Proprietary hospital
- Ambulatory care
- Mental health services

Objectives

After studying this chapter, the student should be able to:

1. Describe the healthcare functions of private and public facilities, inpatient and outpatient services, military facilities, and volunteer facilities.
2. Explain how healthcare systems are financed.

3. Identify the four major types of health services and their functions.

4. Compare the functions of the two major providers of managed care.

5. Explain the concept of diagnosis related groups.

6. Name the major points of the Patient's Bill of Rights.

7. Describe public health, hospital, ambulatory, and mental health services.

Overview of the U.S. Healthcare System

The U.S. healthcare system is extremely varied. Individual healthcare units, which at times overlap, serve a variety of people based on their economic and social status. Individuals and families receive and buy healthcare services based on what they perceive to be their immediate needs. At the present time, physicians in private practice direct delivery of health care. Health care is primarily financed by personal, nongovernment funds or is paid directly by consumers through private health insurance plans. Local and state governments provide public health services.

The federal government provides very few health services directly, preferring to develop new, improved services by furnishing money to buy the developments it wants to see expanded. With minor exceptions—Veterans Administration and the Indian Health Service—the federal government has no authority to provide direct services. This is a function of the private sector and the states. The federal government is involved, however, in financing research and individual health care for the elderly and indigent (via Medicare and Medicaid).

Congress plays a key role in this federal activity by making laws, allocating funds, and doing investigative work through committees. The most important federal agency concerned with health affairs is the *U.S. Department of Health and Human Services (USDHHS)*. The principal unit within this department is the Public Health Service (PHS), which has eight agencies within its domain: National Institutes of Health (NIH); Substance Abuse and Mental Health Services Administration (SAMHSA); Food and Drug Administration (FDA); Centers for Disease Control and Prevention (CDC); Health Resources and Services Administration (HRSA); Agency for Healthcare Research and Quality (AHRQ); Agency for Toxic Substances and Disease Registry (ATSDR); and the Indian Health Service (IHS). The PHS is described more completely later in this chapter.

A wide variety of healthcare facilities are available. These facilities, the places where persons involved in the healthcare industry work, are broadly summarized in this chapter and are individually detailed in succeeding chapters. This discussion of the numerous healthcare fields should assist students in selecting a career and becoming knowledgeable about their chosen fields.

The healthcare industry is a complex system of remedial, therapeutic, and preventive services. Hospitals, clinics, government and volunteer agencies, healthcare professionals, pharmaceutical and medical equipment manufacturers, and private insurance companies provide these services. The healthcare system offers four broad types of services: health promotion, disease prevention, diagnosis and treatment, and rehabilitation.

Health promotion services help clients reduce the risk of illness, maintain optimal function, and follow healthy lifestyles. These services are provided in a variety of ways and settings. Examples include hospitals that offer consumers prenatal nutrition classes and local health departments that offer selected recipients prenatal nutrition classes plus the foods that satisfy their nutrient requirements (the Women, Infants, and Children [WIC] program). Other classes at both hospitals and health departments promote the general health of women and children. Exercise and aerobic classes offered by city recreation departments, adult education programs, and private or nonprofit gymnasiums encourage consumers to exercise and maintain cardiovascular fitness, thus promoting better health through lifestyle changes.

Illness prevention services offer a wide variety of assistance and activities. Educational efforts aimed at involving consumers in their own care include attention to and recognition of risk factors, environmental changes to reduce the threat of illness, occupational safety measures, and public health education programs and legislation. Preventive measures such as these can reduce the overall costs of health care.

Traditionally the *diagnosis and treatment* of illnesses have been the most heavily used of the healthcare services. Normally people waited until they were ill to seek medical attention. However, recent advances in technology and early diagnostic techniques have greatly improved the diagnosis and treatment capacity of the healthcare delivery system—but the advances have also increased the complexity and price of health care.

Rehabilitation involves the restoration of a person to normal or near normal function after a physical or mental illness, including chemical addiction. These programs take place in many settings: homes, community centers, rehabilitation institutions, hospitals, outpatient settings, and extended care facilities. Rehabilitation is a long process, and both the client and family require extra assistance in adjusting to a chronic disability.

Healthcare Facilities

Expansion of the healthcare system and professional specialization has resulted in an increase in the range and types of healthcare settings. A wide variety of *healthcare facilities* are now available. The range includes inpatient, outpatient, community-based, voluntary, institutional, governmental, hospice, and comprehensive health maintenance agencies.

Clients not requiring hospitalization can find health care in physicians' offices, ambulatory care centers, and outpatient clinics. Immediate care clinics exist as freestanding clinics or inside a pharmacy and are staffed by physicians, nurse practitioners or physician assistants who treat minor acute illnesses such as colds, cuts, or sprains. Although physicians with office practices focus mainly on diagnosis and treatment of specific diseases, many clinics and ambulatory centers offer health education and rehabilitation as well.

Community-based agencies provide health care to people within their defined neighborhoods. Such diverse facilities as day care centers, home health agencies, crisis intervention and drug rehabilitation centers, halfway houses, and various support groups all work in a wide variety of ways to maintain the integrity of the community.

Institutions that provide *inpatient* (persons admitted to a facility for diagnosis, treatment, or rehabilitation) services include hospitals, nursing homes, extended care facilities, and rehabilitation centers. Hospitals are the major agency in the healthcare system. They vary greatly in size, depending on location. A rural hospital may have two dozen beds; a hospital in a large city may have more than a thousand.

Hospitals are either private or public. A private hospital is owned and operated by groups such as churches, businesses, corporations, and physicians. Private hospitals are operated in such a way as to make a profit for their owners. A public hospital is financed and operated by a government agency, either at the local or national level. Such facilities are termed *nonprofit* facilities, and they admit many clients who cannot afford to pay for medical care. Clients in private hospitals have insurance, private funds, or medical assistance to pay for their care. Voluntary hospitals are usually nonprofit and often are owned and operated by religious organizations. Community hospitals are independent, nonprofit corporations consisting of local citizens interested in providing hospital care for their community.

Each branch of the military operates and owns hospitals that provide care and treatment for military personnel and their families. The federal government operates Veterans Administration (VA) and Indian Health Service (IHS) hospitals and clinics. The VA provides health care for veterans of the armed services. The IHS is responsible for providing health services to American Indians and Alaska Natives. The IHS currently provides health services to approximately 1.5 million American Indians and Alaska Natives who belong to more than 557 federally recognized tribes in 35 states.

Every state operates hospitals that offer long-term care, if necessary, for treatment of the mentally ill or retarded. These state hospitals are run by state administrative agencies. At the local level, district hospitals are supported by taxes from those who live in the district. These hospitals are not involved with the governments of cities, states, or counties. County hospitals are run by counties and provide services for the poor and private patients. City hospitals are usually controlled by municipal and county governments. Many city hospitals provide care primarily for the poor.

Healthcare professionals working in such widely different facilities encounter diverse challenges that require them to become knowledgeable in specialized areas and to expand their range of services. The healthcare professional who prefers research may choose to work in primary research institutions such as the NIH and agencies that administer health and welfare programs. Two major agencies are the Veterans Administration Hospitals and the Public Health Service. If you choose to practice in Canada, the Canada Health Care System covers medical care for all residents of Canada.

Managed Care

Managed care organizations (MCOs) were the health insurers of choice in 2000. They were divided primarily into *health maintenance organizations (HMOs)* and *preferred provider organizations (PPOs)*.

Some of the most prominent HMOs included Kaiser Permanente in California, Group Health Association in Washington, DC, and the Medical Care Group of Washington University in St. Louis. An HMO provides basic and supplemental health maintenance and treatment services to enrollees who pay a fixed fee. The range of health services delivered depends on the voluntary contractual agreement between the enrollee and the plan. The focus of HMOs is health maintenance, and these agencies employ a large number of healthcare professionals. People belonging to an HMO must use the agency's designated facilities instead of choosing their own, but the services rendered are all prepaid. The consumer's cost is generally less than in other facilities.

Preferred provider organizations offer another option to the consumer for the delivery of health care. PPOs comprise groups of physicians or a hospital that provides companies with comprehensive health services at a discount. They employ paraprofessionals as needed.

Managed care organizations, such as these, showed robust growth in the early and middle 1990s, but experienced a sudden decline in profits in the late 1990s. By the early 2000's MCOs were again showing a profit. The reasons for the losses vary, but the most prevalent ones included the following:

1. The 1990s saw many privately insured employees changing from fee-for-service plans to HMOs, a one-time shift that could save them 10 to 15 percent on their premiums. By late 1990 the majority of employees had made their transition to HMOs and the large gains in enrollment were over.

2. Physicians started to organize to improve their bargaining power with the MCOs. Consumer groups began lobbying their political representatives in Congress and state legislatures to pass consumer protection laws that would provide more choices. These movements also reduced managed care profits.

3. The Balanced Budget Act of 1997 reduced payments to providers, hospitals, and doctors.

The Consumer and Health Care

As discussed in Chapter 1, U.S. society has come to believe that all people have a right to health care regardless of ethnic, social, or economic background. This belief in the 1940s led to the enactment of the *Medicare* and *Medicaid* programs. These programs, with revisions, continue to provide health care for those who cannot afford it, generally the poor and the elderly. However, with escalating medical costs, payments for services have become *prospective*, which means that the rates for reimbursement to healthcare providers are standardized under federal guidelines. The rates are determined on the basis of 492 *diagnosis related groups (DRGs)*. This policy has advantages and disadvantages. On one hand, if Medicare costs are kept from unreasonable increases, the client may be protected in the right to health care. On the other hand, since an agency is reimbursed only a set amount, regardless of its actual costs, the client's right to health care may be threatened because the facility will be reluctant to provide more expensive tests and procedures and in some cases may not accept the client at all.

The Consumer's Rights

In 1973 the American Hospital Association developed a Patient's Bill of Rights, which lists 12 specific rights of hospitalized patients. This bill, while not a legally binding document, states the responsibilities of the hospital and staff toward the client and his or her family. The major tenets are that the client has the right to:

- Receive information pertaining to diagnosis and treatment
- Receive information on fees for services rendered
- Receive continuity of care
- Refuse diagnosis and treatment procedures
- Enjoy privacy and confidentiality from staff and physicians
- Seek a second opinion
- Change physicians and/or facilities if unsatisfied

One of the patient's most important legal rights is *informed consent*; that is, the physician must obtain permission from the client to perform certain actions or procedures. Informed consent must be obtained before beginning any invasive procedure, administering an experimental drug, or entering the client into any research project. Specific criteria must be adhered to in order for informed consent to be valid. The most important requirements state that the client be rational and competent, or represented by someone who is; and that the consent document must be written in language the client can understand, must delineate all the risks involved, must state that participation is voluntary, and must list the benefits of the procedure and any alternatives to it. The client's right to informed consent affects how the healthcare system delivers care. It usually results in increased costs from extra paperwork and other work, but it is necessary for the consumer's protection, and may reduce a care provider's vulnerability to malpractice suits.

In early 1997, President Bill Clinton appointed an Advisory Commission on consumer protection and quality in the healthcare industry that further refined the Patient's Bill of Rights. Its five care provisions were:

- The right to treatment information
- The right to privacy and dignity
- The right to refuse treatment
- The right to emergency care
- The right to an advocate

Each of these rights contains additional provisions to help the consumer understand their meaning and obtain the best care.

Health Teams

The concept of health teams throughout all types of health services has brought about changes in healthcare delivery. The health team consists of a variety of health personnel, each with a specialized function. The membership of the health team varies in accordance with the needs of the client and his or her family.

There are two general types of health teams, functional and patient-centered. Each varies according to the kind of problem to be solved and may dissolve at any given point and regroup to address other special problems. Team members are usually doctors, nurses, dietitians, therapists, and other direct care providers. *Functional teams*, such as the mental health team or the coronary care team, are formed to take care of specific problems. *Patient-centered teams* include patients and family members who are involved in making healthcare decisions together with their doctor and other healthcare professionals.

Medical technologists, radiologic technologists, and pathologists may form a back-up medical care team for the patient. They are not in close contact with the patient, but deal with specific parts of the patient's care, such as his or her X-rays, blood samples, and cultures.

At the outside edge of the interrelated teams are the people who concentrate on the delivery, the costs, the quality, and the availability of services. This healthcare team is composed of public health agents, hospital administrators, health educators, sanitarians, and others.

People working in the health professions must accept the changing nature of health teams and recognize that the combined skills of many professionals contribute to modern health care.

Healthcare Costs

Some major problems plague the healthcare system in the United States. First, the cost of health care is exorbitant and continues to rise. Health insurance premiums are increasing and may approach double-digit increases in the near future. Hospitals are finding it more difficult to maintain profit margins. In 2005, for example, 25 percent of all community hospitals in the United States received inadequate government reimbursement and hospital costs exceeded the amount reimbursed by Medicare and Medicaid by $25 billion. More hospitals, more doctors (80 percent of whom are specialists), more growth in medical science and healthcare technology, greatly expanded research, and expanded insurance coverage have contributed to this phenomenal rise in costs. Second, health care is fragmented. Patients no longer see a family physician with whom they are familiar, but rather a battery of specialists. This fragmentation is confusing and worrisome for the average consumer. Third, the many technological changes taking place can quickly outdate the knowledge and skills of the health practitioner. Fourth, the elderly population is expanding rapidly, increasing the need for special care and technology for this group. Services provided to the poor and the elderly are inadequate. Last, there is an uneven distribution of health services. Although rural areas and towns usually build small clinics or hospitals, the number of rural health workers is low when compared to the number in cities.

There were 47 million uninsured persons in 2006 including 9 million children, and more than 30 million additional underinsured individuals in the United States. Because healthcare costs must be controlled, the government may have to provide essential coverage to the entire population. People who want more and better care will have to pay for it out of their own pockets through private insurance or employer benefits. It is speculated that many employers and employees may separate employment from health care. The employer will just increase wages or provide a supplementary health benefit. This trend will make the future of managed care even more uncertain. The financing of health care is discussed in Chapter 3.

Public Health Services

The threats to health change over time. As one set of diseases, epidemics, and conditions is brought under control or eliminated, new diseases appear. Public health services previously focused on preventing or mitigating the effects of acute infectious diseases such as smallpox, bubonic plague, typhoid fever, childhood diseases, and other highly lethal maladies. As living conditions changed in the twentieth century, degenerative, debilitative diseases, such as chronic obstructive pulmonary disease (COPD), mental and emotional dysfunction, cancer, arthritis, strokes, and coronary heart disease (CHD) replaced infectious diseases. Practitioners in public health, including researchers, study the nature of new threats and organize public measures to combat them. Since the government is usually involved in the financing and policy-making procedures, the term *public health* has come to include research, assessment, and control measures.

Public health services deal primarily with four aspects of care: identifying diseases that cause health or debility; assessing the causes and methods of transmission; finding ways to control or cure diseases and prevent their spread; and educating the public to apply the findings effectively.

The public health system requires cooperation among federal, state, and local governments. Great changes in the roles played by government agencies have occurred over time, with the most important one being the Social Security Act of 1935. This act established annual grants-in-aid from the federal government to the states, part of whose purpose was to fund full-time local health departments. These grants provided for maternal and child health services and extended the services of local public health departments according to the needs of their communities. They were matching-fund grants, in which the states matched, federal money on a dollar-for-dollar basis.

Six basic functions were established for the Public Health Service between 1935 and 1946, and with few revisions they remain the foundation for public health agencies:

- Vital statistics (the recording, reporting, and publication of births, deaths, and diseases)

- Communicable disease control (any disease, such as sexually transmitted disease, that is transmissible between humans)

- Sanitation of the food, milk, and water supply, as well as public eating establishments

- Laboratory services

- Maternal and child health

- Health education

Services added since the basic functions were established have broadened the scope of the American Public Health Association (APHA) and have vested more power in it. The domain now includes such functions as licensing and accrediting health professionals and health facilities, setting standards for automobile safety devices, and supervising the quality of medical payment programs such as Medicaid. Current major goals are:

- Expansion of services and treatment for poor children

- Health promotion, disease prevention, and health maintenance

- Mental health services, especially at the community level

The student desiring to go into public health must be aware of the political battles that are being waged over the structure of the system. New and changing roles for local, state, and federal public health agencies are apparent. The nation will continue to need public health services and leaders who keep abreast of new research and who have a grasp of modern health problems and solutions from both a preventive and curative standpoint. These persons will also need an understanding of the political system and societal expectations and demands. The student who chooses a public health service career will be in a role that is changing in dynamics while still fulfilling fundamental, long-accepted functions.

Hospitals: Development and Services

The hospital is the key resource and center of the U.S. healthcare system. Hospitals not only deliver primary patient care but also train health personnel, conduct research, and disseminate information to consumers.

Since the turn of the century, hospitals have gradually become the professional heart of all medical practice. Accelerating technological advances and changing societal factors have thrust hospitals into the grasp of big business. Hospitals are the third-largest business in the United States. They employ approximately 75 percent of healthcare personnel, with a collective payroll that accounts for at least 40 percent of the nation's health expenditures. Approximately 60 percent of federal health monies and 40 percent of all state and local health monies go to hospitals.

Hospitals also account for the most pressing of today's healthcare system problems—namely, cost inflation. Challenges faced by hospitals include widespread duplication of services, overemphasis on specialized services and diagnostic tests, and a detached manner of caring for the ill.

The major forces affecting the development of hospitals include the following: (1) advances in medical science, most notably discovery of antiseptic techniques and sterilization processes and the use of anesthesia; (2) advances in medical education, with predominant use of scientific theory and standardization of academic training for physicians; and (3) transformation of nursing into a profession by requiring training in caring for the wounded and ill, cleanliness and sanitation procedures, dietary instruction, and simple organized care. These effective, though simple, procedures were a great boon to hospital growth, as the public began to see hospitals as a safe, effective place to go when they were ill. The fourth major force was the development of specialized technology such as X-rays, blood typing, and electrocardiograms, all of which came into being early in the twentieth century.

Hospitals have not responded quickly to the healthcare needs of an aging population. In the late 1980s they finally began to offer nontraditional services such as outpatient care, home health care, extended care units, and rehabilitation. Hospital resources, however, continue to be concentrated on acute care, short-term, curable, and special cases instead of the chronic, long-term illnesses that most often affect the elderly.

The growth of health insurance (discussed in Chapter 3) and of government's increasing role in the hospital industry has had a substantial impact on hospitals. The federal government has financed hospital construction, regulated the type of construction, financed the provision of care, and set policy for the ways in which hospitals are operated. Since 54 percent of all hospital bills are paid by government programs, federal and state agencies are in a position to exert a great deal of control.

The complex hospital industry is usually categorized three ways: (1) function or type of service provided (e.g., hospitals treating a single disease, such as cancer, or those with multiple specialties, usually teaching hospitals); (2) length of stay (from many short-term, where five days is the average length of stay, to fewer long-term, such as psychiatric or chronic disease hospitals, where stays average four to six months); and (3) ownership or source of financial support—government (or public), proprietary (private for profit), or voluntary and religious (private nonprofit) ownership.

Public hospitals are owned by local, state, or federal agencies. Federally owned hospitals are generally reserved for the military, veterans, Native Americans, or other special groups. State government usually operates chronic long-term hospitals, such as mental institutions. Local government has city, county, or district hospitals that are primarily short-term and staffed by physicians who also have private practices. These types of hospitals in small cities and towns are generally small and function as community healthcare facilities. Public hospitals in major urban areas are large and are staffed by salaried physicians and resident physicians. They take care of the economically deprived and furnish all types of services—from drug abuse treatment to family planning.

Proprietary hospitals are operated for the financial benefit of the persons, partnerships, or corporations that own them. The present trend is toward a buyout of substantial numbers of these smaller hospitals by large investment firms, creating large, for-profit hospital systems. Management contracts are also on the rise, not only in for-profit hospitals but also in community hospitals. Both trends are expected to continue, as will adverse reaction to them, especially in regard to management corporations taking over community-based hospitals. Philosophy, policies, and operation change drastically under management systems—sometimes for the better, at other times with dubious benefit. However, the proliferation of multisystem hospitals (corporation owned, leased, or managed) will probably persist. More than 50 percent of community hospitals are part of a corporate system and the mergers will continue in the twenty-first century.

Ambulatory Healthcare Services

Care that is provided outside of institutional settings is considered ambulatory care, and is the most frequent contact that most people have with the healthcare system. Ambulatory care can be any type of care, from simple and routine to complex and specialized.

Probably the most familiar kind of ambulatory care, and the one that most people receive, is in an office of either a solo or group practice, or in a noninstitutional clinic. The type of service is primary or secondary care, and the principal health practitioners are physicians, dentists, nurses, technicians, therapists, and aides. In ambulatory surgical centers there are anesthesiologists as well. If the community can afford an emergency transportation and immediate care system, paramedics and emergency medical technicians are also part of the ambulatory care network. Emergency advice is furnished from community hot lines and poison control centers. Primary and secondary care is given at neighborhood health centers and migrant health centers. Community mental health centers are manned by psychologists and social workers. Home health services and school health services are staffed by nurses who give both primary and preventive care. Public health services, as discussed previously, include targeted programs such as family planning, immunizations, inspections, screening, maternal and child nutrition, and health care and health education. The health practitioners in these settings are physicians, nurses, dietitians, clinical assistants, and aides. The roster may also include environmental health specialists and sanitarians. Pharmacies are ambulatory care facilities staffed by registered pharmacists who dispense drugs and health education. Optical shops with optometrists and opticians provide vision care, while medical technicians give specialized services in medical laboratories. The federal health system, previously detailed, furnishes all types of ambulatory care, as does the prison system.

Many of the ambulatory care services evolve into large, highly complex organizations. For example, an executive committee may be elected to administer the operation. Designated group members may form a credentials committee to screen prospective members, or a building committee may be established. Large group practices usually have a medical director who is responsible for establishing policies regarding scope and quality of care, as well as personnel practices.

Hospitals are expanding their role to include ambulatory services. They have established fully staffed outpatient facilities and clinics. Hospital outpatient clinics include not only primary care, but also specialties such as ophthalmology, neurology, and endocrine care. Teaching hospitals operate many specialty ambulatory clinics that expose medical students and house staff to a greater variety of experiences. Ambulatory surgery centers and emergency medical services have both expanded, with emergency medicine becoming a specialty for physicians, and regional, hospital-based trauma centers springing up in many communities. Forces are at work within communities throughout the nation to enhance primary and specialized health care for all citizens.

Mental Health Services

Mental health facilities in the United States were developed in the nineteenth century (as was the American Psychiatric Association), but were little more than warehouses for large numbers of poor, homeless, and social misfits. They were state hospitals whose primary purpose, rather than treating the patient, was to protect the public. Creation of the National Institute of Mental Health (NIMH) in 1946, and the development of psychopharmaceuticals in the 1950s, were the major breakthroughs leading to real treatment of mental illnesses. Psychotropic drugs enabled thousands of people to return to their communities and to be treated on an outpatient basis. The community mental health center network, conceived in the late 1960s, discharged residents from institutions back into the community with the development of community mental health centers for providing out patient mental health services. Unfortunately, however, this network failed to care for the deinstitutionalized and there are now fewer hospitals specializing in acute psychiatric illness. As a result, visits to community hospital emergency rooms for acute mental health problems have increased. Many people with severe mental illness have returned to institutions for the chronically mentally ill or live in group homes, halfway houses or nursing homes.

Mental health personnel involved in the delivery of mental health services include psychiatrists, medical doctors (MDs) who make a mental diagnosis, prescribe medications, and may provide psychotherapy; and psychologists, clinical social workers, and psychiatric nurses who have advanced degrees and provide case management and/or psychotherapy. A number of allied health fields have developed in response to the growing needs of the community and the availability of funding. These include school counselors and special education teachers, and others such as art, music, and recreational therapists.

Many problems exist within the mental health system, including a surrounding society that clings to the concept of mental illness as a stigma. Over 44 million Americans suffer from a mental disorder and one out of four suffers from mental illness and substance abuse disorders every year. Mental illness and substance abuse disorders are leading causes of disability and death. Adequate and appropriate treatment for mental illness is difficult at best; funding is low and payment is not easy to get from insurance, especially for long-term treatment. Compared to physical illness, most insurance policies limit the number of days in the hospital and the number of outpatient visits for treating mental illness.

Health Care in the Twenty-First Century

From its humble, unscientific, and often haphazard beginnings to the present multibillion-dollar industry, the U.S. healthcare system has undergone broad and often drastic changes. Its present visibility and highly technical orientation have led to thousands of jobs, created new professions, and provided care to millions of people. It is not without the attendant problems of a giant industry, however, and in the twenty-first century the system must face and solve yet more problems. Since healthcare costs are escalating out of control, the most pressing problem of this century will be to bring health care within the reach of everyone without sacrificing quality—a very large order indeed, and one not likely to go away. American ingenuity will face a difficult challenge in formulating a workable, affordable system for all the people.

Summary

The health status of the U.S. population has improved dramatically in the last 30 years. Improvements have been made in public health measures, socioeconomic status, and medical care, especially in preventive clinical services.

The Balanced Budget Act of 1997 set the directions for the twenty-first century. Some of the most pressing issues in health reform remain to be addressed, however. These include:

- Containing mushrooming healthcare costs—the average cost per person now is $6,700 annually

- Providing health security for the middle class

- Providing coverage for the uninsured

- Mitigating the effects of health spending on the federal budget

Objectives for health care, as set forth in *Healthy People 2010*, are to:

1. Increase the quality and years of healthy life. Babies born in 2003 are expected to live an average of 77.5 years. Healthy life is defined as full range of functional capacity at each stage of the life cycle from infancy to old age. The goals are to (1) increase life expectancy; (2) increase the percentage of persons reporting good, very good, or excellent health; and (3) decrease the total death rate.

2. Through new or improved health policy, eliminate health disparities among segments of the population, including differences that occur by gender, race or ethnicity, education or income, disability, geographic location, or sexual orientation.

PAYING FOR HEALTH SERVICES

Key Terms

- Fringe benefits
- Medical technology
- Magnetic resonance imaging (MRI)
- Fiber optics
- Lasers
- Distributive health care
- National health insurance
- Healthcare financing
- American Medical Association (AMA)
- Third-party payers
- Long-term care (LTC)
- Reimbursement
- Fee-for-service payment

- Capitation
- Managed care
- Health maintenance organization (HMO)
- Blue Cross/Blue Shield
- Preferred provider organization (PPO)
- Managed care organization (MCO)
- Deregulation
- Devolution
- Centers for Medicare & Medicaid Services (CMS)
- Telemedicine

Objectives

After studying this chapter, the student should be able to:

1. Identify the major factors that have influenced healthcare financing.

2. Describe the factors that have affected national health insurance.

3. Explain the different methods of payment: (a) private insurance, (b) third-party payment, (c) Medicare, (d) Medicaid, (e) group insurance, (f) individual insurance, (g) managed care, and (h) fee-for-service payment.

4. Discuss ways insurance systems can be abused.

During the 1980s a radical change occurred in the way health care was financed. The term *managed care* came into common usage and remains a significant aspect of the present evolution. Four major factors changed health care: fear, a shift in the balance of power, an excess of doctors, and a shift in the healthcare setting.

Fears that Medicare would go bankrupt prompted the government into invoking policies intended to bring healthcare costs under control. Tax reductions in 1981 induced huge budget deficits, increasing the possibility that the Medicare trust fund would run out of money by 1990. Medicare's costs have always exceeded budgeted monies. In 1983, Congress passed a prospective payment bill, under which hospitals are paid a set amount for each patient in any of the established disease categories and *diagnosis related groups* (DRGs). This means that the government will not pay beyond the fees set for the identified type of illness, no matter how long the patient stays or what services he or she receives. As a result, Medicare hospital admissions dropped and the length of stays shortened, but Medicare payments continued to rise. In 1984, Congress began to regulate direct Medicare payments to physicians by a resource-based relative value scale for payment and established the Physician Payment Review Commission. In 1988, the Commission replaced the CPR (customary, prevailing, and reasonable) system with a fee schedule that was implemented in 1992 in an effort to control healthcare costs. The current Medicare Physician Fee Schedule requires a 10 percent reduction in physician's fees in 2008 and an additional 5 percent reduction each year for the next 10 years.

A shift in the balance of power between unions and management is another dramatic change that has radically altered health care. The 1980s saw a weakening of union bargaining power and a high unemployment rate. These two factors enabled management to decrease employee benefits. Prior to this time, *fringe benefits*, especially those related to health care, had been escalating with the same intensity as healthcare costs. Employees had come to expect increasing health benefits with each ensuing contract. Now employers were able to restrain costs by requiring employees to pay higher deductibles and copayments. Many companies sought out managed care health plans, which direct patients to the most cost-effective source of care.

The oversupply of physicians has led to competition, reorganization of medical practice, advertising for clients, and increased medical costs. It has been widely assumed that there is a shortage of doctors in the United States. The fact is that there is a growing surplus of doctors. The government directly intervened in medical education more than 30 years ago to ensure that there would be enough physicians to keep up with the demands of Medicare. This was accomplished with grants, scholarships, low-interest or no-interest loans, and other incentives, making access to a medical education easy for qualified individuals. The supply of doctors subsequently increased 57 percent from 1970 to 1990, while the population increased only 30 percent. Medical care has shifted from the hospital into the community because revolutionary advances in medical technology created a new dimension in healthcare delivery. Examples of recent advances are portable, mobile units for diagnosing almost every known disease without hospital admission. Magnetic resonance imaging (MRI), mammography, ultrasound, telemedicine and other technological advances are now available in doctors' offices and outpatient clinics and can even be taken into homes. Freestanding surgical centers and outpatient surgery are thriving, facilitated especially by advances made in fiber optics and lasers. These factors together have led to what is called distributive health care, which is changing the healthcare system as well as creating different ways of paying for health care. This chapter discusses the changing objectives of national health insurance, the content of some health insurance proposals, and who pays for health services.

Access to affordable health care has slowly eroded over recent years, despite government attempts to close the gaps through new programs such as Medicare Advantage Programs, the Health Insurance Portability and Accountability Act (HIPAA), expansion of state Medicaid programs through the 10-year, and the $40 billion state children's health insurance program (SCHIP) implemented in 1997. Despite these efforts, the number of Americans without insurance has increased. The economic downturn in 2001, coupled with rapidly rising insurance premiums, has decreased employer-sponsored health insurance. Since 2001, health insurance premiums have increased 78 percent while wages have increased only 19 percent (Kaiser Commission on Medicaid and the Uninsured). The most important trends that account for deterioration of health coverage are the following:

- Employers eliminating coverage because of escalating costs of premiums or shifting more costs to employees by choosing those plans with the highest out-of-pocket payments.

- Rising premium costs, both for those who buy insurance individually and for those insured through an employer plan. In 2007, the annual premium for a family of four was $12,106 (Kaiser Commission on Medicaid and the Uninsured).

- The trend toward temporary and part-time work, which seldom includes health coverage. In 2006, 11 percent of working Americans had part-time jobs and another 10 percent worked as independent contractors. Most of these positions offered no health coverage.

- Limitations of care covered by HMOs.

- Rising costs of "Medigap" coverage for elderly, leading to substantial underinsurance for those with low incomes.

- A crackdown on illegal immigrants and a reduction in services to legal immigrants. Since July 2006, application and renewal of Medicaid benefits requires proof of citizenship status.

As a result of these trends, lack of insurance and underinsurance are becoming widespread problems.

Changing Objectives of National Health Insurance

The costs of sickness include two principal components: the cost of lost earnings and the cost of medical care. The beginnings of national health insurance early in this century aimed at relieving the economic problems of illness. Income loss remains a concern, but concern has shifted during the twentieth century. Reformers shifted their attention, at the individual level, from lost earnings to medical costs as health insurance became more concerned with healthcare financing than with income maintenance.

Health insurance has become increasingly divorced from public health. Health insurance is now viewed as an instrument of institutional reorganization and cost containment. The enormous increases in the costs of medical care and the general changes in U.S. society have shifted the objectives of insurance away from those originally envisioned.

The health insurance business expanded steadily as it shifted from an economic to a medical emphasis. The desirability of expanding medical services became a reality after World War II, when the federal government began subsidizing hospital construction and medical research. The principal goal of public policy then was to expand medical resources rather than to correct distributional inequities. The government aided the expansion of private insurance companies by excluding employers' contributions to health insurance from taxable income. This effectively encouraged employees to accept wage increases as fringe benefits for health insurance instead of as cash. Private insurance companies, forbidden by antitrust laws to limit fees and rates, found it easier to raise their rates than to pursue cost control.

Government policy and the expansion of the private insurance business eventually resulted in a system of health insurance that channeled a greater proportion of national income into health care without infringing on physicians' autonomy or the prerogative of setting their own fees. Medicare and Medicaid did not change this pattern. The government filled the gaps in the private insurance system and continued to accommodate physicians by not challenging their fee structures. Since physicians were paid based on usual and customary fees, those typically charged in their communities, doctors could raise rates to increase reimbursement. Medicare also paid hospitals based on their costs, which did not encourage cost containment, since higher fees meant more reimbursement.

The United States spends more on health per capita than any other country. Costs have gradually increased since the implementation of Medicare in 1965. In 2004, healthcare expenditures totaled $1.9 trillion. The portion of the gross national product (GNP) attributable to health care increased from 5.9 percent to 14 percent between 1965 and 1997 because of the huge surge in medical, hospital, and nursing home costs during this period. Costs continue to rise because of the complexity of health care and the number of elderly requiring care.

Not all increases in medical costs after World War II could be attributed to the insurance system. Overall growth in technological development, public expectations, and public investment in research all contributed to this trend. Inflationary patterns in medical costs were evident in all industrialized nations. An exception was Great Britain, where the medical budget is set at the national level and must compete with defense, education, and other government programs. This system was rejected, however, in the United States, partly due to the fear of "socialized medicine" but also due in large part to the bitter opposition of the American

Medical Association (AMA) and physicians in private practice who believed a national system would take away their autonomy. As a consequence, calls for a national health plan as a means to counteract the escalating cost of health resources repeatedly died out due to lack of both political and popular support.

In the mid-1970s, the United States entered a new stage in the history of health insurance. Prior to this time, the government had accepted the philosophy of increased investment in health care. The dispute that arose over the extent and control of insurance obscured the fact that fee-for-service payment was no longer appropriate or sufficient for managing medical expenses. As one of the four most inflationary sectors of the economy (energy, food, and housing being the top three), medical care logically became a target of anti-inflation measures.

Attempts to slow the increasing costs of health care included industry-wide wage and price controls initiated in 1971, followed by Medicare policies to slow price increases by doctors and hospitals and decrease the unnecessary use of hospital services. This led to the establishment of Peer Review Organizations that also monitor the quality of services.

Medical costs cause concern because of their magnitude and raise questions about their legitimacy. Studies reveal unnecessary surgery, duplication of technology, excess charges, and other discrepancies as major reasons for loss of confidence in the value of medical services.

The rising costs of medical care are of concern to many institutions, among them unions, corporations, and the federal government. All acknowledge the need for change. Today, health insurance programs seem to be more about cost containment and economic management than about efficiency and social equality.

Healthcare Financing

The largest category of expenditures for health is for hospital care (33 percent). Physicians' services rank second in monies spent for health care, at about 23 percent of the total health service budget; the remaining 45 percent of the health dollar is divided among nursing homes, drugs, and miscellaneous health services.

Most of the financing for health care is through government programs and private health insurance (generally referred to as *third-party payers*). Citizens with private insurance have access to sophisticated medical resources and private physicians who are in charge of their care. However, private insurance premiums have escalated to the point that only those people who are economically secure can afford the cost. Most employers now offer managed care options to their employees, and 15 percent of Medicare recipients are in HMOs. Patient care decisions about an illness are now determined by the organization to which patients subscribe, and are primarily based on cost.

Consumers increasingly complain that their doctors are not in control of their care, and that companies are putting their own bottom line first. Not all managed care is equal. There is a strong movement under way to regulate managed care organizations (MCOs).

Healthcare expenditures fall unevenly on the population. If age 65 is the lower limit for the elderly segment of the population, then this group's expenditures are three times higher than the per capita expenditures for younger people, and the expenditures for those 85 years or older are two times higher than for those 65 to 74 years of age. There is a mismatch between acute and chronic care needs, and between the effects and effectiveness of various long-term care (LTC) policies, as the following examples illustrate. The 15 percent of Medicare beneficiaries who have heart failure account for 45 percent of Medicare spending and the 18 percent with diabetes account for 32 percent of Medicare spending.

Women live an average of eight years longer than men, but are in poorer health. A majority of those older than 65 are women, and women become a greater majority in the 85-years-plus age group. While acute fatal diseases are prevalent among men, women experience a high incidence of chronic conditions and higher rates of institutionalization. Older women have lower incomes from every source. Three-fourths of the elderly who live in poverty are women. This gender difference affects access to health care because Medicare covers only one-third of their expenses. Their socioeconomic status, poverty, widowhood, and care giving are affected to a greater extent by government changes, especially program cutbacks, than are the equivalent factors for men.

The predominant method of physician reimbursement is *fee-for-service payment*. The biggest problem with fee-for-service is the definition of a service and what it includes. More services result in a higher income and can lead to abuse. Capitation, defined as paying the physician a fixed amount per person per unit of time without regard to the volume of services provided, is another mechanism for reimbursement. In capitation, insurance pays the physician a set fee to cover all the services; in fee-for-service insurance pays only for the particular itemized service(s) rendered at a given time. A third method of reimbursement is salary. Salary is used only in organizations where various other incentives are provided to the physician to enhance productivity.

Like physicians, hospitals can be reimbursed through several methods. First is reimbursement for specific services (same as fee-for-service). Second is the capitation method. The hospital may also be reimbursed by the number of days of care. Many hospitals average payments among patients instead of individualizing costs.

Health Insurance Coverage in the United States

An estimated 47 million people in the United States were without insurance coverage in 2006. Of those between 18 and 64 years of age, 19.8 percent did not have health insurance and men were more likely than women to lack health insurance. Lack of coverage is a result of the economic downturn in 2001 in combination with rapid increases in health insurance premiums. Great disparities were seen between ethnic groups and within the general population. For example, only 8.5 percent of Minnesota residents lack coverage compared to 25 percent of Texas residents.

- The Medicaid program insured 38.3 million people, but 13.9 million still had no health insurance.

- The foreign-born population was more likely to be without health insurance than natives—34 percent compared with 13 percent in 2006. In addition, 60 percent of poor immigrants had no health insurance.

- Among the general population, 37 percent of poor full-time workers were uninsured in 2006 and of these, 71 percent were in families with at least one full-time worker and 11 percent in families with a part-time worker. Workers most likely to be uninsured are low-wage workers and those employed in small businesses, service industries, and blue-collar jobs.

- The key factors influencing lack of insurance coverage were age, race, educational attainment, and work experience.

- People aged 18 to 24 years were more likely than other groups to lack coverage in 2006. The elderly, because of Medicare, are at the other extreme (1.5 percent without coverage).

- Hispanics had the highest rate of noncoverage; 40 percent lacked coverage in 2004.

- Among all adults, the likelihood of being uninsured declines as education level rises.

- Part-time workers have a higher noncoverage rate than do full-time workers.

Findings concerning children

- Children ages 12 to 17 are less likely to be insured.

- Some 22 percent of Hispanic children were uninsured in 2006 (42 percent were insured by Medicaid).

- Approximately 44 percent of African American children were insured by Medicaid.

- Roughly 21 percent of Asian/Pacific Islander children were covered by Medicaid.

MEDICARE AND MEDICAID

Medicare and Medicaid are government insurance programs designed to pay for the treatment of disease and medically diagnosed conditions. Historically, they have not included payment for preventive services. Only since January 2005 has Medicare Part B covered the cost of preventive services, including screening for diabetes and cardiovascular disease; breast, colon and prostate cancer screenings; bone density measurements to detect osteoporosis; and certain immunizations.

The Medicare program is a federal insurance program for people aged 65 and older, certain disabled people younger than age 65 and any adult with permanent kidney failure (End-Stage Renal Disease). Patients on Medicare are entitled to the same benefits and care as patients in middle-income families with private insurance. The main difference is that the government pays the hospital bills, instead of the individual or private insurance. The Medicare program is administered by the Centers for Medicare and Medicaid Services (CMS) of the U.S. Department of Health and Human Services (USDHHS).

There are four parts to the Medicare program. Part A is hospital insurance, Part B is medical insurance, Part C is supplemental hospital and medical insurance, and Part D is medication insurance. All have deductibles and coinsurance. For Part A in 2008 the patient must pay the first $1,204 of the hospital bill. Medicare then pays only for the first 60 days of hospitalization, or 20 days of skilled nursing care. Beyond these lengths of stay, the patient is required to pay the total cost. Part B of Medicare requires a monthly premium, which was $96.40 in 2008. It carries a $135 deductible and the patient must pay 20 percent of the approved amount and limited charges above that amount. Part C is supplemental or "Medigap" insurance, known as Medicare Advantage, that must be purchased. Part D, the newest part of Medicare benefits, began in 2006; it requires a monthly premium of $27.93, a deductible of $250, and a 25 percent co-pay.

"Approved amount" does not mean that Medicare will pay what the doctor or facility charges. This refers to the DRGs upon which Medicare bases its payments. Third-party and out-of-pocket payments, which include payments for premiums, deductibles, uncovered services, and coinsurance (supplemental insurance), lower the elderly's standard of living. Low-income elderly spend an average of 32 percent of their annual income for medical care. Medicare Advantage programs offer a wide range of options if the employer joins the federal programs. The beneficiaries can establish a medical savings account, make private arrangements with their own physicians, or receive coverage from a PPO. For the elderly poor, who are unable to afford the premiums, Medicaid is available.

Medicaid is the federal–state cooperative health insurance plan for the indigent. People with incomes below the poverty level established by their state can use this government-sponsored health insurance program. Individual states administer Medicaid programs; states receive matching funds from the federal government to help pay for Medicaid coverage. The matching rate ranges from 50 to 76 percent depending on a state's per capita income; wealthier states receive lower federal matches and poorer states receive higher matches. SCHIP is an expansion of Medicaid coverage for uninsured children from families with incomes above that of Medicaid recipients. Medicaid finances over one third (37 percent) of all births in the United States, nearly half (47 percent) of all nursing home spending, and 61 percent of all publicly funded family planning services.[1] Women and children account for 75 percent of all Medicaid beneficiaries. The majority of Medicaid spending, however, funds long-term care services for the elderly, chronically ill, or disabled. In 2004, 60 percent of Medicaid recipients received Medicaid benefits through managed care. Many private facilities and physicians do not accept these patients because of low reimbursement, a conflicting system of payment, or denial of payment for services already rendered.

MANAGED CARE: HMOS AND PPOS

The term *managed care* refers to a system in which employers and health insurers channel patients to the most cost-effective site of care. An umbrella label, health maintenance organization (HMO), was coined in the 1970s to describe independent plans that offer benefits to an enrolled group of subscribers. The benefits cover hospital, physician, and related auxiliary services. These plans offer benefits with the requirement that both hospital care and physician services are contracted through the HMO. An exact number of such organizations in the United States is difficult to ascertain because of many business changes such as bankruptcy, buyouts, mergers, and so on. However, a rough estimate by various private and government agencies includes 500–600 such organizations.

The major characteristic of an HMO is that it combines medical insurance with a broad range of health services. It must compete with commercial insurers and Blue Cross/Blue Shield. Therefore, it has a strong incentive to operate in a cost-effective, efficient manner. The HMO has been seen as a model for encouraging the regulation of healthcare costs through competition. On average, prepaid group practice is less expensive, for the same benefit package, than is traditional underwriting.

The greatest drawback of the HMO lies in the fact that the enrollee must find a physician within the HMO group for services. This often entails geographic challenges, because HMO group physicians tend to practice in large, metropolitan medical centers. If enrollees go outside the HMO for health care, no benefits are available to them.

The most rapid growth among managed care organizations has been among individual practice associations and preferred provider organizations (PPOs). PPOs may be a group of providers who have voluntarily joined together to render health care on a contractual basis, or a group of providers who have been organized by a payer through contractual arrangement for a particular delivery system. These providers can be hospitals, physicians, other healthcare services, or any combination of these. PPOs are fee-for-service systems, as opposed to HMOs, which are capitated (Insurance pays providers a set fee in advance to cover all required services.) Patients subscribing to a PPO have the freedom to go wherever they want for care, including outside the PPO system. From an economic standpoint, however, the incentive to use PPO contract providers is that they are less expensive. Under a PPO contract, standard fee-for-service charges are generally discounted. These discounts range from 10 to 20 percent for hospital services performed by a physician in a hospital environment. The essential elements of a PPO are these: fee-for-service, contractual arrangement, organization of providers, discounts, free choice, and economic incentives. PPOs are an emerging trend. There are currently about 120 to 130 such healthcare providers in the United States. The majority of these are provider-based, and about 48 percent of them are located in California. It is estimated that, as the healthcare field continues to change, at least 20 percent of the fee-for-service market will be in PPO products.

Medicare is gradually expanding its managed care plan, Medicare Advantage. Enrollment has increased 50 percent since 2003 with 8 million, or 20 percent of those who are eligible participating.

The biggest impact on healthcare delivery caused by the managed care explosion is a substantial reduction in hospital use. As more and more people are covered by managed care plans, incentives to cut hospital use will continue to bring the number of hospital stays down. As this trend continues, it is probable that marginal providers will leave the market and that the remainder will compete based on convenience, price, and quality. Health care has not been deregulated in the strict sense that airlines and financial services have been, but there is little doubt that free-market pricing for health care is achieving the same results.

Implications of Devolution

More information is needed regarding the role and effects of managed care organizations (MCOs) on health and human services. Significant questions exist concerning MCOs and their effects on quality of care and nonprofit community-based support. The growing limitation on consumer choice of health plans and practitioners is producing a rising tide of consumer complaints. Many states are considering limiting the growth of HMOs. Physicians and nurses who find their job opportunities limited by managed care have initiated this move. The rapid shift to managed care also raises concerns about access to care for people with chronic mental illness, substance abusers, and the homeless.

Political issues regarding healthcare funding include the following:

- Partisan struggles in Congress and the White House regarding the fate of Medicare and Medicaid

- Governors and state legislatures intent on budget and tax cuts.

- The enhanced ability of proprietary interests to shape public policy creates changes and uncertainty. Nonprofit community care providers are pitted against powerful for-profit nursing homes and managed care.

Economic factors include a rapid rise in for-profit ownership throughout all sectors of medical care. This means increased profitability for owners and shareholders. In addition, the means of achieving cost containment have become ends in themselves. Political and economic attacks on entitlements make the fate of Medicare and Medicaid and the future of long-term care (LTC) uncertain.

Deregulation is one instrument being used selectively to further goals of the federal government: The Unfunded Mandate Reform Act of 1995 limits federal power to adopt mandates for states, localities, and tribal governments without paying for them. Welfare reform and other domestic policy changes are designed to diminish the federal role in health and welfare programs. The responsibility will instead fall on the states.

Business and provider interests are mediating public policy, so problems of access are likely to increase. Accountability issues arise as federal oversight gives way to oversight that depends on variable state and local data. There is little assurance of consistency or uniformity of policy with deregulation, or *devolution*, as it is sometimes called. Devolution is a term that simply means transfer of power or authority from a central government to local governments, delegation to another entity, or in some cases simplification or elimination. The latter definition does not really apply to healthcare issues.

Devolution raises critical questions about policy regarding health care and long-term care of the aging population. The answers to these questions depend on the fiscal condition of individual states, the rapid growth of managed care, and the way in which LTC services will be integrated into managed care programs. Comparing health outcomes, cost, and quality of LTC under both MCOs and fee-for-service programs raises myriad questions.

Continuing Debate

There is a crisis atmosphere surrounding health care. Some reform must be undertaken because the nation cannot afford to continue on its present path. No doubt there will be adverse consequences and many policy makers fear the outcome for themselves and their constituents. Polls in 2007 indicated continuing discontent with the U.S. healthcare system but no agreement about how to reform it. Many people reported going without medical care—not seeing a doctor when ill, not receiving recommended care, or not taking prescribed medications—because of cost. Other complaints were difficulty obtaining a same-day appointment, and fragmented and inefficient care, including medical record and test delays, and time wasted on paperwork.

The United States is committed to changing its healthcare system. It is the only industrialized nation aside from South Africa that does not provide universal health care, or subsidize the education of medical students. Hospitals are a key element in the debate. Not only do they provide essential services to the poor, such as emergency room, inpatient, and outpatient services, but they are also the major centers for graduate medical education. The major problems include loss of faculty practice revenue, threats to clinical research, and trends related to primary care. Many medical centers are making significant organizational changes, such as merging and downsizing.

In the absence of leadership for healthcare reform at the federal level, states and cities are developing healthcare financing at the local level. Massachusetts was the first state to implement near universal coverage; Maine, Vermont, and California also have plans for providing health coverage for nearly all residents. *Healthy San Francisco* is a health plan for uninsured residents; the plan pays for prescription medications, clinic visits, and hospital stays within San Francisco.[2] In 2007, the *Health Coverage Coalition for the Uninsured* (HCCU), a diverse group of 16 major national organizations proposed policy approaches to expand healthcare coverage for the uninsured. Coalition members include the American Medical Association, the American Public Health Association, the American Hospital Association, U.S. Chamber of Commerce and America's Health Insurance Plans. Proposed policy approaches are: (1) increase enrollment of children in SCHIP, (2) create a new family tax credit to cover the cost of insurance premiums, and (3) offer competitive grants to states to cover costs of expanding coverage.

The obstacles to successful and desirable healthcare reform include market failure, high-cost technology, unnecessary care, defensive medical practices, patient complexity, low productivity, and the general disfavor toward sweeping healthcare reform.

Effect on Healthcare Providers

According to the U.S. Department of Labor's most recent statistics, more than 10 million people, or 1 in 10 working Americans, are employed in health care with 45 percent working in hospitals, 17 percent in nursing or personal care facilities, and 27 percent in offices and clinics. Age demographics are predicted to change in 2020 with a 54 percent increase in those 65 years and older and a 57 percent increase in those 85 years and older with almost no corresponding increase in those in the age range of typical healthcare workers, 18 to 64 years old. Predicted growth of available employment in the healthcare professions is twice that of other professions because of the expected aging population. The vast structural shift in healthcare employment in the 1990s affected all health personnel. Redistribution and retooling affect many of the nontechnical and nonprofessional jobs. Hospitals, the industry's largest employers, are predicted to be up to 50 percent fewer by 2010. Those remaining will likely merge into large associations.

There are some winners in the job redistribution. Demands for primary care physicians (family practitioners), physician assistants and nurses with advanced degrees, such as nurse practitioners or nurse midwives, are increasing. More procedures performed outside of hospitals means jobs for skilled laboratory personnel. President Bush's mandate to require all medical records to be in an electronic format by 2014 is expanding opportunities in computer soft-ware and records management. There is an increased need for many rehabilitation specialties, such as therapists of many kinds, home health workers, and geriatric personnel. Large insurance companies will benefit and expand.

The health field of the future remains full of challenges for health personnel. Other issues are discussed in later chapters. Health care as it is known will not disappear, but may take a very changed form.

References

1. Kaiser Foudation (2007).
2. Chicago Tribune (2007).

LONG-TERM CARE

Key Terms

- Long-term health care
- Voluntary nursing homes
- Government nursing homes
- Proprietary nursing homes
- Skilled nursing facility (SNF)
- Intermediate care facility (ICF)
- Assisted living care
- Continuing care
- Community-based care
- Program of All-Inclusive Care for the Elderly (PACE)
- Community health agencies
- Home health agency (HHA)
- Meals on Wheels
- Hospice
- Primary care centers
- Mental health centers
- Shelter care
- The old-old
- The young-old
- Geriatrics
- Shift in the population by age
- The oldest-old
- Frail elderly
- Clinical pharmacology
- Nutrition
- Social services
- Multidisciplinary and interdisciplinary activities
- Optimum potential
- Self-directed services

Objectives

After studying this chapter, the student should be able to:

1. Differentiate between skilled nursing and intermediate care facilities.

2. Describe the services provided by assisted living facilities.

3. Describe the services provided by each of these agencies: (a) home health, (b) hospice, (c) primary care, (d) mental health, and (e) shelter care homes and workshops.

4. Identify the healthcare requirements of long-term care agencies in the twenty-first century.

5. Explain the shifts that must occur in training personnel to care for long-term care patients.

6. Discuss future trends in long-term health care including community-based care.

7. Name four deterrents to progress in long-term care reform.

The aging of the population is a challenge to the U.S. healthcare system. The older population has the greatest incidence of disability and chronic diseases and needs substantially more healthcare services than younger populations. The care of those who are older or disabled is inadequate in the United States, creating a growing burden and many inequities in access to health care. In 2004, life expectancy was 80.4 years for women and 75.2 years for men. Individuals who are 65 now can expect to live to age 83.7 and those who are 85 now can expect to live to age 91.8.

Long-term health care is defined as the help needed by people of any age who are unable to care for themselves because of physical and/or mental impairment. As the term implies, this care is for extended periods, ranging from months to years to a lifetime. An estimated 1.4 million people resided in nearly 16,000 nursing homes in the United States in 2007 with more than half of them 85 years of age or older.[1]

People tend to regard long-term care as being only for the aged, but the fact is that there are more impaired children and adults younger than 65 years of age than there are elderly impaired. However, with the dramatic increase in the population older than age 65, and especially those older than age 80, the need for long-term care is increasing and costs are escalating. Cost containment is a major issue that the aging population is addressing with vigor. (This is discussed at length in Chapter 3.) Adequate personnel needed to provide long-term care is another critical health issue.

While families, friends, and neighbors may be able to help the disabled, family units have become smaller over the years and most able people are working. Frequently, no one is around to take care of the disabled or elderly who cannot cope with the tasks of daily living. For some of these people, community-based services are an alternative to institutional care, but for many others such services are not enough. These individuals include the vast numbers of chronically and/or mentally ill, the frail elderly, impaired children, and the permanently disabled.

Long-term care facilities include more than just nursing homes, although these account for around 70 percent of care provided in long-term facilities. Other long-term care establishments include psychiatric and mental retardation hospitals, chronic disease hospitals, tuberculosis hospitals, and rehabilitation hospitals. Types of long-term care within the system are assisted living facilities, home health services, community and neighborhood health centers, shelter homes and workshops, and hospice programs.

Since the population 65 years of age and older will continue to increase rapidly through the year 2020 and beyond, this chapter focuses on the need for various health services for the elderly, as well as the need for qualified practitioners to carry out these services. The discussion covers nursing homes, community-based health services such as home health agencies and hospices, personnel needs, and trends in the needs for long-term care.

Nursing Homes

Nursing homes originated with county poor houses (alms-houses). They were first established in the nineteenth century to care for the poor and provide food, shelter, and clothing. Over time, they became community dumps for castoff unfortunates. The conditions in these places were atrocious. Society gets what it pays for; many accounts of starving, beating, and murder erupted from time to time, creating scandals. This prompted states to set up regulations governing nursing home care, but most states were unwilling to close the proprietary or voluntary nursing homes because they would then be responsible for the occupants. Instead, they chose to look the other way.

In the twenty-first century, nursing homes that have developed under other sponsorship such as church groups, fraternal organizations, and volunteer groups are proliferating. Many such organizations have started homes to care for their members. It is widely acknowledged that the quality of service in these types of nursing homes is high. The shortcomings of government and proprietary nursing homes continue, however, as do periodic reports of scandal. Homes that cheat patients, physically and mentally abuse patients, neglect care, provide inadequate medical and nursing care, or are firetraps frequently make the news. To make matters worse, the number of people who need good long-term care is growing, and the available beds are insufficient.

Of the available nursing home beds, the proprietary sector clearly led in number, commanding 70 to 80 percent of the market until the late 1990s. The poor and chronically ill who needed nursing home care the most were at the bottom of the list for proprietary nursing homes. Many of these homes also restricted the types of patients they would admit, preferring not to have persons who required a great amount of care or who might damage the property. Long waiting lists for admission of Medicare/Medicaid patients resulted from these restrictions, prompting Congress to enact legislation to construct nonprofit nursing homes. With the rising costs of nursing home care, most of the private paying patients needed to convert to Medicaid as soon as their funds were depleted. Medicare/Medicaid patients are now welcomed at most proprietary institutions.

With the advent of Medicare and Medicaid came federal stipulations governing eligibility. There are now two types of recognized homes: *skilled nursing facilities* and *intermediate care facilities.* A skilled nursing facility (SNF) is a nursing home that provides the level of care closest to hospital care. Twenty-four hour nursing services, medical supervision, rehabilitation, physical therapy, pharmacy and dietetic services, and occupational and recreational therapy are provided in accordance with federal guidelines. Skilled homes are for convalescents and patients with long-term illnesses. They must be recertified every 100 days.

An *intermediate care facility* (ICF) provides less extensive care and services. People in intermediate facilities usually need daily personal care because they are not able to care for themselves or live alone, but they do not need 24-hour care. While nursing care is provided, it does not need to be around the clock. The emphasis in an ICF is on personal care and social services. Some also employ rehabilitative and occupational therapists. These homes must meet federal guidelines to receive government funding. Many general hospitals also have extended care, skilled nursing units within their facilities. With fewer acute care beds occupied, the units can generate income that allows the hospital to remain open.

Assisted living facilities are home to 1 million elderly adults in one of 33,000 facilities in the United States. Residents or their families typically pay the cost, but, Medicaid finances care for 12 percent. Adults eligible for assisted living are those who require assistance with activities of daily living (ADLs) including dressing, bathing, eating or using the bathroom but do not require 24-hour care or medical care. Assisted living may be part of a retirement community, nursing home, senior housing complex, or a stand-alone facility. Licensing requirements vary by state and are known by different names such as residential care, board and care, congregate care, and personal care. Some assisted living facilities are part of a retirement community, known as a continuing care community that allows residents to move from independent living, to assisted living, to a skilled nursing facility as their needs change.

The Omnibus Budget Reconciliation Act of 1987 (OBRA 87) was enacted in response to concerns about the poor quality of care and inadequate regulation in nursing homes in the United States. A change brought about by OBRA 87 required Medicare and Medicaid standards and certification procedures regarding long-term care facilities to merge and intermediate-care facilities standards were upgraded to correspond to those for skilled care facilities. The federal government, through the Centers for Medicare and Medicaid Services (CMS), is responsible for nursing home standards while individual states are responsible for monitoring facilities to assure that standards are met. A new requirement for state surveys of facilities stated that surveys were to be unannounced and include resident interviews and direct observation. The OBRA 87 created minimum standards of care, including staffing requirements and rights for residents. These standards emphasized quality of life issues; and prevention of abuse, mistreatment and neglect, including use of physical and chemical restraints. Rights of residents included the following:

- freedom from abuse, mistreatment, and neglect;

- freedom from physical restraints;

- right to privacy;

- accommodation of medical, physical, psychological, and social needs;

- participation in resident and family groups;

- treatment with dignity;
- exercise of self-determination;
- free communication;
- participation in the review of one's care plan;
- advance notice regarding any changes in care, treatment, or change of status in the facility, and
- ability to voice grievances without discrimination or reprisal.

In the 20 years since OBRA 87, there have been some improvements in the quality of care for residents, but there continue to be problems.[1] An ongoing problem in LTC is the shortage of certified nursing assistants, which is associated with a low level of training and a high level of job turnover, ranging from 70 to over 100 percent turnover in one year.[2] Low wages, lack of benefits, and difficult working conditions account for much of the high staff turnover. [3]

Many of the elderly who make up 85 percent of the population of nursing homes would not need this type of care if more long-term services were available in the community. Community-based long-term care services should continue to grow as the government liberalizes its policies for alternatives to nursing homes. Another reason for the growth of community services is the fact that most people and their families prefer to avoid institutionalization whenever possible.

Community Services

Findings of an NIH committee on personnel needs to address health concerns of the elderly clearly established that the older population would require expansion of a wide range of health services, including preventive, primary, long-term, hospice, and rehabilitative care. Expanded services can help many older people maintain functional independence and remain at home for longer periods. If recent rates of chronic disability and use of health care are maintained, consumer demands for a greater number and variety of health services will more than double by 2020. A wide range of well-educated health personnel, ranging from aides to medical specialists, will be required to respond to these diverse needs. More options are now available for meeting long-term care needs of the elderly who prefer living at home. Examples are home care and community care funded by both Medicare and Medicaid and by private foundations.

The Nursing Home Diversion Modernization Grants Program was included in the reauthorization of the Older Americans Act signed by President Bush in October 2006. A total of $5.7 million in federal funds was awarded to 12 states to provide more choices, including community-based care, for individuals at high risk for nursing home placement.

There are 7 million low-income disabled or elderly Americans eligible for both Medicare and Medicaid. Coordination of care is difficult because Medicare is run by the federal government and Medicaid by individual states. Healthcare costs for these individuals are twice that of other adults on Medicare and eight times higher than children on Medicaid.

For example, the Wisconsin Partnership Program is a dual capitated Medicare/Medicaid program that allows coordination of care much like the PACE program described below.[4]

The *Program of All-Inclusive Care for the Elderly* (PACE) provides comprehensive preventive, primary, acute and long-term care services so older individuals with chronic care needs can continue living in the community. The PACE model of care began in the 1970s in the Chinatown-North Beach area of San Francisco to meet long-term care needs of elderly immigrants. PACE has expanded to 48 sites in urban and rural areas across the United States.   Services include adult day care with physical, occupational and recreational therapy, nutrition counseling, personal care, social services, meals, and medical care. As needs change, participants may receive home, hospital, or nursing home care. PACE programs receive Medicare and Medicaid capitation payments. PACE is available to individuals 55 years of age or older who are certified by their state to need nursing home care but are able to live safely in the community. (http://www.cms.hhs.gov/PACE/)

More research is needed before definite conclusions can be drawn about the effect that liberalized, expanded, community-based long-term care services will have on health costs. The critical issue is not whether these expanded services are less costly than institutional care, but rather how they should be organized to provide maximum efficiency for the increasing numbers of people requiring them.

Community Health Agencies

HOME HEALTH

Home health agencies (HHAs) provide part-time nursing and medical care in patients' homes, as well as other services such as physical, speech, and occupational therapy; social services; and sometimes medical supplies and equipment such as wheelchairs, walkers, and so forth. Homemaker services may also be part of the package. Physicians, physician assistants and nurse practitioners provide medical care at home. The agency may be independently operated, managed by a public health department, or hospital-operated. Patient fees, government grants, private insurance, or Medicare and Medicaid may finance agency services. Variations of HHAs include the well-known Visiting Nurse Association, which most often employs Public Health Service (PHS) nurses. These nurses go to patients' homes and change dressings, give injections, and request other types of services as needed.

A new development in home and community based care is consumer-directed or self-directed home care where the consumer rather than an agency is responsible for hiring home care workers. The federal CMS, under the *Real Choice System Change* and *Independence Plus* grants, has provided funds to assist states in implementing these programs. (http://www.cms.hhs.gov/RealChoice/ and http://www.cms.hhs.gov/IndependencePlus/)

Meals on Wheels is another HHA variation. This agency supplies one hot meal a day (usually lunch) to shut-ins. It may also add a snack for dinner to go along with other foods the patient may have in the house. Patients on therapeutic diets for special conditions can be accommodated. Contracts are made with various agencies, usually hospitals, to provide the meals, which are typically delivered by volunteers.

HOSPICE

In 1967, the hospice movement was resurrected from its beginnings during the medieval era in England. Whereas the first hospices cared for the wounded, sick, and dying, modern hospices care only for the dying. Hospices are operated on the principle that the dying have special needs and wants that hospital personnel are too busy to handle. Hospice care helps manage pain and other symptoms associated with dying when conventional treatment is no longer of value. It allows the dying to spend their last days in their homes among people who are sensitive to their needs and wishes. Hospice seeks to improve the quality of the last days of life. Most hospices offer only home services, though some have added bed care facilities, since they are more likely to be funded by Medicare—this funding comes not as a humanitarian measure, but as an effort to reduce the cost of hospital inpatient care for the terminally ill. The addition of Medicare hospice benefits will achieve significant cost savings as well as serve the needs of the terminally ill elderly more appropriately and humanely.

The U.S. Department of Health and Human Services (USDHHS) funds primary care centers and mental healthcare centers in underserved rural and urban areas and the U.S. Department of Housing and Urban Development provides supportive housing, such as shelters, for the homeless with disabilities, primarily those with severe mental illness, or chronic problems with alcohol or drug abuse.

PRIMARY CARE CENTERS

The U.S. Department of Health and Human Services (USDHHS) funds primary care centers and mental healthcare centers in underserved rural and urban areas and the U.S. Department of Housing and Urban Development provides supportive housing, such as shelters, for the homeless with disabilities, primarily those with severe mental illness, or chronic problems with alcohol or drug abuse.

Community primary care centers provide a limited range of services and focus on primary care. They are expanding rapidly, especially in rural areas, where there is difficulty attracting and retaining health professionals. Usually these centers have one or two family practitioners, a dentist, some nutrition services, some pharmacy services, and perhaps social services. Because the centers are usually in depressed areas, financing by fees is a big problem. The long-term survival of these centers depends on attaining financial stability and retaining professional personnel.

MENTAL HEALTH CENTERS

Community mental health centers were greatly enhanced by the development and subsequent improvement of psychotropic drugs, a movement that began in the 1950s. As local health departments began to report successful treatment outside of institutions, federal legislation was enacted for construction of community mental health centers. They were also provided staffing, conversion, and distress grants. The centers provide inpatient, outpatient, and day care, as well as emergency services. They are required to provide specialized services for the mental health of children and the elderly, and special prevention, treatment, and rehabilitation programs for alcoholics, drug abusers, and drug addicts. The decline of federal monies for local services has affected the comprehensiveness of the centers' services and even the survival of many of them in the places they are needed most—impoverished areas.

SHELTER CARE

Both shelter care homes and sheltered workshops are available to long-term care recipients. If a person needs only to be maintained so that he or she receives the basics—food, shelter, clothing, companionship—and has no major physical problems that require nursing care, then a carefully chosen shelter home may be sufficient. Since 1984 there have been federal regulations in effect that govern shelter home operations. These include, but are not limited to, an adequate balanced diet, acceptable sanitation and safety features, and some consulting services from professionals.

Sheltered workshops exist for the physically and mentally challenged. These are places where the person can learn a repetitive skill and be sheltered from the normal work world. The work and production schedules are not geared to commercial output. The capabilities of the worker are taken into account.

Personnel Needs

It is projected that the population 65 years and older will increase from 35 million to 87 million between 2000 and 2050[5] compared to an increase of less than 1 percent per year for younger persons. The 85-plus segment (the "old-old") will also experience rapid growth from 4 million in 2000 to 21 million in 2050.[5] While only 4 percent of the 65-plus population lived in nursing homes in 2003, the percentages increased dramatically with age, ranging from 1 percent of persons between 65 and 74 years of age, to 5 percent of persons between 75 and 84 years of age, and 17 percent of persons 85 years and older.

If recent rates of chronic disability and health care use continue, consumer demands will more than double by 2020. Requirements for personnel specifically prepared to serve older people will greatly exceed the current supply. Healthcare practitioners will routinely serve older people in the future as part of their regular duties. This care will make up approximately one-third to two-thirds of the workload of physicians and other healthcare personnel.

Although attention to aging and geriatrics has expanded in recent years, most health education programs give little emphasis to these issues. Greatly expanded training programs are required to prepare personnel to provide services in homes, hospices, nursing homes, and other community settings. Financing of geriatric education has come from many sources, including state and local public and private funds and federal programs. Nationwide data are not available as to the extent of this funding.

Personnel needs to ensure adequacy and availability of health care for older persons should be monitored and modifications made in healthcare delivery and financing as needed. To provide responsive care to older persons, greater emphasis on the special needs and conditions of older persons should be included in the education of all health and human service personnel. This education should include skill in the priority services for high-risk groups as well as knowledge of cultural differences. Government funding sources at all levels should support ongoing study and research into the special psychological and physiological characteristics of the elderly.

Demographic Trends and Projections

The staggering statistics of the aging U.S. population emphasize the trend that will occur in future health care as well as concerns regarding how and where that care will be delivered. By the mid-twenty-first century, because of the rapidly increasing population older than age 65, the number of elderly individuals will triple. U.S. Census Bureau projections predict a doubling of the older population between 2010 and 2030 with aging of the Baby Boomers. (65+ in the United States 2005, U.S. Census Bureau.) Between 2000 and 2040 the number of older adults with disabilities requiring long-term care is predicted to double from 10 million to 21 million.[6] The need for LTC (home and nursing home care) and the associated costs will increase tenfold. All of this will put extraordinary demands on the LTC system.

Unrelenting issues of healthcare costs and access, gaps in private insurance protection, negligible LTC insurance coverage, and quality of care for the elderly are all problematic. Though driven by slower growth in spending for hospital care, physician and clinician services, home and nursing home care, Medicare spending nonetheless reached $342 billion in 2005, growing 9.3 percent compared to 10.3 percent in 2004. Out-of-pocket expenses for the elderly continue to increase. Medicare currently covers less than one-half of their health care. Older women pay as much as 42 percent of their annual income for medical expenses not covered by Medicare.

Healthy People 2010 profiled the American people for the year 2000 as follows. In 2000, the overall population grew to 281.4 million people. The population is older. The 35 million people older than age 65 represented about 12 percent of the population. The population of the "oldest-old" (75 to 84 years of age) increased by about 23 percent to a total of 2.3 million.

In 2000, racial and ethnic compositions also differed. Whites represented 77.1 percent. Hispanics increased from 8 to 12.5 percent, or more than 35.8 million. Blacks increased from 12.4 to 12.9 percent. Other groups, including Native Americans, Alaska Natives, and Asians, increased from 3.5 to 4.4 percent of the population. The entry rate of these groups into the workforce was higher than that for whites. Women of all ethnic and racial groups accounted for 47 percent of the workforce. White men accounted for only 25 percent.

By 2000, the American population was predicted, with immigration, to increase by 6 million people. Cities and states on the east and west coasts received the largest number of immigrants. Such data are crucial to decisions regarding health and healthcare programs for the future.

Potential Healthcare Needs

Future healthcare needs will depend in large part on the health and functional status of the growing elderly population. The potential needs discussed here may assist students in determining where future personnel needs might be greatest and how they might best serve in health care.

In the future, the majority of older individuals are likely to be healthy and able to function independently. More than 90 percent of elderly people continue to live in the community, and more than two-thirds of them perceive their health to be good to excellent.

Chronic diseases, arising from both emotional and physical causes, will be the most important of the future disabilities. Chronic disease, which is managed rather than cured, will require continuing services from physicians and other healthcare personnel. Most adults develop one or more chronic health problems. These conditions range from relatively minor to very severe. The minor problems require little care from others, but the severe ones require increasing amounts of care and professional help. Chronic conditions tend to be cumulative, so the elderly, especially the old-old, often experience multiple problems and require a substantial amount of services.

The most prevalent chronic conditions in 2004 among the noninstitutionalized elderly were, in order of prevalence, arthritis, heart disease, diabetes, lung disease, visual impairment, dementia, and hearing impairment. Most chronic conditions tend to increase markedly after 75 years of age, especially visual and hearing impairment and dementia, with dementia present in 30.5 percent of those between 74 and 84 years of age and in 96.1 percent of those 85 years and older.

Mental impairments have serious impact on the functioning of many elderly. These include acute and chronic mental illness, mental retardation, and reactive psychological distress, the most debilitating being depression and schizophrenia. Epidemiological studies indicate that up to 28 percent of the elderly have significant psychiatric symptoms. Depression is more common in those who also have a physical disability. Mental impairment also affects how well the individual handles whatever physical problems there may be, and whether he or she can remain in the community or must be institutionalized. The prevalence of mental impairment increases with age, with an increasing incidence of the dementias. Increased longevity among already impaired individuals, such as the mentally retarded, will contribute to the greater number of persons with all types of mental impairments in the years to come.

Dental needs among the elderly are often serious, especially since Medicare does not include dental care. More than 80 percent of the elderly living in the community experience dental problems. As people live longer, the prevalence of nonlethal disability may increase.

The most debilitating conditions producing functional impairment among the healthy elderly are dementia, stroke, and hip fractures. Those 85 years of age or older are 3 times more likely to have dementia and 10 to 15 times more likely to have a hip fracture than someone 60 to 65 years of age. The number of hip fractures could be as many as 4 million cases annually by 2020. Dementia is also expected to increase from 2.5 million to more than 5 million cases by 2020. In recent years, the old-old have been the fastest growing segment of the population. Furthermore, life expectancy at this advanced age is increasing. Sixty-nine percent of this group is female, mainly widows. The most common causes of disability in the old-old group are arthritis, heart and circulatory disorders, and dementia. This age group, many of whom have serious mental impairments, accounts for more than 40 percent of nursing home residents. Alzheimer's disease is estimated to affect over 20 percent of this age group.

It is noteworthy, however, that of the oldest-old living in the community, at least 40 percent report no limits in their daily activities, and 60 percent of them perceive their health to be good to excellent. Physicians' visits are no more frequent for them than for the young-old. Hospital stays and nursing home residence, however, are much more prevalent than for the young-old.

HEALTH SERVICE NEEDS

A very broad range of services is required to address the health-care needs of the older population. Necessary services include prevention activities, as well as primary, acute, post-acute, rehabilitative, long-term, and hospice care.

Since the old-old population is the one increasing most rapidly, services needed in the twenty-first century will be focused on maintaining the functional capacities of persons of advanced age and on providing long-term care to the frail elderly. After the year 2010, a more rapid expansion will occur in the young-old group. These persons will need more preventive, primary, and acute care services.

Many of the health and related care services for the elderly will take place in community settings. The vast majority of disabled elderly now receive all their care in community settings and this trend is expected to continue. The workplace of some healthcare personnel, therefore, will shift. New sites for health care will need to evolve, such as new residential and living arrangements, and expansion of integrated care systems, involving institutional and community facilities, case management, and cost-sharing arrangements. More emphasis will be placed on rehabilitation and self-care.

Other prospective changes in the health field include increased technology to detect and treat diseases, increased availability of health insurance benefits, more professional and public interest in community-based services, a concentration of the sickest patients in hospitals, new health programs for low-income groups, and a large supply of physicians and other health personnel. These factors will increase the utilization of health services.

SHIFTS IN TRAINING HEALTH PERSONNEL

Health personnel in the coming years will need to develop a broader understanding and competence in geriatrics. An extended curriculum to encompass these goals should be established. It likely will include a variety of clinical settings and short-term, intensive courses to bring practitioners up to current knowledge levels.

Physicians direct the work of other health personnel, and therefore will need to develop additional competencies and leadership roles for the practice of geriatric medicine. All physicians should receive education and training in geriatric medicine as part of their professional preparation. Care of chronically ill, frail elderly persons should be emphasized. Special attention should be focused on clinical pharmacology, especially for patients on multiple medications; sensory loss; dental needs; and nutrition.

Dentists, dental hygienists, and dental assistants will be serving substantially larger numbers of elderly. Like nurses, they should receive education concerning the special needs and conditions of the elderly as part of their basic preparation. Professional nursing students in the past have had limited curricular content focused on the care of aged persons. Innovative educational preparation with a focus on needs and care of the elderly must be emphasized. Nursing personnel need expanded knowledge and skills, with stress on health promotion and nutrition for the elderly. They should be encouraged to go into geriatric nursing or to specialize in advanced gerontology education.

Social work personnel must be prepared to meet the diverse social services needs of the elderly. They will require a specialized knowledge of the aging process and the interpersonal dynamics of the aging and their families.

A large number of other types of health personnel are increasingly involved in the care of older persons, both at the community level and in institutions. Many different occupations and specialties make critical contributions to the care and well-being of the elderly. Often the care of the elderly calls for multidisciplinary and interdisciplinary activities. Diverse competencies and skills are required to respond effectively to the challenge of caring for the aged population; appropriate use of well-prepared allied health professionals and supporting health personnel will be critical to maintaining such a large elderly population at their optimum potential.

Part II of this book describes the work of many health professionals and supporting personnel in great detail. The Bureau of Labor Statistics identified more than 14 million health workers in 200 occupations in 2006, and the projected number for 2016 was 17 million in 250 occupations. More than 400,000 additional jobs are expected in physicians' offices. The most rapid growth, however, is expected to be in offices other than doctors', such as those of physical therapists, outpatient facilities, nurse practitioners, and home health agencies. Each of the professions will need expanded personnel to take care of the aging population. Students considering a career in the health field are encouraged to continue—their services will be greatly needed.

Future Trends

Though the need for health services will increase dramatically in future decades because of the drastic increase in the elderly population, the exact nature and scope of our future healthcare system remain uncertain. Changes in the structure of the healthcare system and uncertainty about how to finance future health care make it difficult to project career situations precisely. Under any conditions, however, the trends indicate a need for substantial increases in the number of health personnel specifically prepared to provide services to older persons.

The use of health services will be concentrated among older and very old persons. This fact has important implications for the education and training of all healthcare personnel. The impact of these changes will have an increasing role in the delivery of health care and on the economy of the United States.

Summary

Prospects for long-term care reform when the baby boom generation needs it will become a major domestic policy issue. If nursing home utilization rates remain constant, on an age-specific basis there will be 5.7 million people in institutions in 2040 compared to 1.6 million in 1990.[7]

The near future for LTC is less certain. There is pessimism about progress regarding LTC due to its private and public costs, tax cuts, financial problems currently evident in Medicare and Social Security, and lack of consensus among policy makers. Few individuals purchase long-term care insurance and after their private funds are depleted for nursing home care, Medicaid covers nursing home costs.

Medicare, which is the universal health insurance for the elderly, does not cover LTC. Medicare is a women's issue. This lack of coverage is especially troubling for older women, who outlive and outnumber men by 3 to 2, with the gap widening with advancing years.[8] Chapter 5 addresses some of the problems of older women's health, access to care, and Medicare issues for the twenty-first century.

References

1. Wiener JM, Frieman MP, Brown D.
2. Decker FH, Gruhn P, Matthew-Martin L, Dollard KJ, Tucker AM, Bizette L.
3. Stone RI, Wiener JM.
4. Robert Wood Johnson Foundation.
5. U.S. Census Bureau.
6. Johnson RW, Toohey D, Wiener JM.
7. U.S. Census.
8. Harrington C, Estes CL.

AGING, HEALTH, AND WOMEN'S ISSUES

Key Terms

- Biological
- Physiological
- Dichotomy
- Alzheimer's disease
- Centers for Medicare & Medicaid Services (CMS) Medicare, Part A, Part B, Part D
- Long-term care (LTC)
- Medicaid
- Managed care
- Caregiver
- Demographics
- Alternative care facilities
- Interdisciplinary

Objectives

After studying this chapter, the student should be able to:

1. Identify the primary cause of the gender gap in women's health care.
2. Name three reasons why women are more dependent on public health programs than men are.
3. Identify three problems related to women's access to health care.

4. Explain the differences between Medicare and Medicaid insurance.

5. Identify the major benefits provided by Medicare Part A.

6. Identify the major benefits provided by Medicare Part B.

7. Identify the benefits provided by Medicare Part D.

8. Name three groups of people who are eligible for Medicaid insurance.

9. List at least three benefits provided by Medicaid that are not provided by Medicare.

10. Explain how financial issues affect the quality of care, particularly for older women.

In Chapter 1, we summarized recent trends in U.S. health care and the need for new strategies to address the health of women. This chapter briefly explores the role that gender and age play in determining women's health care.

Gender-Specific Roles in Health Care

Women's health concerns have traditionally been treated the same as men's, without recognition that women have biological and physiological needs different from those of men. In addition, women have less money, have lower rates of insurance coverage, and are more dependent on public health programs than are men. Although the average lifespan of women has increased significantly since the beginning of the twentieth century, research into outcomes for all health conditions specific to women has lagged far behind, by some 30 years, the research into outcomes for conditions and health concerns specific to men.

Healthcare coverage for women remains a critical issue, although efforts are under way to bridge the gender gap. Low-income and less-educated women are less likely to receive needed services than their higher-income, more-educated counterparts. These facts contribute significantly to deficiencies in the healthcare system.

The health status of older women is a dichotomy. Improvements in nutrition, hygiene, and technological advances in medicine have extended life expectancies, increasing the numbers of older people, including women. On the other hand, although females now live to older ages, they often live their advancing years with multiple illnesses and disabilities. They suffer from higher rates of chronic conditions, and a greater number of conditions, than do men. For example, women are at greater risk for Alzheimer's disease, and they are twice as likely to suffer a major depression, than men.[1]

A woman's access to health care influences her ability to take advantage of the medical progress being made. The availability of Medicare, in turn, determines her access to health care. Women's dependency on Medicare is greater than men's—the result of increased longevity, higher rates of poverty, and poor health status. Insufficient long-term care disproportionately affects older women, who have higher out-of-pocket costs but lower income. As a function of their greater longevity, women account for a greater percentage of Medicare beneficiaries than do men, and therefore need Medicare for more years.

Medicare for Older Women

The Centers for Medicare & Medicaid Services (CMS) oversees the Medicare program. Medicare covered benefits apply mostly to the treatment of patients with acute illnesses. Although chronic conditions are addressed, supportive long-term care (LTC) is not generally covered. Medicare also does not pay for routine foot, dental, or vision care.

Medicare is divided into four parts. Part A is hospital insurance, and all elderly beneficiaries are automatically enrolled. Part B is supplemental medical insurance and is voluntary, although the majority of elderly clients signs on. The current monthly premium is $96.40. Part C is supplemental hospital and medical insurance, and Part D is medication insurance. All have deductibles and coinsurance.

Under Part A, Medicare pays for all reasonable hospital expenses minus a deductible ($1,204) for the first 60 days of each benefit period. Days 61 to 99 require a daily $256 coinsurance payment, and days 91 to 150 require a $512 copayment daily (2008). Part B pays for doctors' services and outpatient hospital services, including emergency room visits, ambulatory services, diagnostic and laboratory tests, durable medical equipment, physical therapy, occupational therapy, speech pathology, medical nutrition therapy, preventive services including screening for diabetes and cardiovascular disease, certain cancers, bone density measurements and certain immunizations. It does not pay for dental, vision, podiatry or routine physical examinations. Medicare B pays 80 percent of the approved amount according to a fee schedule for covered services, in excess of a $135 deductible.

Medicaid for Older Women

Other than being administered by CMS, Medicaid and Medicare structures have little in common. Medicaid is the largest health insurer in the United States, covering medical expenses and LTC for approximately 46 million people in 2001. It pays for covered services for low-income people who are elderly, blind, receiving public assistance, or among the working poor. In recent years important changes in Medicaid have occurred. The greatest change was the expansion of the population deemed eligible for Medicaid—namely, the provision of medical assistance to disabled and elderly people.

Payment of the staggering Medicaid bill ($313.7 billion in 2005) is divided between federal and state governments. The federal share is determined by a formula based on each state's per capita income. States with relatively low per capita incomes receive more federal funding. Medicaid expenditures represent about 40 percent of all federal funds received by states. There is a large variation in eligibility for benefits from state to state, because the states, under federal guidelines, set their own criteria.

Adults and children in low-income families account for three-fourths of Medicaid beneficiaries, but their care accounts for only 30 percent of the total expenditure. Elderly, blind, and disabled persons account for the remainder because of their greater use of acute and LTC services.

Medicaid covers a broad range of services not covered by Medicare, acting as a supplemental insurance for the elderly and disabled. It also pays their Medicare premiums, includes cost-sharing requirements, and covers prescription drugs. A large number of the elderly do not take advantage of Medicaid coverage because of inability to navigate the publicly run system.

Medicaid operates under tight budget constraints, resulting in provider payment rates that are substantially below market rates. This is a problem for the managed care companies, to whom many Medicaid recipients are referred, causing a substantial number of companies not to bid on contracts or to opt out of the system entirely. Many physicians in private practice do not accept Medicaid patients for the same reason. Both factors decrease access to care by the elderly population[2].

Women's Issues and the Healthcare System

The overwhelming majority of healthcare workers are female. Women are treated differently in the healthcare system in significant ways, whether they are patients or providers of health care. Women's roles within the system are also different from men's. Large numbers of women now practice medicine, but the field remains dominated by men. Men hold prestigious posts as professors and deans in medical schools; women work in lower-paying positions, as nurses, technicians, and therapists. Women with less training and education work in the lowest-paying jobs in health care, as nursing assistants, home health aides, housekeeping, and dietary aides.

Women get sick more often than men do and need health services more often. Over a lifetime, they spend more time in hospitals. Both sexes need and use more medical care as they grow older, but women's access to care is often more limited than men's. Finances are the critical issue, as women are far less likely to be able to pay for health care they need. Many healthcare employees lack any insurance coverage or are underinsured, especially those in physician's offices and home health services.

Women as Care Givers

Care giving is the traditional role of women. Nearly two-thirds of caregivers of the elderly are themselves older women. Many care for both grandchildren and older family members. The extent to which women engage in care giving across their lifespan affects their own health as well as their economic security. Higher rates of stress and depression, use of prescription drugs, lack of attention to personal health conditions, and lack of social and recreational activities are among the many consequences.

Conclusion

Three-fourths of the nation's elderly poor are women. By 2020, poverty will be almost exclusive to older women. The current healthcare delivery system, financing, and policy fail to meet the needs of women, especially older women.

The traditional disease-based medical model for health and the separation of women's health from concerns about aging have been missing from public discussions and policy debates regarding reform of the healthcare system. Gender-specific implications when formulating policy changes must be addressed, especially health care for older women.

The unmet needs in older women's health care are myriad: research into the relationship between health and socioeconomic status, healthcare financing and policy, gender bias in the disease-based medical model, health consequences of gendered care giving, the gender-specific impact of LTC policy, limitations on Medicare, employer-based insurance, and prescription drug benefits.

In the twenty-first century, we must seek a solution to make adequate healthcare coverage available to women. We have debated healthcare reform since 1994, and some incremental changes—namely the managed care revolution—have occurred but progress is very slow. In the coming decades many changes in demographics, occupations, economics, and social roles will occur for both women and men. We need to improve research, services, and education about women's health issues now so that all women will have better health in the future.

The Future of Health Care

The healthcare environment will continue to change, but some factors are here to stay. Prospective payment may change in scope and form, but cost containment will remain part of the healthcare environment. The future carries ramifications for financial and ethical decision-making and for the education of health personnel.

1. The elderly population will continue to grow, with the proportion of those older than 65 years of age doubling by 2020 as postwar "baby boomers" reach age 65. The management of chronic, disabling conditions will be a priority issue in health care.

2. Future growth is anticipated in multihospital systems, ambulatory facilities, and alternative delivery systems. The need for extended care facilities will increase because hospitals will care only for short-term, acutely ill people.

3. Problems of access to care and quality of care will continue to multiply and need to be addressed at once. As the number of uninsured grows, health professionals and providers will be faced with very difficult decisions. Consumer expectations of health care may require modification. Alternative care facilities and alternative caregivers may greatly affect the levels and quality of health care. Consumers will need to be educated to become more self-directed in preventive health maintenance and to know what level of care they can expect. It may no longer be possible to provide the highest level of care to all citizens. There may be establishment of minimal levels of care for all patients by government agencies, with additional services for those willing to pay for them.

4. A continued expansion of sophisticated information technology is anticipated, with systems being capable of integrating clinical and financial data. "Medicine by computer" or telemedicine may be the next phase of health care. Allied health personnel may be the link among physicians, computers, and clients.

Future Education for the Health Professions

Healthcare personnel of tomorrow need to begin now to develop some special skills to deal with future changes. First, curricula must include the requirements and care of the elderly population. A second requisite is the need to assume an active role in developing acceptable health policies. Psychosocial needs and health education needs of the population must be taken into consideration. Health professionals must be able to assess needs accurately and teach at all levels. Because healthcare providers will have to address new health issues, policies, technologies, and practice guidelines over the course of their careers, continuing education programs will need to be updated periodically.[1]

Racial and ethnic minority groups account for 25 percent of the U.S. population. Healthy People 2010 recommended that in the health professions, allied and associated health profession fields, and nursing fields, an increased proportion of all degrees be awarded to members of underrepresented racial and ethnic groups.

Health personnel need to become business-oriented. They must be proficient in the use and application of computers in their areas of specialty. Computers must become a part of daily life and continuing education. Personnel must understand the financial management of healthcare delivery. They will need to be able to contribute their part to the cost-effectiveness of services rendered.

Interdisciplinary respect and understanding will be critical for future health professionals. An ideal mechanism to achieve this would be shared educational experiences, with a health science core of studies and laboratories that allow students from many disciplines to interact and jointly provide care. Would-be healthcare professionals must learn to establish strong, effective, collegial relationships with practitioners of all other healthcare disciplines. In this way, the student of today can prepare for a leadership role in guideline development, the political process, and national healthcare planning and research.

As turbulent as the current situation in health care is, and as much as the turbulence is expected to continue in the near future, this is an exciting, challenging time to be preparing for a health career. New ideas, experimentation, risks, and competition do exist in health career paths, and there can be much satisfaction, self-growth, and pride in contributing to the health of the nation.

References

1. *Health People 2010.*
2. Lee PR, Estes CL.

HEALTH CAREER PLANNING

Key Terms

- Inpatient and outpatient facilities and services
- General hospital
- Specialty hospitals
- Industrial health care
- Career alteration due to new technology
- Expanded functions
- Rural and inner city opportunities

- Maldistribution of health personnel
- Primary health care
- Primary care physicians
- Family practitioners
- Alternative choices of careers
- Licensure
- Professional certification
- Professional registration

Objectives

After studying this chapter, the student should be able to:

1. Obtain complete information pertinent to careers in health services.

2. Recognize the specialized knowledge and skills necessary for a given profession.

3. Evaluate employment opportunities.

4. Select an appropriate health career.

5. Locate the appropriate school for training.

Since health care has developed from a small concern into a multibillion-dollar industry and the largest employer in the United States, it is appropriate that this book assist students in obtaining information that will steer them toward satisfying careers in health services. The first five chapters in this book have been devoted to the development of healthcare services, healthcare delivery, and many of the issues involved in meeting the goals set for health care. This chapter focuses on the personnel issues—where and why health professionals are needed.

A vast amount of healthcare knowledge has accumulated since 1900. One result of the knowledge explosion has been a necessary increase in medical personnel who can be grouped by their specialized knowledge and skills important to healthcare activities. The techniques and instruments developed in response to the new knowledge are extremely important; they have affected the staffing patterns and content of educational programs of many of the health services and precipitated the development of new health occupations. Both medicine and dentistry have developed subspecialties, and both are becoming more dependent on the services of additional personnel in the diagnosis and treatment of disease.

Advances in medical technology have improved survival rates of trauma victims who need extensive care from therapists, social workers and supportive personnel. In addition, advances in information technology, such as bedside computer terminals and hand-held computers that record notes on each patient, continue to improve patient care and worker efficiency. For example, information on vital signs and orders for tests is transferred electronically to a main database, eliminating the need for paper and reducing recordkeeping errors.

Health care has grown into a complex system with many important links, which are examined briefly in this chapter. Understanding where the system is and where it might be going should give students important clues to career opportunities. This understanding will help in evaluating where the jobs are likely to be and discerning where a particular health career fits into the entire picture.

Employers of Health Professionals and Health-Related Personnel

The vast healthcare system offers employment in a wide variety of environments. Although hospitals and physicians' offices may come to mind as the most obvious settings for healthcare professionals, other employers abound, in both inpatient and outpatient facilities.

HOSPITALS

As a group, hospitals are the best known and largest single employer of health workers. As discussed in Chapter 2, the general hospital cares for patients with various medical conditions requiring diagnosis and surgical/medical treatment. This is the hospital people are most likely to see in their own community and to visit if they have medical problems. General hospitals represent 87 percent of hospitals. Patients in these hospitals generally stay a short time—a few days to a few weeks.

In specialty hospitals, patients are usually limited to those who have a specific illness or condition. Specialty hospitals may be for psychiatric illness, chronic disease, and rehabilitation of patients. Specialty hospitals are identified as "long-term" because their patients are usually hospitalized for several months before they are well enough to return to their homes.

Both specialty and general hospitals vary in size. Some have as few as 18 hospital beds, while others have well over 1,000 beds.

Nursing Homes and Community Based Care

Nursing homes were almost unknown before the 1930s but have grown rapidly in number since then. By 2007, approximately 1.4 million persons resided in 16,000 nursing homes. An additional 1 million individuals resided in assisted living facilities. Home and community based care is also expanding, especially for the elderly.

Depending on the individual nursing home, the services offered vary from skilled bedside nursing to simple personal care (bathing, dressing, providing meals, and so forth). Although nursing homes are populated mainly by the elderly, adults of any age who are victims of certain conditions or accidents may require nursing home care.

Other Inpatient Facilities

In addition to nursing homes, there are more than 5,000 other residential health facilities for persons who do not need hospitalization or nursing home care. These include residential schools or homes for the mentally retarded, emotionally disturbed, physically handicapped, deaf, blind, alcoholics, and drug abusers. About half of these facilities are for the mentally retarded and emotionally disturbed; these employ three-quarters of the 250,000 workers engaged in inpatient care.

Outpatient and Other Health Facilities or Services

Nearly 500,000 health workers are employed in vital settings or services that are often overlooked as part of the health industry, especially when career opportunities in the health fields are being evaluated. The following list describes some of them.

- Ambulance services transport patients and frequently provide emergency medical services.

- Blood banks draw, process, store, and distribute human whole blood and its derivatives.

- Clinical (medical) laboratories test samples of tissues or fluids to determine the absence or presence and extent of diseases and thereby help physicians diagnose or treat illness.

- Dental laboratories provide services to dentists by making and repairing artificial teeth and other dental appliances.

- Family planning services provide physical examinations, laboratory tests, consultations, education, treatments, and issuance of drugs and contraceptives related to reproduction.

- Home health services provide health care and supportive services to sick or disabled persons at their place of residence when their illnesses do not require hospital or nursing home care or when their disabilities do not allow them to travel to an outpatient facility.

- Opticians' establishments sell and/or make eyeglasses according to the prescription of an optometrist or an ophthalmologist.

- Poison control centers provide comprehensive services to the population regarding the effects of toxic substances and the antidotes available.

- Community mental health centers provide comprehensive services to people with physical, mental, or social disabilities to help them return to satisfying jobs and lifestyles. Certain centers might work with special problems only—rehabilitation of the blind, deaf, or mentally retarded, for example. Certain centers also provide inpatient/outpatient care, day care, and 24-hour emergency, consultation, and educational services for problems related to mental health.

- Migrant health programs provide health services to migrant and seasonal farm workers who would not qualify for health services available to permanent residents of a particular state.

- Neighborhood health centers provide medical, dental, laboratory, radiological, and pharmaceutical services for people living in a particular geographic area within a city.

- Health maintenance organizations (HMOs) provide consumers with comprehensive health services, including hospitalization, office visits, preventive health checkups, and immunizations. Instead of the traditional pay-as-you-go system, consumers and/or their employers pay a fixed monthly fee that covers all these services, no matter how often they are used.

- Health practitioners' offices employ health professionals of various kinds, depending on the size of the practice and the patients who are being served. Some practitioners work alone in private practice, while others share office space and services in a group practice. Practitioners who commonly operate their own offices include medical and osteopathic physicians, dentists, chiropractors, podiatrists, optometrists, psychologists, dietitians, nutritionists, and veterinarians.

- Voluntary health agencies at the national, state, and local levels are concerned with specific health problems or health services. Some of their activities include raising funds for medical research, alerting the public to specific health problems, providing health education programs, and making health services more available at the community level. The American Cancer Society, American Heart Association, and National Foundation–March of Dimes are examples of voluntary health agencies.

- Professional health associations at the national, state, and local levels represent the members of a particular health profession or of a particular type of health facility such as an association of hospitals or community health centers. Their activities often include improving the professional education of their members, establishing standards of practice or operations for their fields, and carrying out research of interest to their members. The American Medical Association, American Hospital Association, American Dietetic Association, and the National Association of Community Health Centers are some examples.

Government Health-Related Activities. At the federal, state, and local levels, the government offers numerous opportunities for health professionals. State and local governments operate health departments that help to control the spread of communicable disease, safeguard the purity of food and water supplies, and promote health education and health measures such as inoculations. At the federal level, the U.S. Department of Health and Human Services' Public Health Service (PHS) is concerned with the health of all citizens.

Other branches of the government also offer opportunities for health-related employment. The U.S. Department of Labor's Occupational Safety and Health Administration (OSHA) enforces standards related to job health and safety. The U.S. Department of Agriculture's state-sponsored programs ensure that meat, poultry, and eggs are disease-free and meet sanitary conditions. The U.S. Army, Navy, Air Force, and Veterans Administration offer employment opportunities in practically every health occupation described in this book.

Industrial Healthcare Employment

Health-related industries not only manufacture prescription drugs and numerous over-the-counter medications but also produce common household health supplies, as well as supplies used by hospitals and other health facilities. Medical devices such as hearing aids, cardiac pacemakers, artificial limbs, and braces are manufactured by industry, as is the sophisticated diagnostic and treatment equipment used in health care today. In addition to producing such items, industrial health care employs thousands of people in research and development to discover new health products and technology.

Many large corporations have started health clinics manned by health professionals within their own companies. Employees receive immediate, in-house health care, and health checkups. Occupational health and safety of workers is a vital concern, and industry employs special health personnel to ensure that employees will not be exposed to unnecessary job hazards.

Employment Opportunities

Health care continually moves in new and different directions. This movement may alter what health workers will be doing, where they will be working, and how many will be employed in a particular occupation. Opportunities may expand in some areas and diminish in others, as has already happened in the case of many careers and will continue to happen as technology and the population change.

No one can predict with absolute certainty the employment outlook for a particular career. The following discussion of current trends gives some clues as to where one might find especially good opportunities today and in the future.

CHANGING OPPORTUNITIES FROM NEW TECHNOLOGY

Advances in technology are frequently responsible for changes in career opportunities. Research is conducted constantly to discover methods of preventing disease and ways to improve diagnosis and treatment. This research often results in the development of a complex machine or a sophisticated medical technique that is subsequently introduced into health care. When this happens, health workers must be trained to operate the machine or to perform the technique correctly and safely.

The first persons selected for training are usually people who are already employed in health and work in a related area. They receive on-the-job training. However, as a new machine or technical innovation becomes better known and more widely used by hospitals and other health facilities, additional trained workers are needed. On-the-job training is often no longer practical, and formal education programs in hospitals or colleges are started. Qualified students—not just healthcare workers—then have the opportunity for training. As the number of these newly trained workers increases, a separate and distinct occupation may emerge.

NEW OPPORTUNITIES THROUGH EXPANDED FUNCTIONS

Several health professions require additional training and knowledge, but certify or license people to perform many tasks that were previously done only by a physician or dentist. Examples include the dental hygienist, the nurse practitioner, and the physician assistant. These professions are described in later chapters in more detail.

OPPORTUNITIES IN RURAL AND INNER CITY COMMUNITIES

In some parts of the country, new health workers are finding it difficult to obtain jobs, while in other places communities cannot find enough workers to fill existing healthcare jobs. This national problem is often referred to as the *maldistribution of health personnel*. Healthcare workers are not distributed according to population or need in many geographic areas. This maldistribution hits low income and overpopulated inner-city areas, and underpopulated rural areas, hardest.

In 1973, 140 rural counties in the United States were without a practicing physician. In impoverished areas of Chicago, 26 physicians practiced for every 100,000 residents, while in Chicago's more affluent areas 210 physicians practiced for every 100,000 people. There is now an overall surplus of doctors in the United States, but some rural areas still lack adequate health care. Areas with shortages continue to need health professionals of all kinds. Addressing this need might require relocation by those healthcare professionals looking to find the best future opportunities.

PRIMARY CARE

Most Americans need primary health care that focuses on prevention, early detection and treatment, and overall responsibility for individual patients. Adequate primary care can often reduce health costs, since it is generally easier and less expensive to prevent problems or treat them in their earliest stages. Although the number of primary care physicians is growing, physicians who practice this kind of basic medicine are still outnumbered 3 to 1 by doctors who specialize in other fields. Primary care services should become increasingly available. Medical schools are encouraging students to go into primary care practice by emphasizing its importance and by exposing students to primary care earlier in their training.

Primary care physicians or generalists include family practice physicians, physicians in general pediatric practice, or those in general internal medicine practice. Family practice physicians deliver comprehensive, primary healthcare services for all family members, while pediatricians provide primary care to infants, children and adolescents, and internists care for adults. This increased emphasis on primary care affects not only the career of the physician but also most other health workers who assist or support the physician. Workplaces are also affected. Facilities that emphasize primary care, such as HMOs and neighborhood health centers, will probably increase in number.

EXPANDING OPPORTUNITIES IN OUTPATIENT HEALTH FACILITIES

In 1978 the United States spent $39 billion on health care. Twelve years later the figure had risen to more than $139 billion. In 2004, the figure rose to $1.9 trillion. Containing costs may be the most important priority of the health field during the coming years. Because the cost of inpatient care in hospitals and nursing homes represents a large part of the nation's healthcare bill, new strategies have been launched to contain these costs. Outpatient alternatives to hospitals or nursing homes are becoming successful. Home care services now enable many ill or aged people to remain in their own homes rather than live as patients in nursing homes. With a growing elderly population, home care services should become increasingly more important, and more workers will be needed to deliver these services.

Ambulatory or "walk-in" patient care in private practitioners' offices, hospital outpatient departments, community health centers, or other health facilities is helping to reduce hospitalization. In the past, many medical procedures, including certain diagnostic tests and simple surgery, were done only on an inpatient hospital basis. Now these same procedures are safely and routinely performed on an outpatient basis in an office setting. This greater emphasis on ambulatory care may shift employment opportunities from hospitals to other kinds of healthcare settings. (See Chapter 2 for details on ambulatory facilities.)

OPPORTUNITIES FOR WOMEN AND MINORITIES

The number of women and minorities is increasing in professions where these groups have been traditionally underrepresented, such as dentistry, veterinary medicine, optometry, podiatry, and health services administration. Congress, federal and state agencies, and professional associations in the health field are making special efforts to create new educational and professional opportunities for women and minorities. As was discussed in Chapter 5, the U.S. Department of Health and Human Services has addressed the need to increase the quality of health services by recommending that an increased proportion of all degrees be awarded to members of underrepresented racial and ethnic groups.[1]

The trends discussed here are not the only ones in health care today, but this discussion may make you more aware of the dynamics of the health field. So while you look into your future as a health worker, watch the healthcare system carefully. Be alert to changes and advances reported in the media. They may affect how and where you become involved in the health field and may help to guide your future.

Health Careers: Something for Everyone

The health field, perhaps more than any other career area, offers wide-ranging opportunities to match almost any interest.

Do you like to work with your hands? Dental technicians, optical mechanics, biomedical equipment technicians, prosthetists, and many other health professionals work with their hands.

Are you interested in working with machines? Respiratory therapists, electroencephalograph (EEG) technologists, and radiologic technologists are a few of the professionals who work with patients and medical machines.

Are you fascinated by photography or the fine arts? Art, music, or dance therapist or biological photographer are among the health careers in which you can use these talents.

Do you enjoy working with people? Nursing, medicine, dentistry, dietetics, optometry, social work, rehabilitation, and mental health are some health career areas that will give you the opportunity to work with and help people of all ages.

The careers just mentioned only begin to enumerate the possibilities. Health careers do offer something for everyone, but too often students say "no" to health careers simply because they do not have the facts. Some common assumptions students make when talking about health careers include such statements as:

"I couldn't work around sick people in a hospital. That's depressing. Besides, I can't stand the sight of blood."

A health career does not automatically mean a hospital job or care of the sick. Health careers have many facets. You can work in health care in research, health planning and administration, health education, disease prevention, environmental protection, and other important areas. Jobs are not just in hospitals. Private doctors' offices, schools, government, industry, and many other places also need and employ health workers.

Do not judge hospital work until you try it, either as a hospital volunteer or as a part-time employee. You may discover by working there and observing trained health professionals that you too can learn to accept the less pleasant parts of helping people get well. You will also find that even in hospitals many jobs are "behind-the-scenes," with little or no direct contact with patients.

"You need science and math for health careers. That's not for me."

Science and mathematics are required for some healthcare jobs, but many others do not emphasize these subjects. Health education, social services, and mental health are just a few areas where psychology, social studies, and other subjects are stressed. However, even when science and math are needed, different skill levels are required. Some occupations, such as optometrist and scientist, require in-depth knowledge, while many other careers require just good basic skills and working knowledge of science and math.

"Training takes too long."

Some careers do take seven or more years of preparation. Most, however, require only two to four years of preparation—not a very big investment considering that most people work more than forty years in their lifetime.

"Training costs too much."

In one sense, the cost of training is only relative. It must be balanced against what one can earn. Figures show that lifetime earnings generally increase with years of education. On the other hand, if you don't think you can afford training, you are not alone. Most students today need and can find financial aid for training. Scholarships and loan repayment programs are available to students who are willing to make a commitment to working in underserved areas or serving in the armed services. The National Health Services Corps (NHSC) and the Indian Health Services (IHS) provide financial assistance in the form of scholarships and loan repayment. The National Health Services Corps[1] place physicians, nurses, and mental health workers in underserved rural and urban areas. The IHS[2] hires health professionals of all kinds for its hospitals and clinics.

"Training is too hard."

Don't sell yourself short. Many students who felt the same way are now working as doctors, nurses, therapists, technologists, or other health professionals. If you fear training may be too hard for you, think twice. A change of attitude, a special remedial program, or additional study may be all you need to succeed. Most community colleges and educational centers offer the special studies needed to prepare you for education in a health career.

Each year many interested, qualified students give up on a health career simply because they have not explored alternatives when their first career choice is not possible. A prime example is the aspiring physician who is not admitted to a medical or an osteopathic school and drops out of the health field entirely. The health field is vast; in it you will find many related careers where you can contribute and find personal satisfaction. Your talents are definitely needed in the health field.

Exploring Health Careers

Career exploration can be a learning experience as you make new discoveries about the world of work and yourself. The reality of the work world is always different from what you learn in school or from what you research in books. One good way to gain firsthand information is to visit several facilities. Make appointments and visit several departments within the facilities. Compare different types of facilities and what people with the same job titles are doing in each one. If you have a particular interest, set up interviews with a health worker in that discipline. This is usually very rewarding for you both. Most health professionals enjoy talking to students and answering questions about their particular fields. Visit laboratories, both private and hospital-based. Visit practitioners in private practice and those in salaried positions. Learn all you can about community-based programs and special services offered by clinics and hospitals. Ask about the philosophy of each facility you visit. Does it provide in-service education for its employees and offer continuing education programs? Does it subscribe to patient education concepts? What are the general amenities offered workers in different kinds of facilities?

Before you go exploring, do your homework. Visit the Web sites of professional organizations listed in certain chapters of this book. Do some more reading in the library. Be prepared to ask pertinent questions that will help you make decisions.

Visit schools that offer majors in the health services. You can find out much about the professions by talking to students and instructors and by spending some time on campus and possibly in the classes. (Most schools permit such visits.)

Some professions stipulate that students have some experience in the field before they are considered for admission to an academic program. Experience can be obtained by summer work, part-time jobs, or volunteer work in a facility. The firsthand experience you gain from such an endeavor will not only help you to make decisions about your career, but may also help get you into the school of your choice.

While you explore, keep an open mind. Investigate many careers, not just those with which you are familiar. The more information you have, the easier your career decisions will be.

Selecting a School

Next to choosing a career, selecting the right school for training is the most important career decision you will need to make. As you read the job requirements for the many careers detailed in Part II of this book, you will discover that health career training is available in many kinds of schools: two-year and four-year colleges and universities; technical institutes; medical, dental, and other professional schools; hospitals; private, vocational, and trade schools; and the military. The secret to selecting the right school lies in answering one important question: Will the school you are interested in prepare you for the career you want? Before you seek the answer to this question, you should understand three basic terms related to employment in the health field: licensure, professional certification, and professional registration.

LICENSURE

Before you can work in many health professions, a state license is required. The qualifications for licensure vary. In general, a student must graduate from a school whose program is approved by the state licensing agency. After graduation, he or she must prove qualification to provide health services by passing a special licensing examination. Licensure is the state's way of protecting the public from unqualified health practitioners.

The health professions that are licensed vary with each state. Some professions, such as registered nurse, practical nurse, physician, dentist, optometrist, podiatrist, pharmacist, social worker, and veterinarian, are licensed in all states. Individual state licensing agencies also vary. The state's Education Department, Department of Higher Education, and Department of Health are usually the responsible agencies. A state agency and a specialty board, such as the Board of Nursing or the Board of Dentistry, may also grant licenses jointly.

PROFESSIONAL CERTIFICATION

Professional certification ensures that health professionals meet established levels of competency. Certification is granted by health professionals' national organizations, not by the individual states, so it carries national recognition. In health professions in which there is no state licensure, professional certification may be required for employment. However, even when certification is not required, it is a strong asset. Most employers prefer to hire certified professionals, and in a tight job market, certification may be the key to getting a job.

In general, to qualify for certification, a student must first complete a program of training recognized by the profession. Usually this means graduating from a program accredited (i.e., approved) by the relevant professional organization. Some organizations accredit programs jointly with the American Medical Assocation (AMA). After graduation, the student must pass a special certification examination.

PROFESSIONAL REGISTRATION

Technically, professional registration means the listing of certified health professionals on an official roster kept by a state agency or health professionals' organization. In practical terms, some health professionals' organizations use the term registration interchangeably with certification.

Using This Book to Select and Plan a Health Career

Part II of this book describes in detail the requirements, including registration, licensure, and certification, of the best-known health professions. In addition to information about requirements, each of the following chapters describes the work and the work environment, employment opportunities and trends, and earnings for a specific category of patient-care career. The chapters also discuss related occupations and additional sources of information about the particular career. Taken together, the career descriptions present a practical, detailed "road map" of the vast healthcare field.

Appendix B has an extensive list of places to begin collecting information on careers and job opportunities. The same sources will help you with job hunting, writing résumés, and successful interviewing. **Appendix C** shows you the basics of creating different types of résumés.

References

1. *Healthy People 2010.*
2. National Health Services Corps.
3. Indian Health Service.

HEALTH PROFESSIONS INVOLVING PATIENT CARE

Objectives

Objectives listed below are for all chapters in Part II. After studying the chapters in this part the student should be able to:

1. Describe the responsibilities and work of each profession.

2. Classify the types of specialties in each profession.

3. Discuss the environment in which the work takes place.

4. Identify any adjunct personnel who assist the professionals with their work.

5. Compare and contrast the following factors among the professions: educational requirements, employment trends, opportunities for advancement, salary potential, and career ladders.

6. Describe the differences in licensing, certification, and registration for careers of interest.

7. Identify the professionals who do similar tasks or have similar responsibilities.

8. Discuss the advantages of the national organizations to which professionals belong.

9. Explain the concept and functions of interdisciplinary teams.

7

MEDICINE

Key Terms

- MD
- DO
- Allopathic
- Surgeons
- Psychiatrists
- Radiologists
- Pediatricians
- Ophthalmologists
- Internists
- Dermatologists
- Anesthesiologists
- Cardiologists

- Primary care physician
- Neurologists
- Gynecologists
- Obstetricians
- Pathologists
- Emergency medicine
- Allergists
- Otolaryngologists
- Preventive medicine/occupational medicine
- Solo practitioners
- Group practice
- Cost of training

Doctors: The Perceptions

Although it is only one of many career paths available to those with the interest and aptitude for a career involving patient care, the profession of physician is one that most readily comes to mind when one thinks of medicine. The title "Dr." traditionally inspires respect—and perhaps envy. Media portrayals through the years have contributed to a popular perception of doctors as public servants of rare intelligence, compassion, and skill; encounters with the medical system have left some consumers convinced that doctors have feet of clay that are shod in gold-plated boots.

Though public perceptions of physicians will undoubtedly persist despite demonstrations of their inapplicability, individuals approaching a career choice should be guided by realities rather than perceptions. The cost of training is a serious consideration for would-be physicians, and, like other healthcare professionals, physicians must adjust to changes in the healthcare system, some of which are potentially constraining to autonomy and earning power.

Doctors: The Realities

WORK DESCRIPTION

Physicians serve a fundamental role in our society and have an effect on all our lives. They diagnose illnesses and prescribe and administer treatment for people suffering from injury or disease. Physicians examine patients, obtain medical histories, and order, perform, and interpret diagnostic tests. They counsel patients on diet, hygiene, and preventive health care.

There are two types of physicians: The MD—Doctor of Medicine—and the DO—Doctor of Osteopathic Medicine. MDs are also known as *allopathic* physicians. While both MDs and DOs may use all accepted methods of treatment, including drugs and surgery, DOs place special emphasis on the body's musculoskeletal system, *preventive medicine*, and holistic patient care.

About one-third of MDs—and more than half of DOs—are primary care physicians. They practice general and family medicine, general internal medicine, or general pediatrics and are usually the first health professionals whom patients consult. Primary care physicians tend to see the same patients on a regular basis for preventive care and to treat a variety of ailments. General and family practitioners emphasize comprehensive health care for patients of all ages and for the family as a group. Those in general internal medicine provide care mainly for adults who may have problems associated with the body's organs. General pediatricians focus on the whole range of children's health issues. When appropriate, primary care physicians refer patients to specialists, who are experts in medical fields such as obstetrics and gynecology, cardiology, psychiatry, or surgery.

DOs are more likely to be primary care providers than are MDs, although they can be found in all specialties. More than half of all DOs practice general or family medicine, general internal medicine, or general pediatrics. Common specialties for DOs include emergency medicine, anesthesiology, obstetrics and gynecology, psychiatry, and surgery.

Dramatic advances in medical technology have expanded the scope of the physician's field. Liver and kidney transplants, laser surgery, and ultrasound and magnetic resonance imaging are but a few of these new technologies. Some are opening entirely new areas of medical practice; others are replacing traditional treatment methods.

The emphasis on technology has implications for the way physicians are trained and the way they practice medicine. High-technology medicine requires extensive skills and training. Its dominant role in U.S. medical care underlies the system of specialty medicine. The cost of technology is largely responsible for making the hospital the site of the most advanced medical care. Only hospitals and very large clinics or group medical practices can afford to purchase the most costly equipment. It is beyond the means of individual physicians or small groups.

The shift from fee-for-service medicine to managed care has altered the practice environment. Examples of managed care systems that set guidelines for medical practice—limiting the kinds of tests physicians may order, for example—include HMOs, PPOs, and various "gatekeeping" schemes. The managed care concept has become widespread, and physicians are subject to more constraints in exercising their professional judgment than has traditionally been the case.

Some commonly encountered types of specialties and their primary focus of practice are described in the following paragraphs.

Surgeons operate so as to treat disease, repair injury, correct deformities, and improve the general health of the patient. Surgeons examine a patient first to determine whether an operation is needed, then choose the best way to operate. A medical history of the patient is most important; this includes information related to past surgeries and potential allergies to drugs or anesthesia.

General surgeons perform many types of surgeries. Neurosurgeons specialize in surgery of the brain, spinal cord, and nervous system. The Neurosurgeons has a major role in treatment of head and spinal injuries caused by accidents. *Orthopedic surgeons* are specialists in the repair of bones and joints. Orthopedic surgeons may also treat patients without surgery by applying casts or braces, or by formulating an exercise program including physiotherapy. *Plastic surgeons* repair malformed or injured parts of the body. Plastic surgeons have a major role in the physiologic and psychological repair of injuries from accidents. *Thoracic surgeons* perform surgery in the chest cavity—for instance, lung and heart surgery.

Psychiatrists help patients recover their mental health. The psychiatrist gathers and analyzes data on the patient's medical and mental history, symptoms, and interaction with the family and society. The psychiatrist diagnoses mental disorders and then formulates a treatment plan. Examples of conditions that are treated by the psychiatrist are anxiety, depression, paranoia, and schizophrenia.

Radiologists diagnose and treat illness by the use of X-rays and radioactive materials. Radiologists treat tumors and other growths with radiation and may inject radioactive materials into the body to make internal organs or structures visible on X-ray. Radiologists are usually involved in one of three areas of specialty: radiation therapy, diagnostic radiology, or nuclear medicine. Nuclear medicine is a new specialty that involves tests using nuclear isotopes. This type of medicine permits physicians to see organs deep within the body from a different perspective than X-rays provide.

Pediatricians care for children from birth to adolescence. They check the health of children, prescribe and administer medicine, vaccinate children against disease, and serve as a reference for parents on medical questions about their children.

Ophthalmologists treat diseases and injuries of the eye. They examine eyes and prescribe corrective lenses, diagnose diseases, perform surgery when necessary, or recommend exercises to strengthen the eye muscles.

Physicians who specialize in internal medicine deal with the internal organs of the body. *Internists* may treat conditions of the lungs, blood, kidneys, heart, and other areas and organs of the body.

Dermatologists treat infections, growths, and injuries related to the skin. They prescribe medicine or treatments and remove growths, cysts, or birthmarks as medically indicated.

Anesthesiologists use drugs and gases to render patients unconscious during surgery. They obtain a detailed history from the patient and then make a decision concerning the type and amount of anesthesia to use during surgery. Several types of anesthesia are available, and anesthesiologists use them singly or in combination according to their judgment. During surgery, the anesthesiologist monitors the progress of the patient and informs the surgeon if any difficulties arise.

Cardiologists treat heart disease. They use many techniques to determine how the patient's heart is functioning. X-rays and electrocardiograms are primary diagnostic tools. The cardiologist prescribes treatment and recommends diet and exercise changes for patients. Cardiovascular surgery of the heart and blood vessels is a subspecialty of cardiology.

The *primary care physician* is involved with the care of the total patient and is prepared educationally to handle most types of illnesses. The recent popularity of the family physician indicates a move away from specialty areas back toward treating the whole patient—and, in many cases, whole families. Primary care physicians are involved in six basic areas: internal medicine, obstetrics and gynecology, surgery, psychiatry, pediatrics, and community medicine. This wide scope of training makes the primary care physician very knowledgeable in treating the whole patient preventively and in coordinating specialty care if necessary.

Neurologists treat disorders of the central nervous system and order tests necessary to detect diseases. They prescribe medicine and treatment based on the neurological diagnosis.

Obstetricians and *gynecologists* are involved in the health care and maintenance of the reproductive system of women. These physicians treat women before and after childbirth and examine women regularly for any abnormal developments or growths in the reproductive system. Obstetricians work with women throughout their pregnancies, deliver infants, and care for the mothers after the delivery.

Pathologists study the characteristics, causes, and progression of diseases. They order and perform laboratory tests. They may perform autopsies to determine cause of death. Many pathologists work in a specialty area such as blood banks or clinical chemistry, and most are actively involved in research.

Emergency medicine is a relatively new specialty. Physicians in this field work specifically in emergency rooms, where they treat acute illnesses and emergency situations. Trauma treatment is a specialized area within emergency medicine, and physicians in this area are knowledgeable in dealing with all kinds of acute illness.

Allergists treat conditions and illnesses caused by allergies or related to the immune system. The allergist is actively involved in ordering tests and evaluating results. They also treat patients who have undergone transplants of organs.

Otolaryngologists are specialists in the treatment of conditions or diseases of the ear, nose, and throat. They may treat patients who have lost the ability to speak or hear. They may perform related surgeries.

Preventive medicine is a specialty that includes occupational medicine, public health, and general preventive treatments. Physicians in this field may work as health officers in infectious disease control or in treatment of illnesses associated with industry. Preventive medicine is a new area of treatment that is rapidly gaining popularity with patients because it helps to decrease the overall cost of medical care.

Some medical specialties also have subspecialties. To become recognized as a specialist, a physician must gain certification from the specific accrediting body for that specialty.

WORK ENVIRONMENT

Many physicians work long, irregular hours. According to the most recent data, more than one-third of all full-time physicians work 60 hours or more per week. They must travel frequently between office and hospital to care for their patients. Increasingly, physicians practice in groups or healthcare organizations that provide back-up coverage and allow for more time off. These physicians often work as part of a team coordinating care for a population of patients; they are less independent than solo practitioners of the past. Physicians who are on-call deal with many patients' concerns over the phone, and they may make emergency visits to hospitals or nursing homes.

EMPLOYMENT OPPORTUNITIES

Physicians and surgeons held about 633,000 jobs in 2006; approximately 15 percent were self-employed. About half of wage–and-salary physicians and surgeons worked in offices of physicians, and 18 percent were employed by hospitals. Others practiced in federal, state, and local governments, including public colleges, universities, and professional schools; private colleges, universities, and professional schools; and outpatient care centers.

Table 7–1 shows the general distribution of physicians in various medical specialties according to the 2006 records of the Department of Labors in the major industrial states in the country.

A growing number of physicians are partners or wage-and-salary employees of group practices. Organized as clinics or as associations of physicians, medical groups can more easily afford expensive medical equipment, can share support staff, and benefit from other business advantages.

According to the AMA, the New England and Middle Atlantic States have the highest ratio of physicians to population; the South Central and Mountain States have the lowest. DOs are more likely than MDs to practice in small cities and towns and in rural areas. MDs tend to locate in urban areas, close to hospitals and education centers.

Table 7–1	**Distribution of practicing physicians in the major industrial states in the United States in 2006**

Medical fields	% Distribution
Primary care	45%
General practice	14%
Pediatrics	8%
Internal medicine	17%
Obstetrics & gynecology	06%
Specialties	55%
Anesthesiology	5%
Psychiatry	5%
Surgery	9%
Others	36%
Total	100%

EDUCATIONAL AND LEGAL REQUIREMENTS

Many years of education and training are required to become a physician: four years of undergraduate school, four years of medical school, and three to eight years of internship and residency, depending on the specialty selected. A few medical schools offer a combined undergraduate and medical school program that lasts six years instead of the customary eight years.

Premedical students must complete undergraduate work in physics, biology, mathematics, English, and inorganic and organic chemistry. Students also take courses in the humanities and the social sciences. Some students choose to volunteer at local hospitals or clinics to gain practical experience in the health professions.

The minimum educational requirement for entry into medical school is three years of college; most applicants, however, have at least a bachelor's degree, and many have advanced degrees. There are 146 medical schools in the United States—126 teach allopathic medicine and award a Doctor of Medicine (MD) degree; 20 teach osteopathic medicine and award the Doctor of Osteopathic Medicine (DO) degree.

The quest to gain acceptance to medical school is very competitive. Applicants must submit transcripts, scores from the Medical College Admission Test, and letters of recommendation. Schools also consider character, personality, leadership qualities, and participation in extracurricular activities. Most schools require an interview with members of the admissions committee.

Students spend most of the first two years of medical school in laboratories and classrooms taking courses such as anatomy, biochemistry, physiology, pharmacology, psychology, microbiology, pathology, medical ethics, and laws governing medicine. They also learn to take medical histories, examine patients, and diagnose illness. During the last two years of medical school, students work with patients under the supervision of experienced physicians in hospitals and clinics to learn acute, chronic, preventive, and rehabilitative care. Through rotations in internal medicine, family practice, obstetrics and gynecology, pediatrics, psychiatry, and surgery, they gain experience in the diagnosis and treatment of illness.

Following medical school, almost all MDs enter a residency—graduate medical education in a specialty that takes the form of paid on-the-job training, usually in a hospital. Most DOs serve a 12-month rotating internship after graduation before entering a residency that may last two to six years. Physicians may benefit from residencies in managed care settings by gaining experience with this increasingly common type of medical practice.

All states, the District of Columbia, and U.S. territories license physicians. To be licensed, physicians must graduate from an accredited medical school, pass a licensing examination, and complete one to seven years of graduate medical education. Although physicians licensed in one state can usually get a license to practice in another state without further examination, some states limit reciprocity. Graduates of foreign medical schools can usually qualify for licensure after passing an examination and completing a U.S. residency.

MDs and DOs seeking board certification in a specialty may spend up to seven years—depending on the specialty—in residency training. A final examination immediately after residency, or after one or two years of practice, is also necessary for board certification by the American Board of Medical Specialists (ABMS) or the American Osteopathic Association (AOA). There are 24 specialty boards, ranging from allergy and immunology to urology. For certification in a subspecialty, physicians usually need another one to two years of residency.

Physicians who want to teach or conduct research may complete graduate work leading to a master's degree or PhD in a field such as biochemistry or microbiology, or spend one year or more in a fellowship devoted to research and advanced clinical training in a specialty area.

A physician's training is costly. According to the Association of American Medical Colleges, in 2004 more than 80 percent of medical school graduates were in debt for educational expenses.

People who wish to become physicians must have a desire to serve patients, be self-motivated, and be able to survive the pressures and long hours of medical education and practice. Physicians must also have a good bedside manner, emotional stability, and the ability to make decisions in emergencies. Prospective physicians must be willing to study throughout their careers to keep up with medical advances. They will also need to be flexible to respond to the changing demands of a rapidly evolving healthcare system.

Employment Trends

Employment of physicians and surgeons is expected to grow faster than the average for all occupations. Job opportunities should be very good, especially for physicians and surgeons willing to practice in specialties—including family practice, internal medicine, and obstetrics and gynecology—or in rural and low-income areas where there is a perceived shortage of medical practitioners.

Employment Change. Employment of physicians and surgeons is projected to grow 14 percent from 2006 to 2016, faster than the average for all occupations. Job growth will occur because of continued expansion of health care related industries. The growing and aging of the U.S. population will drive overall growth in the demand for physician services, as consumers continue to demand high levels of care and access to the latest technologies, diagnostic tests, and therapies.

Demand for physicians' services is highly sensitive to changes in consumer preferences, healthcare reimbursement policies, and legislation. For example, if changes to health coverage result in consumers facing higher out-of-pocket costs, they may demand fewer physician services. Patients relying more on other healthcare providers—such as physician assistants, nurse practitioners, optometrists, and nurse anesthetists—also may temper demand for physician services. In addition, new technologies will increase physician productivity. These technologies include electronic medical records, test and prescription orders, billing, and scheduling.

Job Prospects. Opportunities for individuals interested in becoming physicians and surgeons are expected to be very good. In addition to job openings from employment growth, numerous openings will result from the need to replace physicians and surgeons who retire over the span of the 2006 to 2016 decade.

Unlike their predecessors, newly trained physicians face radically different choices of where and how to practice. New physicians are much less likely to enter solo practice and more likely to take salaried jobs in group medical practices, clinics, and health networks.

Reports of shortages in some specialties, such as general or family practice, internal medicine, and obstetrics and gynecology, or shortages in rural or low-income geographic areas should attract new entrants, encouraging schools to expand programs and hospitals to increase available residency slots. However, because physician training is so lengthy, employment change happens gradually. In the short-term, to meet increased demand, experienced physicians may work longer hours, delay retirement, or take measures to increase productivity, such as using more support staff to provide services. Opportunities should be particularly good in rural and low-income areas, as some physicians find these areas unattractive because of less control over work hours, isolation from medical colleagues, or other reasons.

EARNINGS

Earnings of physicians and surgeons are among the highest of any occupation. **Table 7–2** shows the general earnings of physicians in various medical specialties according to the 2006 records of the Department of Labors in the major industrial states in the country.

Self-employed physicians—those who own or are part owners of their medical practice—generally have higher median incomes than salaried physicians. Earnings vary according to number of years in practice, geographic region, hours worked, skill, personality, and professional reputation. Self-employed physicians and surgeons must provide for their own health insurance and retirement.

Table 7–2	*General earnings of practicing physicians in the major industrial states in the United States in 2006*	
Specialty	**Earnings**	
Anesthesiology	$225,000–270,000	
Surgery	$200,000–230,000	
Obstetrics/gynecology	$195,000–210,000	
Psychiatry	$160,000–190,000	
Internal medicine	$130,000–150,000	
Pediatrics	$120,000–140,000	
Family practice	$120,000–150,000	

RELATED OCCUPATIONS

Physicians work to prevent, diagnose, and treat diseases, disorders, and injuries. Other healthcare practitioners who need similar skills and who exercise critical judgment include chiropractors, dentists, optometrists, physician assistants, podiatrists, registered nurses, and veterinarians.

ADDITIONAL INFORMATION

For a list of medical schools and residency programs, as well as general information on pre-medical education, financial aid, and medicine as a career, contact:

- American Association of Colleges of Osteopathic Medicine, 5550 Friendship Blvd., Suite 310, Chevy Chase, MD 20815. http://www.aacom.org

- Association of American Medical Colleges, Section for Student Services, 2450 N St. NW., Washington, DC 20037. http://www.aamc.org/students

For general information on physicians, contact:

- American Medical Association, 515 N. State St., Chicago, IL 60610. http://www.ama-assn.org

- American Osteopathic Association, Department of Communications, 142 East Ontario St., Chicago, IL 60611. http://www.osteopathic.org

For information about various medical specialties, contact:

- American Academy of Family Physicians, Resident Student Activities Department, 11400 Tomahawk Creek Pkwy., Leawood, KS 66211. http://fmignet.aafp.org

- American Academy of Pediatrics, 141 Northwest Point Blvd., Elk Grove Village, IL 60007. http://www.aap.org

- American Board of Medical Specialties, 1007 Church St., Suite 404, Evanston, IL 60201. http://www.abms.org

- American College of Obstetricians and Gynecologists, 409 12th St. S.W., P.O. Box 96920, Washington, DC 20090. http://www.acog.org

- American College of Physicians, 190 North Independence Mall West, Philadelphia, PA 19106. http://www.acponline.org

- American College of Surgeons, Division of Education, 633 North Saint Clair St., Chicago, IL 60611. http://www.facs.org

- American Psychiatric Association, 1000 Wilson Blvd., Suite 1825, Arlington, VA 22209. http://www.psych.org

- American Society of Anesthesiologists, 520 N. Northwest Hwy., Park Ridge, IL 60068. http://www.asahq.org/career/homepage.htm

Information on federal scholarships and loans is available from the directors of student financial aid at schools of medicine. Information on licensing is available from state boards of examiners.

DENTISTRY

Key Terms

- Orthodontics
- Oral surgery
- Pedodontics
- Periodontics
- Prosthodontics

- Endodontics
- Public health dentistry
- Oral pathology
- Dental hygienists
- Dental assistants

Dentists

WORK DESCRIPTION

Dentists diagnose, prevent, and treat teeth and tissue problems. They remove decay, fill cavities, examine X-rays, place protective plastic sealants on children's teeth, straighten teeth, and repair fractured teeth. They also perform corrective surgery on gums and supporting bones to treat gum diseases. Dentists extract teeth and make models and measurements for dentures to replace missing teeth. They provide instruction on diet, brushing, flossing, the use of fluorides, and other aspects of dental care as well. They also administer anesthetics and write prescriptions for antibiotics and other medications.

Dentists use a variety of equipment, including X-ray machines, drills, and instruments such as mouth mirrors, probes, forceps, brushes, and scalpels. They also wear masks, gloves, and safety glasses to protect themselves and their patients from infectious diseases.

Most dentists are general practitioners who handle a wide variety of dental needs. About 15 percent practice in one of the eight specialty areas recognized by the American Dental Association. *Orthodontists*, the largest group of specialists, straighten teeth. The next largest group, oral and maxillofacial surgeons, operate on the mouth and jaws. The remainder specialize in *pedodontics* (dentistry for children), *periodontics* (treating the gums), *prosthodontics* (making artificial teeth or dentures), *endodontics* (root canal therapy), *public health dentistry* (community dental health), and *oral pathology* (diseases of the mouth).

Today's dentist is involved not only with the treatment of the gums and teeth but also with patients' general health. Many dentists discover symptoms that call for a referral to a physician.

Dentists in private practice oversee a variety of administrative tasks, including bookkeeping and buying equipment and supplies. They may employ and supervise dental hygienists, dental assistants, dental laboratory technicians, and receptionists.

Technological advances in dentistry affect the materials and techniques that dentists employ in their work. For example, dentists now use new composite materials to repair fractured or disfigured teeth. As new technologies are proven and adopted, the nature of dentistry will continue to change.

WORK ENVIRONMENT

Most dental offices are open five days per week, and some dentists have evening hours. Dentists who have offices in retail stores or work for franchised dental outlets may work weekends as well.

Dentists usually work about 42 hours per week, although some spend more than 45 hours per week in the office. Dentists often work fewer hours as they grow older, and a considerable number continue in part-time practice well beyond the usual retirement age.

Important health safeguards for dentists include strict adherence to proper radiologic procedures, compliance with recommended aseptic techniques, including the latest safety precautions, and use of appropriate protective devices such as masks, gloves, and safety glasses. These measures address their own safety as well as the safety of their patients.

EMPLOYMENT OPPORTUNITIES

Most dentists work four or five days a week. Some work evenings and weekends to meet their patients' needs. The number of hours worked varies greatly among dentists. Most full-time dentists work between 35 and 40 hours a week. However, others, especially those who are trying to establish a new practice, work more. Also, experienced dentists often work fewer hours.

EDUCATIONAL AND LEGAL REQUIREMENTS

All 50 states and the District of Columbia require dentists to be licensed. To qualify for a license in most states, candidates must graduate from an accredited dental school and pass written and practical examinations.

Education and Training. In 2006, there were fifty-six dental schools accredited by the American Dental Association (ADA) Commission on Dental Accreditation. Dental schools require a minimum of two years of college-level predental education prior to admittance. Most dental students have at least a bachelor's degree before entering dental school, although a few applicants are accepted to dental school after two or three years of college and complete their bachelor's degree while attending dental school.

High school and college students who want to become dentists should take courses in biology, chemistry, physics, health, and mathematics. College undergraduates planning on applying to dental school are required to take many science courses. Because of this, some choose a major in a science, such as biology or chemistry, while others take the required science coursework while pursuing a major in another subject.

All dental schools require applicants to take the Dental Admissions Test (DAT). When selecting students, schools consider scores earned on the DAT, applicants' grade point averages, and information gathered through recommendations and interviews. Competition for admission to dental school is keen.

Dental school usually lasts four academic years. Studies begin with classroom instruction and laboratory work in science, including anatomy, microbiology, biochemistry, and physiology. Beginning courses in clinical sciences, including laboratory techniques, are also completed. During the last two years, students treat patients, usually in dental clinics, under the supervision of licensed dentists. Most dental schools award the degree of Doctor of Dental Surgery (DDS). Others award an equivalent degree, Doctor of Dental Medicine (DMD).

Some dental school graduates work for established dentists as associates for one to two years to gain experience and save money to equip an office of their own. Most dental school graduates, however, purchase an established practice or open a new one immediately after graduation.

Licensure. A license is required to practice as a dentist. In most states, licensure requires passing written and practical examinations in addition to having a degree from an accredited dental school. Candidates may fulfill the written part of the state licensing requirements by passing the National Board Dental Examinations. Individual states or regional testing agencies administer the written or practical examinations.

In 2006, seventeen states licensed or certified dentists who intended to practice in a specialty area. Requirements include two to four years of postgraduate education and, in some cases, the completion of a special state examination. Most state licenses permit dentists to engage in both general and specialized practice.

Other Qualifications. Dentistry requires diagnostic ability and manual skills. Dentists should have good visual memory; excellent judgment regarding space, shape, and color; a high degree of manual dexterity; and scientific ability. Good business sense, self-discipline, and good communication skills are helpful for success in private practice.

Advancement. Dentists who want to teach or conduct research usually spend an additional two to five years in advanced dental training, in programs operated by dental schools or hospitals. A recent survey by the American Dental Education Association revealed that 11 percent of new graduates are enrolled in postgraduate training programs to prepare for a dental specialty.

EMPLOYMENT OPPORTUNITIES

Dentists held about 161,000 jobs in 2006. Employment was distributed among general practitioners and specialists as shown in **Table 8–1**.

Table 8–1

Projections data from the National Employment Matrix

Occupational title	Employment, 2006	Projected employment, 2016	Change, 2006–2016	
			Number	Percent
Dentists	161,000	176,000	15,000	9
Dentists, general	136,000	149,000	13,000	9
Oral and maxillofacial surgeons	7,700	8,400	700	9
Orthodontists	9,200	10,000	800	9
Prosthodontists	1,000	1,100	100	11
Dentists, all other specialties	6,900	7,400	500	7

NOTE: Data in this table are rounded.

About one-third of dentists were self-employed and not incorporated. Almost all dentists work in private practice. According to the ADA, about three out of four dentists in private practice are sole proprietors, and one in seven belongs to a partnership. A few salaried dentists work in hospitals and offices of physicians.

EMPLOYMENT TRENDS

Average employment growth will generate some job openings, but most openings will result from the need to replace the large number of dentists expected to retire. Job prospects should be good as new dentists take over established practices or start their own.

Employment Change. Employment of dentists is projected to grow nine percent through 2016, about as fast as the average for all occupations. The demand for dental services is expected to continue to increase. The overall population is growing, particularly the number of older people, which will increase the demand for dental care. As members of the baby-boom generation advance into middle age, a large number will need complicated dental work, such as bridges. In addition, elderly people today are more likely to retain their teeth than were their predecessors, so they will require much more care than in the past. The younger generation will continue to need preventive checkups despite an overall increase in the dental health of the public over the last few decades. Recently, some private insurance providers have increased their dental coverage. If this trend continues, those with new or expanded dental insurance will be more likely to visit a dentist than in the past. Also, while they are currently a small proportion of dental expenditures, cosmetic dental services, such as fitting braces for adults as well as children and providing teeth-whitening treatments, have become increasingly popular.

Employment of dentists, however, is not expected to keep pace with the increased demand for dental services. Productivity increases from new technology, as well as having dental hygienists and assistants perform some tasks, will allow dentists to perform more work than they have in the past. As their practices expand, dentists are likely to hire more hygienists and dental assistants to handle routine services.

Dentists will increasingly provide care and instruction aimed at preventing the loss of teeth, rather than simply providing treatments such as fillings. Improvements in dental technology also will allow dentists to offer more effective and less painful treatment to their patients.

Job Prospects. As an increasing number of dentists from the baby-boom generation reach retirement age, many of them will retire or work fewer hours. However, the number of applicants to, and graduates from, dental schools has increased in recent years. Therefore, younger dentists will be able to take over the work from older dentists who retire or cut back on hours, as well as provide dental services to accommodate the growing demand.

Demand for dental services tends to follow the business cycle, primarily because these services usually are paid for either by the patient or by private insurance companies. As a result, during slow times in the economy, demand for dental services can decrease; dentists may have difficulty finding employment, or if already in an established practice, they may work fewer hours because of reduced demand. Table 8–1 shows some projection data provided by the Department of Labor.

EARNINGS

Median annual earnings of salaried dentists were $136,960 in May 2006. Earnings vary according to number of years in practice, location, hours worked, and specialty. Self-employed dentists in private practice tend to earn more than do salaried dentists.

Dentists who are salaried often receive benefits paid by their employer, with health insurance and malpractice insurance being among the most common. However, like other business owners, self-employed dentists must provide their own health insurance, life insurance, retirement plans, and other benefits.

RELATED OCCUPATIONS

Dentists examine, diagnose, prevent, and treat diseases and abnormalities. Chiropractors, optometrists, physicians and surgeons, podiatrists, psychologists, and veterinarians do similar work.

ADDITIONAL INFORMATION

For information on dentistry as a career, a list of accredited dental schools, and a list of state boards of dental examiners contact:

- American Dental Association, Commission on Dental Accreditation, 211 E. Chicago Ave., Chicago, IL 60611. http://www.ada.org

For information on admission to dental schools, contact:

- American Dental Education Association, 1400 K St. NW., Suite 1100, Washington, DC 20005. http://www.adea.org

Persons interested in practicing dentistry should obtain the requirements for licensure from the board of dental examiners of the State in which they plan to work. To obtain information on scholarships, grants, and loans, including Federal financial aid, prospective dental students should contact the office of student financial aid at the schools to which they apply.

Dental Hygienists

WORK DESCRIPTION

Dental hygienists clean teeth and provide other preventive dental care; they also teach patients how to practice good oral hygiene. Hygienists examine patients' teeth and gums, recording the presence of diseases or abnormalities. They remove calculus, stains, and plaque from teeth; take and develop dental X-rays; and apply cavity preventive agents such as fluorides and pit and fissure sealants. In some states, hygienists administer local anesthetics and anesthetic gas; place and carve filling materials, temporary fillings, and periodontal dressings; remove sutures; and smooth and polish metal restorations.

Dental hygienists also help patients develop and maintain good oral health. For example, they may explain the relationship between diet and oral health, inform patients how to select toothbrushes, and show patients how to brush and floss their teeth. Dental hygienists use hand and rotary instruments, lasers, and ultrasonics to clean teeth; X-ray machines to take dental pictures; syringes with needles to administer local anesthetics; and models of teeth to explain oral hygiene.

The nature of the work may vary by practice setting. In schools, for example, hygienists may assist the dentist in examining children's teeth to determine the dental treatment required. Hygienists who have advanced training may teach or conduct research.

WORK ENVIRONMENT

Dental hygienists usually work in clean, well-lighted offices. Important health safeguards for persons in this occupation include regular medical checkups, strict adherence to proper radiologic procedures, compliance with required infection control procedures, including the latest safety precautions, and use of appropriate protective devices when administering nitrous oxide/oxygen analgesia. The occupation is one of several covered by the Consumer-Patient Radiation Health and Safety Board, which sets uniform standards for the training and certification of individuals who perform medical and dental radiologic procedures.

Most hygienists work 30 to 35 hours per week in jobs that may include Saturday or evening hours. Flexible scheduling is a distinctive feature of this job.

EMPLOYMENT OPPORTUNITIES

Dental hygienists held about 167,000 jobs in 2006. Because multiple job holding is common in this field, the number of jobs exceeds the number of hygienists. Almost all jobs for dental hygienists were in offices of dentists. A very small number worked for employment services, offices of physicians, or other industries.

EDUCATIONAL AND LEGAL REQUIREMENTS

Prospective dental hygienists must become licensed in the state in which they wish to practice. A degree from an accredited dental hygiene school is usually required along with licensure examinations.

Education and Training. A high school diploma and college entrance test scores are usually required for admission to a dental hygiene program. High school students interested in becoming a dental hygienist should take courses in biology, chemistry, and mathematics. Also, some dental hygiene programs require applicants to have completed at least one year of college. Specific entrance requirements vary from one school to another.

In 2006, there were 286 dental hygiene programs accredited by the Commission on Dental Accreditation. Most dental hygiene programs grant an associate degree, although some also offer a certificate, a bachelor's degree, or a master's degree. A minimum of an associate degree or certificate in dental hygiene is generally required for practice in a private dental office. A bachelor's or master's degree usually is required for research, teaching, or clinical practice in public or school health programs.

Schools offer laboratory, clinical, and classroom instruction in subjects such as anatomy, physiology, chemistry, microbiology, pharmacology, nutrition, radiography, histology (the study of tissue structure), periodontology (the study of gum diseases), pathology, dental materials, clinical dental hygiene, and social and behavioral sciences.

Licensure. Dental hygienists must be licensed by the state in which they practice. Nearly all states require candidates to graduate from an accredited dental hygiene school and pass both a written and clinical examination. The American Dental Association's Joint Commission on National Dental Examinations administers the written examination, which is accepted by all states and the District of Columbia. State or regional testing agencies administer the clinical examination. In addition, most states require an examination on the legal aspects of dental hygiene practice. Alabama is the only state that allows licensure candidates to take its examinations if they have been trained through a state-regulated on-the-job program in a dentist's office.

Other Qualifications. Dental hygienists should work well with others because they work closely with dentists and dental assistants as well as deal directly with patients. Hygienists also need good manual dexterity, because they use dental instruments within a patient's mouth, with little room for error.

EMPLOYMENT TRENDS

Dental hygienists rank among the fastest growing occupations, and job prospects are expected to remain excellent.

Employment Change. Employment of dental hygienists is expected to grow 30 percent through 2016, much faster than the average for all occupations. This projected growth ranks dental hygienists among the fastest growing occupations, in response to increasing demand for dental care and the greater use of hygienists.

The demand for dental services will grow because of population growth, older people increasingly retaining more teeth, and a growing focus on preventive dental care. To meet this demand, facilities that provide dental care, particularly dentists' offices, will increasingly employ dental hygienists, and more hygienists per office, to perform services that have been performed by dentists in the past.

Job Prospects. Job prospects are expected to remain excellent. Older dentists, who have been less likely to employ dental hygienists, are leaving the occupation and will be replaced by recent graduates, who are more likely to employ one or more hygienists. In addition, as dentists' workloads increase, they are expected to hire more hygienists to perform preventive dental care, such as cleaning, so that they may devote their own time to more complex procedures. **Table 8–2** shows some projection data provided by the Department of Labor.

Table 8-2

Projections data from the National Employment Matrix				
Occupational title	Employment, 2006	Projected employment, 2016	Change, 2006–2016	
			Number	Percent
Dentists hygienists	167,000	217,000	50,000	30

NOTE: Data in this table are rounded.

EARNINGS

Median hourly earnings of dental hygienists were $30.19 in May 2006. The middle 50 percent earned between $24.63 and $35.67 an hour. The lowest 10 percent earned less than $19.45, and the highest 10 percent earned more than $41.60 an hour.

Earnings vary by geographic location, employment setting, and years of experience. Dental hygienists may be paid on an hourly, daily, salary, or commission basis.

Benefits vary substantially by practice setting and may be contingent upon full-time employment. According to the American Dental Association, 86 percent of hygienists receive hospital and medical benefits.

RELATED OCCUPATIONS

Other workers supporting health practitioners in an office setting include dental assistants, medical assistants, occupational therapist assistants and aides, physical therapist assistants and aides, physician assistants, and registered nurses. Dental hygienists sometimes work with radiation technology, as do radiation therapists.

ADDITIONAL INFORMATION

For information on a career in dental hygiene, including educational requirements, contact:

- Division of Education, American Dental Hygienists Association, 444 N. Michigan Ave., Suite 3400, Chicago, IL 60611. http://www.adha.org

- For information about accredited programs and educational requirements, contact:

- Commission on Dental Accreditation, American Dental Association, 211 E. Chicago Ave., Suite 1814, Chicago, IL 60611. http://www.ada.org

- The State Board of Dental Examiners in each state can supply information on licensing requirements.

Dental Assistants

WORK DESCRIPTION

Dental assistants perform a variety of patient care, office, and laboratory duties. They work at chairside as dentists examine and treat patients. They make patients as comfortable as possible in the dental chair, prepare them for treatment, and obtain dental records. Assistants hand instruments and materials to dentists, and keep patients' mouths dry and clear by using suction or other devices. They also sterilize and disinfect instruments and equipment, prepare tray setups for dental procedures, and instruct patients on postoperative and general oral health care.

Some dental assistants prepare materials for making impressions and restorations, expose radiographs, and process dental X-ray film as directed by the dentist. State law determines which clinical tasks a dental assistant may perform, but in most states they may remove sutures, apply anesthetic and caries-preventive agents to the teeth and oral tissue, remove excess cement used in the filling process, and place rubber dams on the teeth to isolate them for individual treatment.

Those with laboratory duties make casts of the teeth and mouth from impressions taken by dentists, clean and polish removable appliances, and make temporary crowns. Dental assistants with office duties arrange and confirm appointments, receive patients, keep treatment records, send bills, receive payments, and order dental supplies and materials. Dental assistants should not be confused with dental hygienists, who are licensed to perform a wider variety of clinical tasks.

WORK ENVIRONMENT

Dental assistants work in a well-lighted, clean environment. Their work area is usually near the dental chair, so they can arrange instruments, materials, and medication and hand them to the dentist when needed. Dental assistants wear gloves and masks to protect themselves from infectious diseases. Following safety procedures minimizes the risks of handling radiographic equipment.

Most dental assistants have a 32 to 40-hour workweek, which may include work on Saturdays or evenings.

EMPLOYMENT OPPORTUNITIES

Dental assistants held about 280,000 jobs in 2006. Almost all jobs for dental assistants were in offices of dentists. A small number of jobs were in the federal, state, and local governments or in offices of physicians. About 35 percent of dental assistants worked part-time, sometimes in more than one dental office.

EDUCATIONAL AND LEGAL REQUIREMENTS

Many assistants learn their skills on the job, although an increasing number are trained in dental-assisting programs offered by community and junior colleges, trade schools, technical institutes, or the armed forces.

Education and Training. High school students interested in a career as a dental assistant should take courses in biology, chemistry, health, and office practices. For those wishing to pursue further education, the Commission on Dental Accreditation within the American Dental Association (ADA) approved 269 dental-assisting training programs in 2006. Programs include classroom, laboratory, and preclinical instruction in dental-assisting skills and related theory. In addition, students gain practical experience in dental schools, clinics, or dental offices. Most programs take one year or less to complete and lead to a certificate or diploma. Two-year programs offered in community and junior colleges lead to an associate degree. All programs require a high school diploma or its equivalent, and some require science or computer-related courses for admission. A number of private vocational schools offer four to six-month courses in dental assisting, but the Commission on Dental Accreditation does not accredit these programs.

A large number of dental assistants learn through on-the-job training. In these situations, the employing dentist or other dental assistants in the dental office teach the new assistant dental terminology, the names of the instruments, how to perform daily duties, how to interact with patients, and other things necessary to help keep the dental office running smoothly. While some things can be picked up easily, it may be a few months before new dental assistants are completely knowledgeable about their duties and comfortable doing all of their tasks without assistance.

A period of on-the-job training is often required even for those who have completed a dental-assisting program or have some previous experience. Different dentists may have their own styles of doing things that need to be learned before an assistant can be comfortable working with them. Office-specific information, such as where files are kept, will need to be learned at each new job. Also, as dental technology changes, dental assistants need to stay familiar with the tools and procedures that they will be using or helping dentists to use. On-the-job training is often sufficient to keep assistants up-to-date on these matters.

Licensure. Most states regulate the duties that dental assistants are allowed to perform. Some states require licensure or registration, which may include passing a written or practical examination. There are a variety of schools offering courses—approximately 10 to 12 months in length—that meet their state's requirements. Other states require dental assistants to complete state-approved education courses of four to twelve hours in length. Some states offer registration of other dental assisting credentials with little or no education required. Some states require continuing education to maintain licensure or registration. A few states allow dental assistants to perform any function delegated to them by the dentist.

Individual states have adopted different standards for dental assistants who perform certain advanced duties. In some states, for example, dental assistants who perform radiological procedures must complete additional training. Completion of the Radiation Health and Safety examination offered by Dental Assisting National Board (DANB) meets the standards in more than 30 states. Some states require completion of a state-approved course in radiology as well.

Certification and Other Qualifications. Certification is available through the Dental Assisting National Board (DANB) and is recognized or required in more than thirty states. Certification is an acknowledgment of an assistant's qualifications and professional competence and may be an asset when one is seeking employment. Candidates may qualify to take the DANB certification examination by graduating from an ADA-accredited dental assisting education program or by having two years of full-time, or four years of part-time, experience as a dental assistant. In addition, applicants must have current certification in cardiopulmonary resuscitation. For annual recertification, individuals must earn continuing education credits. Other organizations offer registration, most often at the state level.

Dental assistants must be a second pair of hands for a dentist; therefore, dentists look for people who are reliable, work well with others, and have good manual dexterity.

Advancement. Without further education, advancement opportunities are limited. Some dental assistants become office managers, dental-assisting instructors, dental product sales representatives, or insurance claims processors for dental insurance companies. Others go back to school to become dental hygienists. For many, this entry-level occupation provides basic training and experience and serves as a stepping-stone to more highly skilled and higher paying jobs.

EMPLOYMENT TRENDS

Employment is expected to increase much faster than average; job prospects are expected to be excellent.

Employment Change. Employment is expected to grow 29 percent from 2006 to 2016, which is much faster than the average for all occupations. In fact, dental assistants are expected to be among the fastest growing occupations over the 2006–2016 projection period.

Population growth, greater retention of natural teeth by middle-aged and older people, and an increased focus on preventive dental care for younger generations will fuel demand for dental services. Older dentists, who have been less likely to employ assistants or have employed fewer, are leaving the occupation and will be replaced by recent graduates, who are more likely to use one or more assistants. In addition, as dentists' workloads increase, they are expected to hire more assistants to perform routine tasks, so that they may devote their own time to more complex procedures.

Job Prospects. Job prospects for dental assistants should be excellent. In addition to job openings due to employment growth, numerous job openings will arise out of the need to

Table 8–3	*Projections data from the National Employment Matrix*			
Occupational title	Employment, 2006	Projected employment, 2016	Change, 2006–2016	
			Number	Percent
Dental assistants	280,000	362,000	82,000	29

NOTE: Data in this table are rounded.

replace assistants who transfer to other occupations, retire, or leave for other reasons. Many opportunities for entry-level positions offer on-the-job training, but some dentists prefer to hire experienced assistants or those who have completed a dental-assisting program. **Table 8–3** shows some projection data provided by the Department of Labor.

EARNINGS

Median hourly earnings of dental assistants were $14.53 in May 2006. The middle 50 percent earned between $11.94 and $17.44 an hour. The lowest 10 percent earned less than $9.87, and the highest 10 percent earned more than $20.69 an hour.

Benefits vary substantially by practice setting and may be contingent upon full-time employment. According to the American Dental Association, 87 percent of dentists offer reimbursement for continuing education courses taken by their assistants.

RELATED OCCUPATIONS

Other workers supporting health practitioners include dental hygienists, medical assistants, surgical technologists, pharmacy aides, pharmacy technicians, occupational therapist assistants and aides, and physical therapist assistants and aides.

ADDITIONAL INFORMATION

Information about career opportunities and accredited dental assistant programs is available from:

- Commission on Dental Accreditation, American Dental Association, 211 East Chicago Ave., Suite 1814, Chicago, IL 60611. http://www.ada.org

For information on becoming a Certified Dental Assistant and a list of state boards of dentistry, contact:

- Dental Assisting National Board, Inc., 676 North Saint Clair St., Suite 1880, Chicago, IL 60611. Internet: http://www.danb.org

For more information on a career as a dental assistant and general information about continuing education, contact:

- American Dental Assistants Association, 35 East Wacker Dr., Suite 1730, Chicago, IL 60601. http://www.dentalassistant.org

For more information about continuing education courses, contact:

- National Association of Dental Assistants, 900 South Washington St., Suite G-13, Falls Church, VA 22046.

9

NURSING

Key Terms

- Registered nurse (RN)
- ADN nurse
- BSN nurse
- Diploma nurse
- Advanced practice nurse (APN)
- Medical regimen
- Hospital nurses

- Nursing home nurses
- Home health nurses
- Clinical nurse specialists
- Certified nurse midwives
- Certified registered nurse anesthetists
- Licensed practical nurse (LPN)

Registered Nurses

WORK DESCRIPTION

Registered nurses (RNs), regardless of specialty or work setting, treat patients, educate patients and the public about various medical conditions, and provide advice and emotional support to patients' family members. RNs record patients' medical histories and symptoms, help perform diagnostic tests and analyze results, operate medical machinery, administer treatment and medications, and assist with patient follow-up and rehabilitation.

RNs teach patients and their families how to manage their illness or injury, explaining post-treatment home care needs; diet, nutrition, and exercise programs; and self-administration of medication and physical therapy. Some RNs work to promote general health by educating the public on warning signs and symptoms of disease. RNs also might run general health screening or immunization clinics, blood drives, and public seminars on various conditions.

When caring for patients, RNs establish a plan of care or contribute to an existing plan. Plans may include numerous activities, such as administering medication, including careful checking of dosages and avoiding interactions; starting, maintaining, and discontinuing intravenous (IV) lines for fluid, medication, blood, and blood products; administering therapies and treatments; observing the patient and recording those observations; and consulting with physicians and other healthcare clinicians. Some RNs provide direction to licensed practical nurses and nursing aids regarding patient care. RNs with advanced educational preparation and training may perform diagnostic and therapeutic procedures and may have prescriptive authority.

RNs can specialize in one or more areas of patient care. There generally are four ways to specialize. RNs can choose a particular work setting or type of treatment, such as *perioperative nurses*, who work in operating rooms and assist surgeons. RNs also may choose to specialize in specific health conditions, as do *diabetes management nurses*, who assist patients to manage diabetes. Other RNs specialize in working with one or more organs or body system types, such as *dermatology nurses*, who work with patients who have skin disorders. RNs also can choose to work with a well-defined population, such as *geriatric nurses*, who work with the elderly. Some RNs may combine specialties. For example, *pediatric oncology nurses* deal with children and adolescents who have cancer.

There are many options for RNs who specialize in a work setting or type of treatment. *Ambulatory care nurses* provide preventive care and treat patients with a variety of illnesses and injuries in physicians' offices or in clinics. Some ambulatory care nurses are involved in telehealth, providing care and advice through electronic communications media such as videoconferencing, the Internet, or by telephone. *Critical care nurses* provide care to patients with serious, complex, and acute illnesses or injuries that require very close monitoring and extensive medication protocols and therapies. Critical care nurses often work in critical or intensive care hospital units. *Emergency*, or *trauma*, *nurses* work in hospital or stand-alone emergency departments, providing initial assessments and care for patients with life-threatening conditions. Some emergency nurses may become qualified to serve as *transport nurses*, who provide medical care to patients who are transported by helicopter or airplane to the nearest medical facility. *Holistic nurses* provide care such as acupuncture, massage and aroma therapy, and biofeedback, which are meant to treat patients' mental and spiritual health in addition to their physical health. *Home healthcare nurses* provide at-home nursing care for patients, often as follow-up care after discharge from a hospital or from a rehabilitation, long-term care, or skilled nursing facility. *Hospice and palliative care nurses* provide care, most often in home or hospice settings, focused on maintaining quality of life for terminally ill patients. *Infusion nurses* administer medications, fluids, and blood to patients through injections into patients' veins. *Long-term care nurses* provide healthcare services on a recurring basis to patients with chronic physical or mental disorders, often in long-term care or skilled nursing facilities. *Medical-surgical nurses* provide health promotion and basic medical care to patients with various medical and surgical diagnoses. *Occupational health nurses* seek to prevent job-related injuries and illnesses, provide monitoring and emergency care services, and help employers implement health and safety standards. *Perianesthesia nurses* provide preoperative and postoperative care to patients undergoing anesthesia during surgery or other procedures. *Perioperative nurses* assist surgeons by selecting and handling instruments, controlling bleeding, and suturing incisions. Some of these nurses also can specialize in plastic and reconstructive surgery. *Psychiatric-mental health nurses* treat patients with personality and mood disorders. *Radiology nurses* provide care to patients undergoing diagnostic radiation procedures such as ultrasounds, magnetic resonance imaging, and radiation therapy for oncology diagnoses. *Rehabilitation nurses* care for patients with temporary and permanent disabilities. *Transplant nurses* care for both transplant recipients and living donors and monitor signs of organ rejection.

RNs specializing in a particular disease, ailment, or healthcare condition are employed in virtually all work settings, including physicians' offices, outpatient treatment facilities, home healthcare agencies, and hospitals. *Addictions nurses* care for patients seeking help with alcohol, drug, tobacco, and other addictions. *Intellectual and developmental disabilities nurses* provide care for patients with physical, mental, or behavioral disabilities; care may include help with feeding, controlling bodily functions, sitting or standing independently, and speaking or other communication. *Diabetes management nurses* help diabetics to manage their disease by teaching them proper nutrition and showing them how to test blood sugar levels and administer insulin injections. *Genetics nurses* provide early detection screenings, counseling, and treatment of patients with genetic disorders, including cystic fibrosis and Huntington's disease. *HIV/AIDS nurses* care for patients diagnosed with HIV and AIDS. *Oncology nurses* care for patients with various types of cancer and may assist in the administration of radiation and chemotherapies and follow-up monitoring. *Wound, ostomy, and continence nurses* treat patients with wounds caused by traumatic injury, ulcers, or arterial disease; provide postoperative care for patients with openings that allow for alternative methods of bodily waste elimination; and treat patients with urinary and fecal incontinence.

RNs specializing in treatment of a particular organ or body system usually are employed in hospital specialty or critical care units, specialty clinics, and outpatient care facilities. *Cardiovascular nurses* treat patients with coronary heart disease and those who have had heart surgery, providing services such as postoperative rehabilitation. *Dermatology nurses* treat patients with disorders of the skin, such as skin cancer and psoriasis. *Gastroenterology nurses* treat patients with digestive and intestinal disorders, including ulcers, acid reflux disease, and abdominal bleeding. Some nurses in this field also assist in specialized procedures such as endoscopies, which examine the gastrointestinal tract using a tube equipped with a light and a camera that can capture images of diseased tissue. *Gynecology nurses* provide care to women with disorders of the reproductive system, including endometriosis, cancer, and sexually transmitted diseases. *Nephrology nurses* care for patients with kidney disease caused by diabetes, hypertension, or substance abuse. *Neuroscience nurses* care for patients with dysfunctions of the nervous system, including brain and spinal cord injuries and seizures. *Ophthalmic nurses* provide care to patients with disorders of the eyes, including blindness and glaucoma, and to patients undergoing eye surgery. *Orthopedic nurses* care for patients with muscular and skeletal problems, including arthritis, bone fractures, and muscular dystrophy. *Otorhinolaryngology nurses* care for patients with ear, nose, and throat disorders, such as cleft palates, allergies, and sinus disorders. *Respiratory nurses* provide care to patients with respiratory disorders such as asthma, tuberculosis, and cystic fibrosis. *Urology nurses* care for patients with disorders of the kidneys, urinary tract, and male reproductive organs, including infections, kidney and bladder stones, and cancers.

RNs who specialize by population provide preventive and acute care in all healthcare settings to the segment of the population in whom they specialize, including newborns (neonatology), children and adolescents (pediatrics), adults, and the elderly (gerontology or geriatrics). RNs also may provide basic health care to patients outside of healthcare settings, in such venues as correctional facilities, schools, summer camps, and the military. Some RNs travel around the United States and abroad providing care to patients in areas with shortages of healthcare workers.

Most RNs work as staff nurses as members of a team providing critical health care. However, some RNs choose to become advanced practice nurses, who work independently or in collaboration with physicians, and may focus on the provision of primary care services. *Clinical nurse specialists* provide direct patient care and expert consultations in one of many nursing specialties, such as psychiatric-mental health. *Nurse anesthetists* provide anesthesia and related care before and after surgical, therapeutic, diagnostic and obstetrical procedures. They also provide pain management and emergency services, such as airway management. *Nurse-midwives* provide primary care to women, including gynecological exams, family planning advice, prenatal care, assistance in labor and delivery, and neonatal care. *Nurse practitioners* serve as primary and specialty care providers, providing a blend of nursing and healthcare services to patients and families. The most common specialty areas for nurse practitioners are family practice, adult practice, women's health, pediatrics, acute care, and geriatrics. Nurse practitioners can choose, however, from a variety of other specialties, including neonatology and mental health. Advanced practice nurses can prescribe medications in all states and in the District of Columbia.

Some nurses have jobs that require little or no direct patient care, but still require an active RN license. *Case managers* ensure that all of the medical needs of patients with severe injuries and severe or chronic illnesses are met. *Forensic nurses* participate in the scientific investigation and treatment of abuse victims, violence, criminal activity, and traumatic accident. *Infection control nurses* identify, track, and control infectious outbreaks in healthcare facilities and develop programs for outbreak prevention and response to biological terrorism. *Legal nurse consultants* assist lawyers in medical cases by interviewing patients and witnesses, organizing medical records, determining damages and costs, locating evidence, and educating lawyers about medical issues. *Nurse administrators* supervise nursing staff, establish work schedules and budgets, maintain medical supply inventories, and manage resources to ensure high-quality care. *Nurse educators* plan, develop, implement, and evaluate educational programs and curricula for the professional development of student nurses and RNs. *Nurse informaticists* manage and communicate nursing data and information to improve decision making by consumers, patients, nurses, and other healthcare providers. RNs also may work as healthcare consultants, public policy advisors, pharmaceutical and medical supply researchers and salespersons, and medical writers and editors.

WORK ENVIRONMENT

Most RNs work in well-lighted, comfortable healthcare facilities. Home health and public health nurses travel to patients' homes, schools, community centers, and other sites. RNs may spend considerable time walking, bending, stretching, and standing. Patients in hospitals and nursing care facilities require 24-hour care; consequently, nurses in these institutions may work nights, weekends, and holidays. RNs also may be on call—available to work on short notice. Nurses who work in offices, schools, and other settings that do not provide 24-hour care are more likely to work regular business hours. About 21 percent of RNs worked part-time in 2006, and 7 percent held more than one job.

Nursing has its hazards, especially in hospitals, nursing care facilities, and clinics, where nurses may be in close contact with individuals who have infectious diseases and with toxic, harmful, or potentially hazardous compounds, solutions, and medications. RNs must observe rigid, standardized guidelines to guard against disease and other dangers, such as those posed by radiation, accidental needle sticks, chemicals used to sterilize instruments, and anesthetics. In addition, they are vulnerable to back injury when moving patients, shocks from electrical equipment, and hazards posed by compressed gases. RNs also may suffer emotional strain from caring for patients suffering unrelieved intense pain, close personal contact with patients' families, the need to make critical decisions, and ethical dilemmas and concerns.

EMPLOYMENT OPPORTUNITIES

As the largest healthcare occupation, registered nurses held about 2.5 million jobs in 2006. Hospitals employed the majority of RNs, with 59 percent of jobs. Other industries also employed large shares of registered nurses. About eight percent of RN jobs were in offices of physicians, five percent in home healthcare services, five percent in nursing care facilities, four percent in employment services, and three percent in outpatient care centers. Remaining RNs worked mostly in government agencies, social assistance agencies, and educational services. About 21 percent of RNs worked part-time.

EDUCATIONAL AND LEGAL REQUIREMENTS

The three major educational paths to registered nursing are a bachelor's degree, an associate degree, and a diploma from an approved nursing program. Nurses most commonly enter the occupation by completing an associate degree or bachelor's degree program. Individuals then must complete a national licensing examination in order to obtain a nursing license. Further training or education can qualify nurses to work in specialty areas, and may help improve advancement opportunities.

Education and Training. There are three major educational paths to registered nursing—a bachelor's of science degree in nursing (BSN), an associate degree in nursing (ADN), and a diploma. BSN programs, offered by colleges and universities, take about 4 years to complete. In 2006, 709 nursing programs offered degrees at the bachelor's level. ADN programs, offered by community and junior colleges, take about two to three years to complete. About 850 RN programs granted associate degrees. Diploma programs, administered in hospitals, last about three years. Only about 70 programs in the United States offered diplomas. Generally, licensed graduates of any of the three types of educational programs qualify for entry-level positions.

Many RNs with an ADN or diploma later enter bachelor's programs to prepare for a broader scope of nursing practice. Often, they can find an entry-level position and then take advantage of tuition reimbursement benefits to work toward a BSN by completing an RN-to-BSN program. In 2006, there were 629 RN-to-BSN programs in the United States. Accelerated master's degree in nursing (MSN) programs also are available by combining one year of an accelerated BSN program with two years of graduate study. In 2006, there were 149 RN-to-MSN programs.

Accelerated BSN programs also are available for individuals who have a bachelor's or higher degree in another field and who are interested in moving into nursing. In 2006, 197 of these programs were available. Accelerated BS programs last 12 to 18 months and provide the fastest route to a BSN for individuals who already hold a degree. MSN programs also are available for individuals who hold a bachelor's or higher degree in another field.

Individuals considering nursing should carefully weigh the advantages and disadvantages of enrolling in a BSN or MSN program because, if they do, their advancement opportunities usually are broader. In fact, some career paths are open only to nurses with a bachelor's or master's degree. A bachelor's degree often is necessary for administrative positions and is a prerequisite for admission to graduate nursing programs in research, consulting, and teaching, and all four advanced practice nursing specialties—clinical nurse specialists, nurse anesthetists, nurse-midwives, and nurse practitioners. Individuals who complete a bachelor's degree receive more training in areas such as communication, leadership, and critical thinking, all of which are becoming more important as nursing care becomes more complex. Additionally, bachelor's degree programs offer more clinical experience in nonhospital settings. Education beyond a bachelor's degree can also help students looking to enter certain fields or increase advancement opportunities. In 2006, 448 nursing schools offered master's degrees, 108 offered doctoral degrees, and 58 offered accelerated BSN-to-doctoral programs.

All four advanced practice nursing specialties require at least a master's degree. Most programs include about two years of full-time study and require a BSN degree for entry; some programs require at least one to two years of clinical experience as an RN for admission. In 2006, there were 342 master's and post-master's programs offered for nurse practitioners, 230 master's and post-master's programs for clinical nurse specialists, 106 programs for nurse anesthetists, and 39 programs for nurse-midwives.

All nursing education programs include classroom instruction and supervised clinical experience in hospitals and other healthcare facilities. Students take courses in anatomy, physiology, microbiology, chemistry, nutrition, psychology and other behavioral sciences, and nursing. Coursework also includes the liberal arts for ADN and BSN students.

Supervised clinical experience is provided in hospital departments such as pediatrics, psychiatry, maternity, and surgery. A growing number of programs include clinical experience in nursing care facilities, public health departments, home health agencies, and ambulatory clinics.

Licensure and Certification. In all states, the District of Columbia, and U.S. territories, students must graduate from an approved nursing program and pass a national licensing examination, known as the NCLEX-RN, in order to obtain a nursing license. Nurses may be licensed in more than one state, either by examination or by the endorsement of a license issued by another state. The Nurse Licensure Compact Agreement allows a nurse who is licensed and permanently resides in one of the member states to practice in the other member states without obtaining additional licensure. In 2006, twenty states were members of the Compact, while two more were pending membership. All states require periodic renewal of licenses, which may require continuing education.

Certification is common, and sometimes required, for the four advanced practice nursing specialties—clinical nurse specialists, nurse anesthetists, nurse-midwives, and nurse practitioners. Upon completion of their educational programs, most advanced practice nurses become nationally certified in their area of specialty. Certification also is available in specialty areas for all nurses. In some states, certification in a specialty is required in order to practice that specialty.

Foreign-educated and foreign-born nurses wishing to work in the United States must obtain a work visa. To obtain the visa, nurses must undergo a federal screening program to ensure that their education and licensure are comparable to that of a U.S. educated nurse, that they have proficiency in written and spoken English, and that they have passed either the Commission on Graduates of Foreign Nursing Schools (CGFNS) Qualifying Examination or the NCLEX-RN. CGFNS administers the VisaScreen Program. (The Commission is an immigration-neutral, nonprofit organization that is recognized internationally as an authority on credentials evaluation in the healthcare field.) Nurses educated in Australia, Canada (except Quebec), Ireland, New Zealand, and the United Kingdom, or foreign-born nurses who were educated in the United States, are exempt from the language proficiency testing. In addition to these national requirements, foreign-born nurses must obtain state licensure in order to practice in the United States. Each state has its own requirements for licensure.

Other Qualifications. Nurses should be caring, sympathetic, responsible, and detail oriented. They must be able to direct or supervise others, correctly assess patients' conditions, and determine when consultation is required. They need emotional stability to cope with human suffering, emergencies, and other stresses.

Advancement. Some RNs start their careers as licensed practical nurses or nursing aides, and then go back to school to receive their RN degree. Most RNs begin as staff nurses in hospitals, and with experience and good performance often move to other settings or are promoted to more responsible positions. In management, nurses can advance from assistant unit manger or head nurse to more senior-level administrative roles of assistant director, director, vice president, or chief nurse. Increasingly, management-level nursing positions require a graduate or an advanced degree in nursing or health services administration. Administrative positions require leadership, communication and negotiation skills, and good judgment.

Some nurses move into the business side of health care. Their nursing expertise and experience on a healthcare team equip them to manage ambulatory, acute, home-based, and chronic care. Employers—hospitals, insurance companies, pharmaceutical manufacturers, and managed care organizations, among others—need RNs for health planning and development, marketing, consulting, policy development, and quality assurance. Other nurses work as college and university faculty or conduct research.

EMPLOYMENT TRENDS

Overall job opportunities for registered nurses are expected to be excellent, but may vary by employment and geographic setting. Employment of RNs is expected to grow much faster than the average for all occupations through 2016 and, because the occupation is very large, many new jobs will result. In fact, positions requiring registered nurses are projected to generate 587,000 new jobs, among the largest number of new jobs for any occupation. Additionally, hundreds of thousands of job openings will result from the need to replace experienced nurses who leave the occupation.

Employment Change. Employment of registered nurses is expected to grow 23 percent from 2006 to 2016, much faster than the average for all occupations. Growth will be driven by technological advances in patient care, which permit a greater number of health problems to be treated, and by an increasing emphasis on preventive care. In addition, the number of older people, who are much more likely than younger people to need nursing care, is projected to grow rapidly.

Employment of RNs will not grow at the same rate, however, in every industry. The projected growth rates for RNs in the industries with the highest employment of registered nurses are listed in **Table 9–1**.

Table 9–1		
Projected growth rates for RNs		
Offices of physicians		39%
Home health care services		39%
Outpatient care centers, except mental health and substance abuse		34%
Employment services		27%
General medical and surgical hospitals, public and private		22%
Nursing care facilities		20%

Employment is expected to grow more slowly in hospitals—health care's largest industry—than in most other healthcare industries. While the intensity of nursing care is likely to increase, requiring more nurses per patient, the number of inpatients (those who remain in the hospital for more than 24 hours) is not likely to grow by much. Patients are being discharged earlier, and more procedures are being done on an outpatient basis, both inside and outside hospitals. Rapid growth is expected in hospital outpatient facilities, such as those providing same-day surgery, rehabilitation, and chemotherapy.

Increasing numbers of sophisticated procedures, once performed only in hospitals, are being performed in physicians' offices and in outpatient care centers, such as freestanding ambulatory surgical and emergency centers. Accordingly, employment is expected to grow very fast in these places as health care in general expands.

Employment in nursing care facilities is expected to grow because of increases in the number of elderly, many of whom require long-term care. This growth, however, will be relatively slower than in other healthcare industries because of patient desire to be treated at home or in residential care facilities, and the increasing availability of these options. The financial pressure on hospitals to discharge patients as soon as possible should produce more admissions to nursing and residential care facilities, as well as to home health care. Job growth also is expected in units that provide specialized long-term rehabilitation for stroke and head injury patients, as well as units that treat Alzheimer's patients.

Employment in home health care is expected to increase rapidly in response to the growing number of older persons with functional disabilities, consumer preference for care in the home, and technological advances that make it possible to bring increasingly complex treatments into the home. The type of care demanded will require nurses who are able to perform complex procedures.

Rapid employment growth in the employment services industry is expected as hospitals, physician's offices, and other healthcare establishments utilize temporary workers to fill short-term staffing needs. And, as the demand for nurses grows, temporary nurses will be needed more often, further contributing to employment growth in this industry.

Job Prospects. Overall job opportunities are expected to be excellent for registered nurses. Employers in some parts of the country and in certain employment settings report difficulty in attracting and retaining an adequate number of RNs, primarily because of an aging RN workforce and a lack of younger workers to fill positions. Enrollments in nursing programs at all levels have increased more rapidly in the past few years as students seek jobs with stable employment. However, many qualified applicants are being turned away because of a shortage of nursing faculty. The need for nursing faculty will only increase as many instructors near retirement. Many employers also are relying on foreign-educated nurses to fill vacant positions.

Even though overall employment opportunities for all nursing specialties are expected to be excellent, they can vary by employment setting. Despite the slower employment growth in hospitals, job opportunities should still be excellent because of the relatively high turnover of hospital nurses. RNs working in hospitals frequently work overtime, or on night and weekend shifts, treating seriously ill and injured patients, all of which can contribute to stress and burnout. Hospital departments in which these working conditions occur most frequently—critical care units, emergency departments, and operating rooms—generally will have more job openings than other departments. To attract and retain qualified nurses, hospitals may offer signing bonuses, family-friendly work schedules, or subsidized training. A growing number of hospitals also are experimenting with online bidding to fill open shifts, in which nurses can volunteer to fill open shifts at premium wages. This practice can decrease the amount of mandatory overtime that nurses are required to work.

Although faster employment growth is projected in physicians' offices and outpatient care centers, RNs may face greater competition for these positions because they generally offer regular working hours and more comfortable working environments. There also may be some competition for jobs in employment services, despite a high rate of employment growth, because a large number of workers are attracted by the industry's relatively high wages and the flexibility of the work in this industry.

Generally, RNs with at least a bachelor's degree will have better job prospects than those without a bachelor's. In addition, all four advanced practice specialties—clinical nurse specialists, nurse practitioners, nurse-midwives, and nurse anesthetists—will be in high demand, particularly in medically underserved areas such as inner cities and rural areas. Relative to physicians, these RNs increasingly serve as lower-cost primary care providers. **Table 9–2** shows some projection data provided by the Department of Labor.

Table 9–2

Projections data from the National Employment Matrix

Occupational title	Employment, 2006	Projected employment, 2016	Change, 2006–2016	
			Number	Percent
Registered nurses	2,505,000	3,092,000	587,000	23

NOTE: Data in this table are rounded.

Earnings. Median annual earnings of registered nurses were $57,280 in May 2006. The middle 50 percent earned between $47,710 and $69,850. The lowest 10 percent earned less than $40,250, and the highest 10 percent earned more than $83,440. Median annual earnings in the industries employing the largest numbers of registered nurses in May 2006 are listed in **Table 9–3**.

Table 9–3

Median annual earnings in the industries employing the largest numbers of registered nurses in May 2006

Employment services	$64,260
General medical and surgical hospitals	$58,550
Home health care services	$54,190
Offices of physicians	$53,800
Nursing care facilities	$52,490

Many employers offer flexible work schedules, child care, educational benefits, and bonuses.

RELATED OCCUPATIONS

Because of the number of specialties for registered nurses, and the variety of responsibilities and duties, many other healthcare occupations are similar in some aspect of the job. Other occupations that deal directly with patients when providing care include licensed practical and licensed vocational nurses, physicians and surgeons, athletic trainers, respiratory therapists, massage therapists, dietitians and nutritionists, occupational therapists, physical therapists, and emergency medical technicians and paramedics. Other occupations that use advanced medical equipment to treat patients include cardiovascular technologists and technicians, diagnostic medical sonographers, radiologic technologists and technicians, radiation therapists, and surgical technologists. Workers who also assist other healthcare professionals in providing care include nursing, psychiatric, and home health aides; physician assistants; and dental hygienists. Some nurses take on a management role, similar to medical and health services managers.

ADDITIONAL INFORMATION

For information on a career as a registered nurse and nursing education, contact:

■ National League for Nursing, 61 Broadway, New York, NY 10006. http://www.nln.org

For information on baccalaureate and graduate nursing education, nursing career options, and financial aid, contact:

■ American Association of Colleges of Nursing, 1 Dupont Circle N.W., Suite 530, Washington, DC 20036. http://www.aacn.nche.edu

For additional information on registered nurses, including credentialing, contact:

■ American Nurses Association, 8515 Georgia Ave., Suite 400, Silver Spring, MD 20910. http://nursingworld.org

For information on the NCLEX-RN exam and a list of individual state boards of nursing, contact:

■ National Council of State Boards of Nursing, 111 E. Wacker Dr., Suite 2900, Chicago, IL 60611. http://www.ncsbn.org

For information on the nursing population, including workforce shortage facts, contact:

■ Bureau of Health Professions, 5600 Fishers Lane, Room 8-05, Rockville, MD 20857. http://bhpr.hrsa.gov

For information on obtaining U.S. certification and work visas for foreign-educated nurses, contact:

■ Commission on Graduates of Foreign Nursing Schools, 3600 Market St., Suite 400, Philadelphia, PA 19104. http://www.cgfns.org

For a list of accredited clinical nurse specialist programs, contact:

■ National Association of Clinical Nurse Specialists, 2090 Linglestown Rd., Suite 107, Harrisburg, PA 17110. http://www.nacns.org

For information on nurse anesthetists, including a list of accredited programs, contact:

■ American Association of Nurse Anesthetists, 222 Prospect Ave., Park Ridge, IL 60068.

For information on nurse-midwives, including a list of accredited programs, contact:

■ American College of Nurse-Midwives, 8403 Colesville Rd., Suite 1550, Silver Spring, MD 20910. http://www.midwife.org

For information on nurse practitioners, including a list of accredited programs, contact:

■ American Academy of Nurse Practitioners, P.O. Box 12846, Austin, TX 78711. http://www.aanp.org

For information on nurse practitioners education, contact:

■ National Organization of Nurse Practitioner Faculties, 1522 K St. NW., Suite 702, Washington, DC 20005. http://www.nonpf.org

For information on critical care nurses, contact:

■ American Association of Critical-Care Nurses, 101 Columbia, Aliso Viejo, CA 92656. http://www.aacn.org

For additional information on registered nurses in all fields and specialties, contact:

■ American Society of Registered Nurses, 1001 Bridgeway, Suite 411, Sausalito, CA 94965. http://www.asrn.org

Licensed Practical and Licensed Vocational Nurses

Work Description

Under the direction of physicians and registered nurses, *licensed practical nurses* (LPNs), or *licensed vocational nurses* (LVNs), care for people who are sick, injured, convalescent, or disabled. (The work of physicians and surgeons and of registered nurses is described elsewhere in this book.) The nature of direction and supervision required varies by state and job setting.

LPNs care for patients in many ways. Often, they provide basic bedside care. Many LPNs measure and record patients' vital signs, such as height, weight, temperature, blood pressure, pulse, and respiration. They also prepare and give injections and enemas, monitor catheters, dress wounds, and give alcohol rubs and massages. To help keep patients comfortable, they assist with bathing, dressing, and personal hygiene, turning in bed, standing, and walking. They might also feed patients who need help eating. Experienced LPNs may supervise nursing assistants and aides.

As part of their work, LPNs collect samples for testing, perform routine laboratory tests, and record food and fluid intake and output. They clean and monitor medical equipment. Sometimes, they help physicians and registered nurses perform tests and procedures. Some LPNs help to deliver, care for, and feed infants.

LPNs also monitor their patients and report adverse reactions to medications or treatments. LPNs gather information from patients, including their health history and how they are currently feeling. They may use this information to complete insurance forms, pre-authorizations, and referrals, and they share information with registered nurses and doctors to help determine the best course of care for a patient. LPNs often teach family members how to care for a relative or teach patients about good health habits.

Most LPNs are generalists and work in all areas of health care. However, some work in a specialized setting, such as a nursing home, a doctor's office, or in home health care. LPNs in nursing care facilities help to evaluate residents' needs, develop care plans, and supervise the care provided by nursing aides. In doctors' offices and clinics, they may be responsible for making appointments, keeping records, and performing other clerical duties. LPNs who work in home health care may prepare meals and teach family members simple nursing tasks. In some states, LPNs are permitted to administer prescribed medicines, start intravenous fluids, and provide care to ventilator-dependent patients.

Work Environment

Most licensed practical nurses in hospitals and nursing care facilities work a 40-hour week, but because hospital patients need round-the-clock care, some work nights, weekends, and holidays. They often stand for long periods and are subject to back injuries when moving patients. LPNs may face hazards from caustic chemicals, radiation, and infectious diseases. They often must deal with the stress of heavy workloads. In addition, the patients they care for may be confused, agitated, or uncooperative.

Employment Opportunities

Licensed practical nurses held about 749,000 jobs in 2006. About 26 percent of LPNs worked in hospitals, 26 percent in nursing care facilities, and another 12 percent in offices of physicians. Others worked for home healthcare services; employment services; residential care facilities; community care facilities for the elderly; outpatient care centers; and federal, state, and local government agencies. About 19 percent of LPNs worked part-time.

Educational and Legal Requirements

Most training programs, lasting about one year, are offered by vocational or technical schools or community or junior colleges. LPNs must be licensed to practice. Successful completion of a practical nurse program and passing an examination are required to become licensed.

Education and Training. All states and the District of Columbia require LPNs to pass a licensing examination, known as the NCLEX-PN, after completing a state-approved practical nursing program. A high school diploma or its equivalent usually is required for entry, although some programs accept candidates without a diploma, and some programs are part of a high school curriculum.

In 2006, there were more than 1,500 state-approved training programs in practical nursing in the United States. Most training programs are available in technical and vocational schools or community and junior colleges. Other programs are available through high schools, hospitals, and colleges and universities.

Most year-long practical nursing programs include both classroom study and supervised clinical practice (patient care). Classroom study covers basic nursing concepts and subjects related to patient care, including anatomy, physiology, medical–surgical nursing, pediatrics, obstetrics, psychiatric nursing, the administration of drugs, nutrition, and first aid. Clinical practice usually takes place in a hospital but sometimes includes other settings.

Licensure. The NCLEX-PN licensing exam is required in order to obtain licensure as an LPN. The exam is developed and administered by the National Council of State Boards of Nursing. The NCLEX-PN is a computer-based exam and varies in length. The exam covers four major categories: safe and effective care environment, health promotion and maintenance, psychosocial integrity, and physiological integrity.

Other qualifications. LPNs should have a caring, sympathetic nature. They should be emotionally stable because working with the sick and injured can be stressful. They also need to be observant, and to have good decision-making and communication skills. As part of a healthcare team, they must be able to follow orders and work under close supervision.

Advancement. In some employment settings, such as nursing homes, LPNs can advance to become *charge nurses* who oversee the work of other LPNs and of nursing aides. Some LPNs also choose to become registered nurses through numerous LPN-to-RN training programs.

EMPLOYMENT TRENDS

Employment of LPNs is projected to grow faster than average. Overall job prospects are expected to be very good, but job outlook varies by industry. The best job opportunities will occur in nursing care facilities and home healthcare services, while applicants for jobs in hospitals may face competition.

Employment Change. Employment of LPNs is expected to grow 14 percent between 2006 and 2016, faster than the average for all occupations, in response to the long-term care needs of an increasing elderly population and the general increase in demand for healthcare services.

Advances in technology now allow many procedures once performed only in hospitals to be performed in physicians' offices and in outpatient care centers, such as ambulatory surgical and emergency medical centers. LPNs care for patients who undergo these and other procedures, so employment of LPNs is projected to decline in traditional hospitals, but is projected to grow faster than average in most settings outside of hospitals. However, some hospitals are assigning a larger share of nursing duties to LPNs, which will temper the employment decline in hospital settings.

Employment of LPNs is expected to grow much faster than average in home healthcare services. Home healthcare agencies will offer a large number of new jobs for LPNs because of an increasing number of older people with functional disabilities, consumer preference for care in the home, and technological advances that make it possible to bring increasingly complex treatments into the home.

Employment of LPNs in nursing care facilities is expected to grow faster than average, and provide the greatest number of new jobs for LPNs, due to the growing number of eldery and disabled people in need of long-term care. In addition, as hospital stays shorten, LPNs will be needed in nursing care facilities to care for the increasing number of patients who have been discharged from the hospital but who are not yet ready to return home.

Job Prospects. Very good job opportunities are expected. Replacement needs will be a major source of job openings for LPNs, as many licensed practical nurses leave the occupation permanently. Rapid employment growth is projected in most healthcare industries, with the best job opportunities occurring in nursing care facilities and in home healthcare services. However, applicants for jobs in hospitals may face competition as the number of hospital jobs for LPNs declines. **Table 9–4** shows some projection data provided by the Department of Labor.

Table 9–4

Projections data from the National Employment Matrix

Occupational title	Employment, 2006	Projected employment, 2016	Change, 2006–2016	
			Number	Percent
Licensed practical and licensed vocational nurses	749,000	854,000	105,000	14

NOTE: Data in this table are rounded.

EARNINGS

Median annual earnings of licensed practical nurses were $36,550 in May 2006. The middle 50 percent earned between $31,080 and $43,640. The lowest 10 percent earned less than $26,380, and the highest 10 percent earned more than $50,480. Median annual earnings in the industries employing the largest numbers of licensed practical nurses in May 2006 are shown in **Table 9–5**.

Table 9–5

Median annual earnings in the industries employing the largest numbers of licensed practical nurses in May 2006

Employment services	$42,110
Nursing care facilities	$38,320
Home health care services	$37,880
General medical and surgical hospitals	$35,000
Offices of physicians	$32,710

RELATED OCCUPATIONS

LPNs work closely with people while helping them. So do emergency medical technicians and paramedics; medical assistants; nursing, psychiatric, and home health aides; registered nurses; athletic trainers; social and human service assistants; pharmacy technicians; pharmacy aides; and surgical technologists.

ADDITIONAL INFORMATION

For information about practical nursing, contact the following organizations:

- National Association for Practical Nurse Education and Service, Inc., P.O. Box 25647, Alexandria, VA 22313. http://www.napnes.org

- National Federation of Licensed Practical Nurses, Inc., 605 Poole Dr., Garner, NC 27529. http://www.nflpn.org

- National League for Nursing, 61 Broadway, New York, NY 10006. http://www.nln.org

Information on the NCLEX-PN licensing exam is available from:

- National Council of State Boards of Nursing, 111 East Wacker Dr., Suite 2900, Chicago, IL 60611. http://www.ncsbn.org

A list of state-approved LPN programs is available from individual state boards of nursing.

10

PHARMACY

Key Terms

- Pharmaceuticals
- Compounding
- Medication profile
- Side effects
- Pharmacotherapists
- Nutrition support pharmacists
- Radiopharmacists/nuclear pharmacists
- Board examination
- Internship
- Pharmaceutical chemistry
- Pharmacy technicians
- Pharmacy aides/assistants

Pharmaceutical Partners

One of the main tools of physicians treating patients is medication. Although doctors prescribe *pharmaceuticals*, the professionals who actually dispense the medication are *pharmacists*. The details of the pharmacist's profession follow in the rest of this chapter.

Pharmacists

WORK DESCRIPTION

Pharmacists advise health professionals and the public on the proper selection and use of medicines. The special knowledge of the pharmacist is needed because of the complexity and potential *side effects* of the large and growing number of pharmaceutical products on the market.

In addition to providing information, pharmacists dispense drugs and medicines prescribed by physicians, dentists, and other health professionals. Pharmacists must understand the use, composition, and effects of drugs and how they are tested for purity and strength. *Compounding*—the actual mixing of ingredients to form powders, tablets, capsules, ointments, and solutions—is now only a small part of a pharmacist's practice, as most medicines are produced by pharmaceutical companies in the dosage and form used by the patient.

Pharmacists practicing in community or retail pharmacies may have other duties. Pharmacists in community or retail pharmacies counsel patients as well as answer questions about prescription drugs, such as those regarding possible adverse reactions or interactions. They provide information about over-the-counter drugs and make recommendations after asking a series of health questions, such as whether the customer is taking any other medications. Such pharmacists also give advice about durable medical equipment and home healthcare supplies. Those who own or manage community pharmacies may sell non-health-related merchandise, hire and supervise personnel, and oversee the general operation of the pharmacy. Some community pharmacists provide specialized services to help patients manage conditions such as diabetes, asthma, smoking cessation, or high blood pressure.

Widespread use of computers in retail stores allows pharmacists to create medication profiles for their customers. A medication profile is a computerized record of the customer's drug therapy. Pharmacists use these profiles to ensure that harmful drug interactions do not occur and to monitor a patient's compliance with the doctor's instructions—by comparing how long it takes the patient to finish the drug versus the recommended daily dosage.

Pharmacists in hospitals and clinics dispense medications and advise the medical staff on the selection and side effects of drugs. They may make sterile solutions, buy medical supplies, teach students majoring in health-related disciplines, and perform administrative duties. They also may be involved in patient education, monitoring of drug regimens, and drug use evaluation. In addition, pharmacists work as consultants to the medical team on drug therapy and patient care. In some hospitals they make hospital rounds with physicians, talking to patients and monitoring pharmaceutical use. Their role is crucial to safe, efficient, and proper therapeutic care.

Pharmacists who work in home health care monitor drug therapy and prepare *infusions*— solutions that are injected into patients—and other medications for use in the home.

Pharmacotherapists specialize in drug therapy and work closely with physicians. They may make hospital rounds with physicians—talking to patients and monitoring pharmaceutical use.

Nutrition support pharmacists help determine and prepare the drugs needed for nutrition. Some pharmacists work in oncology (cancer) and psychiatric drug treatment.

Some pharmacists prepare and dispense *radioactive pharmaceuticals*. Called *radiopharmacists* or *nuclear pharmacists*, they apply the principles and practices of pharmacy and radiochemistry to produce radioactive drugs that are used for diagnosis and therapy.

Pharmacists use their basic educational backgrounds in a host of federal and state positions. At the federal level, pharmacists hold staff and supervisory posts in the U.S. Public Health Service, the Veterans Administration, the Food and Drug Administration, and in all branches of the armed services. Certain of these posts provide commissioned officer status; others come under the heading of civil service.

State and federal boards are boards charged with regulating the practice of pharmacy to preserve and protect public health. These legal boards governing pharmacy practice usually employ pharmacists as full-time executive officers. One or more inspectors, frequently also pharmacists, serve each state. As state health agencies consolidate their purchases, pharmacists are often engaged as purchasers of medical and pharmaceutical supplies on a mass scale.

Nearly every state has an active pharmaceutical association that employs a full-time executive officer. This officer is usually a graduate of a college of pharmacy. Several national professional associations are also guided by pharmacists with an interest and special talent in organizational work.

Other pharmacists are engaged in highly specialized tasks. There are pharmacists in advertising, packaging, technical writing, magazine editing, and science reporting. Pharmacists with legal training serve as patent lawyers or as experts in pharmaceutical law. Pharmacists are found in U.S. space laboratories, aboard ships such as the S.S. Hope, and directing giant manufacturing firms.

WORK ENVIRONMENT

Pharmacists usually work in clean, well-lighted, and well-ventilated areas that resemble small laboratories. Shelves are lined with hundreds of different drug products. In addition, some items are refrigerated, and many substances (narcotics, depressants, and stimulants) are kept under lock and key. Pharmacists spend much time on their feet. When working with dangerous pharmaceutical products, pharmacists must take the proper safety precautions, such as wearing gloves and masks and working with special protective equipment. Because pharmacies in many communities and hospitals are open around the clock, pharmacists in those settings may have to work evenings, nights, weekends, and holidays.

Most full-time salaried pharmacists work approximately 40 hours a week, and about 10 percent work more than 50 hours. *Consultant pharmacists* may travel to nursing homes or other facilities to monitor patients' drug therapy. About 16 percent of pharmacists worked part-time in 2006.

EMPLOYMENT OPPORTUNITIES

Pharmacists held about 243,000 jobs in 2006. About 62 percent worked in community pharmacies that were either independently owned or part of a drugstore chain, grocery store, department store, or mass merchandiser. Most community pharmacists were salaried employees, but some were self-employed owners. About 23 percent of pharmacists worked in hospitals. A small proportion worked in mail-order and Internet pharmacies, pharmaceutical wholesalers, offices of physicians, and the federal government.

EDUCATIONAL AND LEGAL REQUIREMENTS

A license is required in all states, the District of Columbia, and all U.S. territories. In order to obtain a license, pharmacists must earn a Doctor of Pharmacy (PharmD) degree from a college of pharmacy and pass several examinations.

Education and Training. Pharmacists must earn a PharmD degree from an accredited college or school of pharmacy. The PharmD degree has replaced the Bachelor of Pharmacy degree, which is no longer being awarded. To be admitted to a PharmD program, an applicant must have completed at least two years of postsecondary study, although most applicants have completed three or more years. Other entry requirements usually include courses in mathematics and natural sciences, such as chemistry, biology, and physics, as well as courses in the humanities and social sciences. In 2007, 92 colleges and schools of pharmacy were accredited to confer degrees by the Accreditation Council for Pharmacy Education (ACPE). About 70 percent of PharmD programs require applicants to take the Pharmacy College Admissions Test (PCAT).

Courses offered at colleges of pharmacy are designed to teach students about all aspects of drug therapy. In addition, students learn how to communicate with patients and other healthcare providers about drug information and patient care. Students also learn professional ethics, concepts of public health, and medication distribution systems management. In addition to receiving classroom instruction, students in PharmD programs spend about one-fourth of their time in a variety of pharmacy practice settings under the supervision of licensed pharmacists.

During the 2006–2007 academic year, 70 colleges of pharmacy also awarded the Master of Science degree or the PhD degree. Both degrees are awarded after the completion of a PharmD and are designed for those who want additional clinical, laboratory, and research experience. Areas of graduate study include *pharmaceutics* and *pharmaceutical chemistry* (physical and chemical properties of drugs and dosage forms), *pharmacology* (effects of drugs on the body), and *pharmacy administration*. Many Master's and PhD degree holders go on to do research for a drug company or teach at a university.

Other options for pharmacy graduates who are interested in further training include one or two-year residency programs or fellowships. Pharmacy residencies are postgraduate training programs in pharmacy practice and usually require the completion of a research project. These programs are often mandatory for pharmacists who wish to work in hospitals. Pharmacy fellowships are highly individualized programs designed to prepare participants to work in a specialized area of pharmacy, such as clinical practice or research laboratories. Some pharmacists who own their own pharmacy obtain a master's degree in business administration (MBA). Others may obtain a degree in public administration or public health.

Licensure. A license to practice pharmacy is required in all states, the District of Columbia, and all U.S. territories. To obtain a license, a prospective pharmacist must graduate from a college of pharmacy that is accredited by the ACPE and pass a series of examinations. All states, U.S. territories, and the District of Columbia require the North American Pharmacist Licensure Exam (NAPLEX), which tests pharmacy skills and knowledge. Forty-four states and the District of Columbia also require the Multistate Pharmacy Jurisprudence Exam (MPJE), which tests pharmacy law. Both exams are administered by the National Association of Boards of Pharmacy (NABP). Of the eight states and territories that do not require the MJPE, each has its own pharmacy law exam. In addition to the NAPLEX and MPJE, some states and territories require additional exams that are unique to their jurisdiction.

All jurisdictions except California currently grant license transfers to qualified pharmacists who already are licensed by another jurisdiction. Many pharmacists are licensed to practice in more than one jurisdiction. Most jurisdictions require continuing education for license renewal. Persons interested in a career as a pharmacist should check with individual jurisdiction boards of pharmacy for details on license renewal requirements and license transfer procedures.

Graduates of foreign pharmacy schools may also qualify for licensure in some U.S. states and territories. These individuals must apply for certification from the Foreign Pharmacy Graduate Examination Committee (FPGEC). Once certified, they must pass the Foreign Pharmacy Graduate Equivalency Examination (FPGEE), Test of English as a Foreign Language (TOEFL) exam, and Test of Spoken English (TSE) exam. They then must pass all of the exams required by the licensing jurisdiction, such as the NAPLEX and MJPE. Applicants who graduated from programs accredited by the Canadian Council for Accreditation of Pharmacy Programs (CCAPP) between 1993 and 2004 are exempt from FPGEC certification and examination requirements.

Other Qualifications. Prospective pharmacists should possess scientific aptitude, good interpersonal skills, and a desire to help others. They also must be conscientious and pay close attention to detail, because the decisions they make affect human lives.

Advancement. In community pharmacies, pharmacists usually begin at the staff level. Pharmacists in chain drugstores may be promoted to pharmacy supervisor or manager at the store level, then to manager at the district or regional level, and later to an executive position within the chain's headquarters. Hospital pharmacists may advance to supervisory or administrative positions. After they gain experience and secure the necessary capital, some pharmacists become owners or part owners of independent pharmacies. Pharmacists in the pharmaceutical industry may advance into marketing, sales, research, quality control, production, or other areas.

EMPLOYMENT TRENDS

Employment is expected to increase much faster than the average through 2016. As a result of rapid growth and the need to replace workers who leave the occupation, job prospects should be excellent.

Employment Change. Employment of pharmacists is expected to grow by 22 percent between 2006 and 2016, which is much faster than the average for all occupations. The increasing numbers of middle-aged and elderly people—who use more prescription drugs than younger people—will continue to spur demand for pharmacists throughout the projection period. Other factors likely to increase the demand for pharmacists include scientific advances that will make more pharmaceutical products available and increasing coverage of prescription drugs by health insurance plans and Medicare.

As the use of prescription drugs increases, demand for pharmacists will grow in most practice settings, such as community pharmacies, hospital pharmacies, and mail-order pharmacies. As the population ages, assisted living facilities and home care organizations should see particularly rapid growth. Demand will also increase as cost conscious insurers, in an attempt to improve preventive care, use pharmacists in areas such as patient education and administration of vaccines.

Demand is also increasing in managed care organizations where pharmacists analyze trends and patterns in medication use, and in *pharmacoeconomics*—the cost and benefit analysis of different drug therapies. New jobs also are being created in disease management—the development of new methods for curing and controlling diseases—and in sales and marketing. Rapid growth is also expected in *pharmacy informatics*—the use of information technology to improve patient care.

Job Prospects. Excellent opportunities are expected for pharmacists over the 2006 to 2016 period. Job openings will result from rapid employment growth, and from the need to replace workers who retire or leave the occupation for other reasons. **Table 10–1** shows some projection data provided by the Department of Labor.

Table 10–1

Projections data from the National Employment Matrix

Occupational title	Employment, 2006	Projected employment, 2016	Change, 2006–2016	
			Number	Percent
Pharmacists	243,000	296,000	53,000	22

NOTE: Data in this table are rounded.

EARNINGS

The median annual wage-and-salary of pharmacists in May 2006 was $94,520. The middle 50 percent earned between $83,180 and $108,140 a year. The lowest 10 percent earned less than $67,860, and the highest 10 percent earned more than $119,480 a year. Median annual earnings in the industries employing the largest numbers of pharmacists in May 2006 are shown in **Table 10–2**.

According to a 2006 survey by *Drug Topics Magazine*, pharmacists in retail settings earned an average of $92,291 per year, while pharmacists in institutional settings earned an average of $97,545. Full-time pharmacists earned an average of $102,336, while part-time pharmacists earned an average of $55,589.

Table 10–2	*Median annual earnings in the industries employing the largest numbers of pharmacists in May 2006*	
Department stores		$99,050
Grocery stores		$95,600
Pharmacies and drug stores		$94,640
General medical and surgical hospitals		$93,640

RELATED OCCUPATIONS

Pharmacy technicians and *pharmacy aides* also work in pharmacies. Persons in other professions who may work with pharmaceutical compounds include biological scientists, medical scientists, chemists, and materials scientists. Increasingly, pharmacists are involved in patient care and therapy, work that they have in common with physicians and surgeons.

ADDITIONAL INFORMATION

For information on pharmacy as a career, preprofessional and professional requirements, programs offered by colleges of pharmacy, and student financial aid, contact:

- American Association of Colleges of Pharmacy, 1426 Prince St., Alexandria, VA 22314. http://www.aacp.org

General information on careers in pharmacy is available from:

- American Society of Health-System Pharmacists, 7272 Wisconsin Ave., Bethesda, MD 20814. http://www.ashp.org
- National Association of Chain Drug Stores, 413 N. Lee St., P.O. Box 1417-D49, Alexandria, VA 22313-1480. Internet: http://www.nacds.org
- Academy of Managed Care Pharmacy, 100 North Pitt St., Suite 400, Alexandria, VA 22314. http://www.amcp.org
- American Pharmacists Association, 1100 15th Street, NW Suite 400., Washington, DC 20005. http://www.aphanet.org

Information on the North American Pharmacist Licensure Exam (NAPLEX) and the Multistate Pharmacy Jurisprudence Exam (MPJE) is available from:

- National Association of Boards of Pharmacy, 1600 Feehanville Dr., Mount Prospect, IL 60056. http://www.nabp.net

State licensure requirements are available from each state's board of pharmacy. Information on specific college entrance requirements, curricula, and financial aid is available from any college of pharmacy.

Pharmacy Technicians

Pharmacy technicians, assistants, and/or aides help licensed pharmacists provide medication and other healthcare products to patients. Pharmacy technicians usually perform more complex tasks than assistants do, although in some states their duties and job titles overlap. Technicians typically perform routine tasks, such as counting and labeling, to help prepare prescribed medication for patients. A pharmacist must check every prescription before it can be given to a patient, however. Technicians refer any questions regarding prescriptions, drug information, or health matters to the pharmacist. Pharmacy *assistants* or *aides* usually have fewer, less complex responsibilities than pharmacy *technicians* do. Aides and assistants are often clerks or cashiers who primarily answer telephones, handle money, stock shelves, and perform other clerical duties.

Pharmacy technicians who work in retail pharmacies have varying responsibilities depending on state rules and regulations. Technicians receive written prescriptions or requests for prescription refills from patients or representatives. They must verify that the information on the prescription is complete and accurate. To prepare a prescription, technicians must retrieve, count, pour, weigh, measure, and sometimes mix the medication. Then, they must prepare the prescription labels, select the type of prescription container, and affix the prescription and auxiliary labels to the container. Once the prescription is filled, technicians price and file the prescription, which must be checked by a pharmacist before it is given to a patient. Technicians may establish and maintain patient profiles, prepare insurance claim forms, and stock and take inventory of both prescription and over-the-counter medications. Some also clean the pharmacy equipment, help with the maintenance of equipment and supplies, and manage the cash register.

In hospitals, pharmacy technicians have added responsibilities. They read patient charts and prepare and deliver medicines to patients. The pharmacist must check the order before it is delivered to the patient. The technician then copies information regarding the prescribed medication onto the patient's profile. Technicians may also assemble a 24-hour supply of medicine for every patient. They package and label each dose separately. The package is then placed in the medicine cabinet of each patient, until the supervising pharmacist checks it. It is then given to the patient. Technicians are responsible for keeping a running inventory of medicines, chemicals, and other supplies used along the way.

WORK ENVIRONMENT

Pharmacy technicians and assistants work in clean, organized, well-lighted, and well-ventilated areas. Most of their workday is spent on their feet. They may be required to lift heavy boxes or to use stepladders to retrieve supplies from high shelves.

Both technicians and assistants work the same hours as pharmacists do. This schedule includes evenings, nights, weekends, and some holidays. Most technicians work 35 to 45 hours per week. Because some hospital and retail pharmacies are open 24 hours per day, technicians and assistants may work varying shifts. There are many opportunities for part-time work in both retail and hospital settings.

EMPLOYMENT OPPORTUNITIES

Pharmacy technicians held about 285,000 jobs in the United States in 2006. About 71 percent of jobs were in retail pharmacies, either independently owned or part of a drugstore chain, grocery store, department store, or mass retailer. About 18 percent of jobs were in hospitals and a small proportion was in mail-order and Internet pharmacies, offices of physicians, pharmaceutical wholesalers, and the federal government.

EDUCATIONAL AND LEGAL REQUIREMENTS

Most pharmacy technicians are trained on-the-job, but employers favor applicants who have formal training, certification, or previous experience. Strong customer service skills also are important. Pharmacy technicians may become supervisors, may move into specialty positions or into sales, or may become pharmacists.

Education and Training. Although most pharmacy technicians receive informal on-the-job training, employers favor those who have completed formal training and certification. However, there are currently few state and no federal requirements for formal training or certification of pharmacy technicians. Employers who have insufficient resources to give on-the-job training often seek formally educated pharmacy technicians. Formal education programs and certification emphasize the technician's interest in and dedication to the work. In addition to the military, some hospitals, proprietary schools, vocational or technical colleges, and community colleges offer formal education programs.

Formal pharmacy technician education programs require classroom and laboratory work in a variety of areas, including medical and pharmaceutical terminology, pharmaceutical calculations, pharmacy recordkeeping, pharmaceutical techniques, and pharmacy law and ethics. Technicians also are required to learn medication names, actions, uses, and doses. Many training programs include internships, in which students gain hands-on experience in actual pharmacies. After completion, students receive a diploma, a certificate, or an associates degree, depending on the program.

Prospective pharmacy technicians with experience working as an aide in a community pharmacy or volunteering in a hospital may have an advantage. Employers also prefer applicants with experience managing inventories, counting tablets, measuring dosages, and using computers. In addition, a background in chemistry, English, and health education may be beneficial.

Certification and Other Qualifications. Two organizations, the Pharmacy Technician Certification Board and the Institute for the Certification of Pharmacy Technicians, administer national certification examinations. Certification is voluntary in most states, but is required by some states and employers. Some technicians are hired without formal training, but under the condition that they obtain certification within a specified period of time. To be eligible for either exam, candidates must have a high school diploma or GED, no felony convictions of any kind within five years of applying, and no drug or pharmacy related felony convictions at any point. Employers, often pharmacists, know that individuals who pass the exam have a standardized body of knowledge and skills. Many employers also will reimburse the costs of the exam.

Under both programs, technicians must be recertified every two years. Recertification requires 20 hours of continuing education within the two-year certification period. At least one hour must be in pharmacy law. Continuing education hours can be earned from several different sources, including colleges, pharmacy associations, and pharmacy technician training programs. Up to ten hours of continuing education can be earned on the job under the direct supervision and instruction of a pharmacist.

Strong customer service and teamwork skills are needed because pharmacy technicians interact with patients, coworkers, and healthcare professionals. Mathematics, spelling, and reading skills also are important. Successful pharmacy technicians are alert, observant, organized, dedicated, and responsible. They should be willing and able to take directions, but be able to work independently without constant instruction. They must be precise; details are sometimes a matter of life and death. Candidates interested in becoming pharmacy technicians cannot have prior records of drug or substance abuse.

Advancement. In large pharmacies and health-systems, pharmacy technicians with significant training, experience, and certification can be promoted to supervisory positions, mentoring and training pharmacy technicians with less experience. Some may advance into specialty positions such as *chemo therapy technician* and *nuclear pharmacy technician*. Others move into sales. With a substantial amount of formal training, some pharmacy technicians go on to become pharmacists.

EMPLOYMENT TRENDS

Employment is expected to increase much faster than the average through 2016, and job opportunities are expected to be good.

Employment Change. Employment of pharmacy technicians is expected to increase by 32 percent from 2006 to 2016, which is much faster than the average for all occupations. The increased number of middle-aged and elderly people—who use more prescription drugs than younger people—will spur demand for technicians throughout the projection period. In addition, as scientific advances bring treatments for an increasing number of conditions, more pharmacy technicians will be needed to fill a growing number of prescriptions.

As cost-conscious insurers begin to use pharmacies as patient-care centers, pharmacy technicians will assume responsibility for some of the more routine tasks previously performed by pharmacists. In addition, they will adopt some of the administrative duties that were previously performed by pharmacy aides, such as answering phones and stocking shelves.

Reducing the need for pharmacy technicians to some degree, however, will be the growing use of drug dispensing machines. These machines increase productivity by completing some of the pharmacy technician's duties, namely counting pills and placing them into prescription containers. These machines are only used for the most common medications, however, and their effect on employment should be minimal.

Almost all states have legislated the maximum number of technicians who can safely work under a pharmacist at one time. Changes in these laws could directly affect employment.

Job Prospects. Good job opportunities are expected for full-time and part-time work, especially for technicians with formal training or previous experience. Job openings for pharmacy technicians will result from employment growth, and from the need to replace workers who transfer to other occupations or leave the labor force. **Table 10–3** shows some projection data provided by the Department of Labor.

Table 10–3	Projections data from the National Employment Matrix				
Occupational title	**Employment, 2006**	**Projected employment, 2016**	**Change, 2006–2016**		
			Number	**Percent**	
Pharmacy technicians	285,000	376,000	91,000	32	

NOTE: Data in this table are rounded.

EARNINGS

Median hourly earnings of wage-and-salary pharmacy technicians in May 2006 were $12.32. The middle 50 percent earned between $10.10 and $14.92. The lowest 10 percent earned less than $8.56, and the highest 10 percent earned more than $17.65. Median hourly earnings in the industries employing the largest numbers of pharmacy technicians in May 2006 are shown in **Table 10–4**.

Table 10–4	Median hourly earnings in the industries employing the largest numbers of pharmacy technicians in May 2006
General medical and surgical hospitals	$13.86
Grocery stores	$12.78
Pharmacies and drug stores	$11.50

Certified pharmacy technicians may earn more. Shift differentials for working evenings or weekends also can increase earnings. Some technicians belong to unions representing hospital or grocery store workers.

RELATED OCCUPATIONS

This occupation is most closely related to pharmacists and pharmacy aides. Workers in other medical support occupations include dental assistants, medical transcriptionists, medical records and health information technicians, occupational therapist assistants and aides, and physical therapist assistants and aides.

ADDITIONAL INFORMATION

For information on pharmacy technician certification programs, contact:

■ Pharmacy Technician Certification Board, 2215 Constitution Ave. NW, Washington DC 20037-2985. http://www.ptcb.org

■ Institute for the Certification of Pharmacy Technicians, 2536 S. Old Hwy 94, Suite 214, St. Charles, MO 63303. http://www.nationaltechexam.org

For a list of accredited pharmacy technician training programs, contact:

■ American Society of Health-System Pharmacists, 7272 Wisconsin Ave., Bethesda, MD 20814. http://www.ashp.org

For pharmacy technician career information, contact:

■ National Pharmacy Technician Association, P.O. Box 683148, Houston, TX 77268. http://www.pharmacytechnician.org

Pharmacy Aides

WORK DESCRIPTION

Pharmacy aides perform administrative duties in pharmacies. Aides often are clerks or cashiers who primarily answer telephones, handle money, stock shelves, and perform other clerical duties. They work closely with pharmacy *technicians*. Pharmacy technicians usually perform more complex tasks than do aides, although in some states the duties and titles of the jobs overlap. Aides refer any questions regarding prescriptions, drug information, or health matters to a pharmacist.

Pharmacy aides may establish and maintain patient profiles, prepare insurance claim forms, and stock and take inventory of prescription and over-the-counter medications. Accurate record keeping is necessary to help avert dangerous drug interactions. In addition, because many people have medical insurance to help pay for prescriptions, pharmacy aides must correspond efficiently and accurately with third-party insurance providers to obtain payment. Pharmacy aides also maintain inventory and inform the pharmacy supervisor of stock needs so that the pharmacy does not run out of vital medications that customers need. Some aides also help with the maintenance of equipment and supplies.

WORK ENVIRONMENT

Pharmacy aides work in clean, organized, well-lighted, and well-ventilated areas. Most of their workday is spent on their feet. They may be required to lift heavy boxes or to use stepladders to retrieve supplies from high shelves.

Aides work the same hours as pharmacists do. These include evenings, nights, weekends, and some holidays, particularly in facilities that are open 24 hours a day, such as hospitals and some retail pharmacies.

EMPLOYMENT OPPORTUNITIES

Pharmacy aides held about 50,000 jobs in 2006. About 82 percent worked in retail pharmacies, most of which were in drug stores but some of which were in grocery stores, department stores, or mass retailers. About seven percent of aides worked in hospitals.

EDUCATIONAL AND LEGAL REQUIREMENTS

Most pharmacy aides are trained on the job. Employers prefer applicants with previous experience and strong customer service skills. Many pharmacy aides go on to become pharmacy technicians.

Education and Training. Most pharmacy aides receive informal on-the-job training, but employers favor those with at least a high school diploma. Prospective pharmacy aides with experience working as cashiers may have an advantage when applying for jobs. Employers also prefer applicants with experience managing inventories and using computers.

Pharmacy aides begin their training by observing a more experienced worker. After they become familiar with the store's equipment, policies, and procedures, they begin to work on their own. Once they become experienced, aides are not likely to receive additional training, except when new equipment is introduced or when policies or procedures change.

Other Qualifications. Strong customer service and communication skills are essential, as pharmacy aides frequently interact with patients, fellow employees, and other healthcare professionals. Aides entering the field also need strong spelling, reading, and mathematical skills. Successful pharmacy aides are organized, dedicated, friendly, and responsible. They should be willing and able to take direction. Candidates interested in becoming pharmacy aides cannot have prior records of drug or substance abuse.

Advancement. With experience or certification, many pharmacy aides go on to become pharmacy technicians. Some become pharmacists after completing a substantial amount of formal training.

EMPLOYMENT TRENDS

Employment of pharmacy aides is expected to decline rapidly from 2006 to 2016. Job prospects, however, should be good.

Employment Change. Employment of pharmacy aides is expected to decline rapidly, decreasing by 11 percent over the 2006 to 2016 period. Demand for pharmacy aides will fall as pharmacy technicians become increasingly responsible for answering phones, stocking shelves, operating cash registers, and performing other administrative tasks. In addition, with increased training, many pharmacy aides will become pharmacy technicians, which will result in further declines in pharmacy aide jobs.

Job Prospects. Despite declining employment, job opportunities for full-time and part-time work are expected to be good. The frequent need to replace workers who leave the occupation will create opportunities for interested applicants. Aides with related work experience in pharmacies, or as cashiers or stock clerks in other retail settings, should have the best opportunities. **Table 10–5** shows some projection data provided by the Department of Labor.

EARNINGS

Median hourly wage-and-salary earnings of pharmacy aides were $9.35 in May 2006. The middle 50 percent earned between $7.89 and $11.58; the lowest 10 percent earned less than $6.92, and the highest 10 percent earned more than $14.64. Median hourly earnings in the industries employing the largest numbers of pharmacy aides in May 2006 are shown in **Table 10–6**.

Table
10–5

Projections data from the National Employment Matrix

Occupational title	Employment, 2006	Projected employment, 2016	Change, 2006–2016	
			Number	Percent
Pharmacy aides	50,000	45,000	-5,600	-11

NOTE: Data in this table are rounded.

Table
10–6

Median hourly earnings in the industries employing the largest numbers of pharmacy aides in May 2006

General medical and surgical hospitals	$11.53
Grocery stores	$9.87
Pharmacies and drug stores	$8.97

ADDITIONAL INFORMATION

Since pharmacy aide jobs are on-the-job training, specific information is always available from any potential employer.

11

DIETETICS

Key Terms

- Nutritionists
- Clinical dietitians
- Consultant dietitians
- Community dietitians
- Business dietitian
- Management dietitians
- Research dietitians

- Educator dietitian
- American Dietetic Association (ADA)
- Registration
- Internships
- Dietetic technician, registered (DTR)
- Dietetic assistant

Dietitians

WORK DESCRIPTION

Dietitians and *nutritionists* are professionals trained in applying the principles of nutrition to food selection and meal preparation. They help prevent and treat illnesses by promoting healthy eating habits, scientifically evaluating clients' diets, and suggesting diet modifications. They counsel individuals and groups; set up and supervise food service systems for institutions such as schools, hospitals, and prisons; promote sound eating habits through education; and conduct research. Major areas of specialization include clinical, management, community, business and industry, and consultant dietetics. Dietitians also work as educators and researchers.

Clinical dietitians provide nutritional services for patients in hospitals, nursing homes, clinics, or doctors' offices. They assess patients' nutritional needs, develop and implement nutrition programs, and evaluate and report the results. Clinical dietitians confer with doctors and nurses about each patient so as to coordinate nutritional and medical needs.

Expanding knowledge in medical science has led to practice specialties in dietetics. Increasingly, clinical dietitians specialize in such areas as management of obese patients, care of the critically ill, renal care, and diabetes care. Those who care for critically ill patients oversee the preparation of custom-mixed, high-nutrition formulas for patients who require tube or intravenous feedings. Dietitians who specialize in *renal dietetics* treat dialysis patients and other individuals with kidney problems; those who work with diabetics are responsible for establishing long-term nutritional care programs and a system for close monitoring.

Aside from assessing nutritional needs and developing a plan of treatment for individual patients, clinical dietitians may also perform administrative and managerial duties. In a nursing home or small hospital, the dietitian may also manage the food service department.

Consulting has become a significant specialty in dietetics. It has appeal for dietitians who need flexible work time and have a desire to be autonomous. *Consultant dietitians* work under contract with healthcare facilities or in their own private practices. They perform nutrition screenings for their clients, and they offer advice on diet-related concerns such as weight loss or cholesterol reduction. Some work for wellness programs, sports teams, supermarkets, and other nutrition-related businesses. They may consult with food service managers, providing expertise in sanitation, safety procedures, menu development, budgeting, and planning. They advise food and pharmaceutical industries; speak at professional seminars; author food, nutrition, and diet books; counsel patients in nursing homes and medical and dental centers; plan food service systems; and tailor nutrition regimens within fitness programs for athletes, dancers, and others.

Community dietitians counsel individuals and groups on sound nutrition practices to prevent disease and to promote good health. Employed in such places as home health agencies, HMOs, and human service agencies that provide group and home-delivered meals, their job is to evaluate individual needs, establish nutritional care plans, and communicate the principles of good nutrition in a way that individuals and their families can understand. Many community dietitians counsel on food selection in relation to lifestyle. They coordinate nutrition awareness and disease prevention programs in settings such as public health agencies, day care centers, and health clubs.

In addition to evaluating clients, dietitians working in a home health setting may provide informal instruction on nutrition, grocery shopping, or preparation of special infant formulas. In HMOs, dietitians provide nutritional counseling on a range of topics, from weight control to menu planning for diabetics. The dietitian may also collaborate with other HMO staff in conducting information sessions on such subjects as alcoholism, smoking, or hypertension.

Practice opportunities for clinical and community dietitians are becoming more diverse due to increased interest in nutrition and fitness on the part of the public and the medical profession alike. This new awareness has resulted in opportunities for private practitioners in areas such as manufacturing, advertising, and marketing food. Dietitians who work for food manufacturers or grocery store chains may analyze the nutritional content of foods for labeling purposes or marketing efforts. They may also prepare literature for distribution to customers, students, or other interested parties. Dietitians employed by magazines may determine the nutritional content of new recipes, analyze and report on the effectiveness of new diets, or report on important topics in nutrition, such as the importance of dietary fiber or the value of vitamin supplements.

Dietitians are becoming increasingly visible in business. As businesses become more cognizant of the public's desire for accurate nutrition information, they are eager to hire experts. The *business dietitian* works as a professional resource for corporations in product development, food styling, and menu design; as the sales professional or purchasing agent representing food, equipment, or nutrition product accounts; and as a food, nutrition, or marketing expert in public relations and media.

Management dietitians are responsible for large-scale food services in such places as hospitals, company cafeterias, prisons, schools, and colleges and universities. They supervise the planning, preparation, and service of meals; select, train, and direct food service supervisors and workers; budget for and purchase food, equipment, and supplies; enforce sanitary and safety regulations; and prepare records and reports. Increasingly, dietitians use computer programs to plan meals that satisfy nutrition requirements and are economical at the same time. Dietitians who are directors of dietetic departments also decide on departmental policy; coordinate dietetic services with the activities of other departments; and are responsible for the dietetic department's budget, which in large organizations may amount to millions of dollars annually.

Research dietitians usually are employed in academic medical centers or educational institutions, although some work in community health programs. Using established research methods and analytical techniques, they conduct studies in areas that range from basic science to practical applications. Research dietitians may examine changes in the way the body uses food over the course of a lifetime, for example, or the interaction of drugs and diet. They may investigate nutritional needs of persons with particular diseases, behavior modification as it relates to diet and nutrition, or applied topics such as food service systems and equipment. Often research dietitians collaborate with life scientists, physicians, nurses, biomedical engineers, and researchers from other disciplines.

Dietitians have always recognized the need to teach, whether in clinical practice, community settings, or corporations, and some are specifically interested in pursuing careers as health educators. The educator dietitian teaches the science of nutrition and food service systems management in colleges, universities, and hospitals; conducts nutrition and food service systems research; and authors' articles and books on nutrition and food service systems. Dietitians in education usually hold advanced degrees and have considerable experience.

WORK ENVIRONMENT

Most dietitians work 40 hours per week. About one in three dietitians worked part-time in 2006. Those employed in hospitals sometimes work on weekends, while those in commercial food services tend to have irregular hours. Dietitians and nutritionists spend much of their time in clean, well-lighted, and well-ventilated areas such as research laboratories, classrooms, or offices near food preparation areas. However, they may spend time in kitchens and serving areas that are often hot and steamy and where some light lifting may be required. Dietitians and nutritionists in clinical settings may be on their feet for most of the workday. Those involved in consulting spend a significant amount of time traveling.

EMPLOYMENT OPPORTUNITIES

Dietitians and nutritionists held about 57,000 jobs in 2006. More than half of all jobs were in hospitals, nursing care facilities, outpatient care centers, or offices of physicians and other health practitioners. State and local government agencies provided additional jobs—mostly in correctional facilities, health departments, and other public-health-related areas. Some dietitians and nutritionists were employed in special food services, an industry made up of firms providing food services on contract to facilities such as colleges and universities, airlines, correctional facilities, and company cafeterias.

Other jobs were in public and private educational services, community care facilities for the elderly (which includes assisted-living facilities), individual and family services, home healthcare services, and the federal government—mostly in the U.S. Department of Veterans Affairs. Some dietitians were self-employed, working as consultants to facilities such as hospitals and nursing care facilities, or providing dietary counseling to individuals.

Experienced dietitians may advance to assistant, associate, or director of a dietetic department, or they may become self-employed. Some dietitians specialize in areas such as renal or *pediatric dietetics*. Others may leave the occupation to become sales representatives for equipment, pharmaceutical, or food manufacturers. Advancement to higher-level positions in teaching and research requires graduate education; public health nutritionists usually must earn a graduate degree. Graduate study in institutional or business administration is valuable to those interested in management dietetics.

Clinical specialization offers another path to career advancement. Specialty areas for clinical dietitians include kidney disease, diabetes, cancer, heart disease, pediatrics, and gerontology.

EDUCATIONAL AND LEGAL REQUIREMENTS

Dietitians and nutritionists need at least a bachelor's degree. Licensure, certification, or registration requirements vary by state.

Education and training. Becoming a dietitian or nutritionist usually requires at least a bachelor's degree in dietetics, foods and nutrition, food service systems management, or a related area. Graduate degrees also are available. College students in these majors take courses in foods, nutrition, institution management, chemistry, biochemistry, biology, microbiology, and physiology. Other suggested courses include business, mathematics, statistics, computer science, psychology, sociology, and economics. High school students interested in becoming a dietitian or nutritionist should take courses in biology, chemistry, mathematics, health, and communications.

As of 2007, there were 281 bachelor's degree programs and 22 master's degree programs approved by the American Dietetic Association's Commission on Accreditation for Dietetics Education.

Licensure. Of the forty-eight states and jurisdictions with laws governing dietetics, thirty-five require licensure, twelve require statutory certification, and one requires registration. Requirements vary by state. As a result, interested candidates should determine the requirements of the state in which they want to work before sitting for any exam.

In states that require licensure, only people who are licensed can work as dietitians and nutritionists. States that require statutory certification limit the use of occupational titles to people who meet certain requirements; individuals without certification can still practice as a dietitian or nutritionist but without using certain titles. Registration is the least restrictive form of state regulation of dietitians and nutritionists. Unregistered people are permitted to practice as a dietitian or nutritionist.

Certification and other qualifications. Although not required, the Commission on Dietetic Registration of the American Dietetic Association awards the Registered Dietitian credential to those who pass an exam after completing academic coursework and a supervised internship. This certification is different from the statutory certification regulated by some states and discussed in the previous section. To maintain a Registered Dietitian status, workers must complete at least seventy-five credit hours in approved continuing education classes every five years.

A supervised internship, required for certification, can be completed in one of two ways. The first requires the completion of a program accredited by the Commission on Dietetic Registration. As of 2007, there were fifty-three accredited programs that combined academic and supervised practice experience and generally lasted four to five years. The second option requires the completion of 900 hours of supervised practice experience in any of the 265 accredited internships. These internships may be full-time programs lasting six to twelve months or part-time programs lasting two years.

Advancement. Experienced dietitians may advance to management positions, such as assistant director, associate director, or director of a dietetic department, or may become self-employed. Some dietitians specialize in areas such as renal, diabetic, cardiovascular, or pediatric dietetics. Others leave the occupation to become sales representatives for equipment, pharmaceutical, or food manufacturers. A master's degree can help some workers to advance their careers, particularly in career paths related to research, advanced clinical positions, or public health.

EMPLOYMENT TRENDS

Average employment growth is projected. Good job opportunities are expected, especially for dietitians with specialized training, an advanced degree, or certifications beyond the particular State's minimum requirement.

Employment change. Employment of dietitians and nutritionists is expected to increase 9 percent during the 2006–2016 projection decade, *about as fast as the average* for all occupations. Job growth will result from an increasing emphasis on disease prevention through improved dietary habits. A growing and aging population will boost demand for nutritional counseling and treatment in hospitals, residential care facilities, schools, prisons, community health programs, and home healthcare agencies. Public interest in nutrition and increased emphasis on health education and prudent lifestyles also will spur demand, especially in food service management.

Employment growth, however, may be constrained if some employers substitute other workers, such as health educators, food service managers, and dietetic technicians, to do work related to nutrition. Also, demand for nutritional therapy services is related to the ability of patients to pay, either out-of-pocket or through health insurance, and although more insurance plans now cover nutritional therapy services, the extent of such coverage varies among plans. Growth may be curbed by limitations on insurance reimbursement for dietetic services.

Hospitals will continue to employ a large number of dietitians and nutritionists to provide medical nutritional therapy and plan meals. Hospitals also will continue, however, to contract with outside agencies for food service and move medical nutritional therapy to outpatient care facilities, slowing job growth related to food service in hospitals, outpatient facilities, and with other employers.

The number of dietitian positions in nursing care facilities is expected to decline, as these establishments continue to contract with outside agencies for food services. However, employment is expected to grow rapidly in contract providers of food services, in outpatient care centers, and in offices of physicians and other health practitioners.

Finally, with increased public awareness of obesity and diabetes, Medicare coverage may be expanded to include medical nutrition therapy for renal and diabetic patients, creating job growth for dietitians and nutritionists specializing in those diseases.

Job prospects. In addition to employment growth, job openings will result from the need to replace experienced workers who retire or leave the occupation for other reasons. Overall job opportunities will be good for dietitians and nutritionists, particularly for licensed and registered dietitians. Job opportunities should be particularly good in outpatient care facilities, offices of physicians, and food service management. Dietitians and nutritionists without a bachelor's degree will face keen competition for jobs.

Dietitians with specialized training, an advanced degree, or certifications beyond the particular state's minimum requirement will experience the best job opportunities. Those specializing in renal and diabetic nutrition or gerontological nutrition will benefit from the growing number of diabetics and the aging of the population. **Table 11–1** shows some projection data provided by the Department of Labor.

EARNINGS

Median annual earnings of dietitians and nutritionists were $46,980 in May 2006. The middle 50 percent earned between $38,430 and $57,090. The lowest 10 percent earned less than $29,860, and the highest 10 percent earned more than $68,330. Median annual earnings in the industries employing the largest numbers of dietitians and nutritionists in May 2006 are shown in **Table 11–2**.

According to the American Dietetic Association, median annualized wages for registered dietitians in 2005 varied by practice area as follows: $53,800 in consultation and business; $60,000 in food and nutrition management; $60,200 in education and research; $48,800 in clinical nutrition/ambulatory care; $50,000 in clinical nutrition/long-term care; $44,800 in

Table
11–1

Projections data from the National Employment Matrix

Occupational title	Employment, 2006	Projected employment, 2016	Change, 2006–2016	
			Number	Percent
Dietitians and nutritionists	57,000	62,000	4,900	9

NOTE: Data in this table are rounded.

Table
11–2

Median annual earnings in the industries employing the largest numbers of pharmacists in May 2006

Outpatient care centers	$49,950
General medical and surgical hospitals	$47,320
State government	$46,690
Nursing care facilities	$46,660
Local government	$43,250

community nutrition; and $45,000 in clinical nutrition/acute care. Salaries also vary by years in practice, education level, and geographic region.

RELATED OCCUPATIONS

Workers in other occupations who may apply the principles of dietetics include food service managers, health educators, dietetic technicians, and registered nurses.

ADDITIONAL INFORMATION

For a list of academic programs, scholarships, and other information about dietetics, contact:

■ The American Dietetic Association, 120 South Riverside Plaza, Suite 2000, Chicago, IL 60606-6995. http://www.eatright.org

For information on the Registered Dietitian exam and other specialty credentials, contact:

■ The Commission on Dietetic Registration, 120 South Riverside Plaza, Suite 2000, Chicago, IL 60606-6995. http://www.cdrnet.org

Dietetic Technicians

WORK DESCRIPTION

A dietetic technician, registered (DTR), works as a member of the food service, management, and healthcare team, independently or in consultation with a registered dietitian. The dietetic technician supervises support staff, monitors cost-control procedures, interprets and implements quality assurance procedures, counsels individuals or small groups, screens patients/clients for nutritional status, and develops nutrition care plans. The dietetic technician helps to supervise food production and service; plans menus; tests new products for use in the facility; and selects, schedules, and conducts orientation programs for personnel. The technician may also be involved in selecting personnel and providing on-the-job training. The dietetic technician obtains, evaluates, and uses dietary histories to plan nutritional care for patients. Using this information, the technician guides families and individuals in selecting food, preparing it, and planning menus based on nutritional needs. The dietetic technician has an active part in calculating nutrient intakes and dietary patterns.

WORK ENVIRONMENT

Most dietetic technicians work 40 hours per week. They may work weekends as well as early or late shifts, depending on the facility in which they are employed. They spend some of their time in clean, well-lighted, ventilated areas, and some time in hot, steamy kitchens and serving areas. They may be on their feet for most of their working day, and may be required to do some lifting.

EMPLOYMENT OPPORTUNITIES

Job opportunities for dietetic technicians vary depending on the geographic area and the number of hospitals within that area. Job opportunities are available in hospitals, clinics, day care centers, restaurants, health clubs, WIC programs, Meals on Wheels programs, community health programs, and nursing homes. Dietetic technicians also work in university food service operations, some commercial food establishments, correctional facilities, public schools, health clubs, weight management clinics, food companies, and contract food management companies.

EDUCATIONAL AND LEGAL REQUIREMENTS

Individuals interested in becoming a Dietetic Technician, Registered, should expect to study a wide variety of topics focusing on food, nutrition, and management. These areas of study are supported by communication, and by the sciences: biological, physiological, behavioral, and social. Becoming a Dietetic Technician involves a combination of academic preparation and supervised practice culminating in a minimum of an associate degree from an institution sponsoring a program accredited or approved by the Commission on Accreditation for Dietetics Education (CADE) of the American Dietetic Association.

DTRs are trained in food and nutrition and are an integral part of health care and food service management teams. They must meet met the following criteria to earn the DTR credential:

- Achieve at least a two-year associates degree at a U.S. regionally accredited college or university.

- Complete a dietetic technician program approved by the Commission on Accreditation for Dietetics Education of the ADA, including 450 hours of supervised practice experience in various community programs, health care, and food service facilities.

- Pass a national, written examination administered by the Commission on Dietetic Registration.

- Complete continuing professional educational requirements to maintain registration.

EMPLOYMENT TRENDS

The job market for DTRs is assumed to be similar to that for dietitians and nutritionists. According to the U.S. Bureau of Labor Statistics, employment of dietitians and nutritionists is expected to grow faster than the average for all occupations through the year 2014 because of increased emphasis on disease prevention, a growing and aging population, and public interest in nutrition. Employment in hospitals is expected to show little change because of anticipated slow growth and reduced lengths of hospital stay. In contrast, faster growth is anticipated in nursing homes, residential care facilities, and physician clinics.

EARNINGS

The salary levels of DTRs vary with region, employment setting, geographical location, scope of responsibility, and so on. The range in 2006 was $16,000–$35,000.

RELATED OCCUPATIONS

Workers with duties similar to those of dietetic technicians include associate-degree nurses, licensed practical nurses, and dietary managers.

ADDITIONAL INFORMATION

The ADA's Web site (www.eatright.org) includes additional information about careers in dietetics. Access this information directly at www.eatright.org/join/careers.html.

Names, addresses, and directors' names of educational programs that are accredited or approved by the Commission on Accreditation for Dietetics Education of the ADA are online at http://www.eatright.org/cade/. For additional information, such as a course catalog or list of required nutrition classes, contact the CADE-accredited/approved programs that you are interested in attending. For other career guidance information, search ADA's website.

Dietetic Assistants

The dietetic assistant is the third level among personnel involved in the provision of nutritional care. The amount of involvement in patient care depends on education, training, and work experience.

The dietetic assistant, under direct supervision from a food service manager, dietetic technician, or dietitian, works in preparation and serving areas of hospitals and other healthcare facilities. The government, community agencies, restaurants, schools, universities, and the military also offer opportunities.

Dietetic assistant positions have no educational requirements. Assistants frequently receive on-the-job training only, although it is now common practice in accredited facilities to send the worker to a minimum of 45 clock hours of formal classroom/laboratory classes. These classes are often held at junior and community or technical colleges and taught by a registered dietitian. After having passed the course, the student receives a certificate. The assistant must be employed by a health or community agency such as Head Start, school lunch program, or extended care facility to be eligible to take these courses.

Most dietetic assistants are assigned a preceptor who observes and assists them with assigned tasks or projects at the workplace. The assistant performs routine duties as assigned by the manager, dietetic technician, or dietitian according to the job specification.

Others who perform similar tasks are nursing assistants and home health aides. Salaries vary widely within and among geographic locations.

Because requirements for employment vary widely in this job, prospective employees are advised to ask the agency to which they apply if certification will be an expected part of obtaining the job. Employers who want certified dietetic assistants are often willing to pay all or a part of the student's fees.

Dietetic assistants may progress up the career ladder by completing additional coursework and becoming eligible to take an entrance examination given by the Dietary Managers Association to be promoted to dietary manager of a food service. Those who do not belong to the association may take the additional approved courses and obtain jobs as food service supervisors. Accredited healthcare facilities are required to have a person with one or more advanced courses as the head of the dietary department.

12

OPTOMETRY

Key Terms

- Optometrists
- Ophthalmologists
- Dispensing opticians
- Franchises

- Doctor of Optometry
- Video display terminals
- Corrective lens
- Apprenticeship program

Optometrists

WORK DESCRIPTION

More than half the people in the United States wear glasses or contact lenses. *Optometrists* (doctors of optometry) provide much of the vision care these people need.

Optometrists should not be confused with either *ophthalmologists* or *dispensing opticians*. *Ophthalmologists* are physicians (doctors of medicine or osteopathy) who specialize in medical diagnosis and treatment of vision disorders, especially diseases and injuries to the eye. Ophthalmologists may perform eye surgery and prescribe drugs or other eye treatment, as well as lenses. *Dispensing opticians* fit and adjust eyeglasses and may in some states fit contact lenses according to prescriptions written by ophthalmologists or optometrists, but they do not examine eyes or prescribe treatment.

Optometrists are primary eye care providers who examine people's eyes to diagnose and, in some cases, treat vision problems and eye disease. They use instrumentation and observation to evaluate eye health and to test patients' visual acuity, depth and color perception, as well as their ability to focus and coordinate the eyes. They analyze test results and develop a treatment plan. Optometrists prescribe eyeglasses, contact lenses, vision therapy, and low-vision rehabilitation. They administer drugs to patients to aid in the diagnosis of eye vision problems and prescribe drugs to treat some eye diseases. Optometrists often provide preoperative and postoperative care to cataract, laser vision correction, and other eye surgery patients. They also diagnose conditions caused by systemic diseases such as diabetes and high blood pressure, and they refer patients to other health practitioners as needed.

Although most optometrists are in general practice, some specialize in work with the elderly or with children. Others work with partially sighted persons, who use microscopic or telescopic lenses. Still others concentrate on contact lenses or vision therapy. Optometrists teach, do research, consult, and serve on health advisory committees of various kinds.

WORK ENVIRONMENT

Optometrists work in places—usually their own offices—that are clean, well lighted, and comfortable. Most full-time optometrists work about 40 hours a week. Many work weekends and evenings to suit the needs of patients. Emergency calls, once uncommon, have increased with the passage of therapeutic-drug laws expanding optometrists' ability to prescribe medications.

Optometrists who work in solo practice, or with a partner, tend to work longer hours because they must tend to administrative duties in addition to their medical ones. According to the American Optometric Association surveys, optometrists worked about 49 hours per week, on average, in 2004, and were available to see patients about 38 hours per week.

EMPLOYMENT OPPORTUNITIES

Optometrists held about 33,000 jobs in 2006. Salaried jobs for optometrists were primarily in offices of optometrists; offices of physicians, including ophthalmologists; and health and personal care stores, including optical goods stores. A few salaried jobs for optometrists were in hospitals, the federal government, or outpatient care centers including health maintenance organizations. Nearly 25 percent of optometrists are self-employed. According to a 2005 survey by the American Optometric Association, most self-employed optometrists worked in private practice or in partnership with other healthcare professionals. A small number worked for optical chains or franchises or as independent contractors.

EDUCATIONAL AND LEGAL REQUIREMENTS

The Doctor of Optometry degree requires the completion of a four-year program at an accredited optometry school, preceded by at least three years of preoptometric study at an accredited college or university. All states require optometrists to be licensed.

Education and Training. Optometrists need a Doctor of Optometry degree, which requires the completion of a four-year program at an accredited optometry school. In 2006, there were sixteen colleges of optometry in the United States and one in Puerto Rico that offered programs accredited by the Accreditation Council on Optometric Education of the American Optometric Association. Requirements for admission to optometry schools include college courses in English, mathematics, physics, chemistry, and biology. Because a strong background in science is important, many applicants to optometry school major in a science, such as biology or chemistry as undergraduates. Others major in another subject and take many science courses offering laboratory experience.

Admission to optometry school is competitive. Applicants must take the Optometry Admissions Test, which measures academic ability and scientific comprehension. As a result, most applicants take the test after their sophomore or junior year in college, allowing them an opportunity to take the test again and raise their score if necessary. A few applicants are accepted to optometry school after three years of college and complete their bachelor's degree while attending optometry school. However, most students accepted by a school or college of optometry have completed an undergraduate degree. Each institution has its own undergraduate prerequisites, so applicants should contact the school or college of their choice for specific requirements.

Optometry programs include classroom and laboratory study of health and visual sciences, as well as clinical training in the diagnosis and treatment of eye disorders. Courses in pharmacology, optics, vision science, biochemistry, and systemic diseases are included. One-year postgraduate clinical residency programs are available for optometrists who wish to obtain advanced clinical competence. Specialty areas for residency programs include family practice, pediatric, and geriatric optometry; vision therapy and rehabilitation; low-vision rehabilitation; cornea and contact lenses; refractive and ocular surgery; primary eye care optometry; and ocular disease.

Licensure. All states and the District of Columbia require that optometrists be licensed. Applicants for a license must have a Doctor of Optometry degree from an accredited optometry school and must pass both a written National Board examination and a national, regional, or state clinical examination. The written and clinical examinations of the National Board of Examiners in Optometry usually are taken during the student's academic career. Many states also require applicants to pass an examination on relevant state laws. Licenses must be renewed every one to three years and, in all states, continuing education credits are required for license renewal.

Other Qualifications. Business ability, self-discipline, and the ability to deal tactfully with patients are important for success. The work of optometrists also requires attention to detail and manual dexterity.

Advancement. Optometrists wishing to teach or conduct research may study for a master's degree or PhD in visual science, physiological optics, neurophysiology, public health, health administration, health information and communication, or health education.

EMPLOYMENT TRENDS

In response to the vision care needs of a growing and aging population, employment of optometrists is expected to grow as fast as the average for all occupations through 2016. Greater recognition of the importance of vision care, along with growth in employee vision care plans, will also spur job growth.

EMPLOYMENT CHANGE

Employment of optometrists is projected to grow 11 percent between 2006 and 2016. A growing population that recognizes the importance of good eye care will increase demand for optometrists. The increasing number of health insurance plans that include vision care also should generate more job growth.

As the population ages, optometrists and ophthalmologists will see greater numbers of patients experiencing the onset of vision problems that occur at older ages, such as cataracts and glaucoma. Increased incidences of diabetes and hypertension—diseases that often affect eyesight—will generate greater demand for optometric services among the general population as well as in the elderly.

Employment of optometrists would grow more rapidly if not for productivity gains expected to allow each optometrist to see more patients. These expected gains stem from greater use of optometric assistants and other support personnel, who can reduce the amount of time optometrists need with each patient.

The increasing popularity of laser surgery to correct some vision problems may reduce some of the demand for optometrists as patients often do not require eyeglasses afterward. Optometrists still will be needed, however, to provide preoperative and postoperative care for laser surgery patients.

Job Prospects. Job opportunities for optometrists should be very good over the next decade. Demand is expected to be much higher, and because there are only 16 schools of optometry, the number of students who can get a degree in optometry is limited. In addition to growth, the need to replace optometrists who retire or leave the occupation for other reasons will create more employment opportunities. **Table 12–1** shows some projection data provided by the Department of Labor.

EARNINGS

Median annual earnings of salaried optometrists were $91,040 in May 2006. The middle 50 percent earned between $66,530 and $118,490. Median annual earnings of salaried optometrists in offices of optometrists were $86,760. Salaried optometrists tend to earn more initially than do optometrists who set up their own practices. In the long run, however, those in private practice usually earn more.

Table 12–1				
Projections data from the National Employment Matrix				
Occupational title	**Employment, 2006**	**Projected employment, 2016**	**Change, 2006–2016**	
			Number	**Percent**
Optometrists	33,000	36,000	3,700	11

NOTE: Data in this table are rounded.

According to the American Optometric Association, median net annual income for all optometrists, including the self-employed, was $105,000 in 2006. The middle 50 percent earned between $84,000 and $150,000.

Self-employed optometrists, including those working in partnerships, must provide their own benefits. Optometrists employed by others typically enjoy paid vacation, sick leave, and pension contributions.

RELATED OCCUPATIONS

Other workers who apply scientific knowledge to prevent, diagnose, and treat disorders and injuries are chiropractors, dentists, physicians and surgeons, psychologists, podiatrists, and veterinarians.

ADDITIONAL INFORMATION

For information on optometry as a career and a list of accredited optometric institutions of education, contact:

- Association of Schools and Colleges of Optometry, 6110 Executive Blvd., Suite 510, Rockville, MD 20852. http://www.opted.org

Additional career information is available from:

- American Optometric Association, Educational Services, 243 North Lindbergh Blvd., St. Louis, MO 63141. http://www.aoa.org

The board of optometry in each state can supply information on licensing requirements.

For information on specific admission requirements and sources of financial aid, contact the admissions officers of individual optometry schools.

Optician, Dispensing

WORK DESCRIPTION

Dispensing opticians fit eyeglasses and contact lenses, following prescriptions written by ophthalmologists or optometrists. They examine written prescriptions to determine corrective lens specifications. They recommend eyeglass frames, lenses, and lens coatings after considering the prescription and the customer's occupation, habits, and facial features. Dispensing opticians measure clients' eyes, including the distance between the centers of the pupils and the distance between the eye surface and the lens. For customers without prescriptions, dispensing opticians may use a lensometer to record the present eyeglass prescription. They also may obtain a customer's previous record or verify a prescription with the examining optometrist or ophthalmologist.

Dispensing opticians prepare work orders that give *ophthalmic laboratory technicians* the information needed to grind and insert lenses into a frame. The work order includes lens prescriptions and information on lens size, material, color, and style. Some dispensing opticians grind and insert lenses themselves. After the glasses are made, dispensing opticians verify that the lenses have been ground to specifications. They may reshape or bend the frame, by hand or using pliers, so that the eyeglasses fit the customer properly and comfortably. Some also fix, adjust, and refit broken frames. They instruct clients about adapting to, wearing, or caring for eyeglasses.

Some dispensing opticians specialize in fitting contacts, artificial eyes, or cosmetic shells to cover blemished eyes. To fit contact lenses, dispensing opticians measure eye shape and size, select the type of contact lens material, and prepare work orders specifying the prescription and lens size. Fitting contact lenses requires considerable skill, care, and patience. Dispensing opticians observe customers' eyes, corneas, lids, and contact lenses with special instruments and microscopes. During several visits, opticians show customers how to insert, remove, and care for their contacts, and how to ensure the fit is correct. Dispensing opticians keep records on customer prescriptions, work orders, and payments; track inventory and sales; and perform other administrative duties.

Work Environment

Dispensing opticians work indoors in pleasant, quiet surroundings that are well-lighted and well-ventilated. As they sell and service eyeglasses, contact lenses, and other eye-care items, opticians must deal with customers most of the time. They spend part of their time on their feet. If they work in a laboratory where eyeglasses are made, they need to take precautions to guard against the hazards associated with cutting glass and handling various chemical solutions and machines with moving parts. Dispensing opticians generally work a 40-hour week, although a 45- or 50-hour week is not uncommon. Some, especially those employed in retail shops in large shopping centers, work in the evenings and on Saturdays. Some work part-time. Many experienced dispensing opticians go into business for themselves. Others become managers of retail optical stores or sales representatives for wholesalers or manufacturers of eyeglasses or lenses.

Employment Opportunities

Dispensing opticians held about 66,000 jobs in 2006. About one-third of dispensing opticians worked in offices of optometrists. Nearly one-third worked in health and personal care stores, including optical goods stores. Many of these stores offer one-stop shopping. Customers may have their eyes examined, choose frames, and have glasses made on the spot. Some opticians work in optical departments of department stores or other general merchandise stores, such as warehouse clubs and superstores. Eleven percent worked in offices of physicians, primarily ophthalmologists, who sell glasses directly to patients. Two percent of dispensing opticians were self-employed and ran their own unincorporated businesses.

EDUCATIONAL AND LEGAL REQUIREMENTS

Most workers entering this occupation receive their training on the job, mainly through apprenticeship programs that may last two years or longer. Some employers, though, prefer to hire people who have graduated from an opticianry program.

Education and Training. A high school diploma is all that is required to enter this occupation, but most workers have completed at least some college courses or a degree. Classes in physics, basic anatomy, algebra, and trigonometry are particularly valuable, as is experience with computers. This education and experience prepares dispensing opticians to learn job skills, including optical mathematics, optical physics, and the use of precision measuring instruments, along with the use of other necessary machinery and tools.

Most applicants for optician positions do not have any background in the field and learn mainly on the job. Large employers usually offer structured apprenticeship programs; small employers provide more informal, on-the-job training. Apprentices receive technical training and also learn office management and sales. Under the supervision of an experienced optician, optometrist, or ophthalmologist, apprentices work directly with patients, fitting eyeglasses and contact lenses.

Formal training in the field is offered in community colleges and in a few four-year colleges and universities. As of 2007, the Commission on Opticianry Accreditation accredited twenty-one associate degree programs. Graduation from an accredited program in opticianry provides a nationally recognized credential. There also are shorter programs of one year or less.

Licensure. Twenty-one states require dispensing opticians to be licensed. States may require individuals to pass one or more of the following for licensure: a state practical examination, a state written examination, and certification examinations offered by the American Board of Opticianry (ABO) and the National Contact Lens Examiners (NCLE). To qualify for the examinations, states often require applicants to complete postsecondary training or work as apprentices for two to four years.

Some states that license dispensing opticians allow graduates of opticianry programs to take the licensure exam immediately upon graduation; others require a few months to a year of experience. Continuing education is commonly required for licensure renewal. Information about specific licensing requirements is available from individual state boards of occupational licensing.

Certification and Other Qualifications. Any optician can apply to the ABO and the NCLE for certification of their skills, whether or not their state requires it. Certification signifies to customers and employers that an optician has a certain level of expertise. All applicants age 18 or older who have a high school diploma or equivalent are eligible for the exam, but some state licensing boards have additional eligibility requirements. Certification must be renewed every three years through continuing education. The State of Texas offers voluntary registration for the occupation.

Dispensing opticians deal directly with the public, so they should be tactful, pleasant, and communicate well. Manual dexterity and the ability to do precision work are essential.

Advancement. Many experienced dispensing opticians open their own optical stores. Others become managers of optical stores or sales representatives for wholesalers or manufacturers of eyeglasses or lenses.

EMPLOYMENT TRENDS

Employment of dispensing opticians is expected to grow about as fast as average for all occupations through 2016, as the population ages and demand for corrective lenses increases. Good job prospects are expected, but the occupation itself will remain relatively small.

Employment Change. Employment in this occupation is expected to rise nine percent over the 2006–2016 decade. Middle age is a time when many individuals use corrective lenses for the first time, and elderly persons generally require more vision care than others. As the share of the population in these older age groups increases, more opticians will be needed to provide service to them. In addition, awareness is increasing of the importance of regular eye exams across all age groups. A small, but growing, number of states require children as young as five years old to get eye exams. This is expected to increase the need for eye care services in those states. Fashion also influences demand. Frames come in a growing variety of styles, colors, and sizes, encouraging people to buy more than one pair.

Moderating the need for optician services is the increasing use of laser surgery to correct vision problems. Although the surgery remains relatively more expensive than eyewear, patients who successfully undergo this surgery may not require glasses or contact lenses for several years. In addition, new technology allows people with minimal training to make the measurements needed to fit glasses and may allow dispensing opticians to work faster, limiting the need for more workers. Proposed legislation may require contact lens manufacturers to make lenses available to nonoptical retail outlets, which may allow them to be sold over the Internet, reducing the need for opticians to provide contact lens services.

Job Prospects. Job prospects for entering the profession should remain good as those who leave the occupation or retire are replaced. Nevertheless, the number of job openings will be limited because the occupation is small. In addition, dispensing optician is among the occupations vulnerable to changes in the business cycle because eyewear purchases often can be deferred for a time. Job prospects will be best for those who have taken formal opticianry classes and those who master new technology, including new refraction systems, framing materials, and edging techniques. **Table 12–2** shows some projection data provided by the Department of Labor.

EARNINGS

Median annual earnings of dispensing opticians were $30,300 in May 2006. The middle 50 percent earned between $23,560 and $38,950. The lowest 10 percent earned less than $19,290, and the highest 10 percent earned more than $47,630. Median annual earnings in the industries employing the largest numbers of dispensing opticians in May 2006 are shown in **Table 12–3**.

Benefits for opticians are generally determined by the industries in which they are employed. Those opticians who work part-time or in small retail shops generally have fewer benefits than those who may work for large optical chains or department stores. Self-employed opticians must provide their own benefits.

Table 12–2	Projections data from the National Employment Matrix				
Occupational title	**Employment, 2006**	**Projected employment, 2016**	**Change, 2006–2016**		
			Number	**Percent**	
Opticians, dispensing	66,000	72,000	5,700	9	

NOTE: Data in this table are rounded.

Table 12–3	Median annual earnings in the industries employing the largest numbers of dispensing opticians in May 2006	
Offices of physicians		$32,770
Health and personal care stores		$31,850
Offices of health practitioner		$29,200
Offices of optometrists		$29,190

RELATED OCCUPATIONS

Other workers who deal with customers and perform delicate work include jewelers and precious stone and metal workers; orthotists and prosthetists; and precision instrument and equipment repairers. Ophthalmic laboratory technicians also perform many of the tasks that opticians perform. And because many opticians work in the retail industry, retail sales workers also perform some of the same duties.

ADDITIONAL INFORMATION

To learn about voluntary certification for opticians who fit eyeglasses, as well as a list of state licensing boards for opticians, contact:

■ American Board of Opticianry, 6506 Loisdale Rd., Suite 209, Springfield, VA 22150. http://www.abo.org

For information on voluntary certification for dispensing opticians who fit contact lenses, contact:

■ National Contact Lens Examiners, 6506 Loisdale Rd., Suite 209, Springfield, VA 22150. http://www.abo-ncle.org

13

PHYSICIAN ASSISTANT

Key Terms

- Middle-level health workers
- Primary care
- Biological sciences
- Telemedicine

A Relatively New Profession

The occupation of physician assistant (PA) came into being during the mid-1960s in response to a shortage of primary care physicians. The purpose of the PA in primary care is to help physicians provide personal health services to patients under their care. PAs are skilled health practitioners, qualified through academic and clinical training to serve patients with and under the supervision of a doctor of medicine (MD) or osteopathy (DO) who is responsible for the performance of that particular assistant. PAs are also responsible for their own actions. They are *middle-level health workers* with skills beyond those of a registered nurse and short those of a licensed physician.

Physician Assistant

WORK DESCRIPTION

Physician assistants are formally trained to provide routine diagnostic, therapeutic, and preventive healthcare services under the direction and supervision of a physician. They take medical histories, examine patients, order and interpret laboratory tests and X-rays, and make preliminary diagnoses. They also treat minor injuries by suturing, splinting, and casting. PAs record progress notes, instruct and counsel patients, and order or carry out therapy. In 46 states and the District of Columbia, Physician assistants may prescribe medications. PAs may have managerial duties, too. Some order medical and laboratory supplies and equipment; others supervise technicians and assistants.

Physician assistants always work under the supervision of a physician. The extent of supervision, however, depends on the work setting. For example, PAs working in rural or inner-city clinics, where a physician may be available just one or two days each week, may provide most of the health care for patients and consult with the supervising physician and other medical professionals as needed or required by law. Other PAs may make house calls or go to hospitals and nursing homes to check on patients and report to the physician.

Physician assistants assist physicians in a variety of practice settings and specialty areas. The most important practice settings are hospitals, clinics, and physicians' offices. Leading medical specialties using PAs are family practice, internal medicine, general surgery, emergency medicine, pediatrics, orthopedic surgery, thoracic surgery, and geriatrics.

The duties of physician assistants are determined by the supervising physician and by state law. Aspiring PAs should investigate the laws and regulations in the states where they wish to practice.

WORK ENVIRONMENT

Although PAs generally work in a comfortable, well-lighted environment, they often must stand for long periods and do considerable walking.

The work week and schedule vary according to practice setting. Some emergency room PAs work 24-hour shifts twice weekly, and others work three 12-hour shifts each week. The work week of PAs who work in physicians' offices may include weekends, night hours, or early morning hospital rounds to visit patients. PAs in clinics usually work a five-day, 40-hour week.

EMPLOYMENT OPPORTUNITIES

Physician assistants held about 66,000 jobs in 2006. The number of jobs is greater than the number of practicing PAs because some hold two or more jobs. For example, some PAs work with a supervising physician, but also work in another practice, clinic, or hospital. According to the American Academy of Physician Assistants, about 15 percent of actively practicing PAs worked in more than one clinical job concurrently in 2006.

More than half of jobs for PAs were in the offices of physicians. About a quarter were in public or private hospitals. The rest were mostly in outpatient care centers, including health maintenance organizations; the federal government; and public or private colleges, universities, and professional schools. A few PAs were self-employed.

EDUCATIONAL AND LEGAL REQUIREMENTS

Physician assistant programs usually last at least two years. Admission requirements vary by program, but many require at least two years of college and some healthcare experience. All states require that PAs complete an accredited, formal education program and pass a national exam to obtain a license.

Education and Training. Physician assistant education programs usually last at least two years and are full-time. Most programs are in schools of allied health, academic health centers, medical schools, or four-year colleges; a few are in community colleges, the military, or hospitals. Many accredited PA programs have clinical teaching affiliations with medical schools.

In 2007, 136 education programs for physician assistants were accredited or provisionally accredited by the American Academy of Physician Assistants. More than 90 of these programs offered the option of a master's degree, and the rest offered either a bachelor's degree or an associate degree. Most applicants to PA educational programs already have a bachelor's degree.

Admission requirements vary, but many programs require two years of college and some work experience in the healthcare field. Students should take courses in biology, English, chemistry, mathematics, psychology, and the social sciences. Many PAs have prior experience as registered nurses, and others come from varied backgrounds, including military corpsmen or medics, and allied health occupations, such as respiratory therapists, physical therapists, and emergency medical technicians and paramedics.

PA education includes classroom instruction in biochemistry, pathology, human anatomy, physiology, microbiology, clinical pharmacology, clinical medicine, geriatric and home health care, disease prevention, and medical ethics. Students obtain supervised clinical training in several areas, including family medicine, internal medicine, surgery, prenatal care and gynecology, geriatrics, emergency medicine, psychiatry, and pediatrics. Sometimes, PA students serve one or more of these rotations under the supervision of a physician who is seeking to hire a PA. The rotations often lead to permanent employment.

Licensure. All states and the District of Columbia have legislation governing the qualifications or practice of physician's assistants. All jurisdictions require physician assistants to pass the Physician Assistant National Certifying Examination, administered by the National Commission on Certification of Physician Assistants (NCCPA) and open only to graduates of accredited PA education programs. Only those successfully completing the examination may use the credential "Physician Assistant-Certified." To remain certified,

PAs must complete 100 hours of continuing medical education every two years. Every six years, they must pass a recertification examination or complete an alternative program combining learning experiences and a take-home examination.

Other Qualifications. Physician assistants must have a desire to serve patients and be self-motivated. PAs also must have a good bedside manner, emotional stability, and the ability to make decisions in emergencies. Physician assistants must be willing to study throughout their career to keep up with medical advances.

Certification and Advancement. Some PAs pursue additional education in a specialty such as surgery, neonatology, or emergency medicine. PA postgraduate educational programs are available in areas such as internal medicine, rural primary care, emergency medicine, surgery, pediatrics, neonatology, and occupational medicine. Candidates must be graduates of an accredited program and be certified by the NCCPA.

As they attain greater clinical knowledge and experience, PAs can advance to added responsibilities and higher earnings. However, by the very nature of the profession, clinically practicing PAs always are supervised by physicians.

EMPLOYMENT TRENDS

Employment is expected to grow much faster than the average as healthcare establishments increasingly use physician assistants to contain costs. Job opportunities for PAs should be good, particularly in rural and inner city clinics, as these settings typically have difficulty attracting physicians.

Employment Change. Employment of physician assistants is expected to grow 27 percent from 2006 to 2016, much faster than the average for all occupations. Projected rapid job growth reflects the expansion of healthcare industries and an emphasis on cost containment, which results in increasing use of PAs by healthcare establishments.

Physicians and institutions are expected to employ more PAs to provide primary care and to assist with medical and surgical procedures because PAs are cost-effective and productive members of the healthcare team. Physician assistants can relieve physicians of routine duties and procedures. Telemedicine—using technology to facilitate interactive consultations between physicians and physician assistants—also will expand the use of physician assistants.

Besides working in traditional office-based settings, PAs should find a growing number of jobs in institutional settings such as hospitals, academic medical centers, public clinics, and prisons. PAs also may be needed to augment medical staffing in inpatient teaching hospital settings as the number of hours physician residents are permitted to work is reduced, encouraging hospitals to use PAs to supply some physician resident services.

Job Prospects. Job opportunities for PAs should be good, particularly in rural and inner-city clinics because those settings have difficulty attracting physicians. In addition to job openings from employment growth, openings will result from the need to replace physician assistants who retire or leave the occupation permanently during the 2006–2016 decade. Opportunities will be best in states that allow PAs a wider scope of practice, such as allowing them to prescribe medications. **Table 13–1** shows some projection data provided by the Department of Labor.

Table 13–1	Projections data from the National Employment Matrix				
Occupational title	Employment, 2006	Projected employment, 2016	Change, 2006–2016		
			Number	Percent	
Physician assistants	33,000	36,000	3,700	11	

NOTE: Data in this table are rounded.

EARNINGS

Median annual earnings of wage-and-salary physician assistants were $74,980 in May 2006. The middle 50 percent earned between $62,430 and $89,220. The lowest 10 percent earned less than $43,100, and the highest 10 percent earned more than $102,230. Median annual earnings in the industries employing the largest numbers of physician assistants in May 2006 are shown in **Table 13–2**.

According to the American Academy of Physician Assistants, median income for physician assistants in full-time clinical practice was $80,356 in 2006; median income for first-year graduates was $69,517. Income varies by specialty, practice setting, geographic location, and years of experience. Employers often pay for their employees' liability insurance, registration fees with the Drug Enforcement Administration, state licensing fees, and credentialing fees.

Table 13–2	Median annual earnings in the industries employing the largest numbers of physician assistants in May 2006
Outpatient care centers	$80,960
General medical and surgical hospitals	$76,710
Offices of physicians	$74,160

RELATED OCCUPATIONS

Other healthcare workers who provide direct patient care that requires a similar level of skill and training include audiologists, occupational therapists, physical therapists, registered nurses, and speech-language pathologists.

Additional Information

For information on a career as a physician assistant, including a list of accredited programs, contact:

- ■ American Academy of Physician Assistants Information Center, 950 North Washington St., Alexandria, VA 22314. http://www.aapa.org

For eligibility requirements and a description of the Physician Assistant National Certifying Examination, contact:

- ■ National Commission on Certification of Physician Assistants, Inc., 12000 Findley Rd., Suite 200, Duluth, GA 30097. http://www.nccpa.net

COMMUNICATION IMPAIRMENTS

Key Terms

- Language disorder
- Grammatical patterns
- Speech disorder
- Hearing impairment
- Speech-language pathologists
- Communication disorders
- Audiologists

- Consultants
- Telecommunications
- Certificate of Clinical Competence in Speech-Language Pathology (CCC-SLP)
- Certificate of Clinical Competence in Audiology (CCC-A)
- Rehabilitative services

Speech, Language, and Hearing Impairments: An Overview

Speech, language, and hearing impairments hinder communication and can cause problems throughout life. Children who have difficulty speaking, hearing, or understanding language, for instance, cannot participate fully with others in play or classroom activities. Sometimes these children are thought to have mental or emotional problems when, in fact, the problem is one of language or hearing. Adults with speech, language, or hearing impairments may have problems on the job and may withdraw socially to avoid frustration and embarrassment. The aging process almost invariably brings some degree of hearing loss. Severe loss, if not treated, can result in diminished pleasure in everyday activities, social isolation, and, even worse, wrongful labeling of elderly people as demented or "confused."

A *language disorder* is defined as an inability to use the symbols of language through appropriate *grammatical patterns*, proper use of words and their meanings, and the correct use of speech sounds. A *speech disorder* is identified by an individual's difficulty in producing speech sounds, controlling voice production, and maintaining speech rhythm. Individuals with speech and language disorders also include those with physical conditions such as a stroke or head injury, cleft palate, or cerebral palsy. Other causes of speech and language disorders are hearing loss, viral diseases, certain drugs, poor speech and language models in the home, or a short attention span.

Hearing impairment can take many forms. It can be an inability to hear speech and other sounds clearly, even though the sounds are sufficiently loud. It can be an inability to understand and use speech in communication, though speech is sufficiently loud and can be heard clearly. It can be the inability to hear speech and other sounds loudly enough, which is considered a loss of hearing sensitivity. A person can experience these three types of hearing impairments in combination. Thus, hearing impairment is more complex than simply the inability to hear speech or other sounds well enough. Some hearing impairments can be subtle and difficult to recognize. Hearing impairment can be a serious problem because the ability to communicate is our most human characteristic. Many individuals with hearing impairments experience social, emotional, and educational isolation. Hearing impairments can be caused by viral infections, head injury, birth defects, excessively loud noises, drugs, tumors, heredity, and the aging process. Hearing impairment is the disorder most frequently reported to physicians. Approximately half of the people in the United States who have hearing impairments are 65 year of age or older.

Speech-Language Pathologists

WORK DESCRIPTION

Speech-language pathologists, sometimes called *speech therapists*, assess, diagnose, treat, and help to prevent disorders related to speech, language, cognitive-communication, voice, swallowing, and fluency.

Speech-language pathologists work with people who cannot produce speech sounds or cannot produce them clearly; those with speech rhythm and fluency problems, such as stuttering; people with voice disorders, such as inappropriate pitch or harsh voice; those with problems understanding and producing language; those who wish to improve their communication skills by modifying an accent; and those with cognitive communication impairments, such as attention, memory, and problem solving disorders. They also work with people who have swallowing difficulties.

Speech, language, and swallowing difficulties can result from a variety of causes including stroke, brain injury or deterioration, developmental delays or disorders, learning disabilities, cerebral palsy, cleft palate, voice pathology, mental retardation, hearing loss, or emotional problems. Problems can be congenital, developmental, or acquired. Speech-language pathologists use special instruments and qualitative and quantitative assessment methods, including standardized tests, to analyze and diagnose the nature and extent of impairments.

Speech-language pathologists develop an individualized plan of care, tailored to each patient's needs. For individuals with little or no speech capability, speech-language pathologists may select augmentative or alternative communication methods, including automated devices and sign language, and teach their use. They teach patients how to make sounds, improve their voices, or increase their oral or written language skills to communicate more effectively. They also teach individuals how to strengthen muscles or use compensatory strategies to swallow without choking or inhaling food or liquid. Speech-language pathologists help patients develop, or recover, reliable communication and swallowing skills so patients can fulfill their educational, vocational, and social roles.

Speech-language pathologists keep records on the initial evaluation, progress, and discharge of clients. This helps pinpoint problems, tracks client progress, and justifies the cost of treatment when applying for reimbursement. They counsel individuals and their families concerning communication disorders and how to cope with the stress and misunderstanding that often accompany them. They also work with family members to recognize and change behavior patterns that impede communication and treatment, and instruct them in communication-enhancing techniques to use at home.

Most speech-language pathologists provide direct clinical services to individuals with communication or swallowing disorders. In medical facilities, they may perform their job in conjunction with physicians, social workers, psychologists, and other therapists. Speech-language pathologists in schools collaborate with teachers, special educators, interpreters, other school personnel, and parents to develop and implement individual or group programs, provide counseling, and support classroom activities.

Some speech-language pathologists conduct research on how people communicate. Others design and develop equipment or techniques for diagnosing and treating speech problems.

WORK ENVIRONMENT

Speech-language pathologists usually work at a desk or table in clean comfortable surroundings. In medical settings, they may work at the patient's bedside and assist in positioning the patient. In schools, they may work with students in an office or classroom. Some work in the client's home.

Although the work is not physically demanding, it requires attention to detail and intense concentration. The emotional needs of clients and their families may be demanding. Most full-time speech-language pathologists work 40 hours per week. Those who work on a contract basis may spend a substantial amount of time traveling between facilities.

EMPLOYMENT OPPORTUNITIES

Speech-language pathologists held about 110,000 jobs in 2006. About half were employed in educational services, primarily in preschools and elementary and secondary schools. Others worked in hospitals; offices of other health practitioners, including speech-language pathologists; nursing care facilities; home healthcare services; individual and family services; outpatient care centers; and child day care centers.

A few speech-language pathologists are self-employed in private practice. They contract to provide services in schools, physicians' offices, hospitals, or nursing care facilities. Some work as consultants to industry.

EDUCATIONAL AND LEGAL REQUIREMENTS

A master's degree is the most common level of education among speech-language pathologists. Licensure or certification requirements also exist, but vary by state.

Education and Training. Most speech-language pathologist jobs require a master's degree. In 2007, more than 230 colleges and universities offered graduate programs in speech-language pathology accredited by the Council on Academic Accreditation in Audiology and Speech-Language Pathology. While graduation from an accredited program is not always required to become a speech-language pathologist, it may be helpful in obtaining a license or may be required to obtain a license in some states.

Speech-language pathology courses cover anatomy, physiology, and the development of the areas of the body involved in speech, language, and swallowing; the nature of disorders; principles of acoustics; and psychological aspects of communication. Graduate students also learn to evaluate and treat speech, language, and swallowing disorders and receive supervised clinical training in communication disorders.

Licensure and Certification. In 2007, 47 states regulated speech-language pathologists through licensure or registration. A passing score on the national examination on speech-language pathology, offered through the Praxis Series of the Educational Testing Service, is required. Other usual requirements include 300 to 375 hours of supervised clinical experience and nine months of postgraduate professional clinical experience. Forty-one states have continuing education requirements for licensure renewal. Medicaid, Medicare, and private health insurers generally require a practitioner to be licensed to qualify for reimbursement.

Only 12 states require this same license to practice in the public schools. The other states issue a teaching license or certificate that typically requires a master's degree from an approved college or university. Some states will grant a provisional teaching license or certificate to applicants with a bachelor's degree, but a master's degree must be earned within three to five years. A few states grant a full teacher's certificate or license to bachelor's degree applicants.

In some states, the *Certificate of Clinical Competence in Speech-Language Pathology (CCC-SLP)* offered by the American Speech-Language-Hearing Association meets some or all of the requirements for licensure. To earn a CCC, a person must have a graduate degree from an accredited university, complete 400 hours of supervised clinical experience, complete a 36-week postgraduate clinical fellowship, and pass the Praxis Series examination in speech-language pathology administered by the Educational Testing Service. Contact your state's licensing board for details on your state's requirements.

Other Qualifications. Speech-language pathologists should be able to effectively communicate diagnostic test results, diagnoses, and proposed treatment in a manner easily understood by patients and their families. They must be able to approach problems objectively and be supportive. Because a patient's progress may be slow, patience, compassion, and good listening skills are necessary.

Advancement. As speech-language pathologists gain clinical experience and engage in continuing professional education, many develop expertise with certain populations, such as preschoolers and adolescents, or with particular disorders, such as aphasia and learning disabilities. Some may obtain board recognition in a specialty area, such as child language, fluency, or feeding and swallowing. Experienced clinicians may become mentors or supervisors of other therapists or be promoted to administrative positions.

EMPLOYMENT TRENDS

Average employment growth is projected. Job opportunities are expected to be excellent.

Employment Change. Employment of speech-language pathologists is expected to grow 11 percent from 2006 to 2016, about as fast as the average for all occupations. As the members of the baby boom generation continue to age, the possibility of neurological disorders and associated speech, language, and swallowing impairments increases. Medical advances continue to improve the survival rate of premature infants and trauma and stroke victims, who often then need assessment and sometimes treatment by speech-language pathologists.

Employment of speech-language pathologists in educational services will increase with the growth in elementary and secondary school enrollments, including enrollment of special education students. Federal law guarantees special education and related services to all eligible children with disabilities. Greater awareness of the importance of early identification and diagnosis of speech and language disorders in young children will also increase employment.

In healthcare facilities, restrictions on reimbursement for therapy services may limit the growth of speech-language pathologist jobs in the near term. However, the long-term demand for therapists should continue to rise as growth in the number of individuals with disabilities or limited function spurs demand for therapy services. The number of speech-language pathologists in private practice will rise because of the increasing use of contract services by hospitals, schools, and nursing care facilities.

Job Prospects. The combination of growth in the occupation and an expected increase in retirements over the coming years should create excellent job opportunities for speech-language pathologists. Opportunities should be particularly favorable for those with the ability to speak a second language, such as Spanish. Job prospects also are expected to be especially favorable for those who are willing to relocate, particularly to areas experiencing difficulty in attracting and hiring speech-language pathologists. **Table 14–1,** shows some projection data provided by the Department of Labor.

Table 14–1	Projections data from the National Employment Matrix				
	Occupational title	Employment, 2006	Projected employment, 2016	Change, 2006–2016	
				Number	Percent
Speech-language pathologists	110,000	121,000	12,000	11	

NOTE: Data in this table are rounded.

Median annual earnings of wage-and-salary speech-language pathologists were $57,710 in May 2006. The middle 50 percent earned between $46,360 and $72,410. The lowest 10 percent earned less than $37,970, and the highest 10 percent earned more than $90,400. Median annual earnings in the industries employing the largest numbers of speech-language pathologists are shown in **Table 14–2.**

Some employers may reimburse speech-language pathologists for their required continuing education credits.

Table 14–2	Median annual earnings in the industries employing the largest numbers of speech-language pathologists	
	Nursing care facilities	$70,180
	Offices of other health practitioners	$63,240
	General medical and surgical hospitals	$61,970
	Elementary and secondary schools	$53,110

RELATED OCCUPATIONS

Speech-language pathologists specialize in the prevention, diagnosis, and treatment of speech and language problems. Workers in related occupations include audiologists, occupational therapists, optometrists, physical therapists, psychologists, and recreational therapists. Speech-language pathologists in school systems often work closely with special education teachers in assisting students with disabilities.

ADDITIONAL INFORMATION

State licensing boards can provide information on licensure requirements. State departments of education can supply information on certification requirements for those who wish to work in public schools.

For information on careers in speech-language pathology, a description of the CCC-SLP credential, and a listing of accredited graduate programs in speech-language pathology, contact:

- American Speech-Language-Hearing Association, 10801 Rockville Pike, Rockville, MD 20852. http://www.asha.org

Audiologists

WORK DESCRIPTION

Audiologists work with people who have hearing, balance, and related ear problems. They examine individuals of all ages and identify those with the symptoms of hearing loss and other auditory, balance, and related sensory and neural problems. They then assess the nature and extent of the problems and help the individuals manage them. Using audiometers, computers, and other testing devices, they measure the loudness at which a person begins to hear sounds, the ability to distinguish between sounds, and the impact of hearing loss on an individual's daily life. In addition, audiologists use computer equipment to evaluate and diagnose balance disorders. Audiologists interpret these results and may coordinate them with medical, educational, and psychological information to make a diagnosis and determine a course of treatment.

Hearing disorders can result from a variety of causes, including trauma at birth, viral infections, genetic disorders, exposure to loud noise, certain medications, or aging. Treatment may include examining and cleaning the ear canal, fitting and dispensing hearing aids, and fitting and programming cochlear implants. Audiologic treatment also includes counseling on adjusting to hearing loss, training on the use of hearing instruments, and teaching communication strategies for use in a variety of environments. For example, audiologists may provide instruction in listening strategies. They also may recommend, fit, and dispense personal or large area amplification systems and alerting devices.

In audiology clinics, audiologists may independently develop and carry out treatment programs. They keep records on the initial evaluation, progress, and discharge of patients. In other settings, audiologists may work with other health and education providers as part of a team in planning and implementing services for children and adults. Audiologists who diagnose and treat balance disorders often work in collaboration with physicians and physical and occupational therapists.

Some audiologists specialize in work with the elderly, children, or hearing-impaired individuals who need special treatment programs. Others develop and implement ways to protect workers' hearing from on-the-job injuries. They measure noise levels in workplaces and conduct hearing protection programs in factories, schools, and communities.

Audiologists who work in private practice also manage the business aspects of running an office, such as developing a patient base, hiring employees, keeping records, and ordering equipment and supplies. Some audiologists research hearing, balance, and related disorders, and their treatment. Others design and develop equipment or techniques for diagnosing and treating these disorders.

WORK ENVIRONMENT

Audiologists usually work at a desk or table in clean, comfortable surroundings. The job is not physically demanding but does require attention to detail and intense concentration. The emotional needs of patients and their families may be demanding. Most full-time audiologists work about 40 hours per week, which may include weekends and evenings in order to meet the needs of patients. Some work part-time. Those who work on a contract basis may spend a substantial amount of time traveling between facilities.

EMPLOYMENT OPPORTUNITIES

Audiologists held about 12,000 jobs in 2006. More than half of all jobs were in healthcare facilities, such as physicians' offices; the offices of other health practitioners, including audiologists; hospitals; and outpatient care centers. About 13 percent of jobs were in educational services, including elementary and secondary schools. Other jobs for audiologists were in health and personal care stores, including hearing aid stores; scientific research and development services; and state and local governments.

A small number of audiologists were self-employed in private practice. They provided services in their own offices or worked under contract for schools, healthcare facilities, or other establishments.

EDUCATIONAL AND LEGAL REQUIREMENTS

All states require audiologists to be licensed or registered. Licensure or registration requires at least a master's degree in audiology, however, a first professional, or doctoral, degree is becoming increasingly necessary.

Education and Training. Individuals must have at least a master's degree in audiology to qualify for a job. However, a first professional or doctoral degree is becoming more common. As of early 2007, eight states required a doctoral degree or its equivalent. The professional doctorate in audiology (Au.D.) requires approximately eight years of university training and supervised professional experience.

In early 2007, the Accreditation Commission of Audiology Education accredited more than 50 AuD programs and the Council on Academic Accreditation in Audiology and Speech-Language Pathology (CAA) accredited over 70 graduate programs in audiology. Graduation from an accredited program may be required to obtain a license in some states. Requirements for admission to programs in audiology include courses in English, mathematics, physics, chemistry, biology, psychology, and communication. Graduate coursework in audiology includes anatomy; physiology; physics; genetics; normal and abnormal communication development; auditory, balance, and neural systems assessment and treatment; diagnosis and treatment; pharmacology; and ethics.

Licensure and Certification. Audiologists are regulated by licensure or registration in all fifty states. While forty-one states have continuing education requirements for licensure renewal, the number of hours required varies by state. Twenty states and the District of Columbia also require audiologists to have a Hearing Aid Dispenser license to dispense hearing aids; the remaining thirty states require an audiologist license to do so. Third-party payers generally require practitioners to be licensed to qualify for reimbursement. States set requirements for education, mandating a master's or doctoral degree, as well as other requirements. For information on the specific requirements of your state, contact your state's licensing board.

In some states, specific certifications from professional associations satisfy some or all of the requirements for state licensure. Certification can be obtained from two certifying bodies. Audiologists can earn the *Certificate of Clinical Competence in Audiology (CCC-A)* offered by the American Speech-Language-Hearing Association; they may also be certified through the American Board of Audiology.

Other Qualifications. Audiologists should be able to effectively communicate diagnostic test results, diagnoses, and proposed treatments in a manner easily understood by their patients. They must be able to approach problems objectively and provide support to patients and their families. Because a patient's progress may be slow, patience, compassion, and good listening skills are necessary.

It is important for audiologists to be aware of new diagnostic and treatment technologies. Most audiologists participate in continuing education courses to learn new methods and technologies.

Advancement. With experience, audiologists can advance to open their own private practice. Audiologists working in hospitals and clinics can advance to management or supervisory positions.

Employment Trends

Average employment growth is projected. However, because of the small size of the occupation, few job openings are expected. Job prospects will be favorable for those possessing the AuD degree.

Employment Change. Employment of audiologists is expected to grow 10 percent from 2006 to 2016, about as fast as the average for all occupations. Hearing loss is strongly associated with aging, so rapid growth in older population groups will cause the number of people with hearing and balance impairments to increase markedly. Medical advances continue to improve the survival rate of premature infants and trauma victims, who then often need assessment and sometimes treatment by audiologists. Greater awareness of the importance of early identification and diagnosis of hearing disorders in infants also will increase employment. A number of states require that newborns be screened for hearing loss and receive appropriate early intervention services. Employment in educational services will increase along with growth in elementary and secondary school enrollments, including enrollment of special education students. Growth in employment of audiologists will be moderated by limitations on reimbursements made by third-party payers for the tests and services audiologists provide.

Job Prospects. Job prospects will be favorable for those possessing the AuD degree. Only a few job openings for audiologists will arise from the need to replace those who leave the occupation, because the occupation is relatively small and workers tend to stay in this occupation until they retire. **Table 14–3** shows some projection data provided by the Department of Labor.

Table 14–3	Projections data from the National Employment Matrix			
Occupational title	Employment, 2006	Projected employment, 2016	Change, 2006–2016	
			Number	Percent
Audiologists	12,000	13,000	1,200	10

NOTE: Data in this table are rounded.

EARNINGS

Median annual earnings of wage-and-salary audiologists were $57,120 in May 2006. The middle 50 percent earned between $47,220 and $70,940. The lowest 10 percent earned less than $38,370, and the highest 10 percent earned more than $89,160. Some employers may pay for continuing education courses.

RELATED OCCUPATIONS

Audiologists specialize in the prevention, diagnosis, and treatment of hearing problems. Workers in related occupations include occupational therapists, optometrists, physical therapists, psychologists, recreational therapists, rehabilitation counselors, and speech-language pathologists.

ADDITIONAL INFORMATION

State licensing boards can provide information on licensure requirements. State departments of education can supply information on certification requirements for those who wish to work in public schools.

For information on the specific requirements of your state, contact your state's licensing board. Career information, a description of the CCC-A credential, and information on state licensure is available from:

- American Speech-Language-Hearing Association, 10801 Rockville Pike, Rockville, MD 20852. http://www.asha.org

Information on American Board of Audiology certification is available from:

- American Board of Audiology, 11730 Plaza America Dr., Suite 300, Reston, VA 20190. http://www.americanboardofaudiology.org

For information on the AuD degree, contact:

- Audiology Foundation of America, 8 N. 3rd St., Suite 406, Lafayette, IN 47901. http://www.audfound.org

EMERGENCY MEDICAL TECHNICIANS AND PARAMEDICS

Key Terms

- Emergency medical technician-paramedics (EMT-Paramedics)
- Advanced life support units
- Trauma centers
- National Registry of Emergency Medical Technicians (NREMT)

- EMT-Basic
- EMT-Intermediate
- Defibrillator
- Endotracheal intubation

High Drama in Health Care

Paramedics, or *emergency medical technicians (EMTs)*, have a career that is often very dramatic, calling for immediate, calm application of the EMT's skills amid sometimes dangerous conditions. The September 11, 2001, attack on the World Trade Center was the most dramatic and deadly situation that paramedics, along with teams of firefighters and police, have ever faced, and they lived up to their potential and training with great heroism. If you watched the terrible events unfolding at that scene, you saw many of them in action as their ambulances drove through dangerous smoke, fire, and rubble to help rescue and transport the critically injured to hospitals. Their bravery in the face of peril speaks well of the crucial role played by paramedics in times of crisis as well as in everyday life.

Although not every call received by a paramedic team is a life-or-death situation, the potential for drama always exists. The remainder of this chapter details the dramatic as well as the mundane aspects of this healthcare profession.

EMT-Paramedics

WORK DESCRIPTION

People's lives often depend on the quick reaction and competent care of emergency medical technicians (EMTs) and paramedics. Incidents as varied as automobile accidents, heart attacks, slip and falls, childbirth, and gunshot wounds all require immediate medical attention. EMTs and paramedics provide this vital service as they care for and transport the sick or injured to a medical facility.

In an emergency, EMTs and paramedics are typically dispatched by a 911 operator to the scene, where they often work with police and fire fighters. Once they arrive, EMTs and paramedics assess the nature of the patient's condition while trying to determine whether the patient has any pre-existing medical conditions. Following medical protocols and guidelines, they provide appropriate emergency care and, when necessary, transport the patient. Some paramedics are trained to treat patients with minor injuries on the scene of an accident, or they may treat them at their home, without transporting them to a medical facility. Emergency treatment is carried out under the medical direction of physicians.

EMTs and paramedics may use special equipment, such as backboards, to immobilize patients before placing them on stretchers and securing them in the ambulance for transport to a medical facility. These healthcare workers generally go out in teams. During the transport of a patient, one EMT or paramedic drives while the other monitors the patient's vital signs and gives additional care as needed. Some paramedics work as part of a helicopter's flight crew to transport critically ill or injured patients to hospital trauma centers.

At the medical facility, EMTs and paramedics help transfer patients to the emergency department, report their observations and actions to emergency department staff, and may provide additional emergency treatment. After each run, EMTs and paramedics replace used supplies and check equipment. If a transported patient had a contagious disease, EMTs and paramedics decontaminate the interior of the ambulance and report cases to the proper authorities.

EMTs and paramedics also provide transportation for patients from one medical facility to another, particularly if they work for private ambulance services. Patients often need to be transferred to a hospital that specializes in their injury or illness or to a nursing home.

Beyond these general duties, the specific responsibilities of EMTs and paramedics depend on their level of qualification and training. The *National Registry of Emergency Medical Technicians (NREMT)* certifies emergency medical service providers at five levels: First Responder; *EMT-Basic*; *EMT-Intermediate*, which has two levels called 1985 and 1999; and *Paramedic*. Some states, however, have their own certification programs and use distinct names and titles.

The EMT-Basic represents the first component of the emergency medical technician system. An EMT trained at this level is prepared to care for patients at the scene of an accident and while transporting patients by ambulance to the hospital under medical direction. The EMT-Basic has the emergency skills to assess a patient's condition and manage respiratory, cardiac, and trauma emergencies.

The EMT-Intermediate has more advanced training. However, the specific tasks that those certified at this level are allowed to perform varies greatly from one state to another. EMT-Paramedics provide the most extensive pre-hospital care. In addition to carrying out the procedures of the other levels, paramedics may administer drugs orally and intravenously, interpret electrocardiograms (EKGs), perform *endotracheal intubations*, and use monitors and other complex equipment. However, as with EMT-Intermediate, what paramedics are permitted to do varies by state.

WORK ENVIRONMENT

EMTs and paramedics work both indoors and out, in all types of weather. They are required to do considerable kneeling, bending, and heavy lifting. These workers risk noise-induced hearing loss from sirens and back injuries from lifting patients. In addition, EMTs and paramedics may be exposed to diseases such as hepatitis-B and AIDS, as well as violence from mentally unstable patients. The work is not only physically strenuous but can be stressful, sometimes involving life-or-death situations and suffering patients. Nonetheless, many people find the work exciting and challenging and enjoy the opportunity to help others.

EMTs and paramedics employed by fire departments work about 50 hours a week. Those employed by hospitals frequently work between 45 and 60 hours a week, and those in private ambulance services, between 45 and 50 hours. Some of these workers, especially those in police and fire departments, are on call for extended periods. Because emergency services function 24 hours a day, EMTs and paramedics have irregular working hours.

EMPLOYMENT OPPORTUNITIES

EMTs and paramedics held about 201,000 jobs in 2006. Most career EMTs and paramedics work in metropolitan areas. Volunteer EMTs and paramedics are more common in small cities, towns, and rural areas. These individuals volunteer for fire departments, emergency medical services, or hospitals and may respond to only a few calls per month. About 30 percent of EMTs or paramedics belong to a union.

Paid EMTs and paramedics were employed in a number of industries. About 4 out of 10 worked as employees of private ambulance services. About 3 out of 10 worked in local government for fire departments, public ambulance services, and emergency medical services. Another 2 out of 10 worked full-time within hospitals or responded to calls in ambulances or helicopters to transport critically ill or injured patients. The remainder worked in various industries providing emergency services.

EDUCATIONAL AND LEGAL REQUIREMENTS

Generally, a high school diploma is required to enter a training program to become an EMT or paramedic. Workers must complete a formal training and certification process.

Education and Training. A high school diploma usually is required to enroll in a formal emergency medical technician training program. Training is offered at progressive levels: EMT-Basic, EMT-Intermediate, and EMT-Paramedic.

At the EMT-Basic level, coursework emphasizes emergency skills, such as managing respiratory, trauma, and cardiac emergencies, and patient assessment. Formal courses are often combined with time in an emergency room or ambulance. The program provides instruction and practice in dealing with bleeding, fractures, airway obstruction, cardiac arrest, and emergency childbirth. Students learn how to use and maintain common emergency equipment, such as backboards, suction devices, splints, oxygen delivery systems, and stretchers. Graduates of approved EMT-Basic training programs must pass a written and practical examination administered by the state certifying agency or the NREMT.

At the EMT-Intermediate level, training requirements vary by state. The nationally defined levels (EMT-Intermediate 1985 and EMT-Intermediate 1999) typically require 30 to 350 hours of training based on scope of practice. Students learn advanced skills, such as the use of advanced airway devices, intravenous fluids, and some medications.

The most advanced level of training for this occupation is EMT-Paramedic. At this level, the caregiver receives training in anatomy and physiology as well as advanced medical skills. Most commonly, the training is conducted in community colleges and technical schools over one to two years and may result in an associates degree. Such education prepares the graduate to take the NREMT examination and become certified as a Paramedic. Extensive related coursework and clinical and field experience is required. Refresher courses and continuing education are available for EMTs and paramedics at all levels.

Licensure. All fifty states require certification for each of the EMT levels. In most states and the District of Columbia registration with the NREMT is required at some or all levels of certification. Other states administer their own certification examination or provide the option of taking either the NREMT or state examination. To maintain certification, EMTs and paramedics must recertify, usually every two years. Generally, they must be working as an EMT or paramedic and meet a continuing education requirement.

Other Qualifications. EMTs and paramedics should be emotionally stable, have good dexterity, agility, and physical coordination, and be able to lift and carry heavy loads. They also need good eyesight—corrective lenses may be used—with accurate color vision.

Advancement. Paramedics can become supervisors, operations managers, administrative directors, or executive directors of emergency services. Some EMTs and paramedics become instructors, dispatchers, or physician assistants; others move into sales or marketing of emergency medical equipment. A number of people become EMTs and paramedics to test their interest in health care before training as registered nurses, physicians, or other health workers.

EMPLOYMENT TRENDS

Employment for EMTs and paramedics is expected to grow faster than the average for all occupations through 2016. Job prospects should be good, particularly in cities and private ambulance services.

Employment Change. Employment of emergency medical technicians and paramedics is expected to grow by 19 percent between 2006 and 2016, which is faster than the average for all occupations. Full-time paid EMTs and paramedics will be needed to replace unpaid volunteers. It is becoming increasing difficult for emergency medical services to recruit and retain unpaid volunteers because of the amount of training and the large time commitment these positions require. As a result, more paid EMTs and paramedics are needed. Furthermore, as a large segment of the population—aging members of the baby boom generation—becomes more likely to have medical emergencies, demand will increase for EMTs and paramedics. Demand for part-time, volunteer EMTs and paramedics will continue in rural areas and smaller metropolitan areas.

Job Prospects. Job prospects should be favorable. Many job openings will arise from growth and from the need to replace workers who leave the occupation because of the limited potential for advancement, as well as the modest pay and benefits in private-sector jobs.

Job opportunities should be best in private ambulance services. Competition will be greater for jobs in local government, including fire, police, and independent third-service rescue squad departments which tend to have better salaries and benefits. As clients and patients expect and demand higher levels of care before arriving at the hospital, EMTs and paramedics who have advanced education and certifications, such as Paramedic level certification, should enjoy the most favorable job prospects. **Table 15–1** shows some projection data provided by the Department of Labor.

Table 15–1

Projections data from the National Employment Matrix				
Occupational title	Employment, 2006	Projected employment, 2016	Change, 2006–2016	
			Number	Percent
Emergency medical technicians and paramedics	201,000	240,000	39,000	19

NOTE: Data in this table are rounded.

EARNINGS

Earnings of EMTs and paramedics depend on the employment setting and geographic location of their jobs, as well as their training and experience. Median annual earnings of EMTs and paramedics were $27,070 in May 2006. The middle 50 percent earned between $21,290 and $35,210. The lowest 10 percent earned less than $17,300, and the highest 10 percent earned more than $45,280. Median annual earnings in the industries employing the largest numbers of EMTs and paramedics in May 2006 were $23,250 in general medical and surgical hospitals and $20,350 in ambulance services.

Those in emergency medical services who are part of fire or police departments typically receive the same benefits as firefighters or police officers. For example, many are covered by pension plans that provide retirement at half pay after 20 or 25 years of service or if the worker is disabled in the line of duty.

RELATED OCCUPATIONS

Other workers in occupations that require quick and level-headed reactions to life-or-death situations are air traffic controllers, firefighters, physician assistants, police and detectives, and registered nurses.

ADDITIONAL INFORMATION

General information about emergency medical technicians and paramedics is available from:

■ National Association of Emergency Medical Technicians, P.O. Box 1400, Clinton, MS 39060-1400. http://www.naemt.org

■ National Highway Traffic Safety Administration, EMS Division, 400 7th St. SW., NTS-14, Washington, DC 20590. http://www.nhtsa.dot.gov

■ National Registry of Emergency Medical Technicians, Rocco V. Morando Bldg., 6610 Busch Blvd., P.O. Box 29233, Columbus, OH 43229. http://www.nremt.org

IMAGING MODALITIES

Key Terms

- Diagnostic imaging
- Ultrasound machines
- Magnetic resonance scanner/imaging (MRI)
- Positron emission scanners/tomography (PET)
- Radiologist
- Radiologic technician/radiographer/X-ray technician
- Fluoroscopy
- Contrast medium
- CT technologist

- Magnetic resonance imaging (MRI) technologist
- Radiation therapy
- Dosimetrist
- Sonographer/ultrasound technologist
- Diagnostic medical sonography
- American Registry of Radiologic Technologists (ARRT)
- American Registry of Diagnostic Medical Sonographers (ARDMS)
- Computerized tomography (CT)
- Echocardiograph (EKG)

X-rays and Beyond

Perhaps the most familiar use of the X-ray is the diagnosis of broken bones. Although this remains a major use, medical uses of radiation go far beyond that. Today, radiation is used not only to produce images of the interior of the body, but also to treat disease. The rapidly growing use of imaging techniques that do not involve X-rays has transformed the field, and the term diagnostic imaging embraces procedures such as ultrasound and magnetic resonance scans in addition to the familiar X-ray.

With the application of computer technology to radiology, the field has been revolutionized. Computer-enhanced equipment produces amazingly clear and sharp images. Thanks in part to the speed with which computerized scanners can read and organize the millions of messages involved in a single test, it is now possible to view soft tissues and organs such as the heart and brain, parts of the body that until quite recently could be examined only through invasive techniques such as exploratory surgery.

Remarkable strides have occurred in the development of imaging equipment that does not involve the use of radiation, thereby reducing the risk of adverse side effects. Examples include ultrasound machines, which use sound waves; magnetic resonance scanners, which use radio waves; and positron emission scanners. Although discovered many years ago, some of these imaging techniques became clinically practical only during the 1990s, as a result of improvements in electronic circuitry that enable computers to handle the vast amount of data involved.

Future generations of imaging equipment are certain to be even more sophisticated than machines in use today. Physicians seeking to confirm a diagnosis or monitor a patient's condition will obtain better information, and patients will be subjected to less risk or discomfort. There is ample reason to believe that technological advances in this field will continue to occur very rapidly, and that the clinical benefits will spur even more extensive use of diagnostic imaging procedures.

Radiologic Technologists and Technicians

WORK DESCRIPTION

Radiologic technologists take X-rays and administer nonradioactive materials into patients' bloodstreams for diagnostic purposes.

Radiologic technologists, also referred to as *radiographers*, produce X-ray films (radiographs) of parts of the human body for use in diagnosing medical problems. They prepare patients for radiologic examinations by explaining the procedure, removing jewelry and other articles through which X-rays cannot pass, and positioning patients so that the parts of the body can be appropriately radiographed. To prevent unnecessary exposure to radiation, these workers surround the exposed area with radiation protection devices, such as lead shields, or limit the size of the X-ray beam. Radiographers position radiographic equipment at the correct angle and height over the appropriate area of a patient's body. Using instruments similar to a measuring tape, they may measure the thickness of the section to be radiographed and set controls on the X-ray machine to produce radiographs of the appropriate density, detail, and contrast. They place the X-ray film under the part of the patient's body to be examined and make the exposure. They then remove the film and develop it.

Radiologic technologists must follow physicians' orders precisely and conform to regulations concerning the use of radiation to protect themselves, their patients, and their coworkers from unnecessary exposure.

In addition to preparing patients and operating equipment, radiologic technologists keep patient records and adjust and maintain equipment. They also may prepare work schedules, evaluate purchases of equipment, or manage a radiology department.

Experienced radiographers may perform more complex imaging procedures. When performing *fluoroscopies*, for example, radiographers prepare a solution of *contrast medium* for the patient to drink, allowing the radiologist (a physician who interprets radiographs) to see soft tissues in the body.

Some radiographers specialize in *computed tomography* (CT), and are sometimes referred to as *CT technologists*. CT scans produce a substantial number of cross-sectional X-rays of an area of the body. From those cross-sectional X-rays, a three-dimensional image is made. The CT uses ionizing radiation; therefore, it requires the same precautionary measures that radiographers use with other X-rays.

Radiographers also can specialize in *magnetic resonance imaging* as an *MR technologist*. MR, like CT, produces multiple cross-sectional images to create a 3-dimensional image. Unlike CT, MR uses non-ionizing radio frequency to generate image contrast. Another common specialty for radiographers is mammography. Mammographers use low dose X-ray systems to produce images of the breast.

In addition to radiologic technologists, others who conduct diagnostic imaging procedures include:

- Medical diagnostic sonographers

- Cardiovascular technologists and technicians

- Nuclear medicine technologists

The first of these occupations is discussed in the third part of this chapter and the other two are discussed in a later chapter of this book.

WORK ENVIRONMENT

Physical stamina is important in this occupation because technologists are on their feet for long periods and may lift or turn disabled patients. Technologists work at diagnostic machines but also may perform some procedures at patients' bedsides. Some travel to patients in large vans equipped with sophisticated diagnostic equipment.

Although radiation hazards exist in this occupation, they are minimized by the use of lead aprons, gloves, and other shielding devices, as well as by instruments monitoring exposure to radiation. Technologists wear badges measuring radiation levels in the radiation area, and detailed records are kept on their cumulative lifetime dose.

Most full-time radiologic technologists work about 40 hours a week. They may, however, have evening, weekend, or on-call hours. Opportunities for part-time and shift work also are available.

Employment Opportunities

Radiologic technologists held about 196,000 jobs in 2006. More than 60 percent of all jobs were in hospitals. Most other jobs were in offices of physicians; medical and diagnostic laboratories, including diagnostic imaging centers; and outpatient care centers.

Educational and Legal Requirements

Preparation for this profession is offered in hospitals, colleges and universities, and less frequently at vocational-technical institutes. Hospitals employ most radiologic technologists. Employers prefer to hire technologists with formal training.

Education and Training. Formal training programs in radiography range in length from one to four years and lead to a certificate, an associate degree, or a bachelor's degree. Two-year associate degree programs are most prevalent.

Some one-year certificate programs are available for experienced radiographers or individuals from other health occupations, such as medical technologists and registered nurses, who want to change fields. A bachelor's or master's degree in one of the radiologic technologies is desirable for supervisory, administrative, or teaching positions.

The Joint Review Committee on Education in Radiologic Technology accredits most formal training programs for the field. The committee accredited more than 600 radiography programs in 2007. Admission to radiography programs requires, at a minimum, a high school diploma or the equivalent. High school courses in mathematics, physics, chemistry, and biology are helpful. The programs provide both classroom and clinical instruction in anatomy and physiology, patient care procedures, radiation physics, radiation protection, principles of imaging, medical terminology, positioning of patients, medical ethics, radiobiology, and pathology.

Licensure. Federal legislation protects the public from the hazards of unnecessary exposure to medical and dental radiation by ensuring that operators of radiologic equipment are properly trained. Under this legislation, the federal government sets voluntary standards that the states may use for accrediting training programs and licensing individuals who engage in medical or dental radiography. In 2007, 40 states required licensure for practicing radiologic technologists and technicians.

Certification and Other Qualifications. The *American Registry of Radiologic Technologists (ARRT)* offers voluntary certification for radiologic technologists. In addition, 35 States use ARRT-administered exams for state licensing purposes. To be eligible for certification, technologists generally must graduate from an accredited program and pass an examination. Many employers prefer to hire certified radiographers. To be recertified, radiographers must complete 24 hours of continuing education every two years.

Radiologic technologists should be sensitive to patients' physical and psychological needs. They must pay attention to detail, follow instructions, and work as part of a team. In addition, operating complicated equipment requires mechanical ability and manual dexterity.

Advancement. With experience and additional training, staff technologists may become specialists, performing CT scanning, MR, and angiography, a procedure during which blood vessels are X-rayed to find clots. Technologists also may advance, with additional education and certification, to become a radiologist assistant.

Experienced technologists also may be promoted to supervisor, chief radiologic technologist, and, ultimately, department administrator or director. Depending on the institution, courses or a master's degree in business or health administration may be necessary for a directorship.

Some technologists progress by specializing in the occupation to become instructors or directors in radiologic technology programs; others take jobs as sales representatives or instructors with equipment manufacturers.

EMPLOYMENT TRENDS

Employment is projected to grow faster than average, and job opportunities are expected to be favorable.

Employment Change. Employment of radiologic technologists is expected to increase by about 15 percent from 2006 to 2016, faster than the average for all occupations. As the population grows and ages, there will be an increasing demand for diagnostic imaging. Although healthcare providers are enthusiastic about the clinical benefits of new technologies, the extent to which they are adopted depends largely on cost and reimbursement considerations. As technology advances, many imaging modalities are becoming less expensive and their adoption is becoming more widespread. For example, digital imaging technology can improve the quality of the images and the efficiency of the procedure, but it remains slightly more expensive than analog imaging, a procedure during which the image is put directly on film. Despite this, digital imaging is becoming more widespread in many imaging facilities because of the advantages it provides over analog.

Although hospitals will remain the principal employer of radiologic technologists, a number of new jobs will be found in offices of physicians and diagnostic imaging centers. Health facilities such as these are expected to grow through 2016, because of the shift toward outpatient care, encouraged by third-party payers and made possible by technological advances that permit more procedures to be performed outside the hospital.

Job Prospects. In addition to job growth, job openings also will arise from the need to replace technologists who leave the occupation. Radiologic technologists who are willing to relocate and who also are experienced in more than one diagnostic imaging procedure—such as CT, MR, and mammography—will have the best employment opportunities as employers seek to control costs by using multi-credentialed employees.

CT is becoming a frontline diagnostic tool. Instead of taking X-rays to decide whether a CT is needed, as was the practice before, it is often the first choice for imaging because of its accuracy. MR also is increasing in frequency of use. Technologists with credentialing in either of these specialties will be very marketable to employers. **Table 16–1** shows some projection data provided by the Department of Labor.

Table 16–1 **Projections data from the National Employment Matrix**				
Occupational title	**Employment, 2006**	**Projected employment, 2016**	**Change, 2006–2016**	
			Number	**Percent**
Radiologic technologists and technicians	196,000	226,000	30,000	15

NOTE: Data in this table are rounded.

EARNINGS

Median annual earnings of radiologic technologists were $48,170 in May 2006. The middle 50 percent earned between $39,840 and $57,940. The lowest 10 percent earned less than $32,750, and the highest 10 percent earned more than $68,920. Median annual earnings in the industries employing the largest numbers of radiologic technologists in 2006 are shown in **Table 16–2**.

Table 16–2 **Median annual earnings in the industries employing the largest numbers of radiologic technologists in 2006**	
Medical and diagnostic laboratories	$51,280
General medical and surgical hospitals	$48,830
Offices of physicians	$45,500

RELATED OCCUPATIONS

Radiologic technologists operate sophisticated equipment to help physicians, dentists, and other health practitioners diagnose and treat patients. Workers in related occupations include cardiovascular technologists and technicians, clinical laboratory technologists and technicians, nuclear medicine technologists, and respiratory therapists.

ADDITIONAL INFORMATION

For information on careers in radiologic technology, contact:

■ American Society of Radiologic Technologists, 15000 Central Ave. SE., Albuquerque, NM 87123-3917. http://www.asrt.org

For the current list of accredited education programs in radiography, write to:

■ Joint Review Committee on Education in Radiologic Technology, 20 N. Wacker Dr., Suite 2850, Chicago, IL 60606-3182. http://www.jrcert.org

For certification information, contact:

■ American Registry of Radiologic Technologists, 1255 Northland Dr., St. Paul, MN 55120-1155. http://www.arrt.org

Radiation Therapists

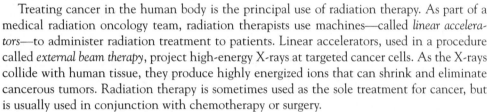

WORK DESCRIPTION

Treating cancer in the human body is the principal use of radiation therapy. As part of a medical radiation oncology team, radiation therapists use machines—called *linear accelerators*—to administer radiation treatment to patients. Linear accelerators, used in a procedure called *external beam therapy*, project high-energy X-rays at targeted cancer cells. As the X-rays collide with human tissue, they produce highly energized ions that can shrink and eliminate cancerous tumors. Radiation therapy is sometimes used as the sole treatment for cancer, but is usually used in conjunction with chemotherapy or surgery.

The first step in the radiation therapy process is simulation. During simulation, the radiation therapist uses an X-ray imaging machine or computer tomography (CT) scan to pinpoint the location of the tumor. The therapist then positions the patient and adjusts the linear accelerator so that, when treatment begins, radiation exposure is concentrated on the tumor cells. The radiation therapist then develops a treatment plan in conjunction with a *radiation oncologist* (a physician who specializes in therapeutic radiology), and a *dosimetrist* (a technician who calculates the dose of radiation that will be used for treatment). The therapist later explains the treatment plan to the patient and answers any questions that the patient may have.

The next step in the process is treatment. To begin, the radiation therapist positions the patient and adjusts the linear accelerator according to the guidelines established in simulation. From a separate room protected from radiation, the therapist then operates the linear accelerator and monitors the patient's condition through a television monitor and an intercom system. Treatment can take anywhere from ten to thirty minutes and is usually administered once a day, five days a week, for two to nine weeks.

During the treatment phase, the radiation therapist monitors the patient's physical condition to determine if any adverse side effects are occurring. The therapist must also be aware of the patient's emotional well-being. Many patients undergoing radiation therapy are under stress and emotionally fragile. It is important for the therapist to maintain a positive attitude and provide emotional support.

Radiation therapists keep detailed records of their patients' treatments. These records include information such as the dose of radiation used for each treatment, the total amount of radiation used to date, the area treated, and the patient's reactions. Radiation oncologists and dosimetrists review these records to ensure that the treatment plan is working, to monitor the amount of radiation exposure that the patient has received, and to keep side effects to a minimum.

Radiation therapists also assist *medical radiation physicists*, specialists who monitor and adjust the linear accelerator. Radiation therapists often work alone during the treatment phase, however, they need to be able to check the linear accelerator for problems and make any necessary adjustments. Therapists also may assist dosimetrists with routine aspects of dosimetry, the process used to calculate radiation dosages.

Work Environment. Radiation therapists work in hospitals or in cancer treatment centers. These places are clean, well-lighted, and well-ventilated. Therapists do a considerable amount of lifting and must be able to help disabled patients get on and off treatment tables. They spend most of their time on their feet.

Radiation therapists generally work 40 hours a week, and unlike many in other healthcare occupations, they normally work only during the day. Radiation therapy emergencies do occur, however, and some therapists are required to be on call and may have to work outside of their normal hours.

Working with cancer patients can be stressful, but many radiation therapists also find it rewarding. Because they work around radioactive materials, radiation therapists take great care to ensure that they are not exposed to dangerous levels of radiation. Following standard safety procedures can prevent overexposure.

EMPLOYMENT OPPORTUNITIES

Radiation therapists held about 15,000 jobs in 2006. About 73 percent of them worked in hospitals, and about 17 percent worked in physicians' offices. A small proportion worked in outpatient care centers.

EDUCATIONAL AND LEGAL REQUIREMENTS

A bachelor's degree, associate degree, or certificate in radiation therapy generally is required. Many states also require radiation therapists to be licensed. With experience, therapists can advance to managerial positions.

Education and Training. Employers usually require applicants to complete an associate or a bachelor's degree program in radiation therapy. Individuals also may become qualified by completing an associate or a bachelor's degree program in radiography, which is the study of radiological imaging, and then completing a 12-month certificate program in radiation therapy. Radiation therapy programs include core courses on radiation therapy procedures and the scientific theories behind them. In addition, such programs often include courses on human anatomy and physiology, physics, algebra, precalculus, writing, public speaking, computer science, and research methodology. In 2007 there were 123 radiation therapy programs accredited by the *American Registry of Radiologic Technologists (ARRT)*.

Licensure. In 2007, 32 states required radiation therapists to be licensed by a state accrediting board. Licensing requirements vary by state, but many states require applicants to pass the ARRT certification examination. Further information is available from individual state licensing offices.

Certification and Other Qualifications. Some states, as well as many employers, require that radiation therapists be certified by ARRT. To become ARRT-certified, an applicant must complete an accredited radiation therapy program, adhere to ARRT ethical standards, and pass the ARRT certification examination. The examination and accredited academic programs cover radiation protection and quality assurance, clinical concepts in radiation oncology, treatment planning, treatment delivery, and patient care and education. Candidates also must demonstrate competency in several clinical practices including patient care activities; simulation procedures; dosimetry calculations; fabrication of beam modification devices; low-volume, high-risk procedures; and the application of radiation.

Certification by ARRT is valid for one year, after which therapists must renew it. Requirements for renewal include abiding by the ARRT ethical standards, paying annual dues, and satisfying continuing education requirements. Continuing education requirements must be met every two years and include either the completion of 24 credits of radiation therapy-related courses or the attainment of ARRT certification in a discipline other than radiation therapy. Certification renewal, however, may not be required by all states or employers that require initial certification.

All radiation therapists need good communication skills because their work involves a great deal of patient interaction. Individuals interested in becoming radiation therapists should be psychologically capable of working with cancer patients. They should be caring and empathetic because they work with patients who are ill and under stress. They should be able to keep accurate, detailed records. They also should be physically fit because they work on their feet for long periods and lift and move disabled patients.

Advancement. Experienced radiation therapists may advance to manage radiation therapy programs in treatment centers or other healthcare facilities. Managers generally continue to treat patients while taking on managerial responsibilities. Other advancement opportunities include teaching, technical sales, and research. With additional training and certification, therapists also can become dosimetrists, who use complex mathematical formulas to calculate proper radiation doses.

EMPLOYMENT TRENDS

Employment is expected to increase much faster than the average from 2006 to 2016, and job prospects should be good.

Employment Change. Employment of radiation therapists is projected to grow by 25 percent between 2006 and 2016, which is much faster than the average for all occupations. As the U.S. population grows and an increasing share of it moves into older age groups, the number of people needing treatment is expected to increase and to spur demand for radiation therapists. In addition, as radiation technology advances and is able to treat more types of cancer, radiation therapy will be prescribed more often.

Job Prospects. Job prospects are expected to be good. Job openings will result from employment growth and from the need to replace workers who retire or leave the occupation for other reasons. Applicants who are certified should have the best opportunities. **Table 16–3** shows some projection data provided by the Department of Labor.

EARNINGS

Median annual earnings of wage-and-salary radiation therapists were $66,170 in May 2006. The middle 50 percent earned between $54,170 and $78,550. The lowest 10 percent

Table 16–3	Projections data from the National Employment Matrix				
Occupational title	Employment, 2006	Projected employment, 2016	Change, 2006–2016		
			Number	Percent	
Radiation therapists technicians	15,000	18,000	3,600	25	

NOTE: Data in this table are rounded.

earned less than $44,840, and the highest 10 percent earned more than $92,110. Median annual earnings in the industries that employed the largest numbers of radiation therapists in May 2006 are shown in **Table 16–4**.

Some employers also reimburse their employees for the cost of continuing education.

Table 16–4	Median annual earnings in the industries that employed the largest numbers of radiation therapists in May 2006
Outpatient care centers	$73,810
Physicians' offices	$70,050
General medical and surgical hospitals	$63,580

RELATED OCCUPATIONS

Radiation therapists use advanced machinery to administer medical treatment to patients. Other occupations that perform similar duties include nuclear medicine technologists, cardiovascular technologists and technicians, dental hygienists, respiratory therapists, physical therapist assistants and aides, registered nurses, and physicians and surgeons.

Other healthcare workers who build relationships with patients and provide them with emotional support include nurses; psychiatric and home health aides; counselors; psychologists; social workers; and social and human service assistants.

ADDITIONAL INFORMATION

Information on certification by the American Registry of Radiologic Technologists and on accredited radiation therapy programs may be obtained from:

■ American Registry of Radiologic Technologists, 1255 Northland Dr., St. Paul, MN 55120. http://www.arrt.org

Information on careers in radiation therapy may be obtained from:

■ American Society of Radiologic Technologists, 15000 Central Ave., S.E., Albuquerque, NM 87123. http://www.asrt.org

Diagnostic Medical Sonographers

WORK DESCRIPTION

Diagnostic imaging embraces several procedures that aid in diagnosing ailments. The most familiar procedures are the X-ray and magnetic resonance imaging, however, not all imaging technologies use ionizing radiation or radio waves. Sonography, or ultrasonography, uses sound waves to generate an image for the assessment and diagnosis of various medical conditions. Sonography commonly is associated with obstetrics and the use of ultrasound imaging during pregnancy, but this technology has many other applications in the diagnosis and treatment of medical conditions throughout the body.

Diagnostic medical sonographers use special equipment to direct nonionizing, high frequency sound waves into areas of the patient's body. Sonographers operate the equipment, which collects reflected echoes and forms an image that may be videotaped, transmitted, or photographed for interpretation and diagnosis by a physician.

Sonographers begin by explaining the procedure to the patient and recording any medical history that may be relevant to the condition being viewed. They then select appropriate equipment settings and direct the patient to move into positions that will provide the best view. To perform the exam, sonographers use a transducer, which transmits sound waves in a cone or rectangle-shaped beam. Although techniques vary with the area being examined, sonographers usually spread a special gel on the skin to aid the transmission of sound waves.

Viewing the screen during the scan, sonographers look for subtle visual cues that contrast healthy areas with unhealthy ones. They decide whether the images are satisfactory for diagnostic purposes and select which ones to store and show to the physician. Sonographers take measurements, calculate values, and analyze the results in preliminary findings for the physicians.

In addition to working directly with patients, diagnostic medical sonographers keep patient records, and adjust and maintain equipment. They also may prepare work schedules, evaluate equipment purchases, or manage a sonography or diagnostic imaging department.

Diagnostic medical sonographers may specialize in obstetric and gynecologic sonography (the female reproductive system), abdominal sonography (the liver, kidneys, gallbladder, spleen, and pancreas), neurosonography (the brain), or breast sonography. In addition, sonographers may specialize in vascular sonography or cardiac sonography. (The work of vascular sonographers and cardiac sonographers is covered in the chapter on cardiovascular technologists and technicians.)

Obstetric and gynecologic sonographers specialize in the imaging of the female reproductive system. Included in the discipline is one of the better known uses of sonography: examining the fetus of a pregnant woman to track the baby's growth and health.

Abdominal sonographers inspect a patient's abdominal cavity to help diagnose and treat conditions primarily involving the gallbladder, bile ducts, kidneys, liver, pancreas, spleen, and male reproductive system. Abdominal sonographers also are able to scan parts of the chest, although studies of the heart using sonography usually are done by *echocardiographers*.

Neurosonographers focus on the nervous system, including the brain. In neonatal care, neurosonographers study and diagnose neurological and nervous system disorders in premature infants. They also may scan blood vessels to check for abnormalities indicating a stroke in infants diagnosed with sickle-cell anemia. Like other sonographers, neurosonographers operate transducers to perform the sonogram, but use frequencies and beam shapes different from those used by obstetric and abdominal sonographers.

Breast sonographers use sonography to study diseases of the breasts. Sonography aids mammography in the detection of breast cancer. Breast sonography can also track tumors, blood supply conditions, and assist in the accurate biopsy of breast tissue. Breast sonographers use high-frequency transducers, made exclusively to study breast tissue.

WORK ENVIRONMENT

Sonographers typically work in clean and well-maintained healthcare facilities. They usually work at diagnostic imaging machines in darkened rooms, but also may perform procedures at patients' bedsides. Sonographers may be on their feet for long periods of time and may have to lift or turn disabled patients. In addition, the nature of their work can put sonographers at an increased risk for musculoskeletal disorders such as carpal tunnel syndrome, or neck, back, and eye strain. Increasing use of ergonomically correct equipment, combined with an increasing awareness of potential problems, will help to minimize such risks.

Some sonographers work as contract employees and may travel to several different healthcare facilities within a given area. Similarly, some sonographers travel with mobile imaging service providers and bring mobile diagnostic imaging services to patients in areas that otherwise lack access to them.

Most full-time sonographers work about 40 hours a week. Hospital-based sonographers may have evening and weekend hours, including times when they are on call and must be ready to report to work on short notice.

EMPLOYMENT OPPORTUNITIES

Diagnostic medical sonographers held about 46,000 jobs in 2006. More than half of all sonographer jobs were in public and private hospitals. The remainder were typically in physicians' offices, medical and diagnostic laboratories, and with mobile imaging services.

EDUCATIONAL AND LEGAL REQUIREMENTS

Employers hiring in diagnostic medical sonography recognize and accept several levels of education and methods of acquiring it. Although no one level of education is preferred, employers do prefer registered sonographers who trained in accredited programs.

Education and Training. Several avenues exist for entry into the field of diagnostic medical sonography. Sonographers may train in hospitals, vocational-technical institutions, colleges and universities, or the armed forces. Some training programs prefer applicants with a background in science or experience in other healthcare professions. Some training programs also may consider high school graduates with courses in mathematics and science, as well as applicants with liberal arts backgrounds, but this practice is infrequent.

Colleges and universities offer formal training in both two- and four-year programs, culminating in an associate or a bachelor's degree. Two-year programs are most prevalent. Course work includes classes in anatomy, physiology, instrumentation, basic physics, patient care, and medical ethics.

A few one-year programs, some of which result in a certificate, also are accepted as appropriate education by employers. These programs typically are satisfactory education and training for workers already in health care who seek to increase their marketability by training in sonography. These programs are not accredited.

The Commission on Accreditation for Allied Health Education Programs (CAAHEP) accredited 147 diagnostic medical sonography training programs in 2006. These programs typically are the formal training programs offered by colleges and universities. Some hospital programs are accredited as well.

Certification and Other Qualifications. Although no state requires licensure in diagnostic medical sonography, organizations such as the *American Registry for Diagnostic Medical Sonography (ARDMS)* certify the skills and knowledge of sonographers through credentialing, including registration. Registration provides an independent, objective measure of an individual's professional standing, and many employers prefer to hire registered sonographers. Sonographers registered by the ARDMS are referred to as *Registered Diagnostic Medical Sonographers (RDMS)*. Registration with ARDMS requires passing a general physical principles and instrumentation examination, in addition to passing an exam in a specialty such as obstetric and gynecologic sonography, abdominal sonography, or neurosonography. Sonographers must complete a required number of continuing education hours to maintain registration with the ARDMS and to stay abreast of technological advancements related to the occupation.

Sonographers need good communication and interpersonal skills because they must be able to explain technical procedures and results to their patients, some of whom may be nervous about the exam or the problems it may reveal. Good hand-eye coordination is particularly important to obtaining quality images. Sonographers should also enjoy learning because continuing education is the key to them staying abreast of the ever-changing field of diagnostic medicine. A background in mathematics and science is helpful for sonographers as well.

Advancement. Sonographers specializing in one particular discipline often seek competency in other specialties. For example, obstetric sonographers might seek training in abdominal sonography to broaden their opportunities and increase their marketability.

Sonographers may also have advancement opportunities in education, administration, research, sales, or technical advising.

EMPLOYMENT TRENDS

Faster-than-average employment growth is expected. Job opportunities should be favorable.

Employment Change. As the U.S. population ages, demand for diagnostic imaging and therapeutic technology will increase. Employment of diagnostic medical sonographers is expected to increase by about 19 percent through 2016—faster than the average for all occupations.

Additional job growth also is expected as patients seek safer treatment methods and sonography becomes an increasingly attractive alternative to radiologic procedures Unlike most diagnostic imaging methods, sonography does not involve radiation, so harmful side effects and complications from repeated use are less likely for both the patient and the sonographer. Sonographic technology is expected to evolve rapidly and to spawn many new sonography procedures, such as 3D- and 4D-sonography for use in obstetric and ophthalmologic diagnosis. However, high costs and necessary approval by the federal government may limit the rate at which some promising new technologies are adopted.

Hospitals will remain the principal employer of diagnostic medical sonographers. However, employment is expected to grow more rapidly in physicians' offices and in medical and diagnostic laboratories, including diagnostic imaging centers. Healthcare facilities such as these are expected to increase very rapidly through 2016 because of the strong shift toward outpatient care, encouraged by third-party payers and made possible by technological advances that permit more procedures to be performed outside the hospital.

Job Prospects. Job opportunities should be favorable. In addition to job openings from growth, some openings will arise from the need to replace sonographers who retire or leave the occupation permanently for some other reason. Pain caused by musculoskeletal disorders has made it difficult for some sonographers to perform well. Some are forced to leave the occupation early because of such disorders. **Table 16–5** shows some projection data provided by the Department of Labor.

Table 16–5

			Change, 2006–2016	
Occupational title	Employment, 2006	Projected employment, 2016	Number	Percent
Diagnostic medical sonographers	46,000	54,000	8,700	19

Projections data from the National Employment Matrix

NOTE: Data in this table are rounded.

EARNINGS

Median annual earnings of diagnostic medical sonographers were $57,160 in May 2006. The middle 50 percent earned between $48,890 and $67,670 a year. The lowest 10 percent earned less than $40,960, and the highest 10 percent earned more than $77,520. Median annual earnings of diagnostic medical sonographers in May 2006 were $56,970 for those employed in physicians' offices and $56,850 for those working in general medical and surgical hospitals.

RELATED OCCUPATIONS

Diagnostic medical sonographers operate sophisticated equipment to help physicians and other health practitioners diagnose and treat patients. Workers in related occupations include cardiovascular technologists and technicians, clinical laboratory technologists and technicians, nuclear medicine technologists, and respiratory therapists.

ADDITIONAL INFORMATION

For information on a career as a diagnostic medical sonographer, contact:

- Society of Diagnostic Medical Sonography, 2745 Dallas Pkwy., Suite 350, Plano, TX 75093-8730. http://www.sdms.org

For information on becoming a registered diagnostic medical sonographer, contact:

- American Registry for Diagnostic Medical Sonography, 51 Monroe St., Plaza East 1, Rockville, MD 20850-2400. http://www.ardms.org

For more information on ultrasound in medicine, contact:

- American Institute of Ultrasound in Medicine, 14750 Sweitzer Lane, Suite 100, Laurel, MD 20707-5906. http://www.aium.org

For a current list of accredited education programs in diagnostic medical sonography, contact:

- Joint Review Committee on Education in Diagnostic Medical Sonography, 2025 Woodlane Dr., St. Paul, MN 55125-2998. http://www.jrcdms.org

- Commission on Accreditation for Allied Health Education Programs, 35 East Wacker Dr., Suite 1970, Chicago, IL 60601. http://www.caahep.org

17

SOCIAL WORKERS

Key Terms

- Health professions involving patient care
- Environmental factors
- Psychological treatment
- Emotional stress
- Health care social worker
- Clinical social worker
- Child welfare/family services social worker
- Child or adult protective services social worker

- Mental health social worker
- School social worker
- Criminal justice social worker
- Occupational social worker
- Gerontology social worker
- Social work administrator
- Social work planners and policy makers
- Human service workers and assistants

Social, Economic, and Other Factors Related to Health

Health has been defined as not merely the absence of disease but as a condition of complete physical, mental, and social well-being. The effect of social, economic, and environmental factors on an individual's state of health is an accepted fact, and studies reveal a definite relationship between these factors and occurrence of disease. Recognizing this, health officials are placing increasing emphasis on the psychological treatment as well as the clinical treatment of patients in health facilities. Very often a patient's restoration to and maintenance of health is influenced by many factors that can be dealt with by other professionals, including competently trained social workers.

Social work in the health field involves programs and services that meet the special needs of the ill, disabled, elderly, or otherwise handicapped. Social workers deal with the total emotional, social, cultural, and physical needs of patients in whom the effects of illness go far beyond bodily discomfort. Such problems usually lie in three areas—problems within the patient, problems between the patient and family, or problems between the patient and the patient's environment. Illness invariably results in emotional stress and often causes significant changes in the lives of patients and their families. Medical care alone, even if it is of the highest quality, is often not sufficient. Social workers help patients and members of the health team to deal with these problems by providing a skilled appraisal of the source and significance of social, emotional, environmental, and economic factors affecting health. Their efforts with individual patients or groups of patients help to bring about constructive and meaningful changes in terms of total health.

Social Workers

WORK DESCRIPTION

Social work is a profession for those with a strong desire to help improve people's lives. Social workers assist people by helping them cope with issues in their everyday lives, deal with their relationships, and solve personal and family problems. Some social workers help clients who face a disability or a life-threatening disease or a social problem, such as inadequate housing, unemployment, or substance abuse. Social workers also assist families that have serious domestic conflicts, sometimes involving child or spousal abuse. Some social workers conduct research, advocate for improved services, engage in systems design, or are involved in planning and policy development. Many social workers specialize in serving a particular population or working in a specific setting.

Child, family, and school social workers provide social services and assistance to improve the social and psychological functioning of children and their families and to maximize the well-being of families and the academic functioning of children. They may assist single parents, arrange adoptions, or help find foster homes for neglected, abandoned, or abused children. Some specialize in services for senior citizens. These social workers may run support groups for the children of aging parents; advise elderly people or family members about housing, transportation, long-term care, and other services; and coordinate and monitor these services. Through employee assistance programs, social workers may help people cope with job-related pressures or with personal problems that affect the quality of their work.

In schools, social workers often serve as the link between students' families and the school, working with parents, guardians, teachers, and other school officials to ensure students reach their academic and personal potential. In addition, they address problems such as misbehavior, truancy, and teenage pregnancy, and advise teachers on how to cope with difficult students. Increasingly, school social workers teach workshops to entire classes.

Child, family, and school social workers may also be known as child welfare social workers, family services social workers, child protective services social workers, occupational social workers, or gerontology social workers. They often work for individual and family service agencies, schools, or state and local governments.

Medical and public health social workers provide psychosocial support to people, families, or vulnerable populations so they can cope with chronic, acute, or terminal illnesses, such as Alzheimer's disease, cancer, or AIDS. They also advise family caregivers, counsel patients, and help plan for patients' needs after discharge from hospitals. They may arrange for at-home services, such as meals-on-wheels or home care. Some work on interdisciplinary teams that evaluate certain kinds of patients—geriatric or organ transplant patients, for example. Medical and public health social workers may work for hospitals, nursing and personal care facilities, individual and family service agencies, or local governments.

Mental health and substance abuse social workers assess and treat individuals with mental illness or substance abuse problems, including abuse of alcohol, tobacco, or other drugs. Such services include individual and group therapy, outreach, crisis intervention, social rehabilitation, and teaching skills needed for everyday living. They also may help plan for supportive services to ease clients' return to the community. Mental health and substance abuse social workers are likely to work in hospitals, substance abuse treatment centers, individual and family service agencies, or local governments. These social workers may be known as clinical social workers. Other types of social workers include social work administrators, planners and policymakers, who develop and implement programs to address issues such as child abuse, homelessness, substance abuse, poverty, and violence. These workers research and analyze policies, programs, and regulations. They identify social problems and suggest legislative and other solutions. They may help raise funds or write grants to support these programs.

WORK ENVIRONMENT

Social workers usually spend most of their time in an office or residential facility, but they also may travel locally to visit clients, meet with service providers, or attend meetings. Some may meet with clients in one of several offices within a local area. Social work, while satisfying, can be challenging. Understaffing and large caseloads add to the pressure in some agencies. To tend to patient care or client needs, many hospitals and long-term care facilities employ social workers on teams with a broad mix of occupations, including clinical specialists, registered nurses, and health aides. Full-time social workers usually work a standard 40-hour week, but some occasionally work evenings and weekends to meet with clients, attend community meetings, and handle emergencies. Some work part-time, particularly in voluntary nonprofit agencies.

EMPLOYMENT OPPORTUNITIES

Social workers held about 595,000 jobs in 2006. About five out of ten jobs were in health care and social assistance industries and three out of ten are employed by state and local government agencies, primarily in departments of health and human services. Although most social workers are employed in cities or suburbs, some work in rural areas. Employment by type of social worker in 2006 is shown in **Table 17–1**.

Table
17–1

Employment by type of social worker in 2006

Child, family, and school social workers	282,000
Medical and public health social workers	124,000
Mental health and substance abuse social workers	122,000
Social workers, all other	66,000

EDUCATIONAL AND LEGAL REQUIREMENTS

A bachelor's degree is the minimum requirement for entry into the occupation, but many positions require an advanced degree. All states and the District of Columbia have some licensure, certification, or registration requirement, but the regulations vary.

Education and Training. A bachelor's degree in social work (BSW) is the most common minimum requirement to qualify for a job as a social worker, however, majors in psychology, sociology, and related fields may qualify for some entry-level jobs, especially in small community agencies. Although a bachelor's degree is sufficient for entry into the field, an advanced degree has become the standard for many positions. A master's degree in social work (MSW) is typically required for positions in health settings and is required for clinical work as well. Some jobs in public and private agencies also may require an advanced degree, such as a master's degree in social services policy or administration. Supervisory, administrative, and staff training positions usually require an advanced degree. College and university teaching positions and most research appointments normally require a doctorate in social work (DSW or PhD).

As of 2006, the Council on Social Work Education accredited 458 bachelor's programs and 181 master's programs. The Group for the Advancement of Doctoral Education listed 74 doctoral programs in social work (DSW or PhD) in the United States. Bachelor's degree programs prepare graduates for direct service positions, such as caseworker, and include courses in social work values and ethics, dealing with a culturally diverse clientele and at-risk populations, promotion of social and economic justice, human behavior and the social environment, social welfare policy and services, social work practice, social research methods, and field education. Accredited programs require a minimum of 400 hours of supervised field experience.

Master's degree programs prepare graduates for work in their chosen field of concentration and continue to develop the skills required to perform clinical assessments, manage large case-loads, take on supervisory roles, and explore new ways of drawing upon social services to meet the needs of clients. Master's programs last two years and include a minimum of 900 hours of supervised field instruction or internship. A part-time program may take four years. Entry into a master's program does not require a bachelor's degree in social work, but courses in psychology, biology, sociology, economics, political science, and social work are recommended. In addition, a second language can be very helpful. Most master's programs offer advanced standing for those with a bachelor's degree from an accredited social work program.

Licensure. All states and the District of Columbia have licensing, certification, or registration requirements regarding social work practice and the use of professional titles. Although standards for licensing vary by state, a growing number of states are placing greater emphasis on communication skills, professional ethics, and sensitivity to cultural diversity issues. Most states require two years (3,000 hours) of supervised clinical experience for licensure of clinical social workers.

Other Qualifications. Social workers should be emotionally mature, objective, and sensitive to people and their problems. They must be able to handle responsibility, work independently, and maintain good working relationships with clients and coworkers. Volunteer or paid jobs as a social work aide can help people test their interest in this field.

Certification and Advancement. The National Association of Social Workers offers voluntary credentials. Social workers with a master's degree in social work may be eligible for the Academy of Certified Social Workers (ACSW), the Qualified Clinical Social Worker (QCSW), or the Diplomate in Clinical Social Work (DCSW) credential, based on their professional experience. Credentials are particularly important for those in private practice; some health insurance providers require social workers to have them in order to be reimbursed for services.

Advancement to supervisor, program manager, assistant director, or executive director of a social service agency or department usually requires an advanced degree and related work experience. Other career options for social workers include teaching, research, and consulting. Some of these workers also help formulate government policies by analyzing and advocating policy positions in government agencies, in research institutions, and on legislators' staffs.

Some social workers go into private practice. Most private practitioners are clinical social workers who provide psychotherapy, usually paid for through health insurance or by the client themselves. Private practitioners must have at least a master's degree and a period of supervised work experience. A network of contacts for referrals also is essential. Many private practitioners split their time between working for an agency or hospital and working in their private practice. They may continue to hold a position at a hospital or agency in order to receive health and life insurance.

EMPLOYMENT TRENDS

Employment for social workers is expected grow much faster than the average for all occupations through 2016. Job prospects are expected to be favorable, particularly for social workers who specialize in the aging population or work in rural areas.

Employment Change. Employment of social workers is expected to increase by 22 percent during the 2006 to 2016 decade, which is much faster than the average for all occupations. The growing elderly population and the aging baby boom generation will create greater demand for health and social services, resulting in rapid job growth among gerontology social workers. Employment of social workers in private social service agencies also will increase. However, agencies increasingly will restructure services and hire more social and human service assistants, who are paid less, instead of social workers. Employment in state and local government agencies may grow somewhat in response to growing needs for public welfare, family services, and child protective services, but many of these services will be contracted out to private agencies. Employment levels in public and private social service agencies may fluctuate, depending on need and government funding levels.

Opportunities for social workers in private practice will expand, but growth may be somewhat hindered by restrictions that managed care organizations put on mental health services. The growing popularity of employee assistance programs is expected to spur demand for private practitioners, some of whom provide social work services to corporations on a contractual basis. The popularity of employee assistance programs, however, will fluctuate with the business cycle because businesses are not likely to offer these services during recessions.

Employment of child, family and school social workers is expected to grow by 19 percent, which is faster than the average for all occupations. One of the major contributing factors will be the rise in the elderly population. Social workers, particularly family social workers, will be needed to assist in finding the best care for the aging and to support their families. Furthermore, demand for school social workers will increase and lead to more jobs as efforts are expanded to respond to rising student enrollments as well as the continued emphasis on integrating disabled children into the general school population. There could be competition for school social work jobs in some areas because of the limited number of openings. The availability of federal, state, and local funding will be a major factor in determining the actual job growth in schools. The demand for child and family social workers may also be tied to the availability of government funding.

Employment of mental health and substance abuse social workers will grow by 29 percent, which is much faster than the average, over the 2006 to 2016 decade. In particular, social workers specializing in substance abuse will experience strong demand. Substance abusers are increasingly being placed into treatment programs instead of being sentenced to prison. In addition, growing numbers of the substance abusers sentenced to prison or probation are being required by correctional systems to have substance abuse treatment added as a condition to their sentence or probation. As this trend grows, demand will strengthen for treatment programs and social workers to assist abusers on the road to recovery.

Growth of medical and public health social workers is expected to be 24 percent, which is much faster than the average for all occupations. Hospitals continue to limit the length of patient stays, so the demand for social workers in hospitals will grow more slowly than in other areas. But hospitals are releasing patients earlier than in the past, so social worker employment in home healthcare services is growing. However, the expanding senior population is an even larger factor. Employment opportunities for social workers with backgrounds in gerontology should be good in the growing numbers of assisted-living and senior-living communities. The expanding senior population also will spur demand for social workers in nursing homes, long-term care facilities, and hospices. However, in these settings other types of workers are often being given tasks that were previously done by social workers.

Job Prospects. Job prospects are generally expected to be favorable. Many job openings will stem from growth and the need to replace social workers who leave the occupation. However, competition for social worker jobs is expected in cities, where training programs for social workers are prevalent. Opportunities should be good in rural areas, where it is often difficult to attract and retain qualified staff. By specialty, job prospects may be best for those social workers with a background in gerontology and substance abuse treatment. **Table 17–2** shows some projection data provided by the Department of Labor.

Table 17–2

Projections data from the National Employment Matrix

Occupational title	Employment, 2006	Projected employment, 2016	Change, 2006–2016	
			Number	Percent
Social workers	595,000	727,000	132,000	22
Child, family, and school social workers	282,000	336,000	54,000	19
Medical and public health social workers	124,000	154,000	30,000	24
Mental health and substance abuse social workers	122,000	159,000	37,000	30
Social workers, all other	66,000	78,000	12,000	18

NOTE: Data in this table are rounded.

Earnings Median annual earnings of child, family, and school social workers were $37,480 in May 2006. The middle 50 percent earned between $29,590 and $49,060. The lowest 10 percent earned less than $24,480, and the top 10 percent earned more than $62,530. Median annual earnings in the industries employing the largest number of child, family, and school social workers in May 2006 are shown in **Table 17–3**.

Median annual earnings of medical and public health social workers were $43,040 in May 2006. The middle 50 percent earned between $34,110 and $53,740. The lowest 10 percent earned less than $27,280, and the top 10 percent earned more than $64,070. Median annual earnings in the industries employing the largest number of medical and public health social workers in May 2006 are shown in **Table 17–4**.

Median annual earnings of mental health and substance abuse social workers were $35,410 in May 2006. The middle 50 percent earned between $27,940 and $45,720. The lowest 10 percent earned less than $22,490, and the top 10 percent earned more than $57,630. Median

Table
17–3

Median annual earnings in the industries employing the largest numbers of child, family, and school social workers in May 2006

Elementary and secondary schools	$48,360
Local government	$43,500
State government	$39,000
Individual and family services	$32,680
Other residential care facilities	$32,590

Table
17–4

Median annual earnings in the industries employing the largest numbers of medical and public health social workers in May 2006

General medical and surgical hospitals	$48,420
Home health care services	$44,470
Local government	$41,590
Nursing care facilities	$38,550
Individual and family services	$35,510

annual earnings in the industries employing the largest number of mental health and substance abuse social workers in May 2006 are shown in **Table 17–5**.

Median annual earnings of social workers, all other, were $43,580 in May 2006. The middle 50 percent earned between $32,530 and $56,420. The lowest 10 percent earned less than $25,540, and the top 10 percent earned more than $68,500. Median annual earnings in the industries employing the largest numbers of social workers, all other, in May 2006 are shown in **Table 17–6**.

About 20 percent of social workers are members of a union. Many belong to a union representing workers in other occupations at their place of employment.

RELATED OCCUPATIONS

Through direct counseling or referral to other services, social workers help people solve a range of personal problems. Workers in occupations with similar duties include the clergy, counselors, probation officers, correctional treatment specialists, psychologists, and social and human services assistants.

Table
17–5

Median annual earnings in the industries employing the largest number of mental health and substance abuse social workers in May 2006

Local government	$39,550
Psychiatric and substance abuse hospitals	$39,240
Individual and family services	$34,920
Residential mental retardation, mental health and substance abuse facilities	$30,590
Outpatient mental health and substance abuse centers	$34,290

Table
17–6

Median annual earnings in the industries employing the largest numbers of social workers, all other in May 2006

Local government	$46,330
State government	$45,070
Individual and family services	$35,150

ADDITIONAL INFORMATION

For information about career opportunities in social work and voluntary credentials for social workers, contact:

■ National Association of Social Workers, 750 First St. N.E., Suite 700, Washington, DC 20002-4241. http://www.socialworkers.org

For a listing of accredited social work programs, contact:

■ Council on Social Work Education, 1725 Duke St., Suite 500, Alexandria, VA 22314-3457. http://www.cswe.org

■ Information on licensing requirements and testing procedures for each state may be obtained from state licensing authorities, or from:

■ Association of Social Work Boards, 400 South Ridge Pkwy., Suite B, Culpeper, VA 22701. http://www.aswb.org

Social and Human Service Assistants

WORK DESCRIPTIONS

Social and human service assistants help social workers, healthcare workers, and other professionals to provide services to people. Social and human service assistant is a generic term for workers with a wide array of job titles, including human service worker, case management aide, social work assistant, community support worker, mental health aide, community outreach worker, life skills counselor, or gerontology aide. They usually work under the direction of workers from a variety of fields, such as nursing, psychiatry, psychology, rehabilitative or physical therapy, or social work. The amount of responsibility and supervision they are given varies a great deal. Some have little direct supervision—they may run a group home, for example. Others work under close supervision.

Social and human service assistants provide services to clients to help them improve their quality of life. They assess clients' needs, investigate their eligibility for benefits and services such as food stamps, Medicaid, or welfare, and help clients obtain these services. They also arrange for transportation and escorts, if necessary, and provide emotional support. Social and human service assistants monitor and keep case records on clients and report progress to supervisors and case managers.

Social and human service assistants play a variety of roles in a community. They may organize and lead group activities, assist clients in need of counseling or crisis intervention, or administer food banks or emergency fuel programs. In halfway houses, group homes, and government-supported housing programs, they assist adults who need supervision with personal hygiene and daily living skills. They review clients' records, ensure that they take their medication, talk with family members, and confer with medical personnel and other caregivers to provide insight into clients' needs. Social and human service assistants also give emotional support and help clients become involved in community recreation programs and other activities.

In psychiatric hospitals, rehabilitation programs, and outpatient clinics, social and human service assistants work with psychiatrists, psychologists, social workers, and others to help clients master everyday living skills, communicate more effectively, and live well with others. They support the client's participation in a treatment plan, such as individual or group counseling or occupational therapy. The work, while satisfying, can be emotionally draining. Understaffing and relatively low pay may add to the pressure.

WORK ENVIRONMENT

Working conditions of social and human service assistants vary. Some work in offices, clinics, and hospitals, while others work in group homes, shelters, sheltered workshops, and day programs. Traveling to see clients is also required for some jobs. Sometimes working with clients can be dangerous even though most agencies do everything they can to ensure their workers' safety. Most assistants work 40 hours a week; some work in the evening and on weekends.

EMPLOYMENT OPPORTUNITIES

Social and human service assistants held about 339,000 jobs in 2006. Over 60 percent were employed in the health care and social assistance industries. Nearly 3 in 10 were employed by state and local governments, primarily in public welfare agencies and facilities for mentally disabled and developmentally challenged individuals.

EDUCATIONAL AND LEGAL REQUIREMENTS

A bachelor's degree is not required for most jobs in this occupation, but employers increasingly seek individuals with relevant work experience or education beyond high school.

Education and Training. Many employers prefer to hire people with some education beyond high school. Certificates or associate degrees in subjects such as human services, gerontology or one of the social or behavioral sciences meet many employers' requirements. Some jobs may require a bachelor's or master's degree in human services or a related field, such as counseling, rehabilitation, or social work.

Human services degree programs have a core curriculum that trains students to observe patients and record information, conduct patient interviews, implement treatment plans, employ problem-solving techniques, handle crisis intervention matters, and use proper case management and referral procedures. Many programs utilize field work to give students hands-on experience. General education courses in liberal arts, sciences, and the humanities also are part of most curricula. Most programs also offer specialized courses related to addictions, gerontology, child protection, and other areas. Many degree programs require completion of a supervised internship.

Workers' level of education often influences the kind of work assigned and the degree of responsibility given. For example, workers with no more than a high school education are likely to receive extensive on-the-job training to work in direct-care services, helping clients to fill out paperwork, for example. Workers with a college degree, however, might do supportive counseling, coordinate program activities, or manage a group home. Social and human service assistants with proven leadership ability, especially from paid or volunteer experience in social services, often have greater autonomy in their work. Regardless of the academic or work background of employees, most employers provide some form of in-service training to their employees such as seminars and workshops.

Other Qualifications. These workers should have a strong desire to help others, effective communication skills, a sense of responsibility, and the ability to manage time effectively. Many human service jobs involve direct contact with people who are vulnerable to exploitation or mistreatment; so patience and understanding are also highly valued characteristics. It is becoming more common for employers to require a criminal background check, and in some settings, workers may be required to have a valid driver's license.

Advancement. Formal education is almost always necessary for advancement. In general, advancement to case management, rehabilitation, or social work jobs requires a bachelor's or master's degree in human services, counseling, rehabilitation, social work, or a related field.

EMPLOYMENT TRENDS

Employment of social and human service assistants is expected to grow by nearly 34 percent through 2016. Job prospects are expected to be excellent, particularly for applicants with appropriate postsecondary education.

EMPLOYMENT CHANGE

The number of social and human service assistants is projected to grow by nearly 34 percent between 2006 and 2016, which is much faster than the average for all occupations. This occupation will have a very large number of new jobs arise, about 114,000 over the 2006 to 2016 projection decade. Faced with rapid growth in the demand for social and human services, many employers increasingly rely on social and human service assistants.

Demand for social services will expand with the growing elderly population, who are more likely to need adult day care, meal delivery programs, support during medical crises, and other services. In addition, more social and human service assistants will be needed to provide services to pregnant teenagers, the homeless population, people who are mentally disabled or developmentally challenged, and those who are substance abusers.

Job training programs are also expected to require additional social and human service assistants. As social welfare policies shift focus from benefit-based programs to work-based initiatives, there will be more demand for people to teach job skills to people entering or returning to the workforce.

Residential care establishments face increased pressures to respond to the needs of the mentally and physically disabled. The number of people who are disabled is increasing, and many need help to look after themselves. More community-based programs and supportive independent-living sites are expected to be established to house and assist the homeless and the mentally and physically disabled. Furthermore, as substance abusers are increasingly being sent to treatment programs instead of prison, employment of social and human service assistants in substance abuse treatment programs also will grow.

Opportunities are expected to be good in private social service agencies. Employment in private agencies will grow as state and local governments continue to contract out services to the private sector in an effort to cut costs. Also, some private agencies have been employing more social and human service assistants in place of social workers, who are more educated and more highly paid.

The number of jobs for social and human service assistants in local governments will grow, but not as fast as employment for social and human service assistants in other industries. Employment in the public sector may fluctuate with the level of funding provided by state and local governments and with the number of services contracted out to private organizations.

Job Prospects. Job prospects for social and human service assistants are expected to be excellent, particularly for individuals with appropriate postsecondary education. Job openings will come from job growth, but also from the need to replace workers who advance into new positions, retire, or leave the workforce for other reasons. Competition for jobs in urban areas will outweigh competition in rural areas, but qualified applicants should have little difficulty finding employment anywhere. **Table 17–7** shows some projection data provided by the Department of Labor.

Table 17–7	Projections data from the National Employment Matrix				
Occupational title	**Employment, 2006**	**Projected employment, 2016**	**Change, 2006–2016**		
			Number	**Percent**	
Social and human service assistants	339,000	453,000	114,000	34	

NOTE: Data in this table are rounded.

EARNINGS

Median annual earnings of social and human service assistants were $25,580 in May 2006. The middle 50 percent earned between $20,350 and $32,440. The top 10 percent earned more than $40,780, while the lowest 10 percent earned less than $16,180.

Median annual earnings in the industries employing the largest number of social and human service assistants in May 2006 are shown in **Table 17–8.**

Table 17–8	Median annual earnings in the industries employing the largest numbers of social and human service assistants in May 2006
Local government	$30,510
State government	$29,810
Individual and family services	$24,490
Vocational rehabilitation services	$22,530
Residential mental retardation, mental health and substance abuse facilities	$22,380

RELATED OCCUPATIONS

Workers in other occupations that require skills similar to those of social and human service assistants include social workers; clergy; counselors; child care workers; occupational therapist assistants and aides; physical therapist assistants and aides; and nursing, psychiatric, and home health aides.

ADDITIONAL INFORMATION

For information on programs and careers in human services, contact:

- Council for Standards in Human Services Education, PMB 703, 1050 Larrabee Avenue, Suite 104, Bellingham, WA 98225-7367. http://www.cshse.org

- National Organization for Human Services, 90 Madison Street, Suite 206, Denver, CO 80206. http://www.nationalhumanservices.org

Social Assistance, Except Child Day Care

WORK DESCRIPTIONS

Many people at times need help to live a full and productive life. They may need assistance finding a job or appropriate child care, learning skills to find employment, locating safe and adequate housing, and getting nutritious food for their family. The social assistance industry provides help to individuals and families to aid them in becoming healthy and productive members of society.

Goods and Services. Social assistance establishments provide a wide array of services that include helping the homeless, counseling troubled and emotionally disturbed individuals, training the unemployed or underemployed, and helping the needy to obtain financial assistance. In general, organizations in this industry work to improve the lives of the individuals and families they serve and to enrich their communities. The specific services provided vary greatly depending on the population the establishment is trying to serve and its goals or mission.

Social assistance consists of four segments—individual and family services; community food and housing, along with emergency and other relief services; vocational rehabilitation services; and child day care services. This chapter details all but the last segment.

Establishments in the *individual and family services* sector work to provide the skills and resources necessary for individuals to be more self-sufficient and for families to live in a stable and safe environment. Many of the services in this sector are aimed at a particular population, such as children, the elderly, or those with mental or physical disabilities. Services targeted at children can vary greatly based on the goal of the establishment providing the assistance. Some programs provide youth services, such as afterschool programs or youth centers. These programs are generally aimed at giving children a safe, supportive environment in which to spend their time after school or on weekends. Planned activities often include field trips, assistance with homework, games, and sports. Foster care and adoption agencies also provide services directly aimed at assisting children. These organizations are responsible for locating safe families and environments for children in the foster care system. Other services aimed at children include drug prevention and mentoring programs.

Services provided to the elderly include senior centers, which hold activities geared towards senior citizens, and are often used as a place for seniors to gather to talk or play games. Some services, like adult day care, home care services, and support groups, are aimed at assisting both the elderly and disabled population. This sector of the industry also provides various support services to individuals and families. These often include programs for people addicted to drugs or alcohol, parenting support groups, and rape or abuse crisis centers.

Establishments specializing in *community food and housing, and emergency and other relief services*, provide various types of assistance to community members. This segment of social assistance consists of three subsectors: community food services, community housing services, and emergency and other relief services.

Establishments in the *community food services* subsector collect, prepare, and deliver food for the needy. They may prepare and deliver meals to persons who, because of age, disability, or illness are unable to prepare meals for themselves. They may also collect and distribute salvageable or donated food, prepare and provide meals at fixed or mobile locations, and distribute clothing and blankets. Food banks, meal delivery programs, and soup kitchens are included in this subsector of the social assistance industry.

Establishments in the *community housing service* sector provide short-term emergency shelter for victims of domestic violence, sexual assault, or child abuse. These establishments may operate their own shelter or may provide subsidized housing using existing homes. This sector also includes establishments that provide transitional housing for low-income individuals and families, as well as those that provide temporary residential shelter for the homeless, runaway youths, and patients or families caught in medical crises. Community housing establishments also voluntarily construct or repair low-cost housing or homes belonging to the elderly or disabled—sometimes working in partnership with the future homeowner, who may assist with construction or repair work.

Establishments in the *emergency and other relief services* sector provide assistance to those who have been directly affected by a disaster. These establishments may set up emergency shelters for those who have been evacuated from their homes. They may also provide medical assistance to those who have been injured in the disaster. In the aftermath, they may supply food and clothing, assist with resettlement, and provide counseling to victims of local, national, or international disasters and conflicts.

Vocational rehabilitation service establishments provide vocational rehabilitation or life skills services. They generally work with people who are disabled, either from birth or as a result of an illness or injury. They teach clients the skills necessary to live independently and search for employment. Often, they help assess the abilities of their clients to determine what occupations might be appropriate for them. They may also provide job counseling and assist in locating training and educational programs. Thousands of other establishments, mainly in state and local government, provide additional social assistance.

Industry Organization. About 77,000 establishments in the private sector provided social assistance in 2006. Of that, 59,000 establishments specialized in individual and family services, about 9,000 in community food and housing, and emergency and other relief services, and 9,000 in vocational rehabilitation services. Establishments in this industry tend to be smaller than the average for all establishments. In 2006, half of social assistance establishments employed fewer than five workers, however, larger establishments, while small in number, accounted for most jobs.

WORK ENVIRONMENT

Some social assistance establishments operate around the clock, and evening, weekend, and holiday work is common. Some establishments may be understaffed, resulting in large caseloads for each worker. Jobs in voluntary, nonprofit agencies often are part-time.

Some workers spend a substantial amount of time traveling within the local area. For example, home health and personal care aides routinely visit clients in their homes; social workers and social and human service assistants also may make home visits.

EMPLOYMENT OPPORTUNITIES

Social assistance provided 1.5 million nongovernment wage-and-salary jobs in 2006. About 65 percent were in individual and family services (**Table 17–9**).

Table 17–9	*Employment in social assistance, except child day care by industry segment, 2006 and projected change, 2006–2016. (Employment in thousands)*	
Industry segment	**2006, Employment**	**2006–2016, Percent change**
Social assistance, except child day care, total	1,502	54.8
Individual and family services	974	73.3
Vocational rehabilitation services	399	21.5
Community food and housing, and emergency and other relief services	129	18.6

Jobs in social assistance are concentrated in large states with heavily populated urban areas, such as New York and California.

Careers in social assistance appeal to people with a strong desire to make life better and easier for others. Workers in this industry are usually good communicators and enjoy interacting with people. Many jobs in this industry are professional positions that require at least a bachelor's degree, while other occupations require little education beyond a high school diploma.

Professional and Related Occupations. More than 35 of all nongovernment social assistance jobs were in professional and related occupations in 2006 (**Table 17–10**).

Some of these workers may have direct interaction with clients, while others have limited interaction with the population they serve. These workers may spend their time on tasks like planning programs or events, organizing classes or workshops, grant writing, or creating educational material to be used by clients. Professional and related occupations within this

Table
17–10

Employment of wage-and-salary workers in social assistance, except child day care, according to occupation in 2006 and with projected change, 2006–2016. (Employment in thousands)

Occupation	Employment, 2006		Percent change, 2006–2016
	Number	Percent	
All occupations	1,502	100.0	54.8
Management, business, and financial occupations	132	8.8	43.1
General and operations managers	20	1.3	31.7
Social and community service managers	40	2.6	48.4
Human resources, training, and labor relations specialists	22	1.5	36.3
Professional and related occupations	532	35.4	56.7
Clinical, counseling, and school psychologists	9	0.6	57.2
Substance abuse and behavioral disorder counselors	13	0.9	58.4
Educational, vocational, and school counselors	23	1.6	33.8
Marriage and family therapists	9	0.6	63.6
Mental health counselors	19	1.2	58.3
Rehabilitation counselors	59	3.9	34.7
Child, family, and school social workers	61	4.1	58.0
Medical and public health social workers	16	1.1	57.0
Mental health and substance abuse social workers	26	1.7	56.0
Health educators	10	0.7	78.1
Social and human service assistants	107	7.1	76.4
Preschool teachers, except special education	16	1.1	57.5
Adult literacy, remedial education, and GED teachers and instructors	6	0.4	42.3

Table
17–10

Continued

Employment of wage-and-salary workers in social assistance, except child day care, according to occupation in 2006 and with projected change, 2006–2016. (Employment in thousands)

Occupation	Employment, 2006		Percent change, 2006–2016
	Number	Percent	
Self-enrichment education teachers	11	0.8	40.4
Teacher assistants	23	1.5	53.4
Registered nurses	17	1.1	52.8
Therapists	11	0.7	45.2
Service occupations	539	35.9	67.0
Home health aides	123	8.2	79.0
Nursing aides, orderlies, and attendants	14	0.9	55.6
Cooks, institution and cafeteria	11	0.7	46.6
Janitors and cleaners, except maids and housekeeping cleaners	31	2.1	36.3
Child care workers	26	1.7	54.3
Personal and home care aides	233	15.5	79.0
Recreation workers	23	1.5	47.5
Residential advisors	10	0.7	34.2
Office and administrative support occupations	180	12.0	38.9
Bookkeeping, accounting, and auditing clerks	18	1.2	47.2
Receptionists and information clerks	19	1.2	47.4
Secretaries and administrative assistants	45	3.0	40.7
Office clerks, general	40	2.7	44.8

Table 17–10	*Continued*

Employment of wage-and-salary workers in social assistance, except child day care, according to occupation in 2006 and with projected change, 2006–2016. (Employment in thousands)

Occupation	Employment, 2006		Percent change, 2006–2016
	Number	Percent	
Transportation and material moving occupations	54	3.6	31.5
Bus drivers, school	13	0.9	49.2
Taxi drivers and chauffeurs	10	0.7	47.4
Laborers and material movers, hand	18	1.2	8.5

NOTE: Columns may not add to totals due to omission of occupations with small employment

industry include: social workers, counselors, health educators, teachers in adult literacy and remedial education, and assistants in social and human services.

Social workers help clients function within the limitations of their environment, improve their relationships, and solve personal and family problems. Often, this includes counseling and assessing the needs of clients, referring them to the appropriate sources of help, and monitoring their progress. Many social workers specialize in a particular field. *Child, family and school social workers* aim to improve the social and psychological functioning of children and their families. This may involve work with single parents, parents seeking to adopt a child, or children in foster care. *Medical and public health social workers* provide support to individuals or families coping with illness or diseases; at times, this may include both terminal and chronic illnesses. They may help arrange for additional services to assist in caring for patients, including services such as meals-on-wheels or other home care services. *Mental health and substance abuse social workers* evaluate and treat individuals with mental health and substance abuse problems. They may provide treatment through group or individual therapy or work on community outreach and crisis intervention.

Counselors help people evaluate their interests and abilities, and advise and assist them with personal and social problems. Counselors generally specialize enough that their job duties vary greatly based on the population they serve. *Educational, vocational, and school counselors* in this industry generally work in what is more commonly known as career counseling. They assist clients in determining what field of work they should enter and help them with job search activities, such as locating available job openings for which they might apply, or coaching them on proper interview conduct. *Rehabilitation counselors* assist people in living with the social, personal, and vocational effects of a disability. In some cases, they assist people who are adjusting to a disability caused by injury or illness, but they also counsel those who have had disabilities from birth. These counselors evaluate the abilities and limitations of the individual and arrange for vocational training, medical care and job placement. *Men-*

tal health counselors work with individuals and families to treat mental and emotional disorders. This often is done through individual or group therapy. *Substance abuse and behavioral disorder counselors* work with individuals who are addicted to substances, such alcohol, tobacco or other drugs, or behaviors, like gambling or eating disorders. They often use group or individual therapy and, in some settings, they may be involved in crisis intervention and community outreach. *Marriage and family therapists* aim to improve an individual's or family's mental and emotional health through therapeutic techniques that focus on the family system. This is frequently done through individual, family, or group therapy.

Health educators encourage healthy lifestyles and wellness by educating individuals and communities about behaviors that promote health and prevent illness and diseases. They use many different methods to get their message to their target audience. They often teach classes or entire courses, plan events or programs on health related topics, publish pamphlets and other written materials, and organize screenings for illnesses. In the social assistance industry, they may be responsible for writing grant applications.

Adult literacy and remedial education teachers instruct adults and out-of-school youth in reading, writing, speaking English, and basic math skills. These teachers may work with adults who are in need of basic education or who are pursuing their General Educational Development (GED) certificate. They may also work with adults and children who are learning English as a second language.

Social and human service assistants work in a variety of social and human service delivery settings. However, in general, they provide services, either directly or indirectly, to ensure that individuals in their care can function to the best of their ability. Job titles and duties of these workers vary, but they include human service worker, case management aide, social work assistant, mental health aide, child abuse worker, community outreach worker, and gerontology aide.

Service Occupations. About 36 percent of the jobs in the social assistance industry are in service occupations. These workers generally provide direct services to their clients. Many do work that requires hands-on interaction with clients. These workers include personal and home care aides and home health aides who help elderly, disabled, and ill persons live in their own homes, instead of in institutions. *Personal and home care aides* provide routine personal care services. They generally do non-medical tasks, such as cooking meals, basic cleaning, assisting the client to bathe or dress and, in some cases, accompanying the client to appointments. *Home health aides* provide health related services, like administering oral medication, or checking the client's pulse rate or temperature. They may assist the client in performing exercises and help them bathe, dress, and groom themselves.

Other Occupations. Social and community service managers plan, organize, and coordinate the activities of a social service program or community outreach program. This generally includes overseeing the budget and the execution of programs, events, and services. They often may direct and supervise those who are providing both direct and indirect services to the population they serve. In some situations, they may be responsible for fundraising activities or speaking to donors.

As in most industries, office and administrative support workers—secretaries and bookkeepers, for example—help with recordkeeping and other administrative tasks.

EDUCATIONAL AND LEGAL REQUIREMENTS

Training requirements within this industry vary greatly based on occupation, state licensure requirements, and the setting in which the work is done. Many workers begin in this industry by working as a volunteer. Volunteering with a student, religious, or charitable organization is a good way for job seekers to test their interest in social assistance, and may provide an advantage when applying for jobs in this industry. However, for many occupations, a bachelor's or master's degree is required for entrance into the industry.

Professional and Related Occupations. Entry requirements vary based on occupational specialty and state licensure and certification requirements. A bachelor's degree is the minimum educational requirement for entry-level positions as social workers, health educators, marriage and family therapists and counselors. However, some specialties and employers may require additional education, like a master's degree, or some previous experience. In some settings and specialties, social workers, marriage and family therapists and counselors may be required to obtain a state-issued license. Licensure requirements vary from state to state, but most states require a master's degree and two years or 3,000 hours of supervised clinical experience.

Educational requirements are less stringent for social and human service assistants. Some employers do not require any education beyond high school, but they may prefer some related work experience. Other employers favor workers who have completed some coursework in human services, social work, or another social or behavioral science. Other employers prefer an associate degree or a bachelor's degree in human services or social work. A number of employers also provide in-service training, such as seminars and workshops.

Professional workers in this industry often advance to a supervisory position, such as supervisor, program manager, assistant director, or executive director. Generally, advancing to this level requires a master's degree and the appropriate licenses. Some workers opt to move away from positions that provide services directly to clients and become involved in policymaking, grant writing, or research. Others enter private practice and provide psychotherapeutic counseling and other services on a contractual basis.

Service Occupations. Service occupations within this industry generally require little to no education beyond a high school diploma. Personal and home care aides generally receive some basic on-the-job training. The federal government has guidelines for home health aides whose employers receive reimbursement from Medicare and requires home health aides to pass a competency test covering a wide range of topics, including documentation of patient status and care provided; reading and recording of vital signs; basic infection-control procedures; and basic bodily functions. As a result, many home health aides receive some training prior to taking the exam.

Workers in service occupations may opt to get some additional training and may advance to, for example, licensed practical nurse. Some personal and home care aides may opt to open their own business.

EMPLOYMENT TRENDS

Job opportunities in social assistance should be plentiful because employment is expected to grow rapidly and many workers leave the industry and need to be replaced.

Employment Change. Employment within this industry is expected to grow rapidly relative to all other industries through 2016. The number of nongovernment wage-and-salary jobs is expected to increase 59 percent, compared with only 11 percent for all industries combined. However, growth will not be evenly distributed amongst the industry's subsectors. The individual and family services industry is expected to grow by 73 percent, making it one of the fastest growing industries in the economy. Community food and housing and emergency and other relief services is expected to grow by 19 percent. Vocational rehabilitation services is expected to grow 22 percent over the 2006–2016 projection period.

Growth of employment in the social assistance industry may depend, in large part, on the amount of funding made available by the government and managed-care organizations. Employment in private social service agencies may grow if state and local governments contract out some of their social services functions in an effort to cut costs.

Projected job growth in individual and family services will be due mostly to an increase in the population that will demand additional services from this sector. As baby boomers age, there is expected to be an increase in the elderly population, one of the primary segments of the population that requires services from this industry. Programs that serve the elderly will expand, including adult day care or services that allow the elderly to remain in their homes for as long as possible. Furthermore, the number of small children and immigrants is expected to rise during the projections decade, increasing demand for programs aimed at assisting families. These may include after-school programs and mentoring programs or classes in English as a second language. Similarly, services for the mentally ill, the physically disabled, and families in crisis will be expanded and demand will increase for drug and alcohol abuse prevention programs.

The community housing and food, and emergency and other services segment of social services will grow as a result of increases in urbanization. As cities become more densely populated, more people will be affected by natural disasters, increasing the demand for disaster relief. Furthermore, demand for housing and food assistance will remain steady. However, charitable giving has been on the rise in recent years, so shelters and food banks may be able to respond to some of the growing demand for assistance.

Employment growth is expected in vocational rehabilitation services due to a steady demand for services from individuals with some form of physical or mental disability. Workers in this sector will continue to serve people who are injured on the job and need assistance moving back into the work environment. The main demand for services from this sector will be from injuries that are covered by worker's compensation, which are expected to increase as the population expands.

Some of the fastest growing occupations in the nation are concentrated in social assistance. The number of home health aides within social assistance is projected to grow 79 percent and employment of personal and home care is expected to grow by 79 percent between 2006 and 2016. Employment growth for these two occupations is driven predominantly by the need to provide services to the elderly and ill in their homes and avoid expensive hospital or nursing home care. The number of social and human service assistants is expected to grow by 76 percent as the work of many social services is restructured to employ more assistants and fewer higher-paid social workers and counselors.

Job Prospects. Besides job openings arising from employment growth, many additional openings will stem from the need to replace workers who transfer to other occupations or stop working. Workers leave jobs in this industry at a higher rate than the rest of the economy, making job prospects excellent.

EARNINGS

Industry Earnings. Average earnings in the social assistance industry are lower than the average for all industries, as shown in **Table 17–11**.

Table 17–11

Average earnings of nonsupervisory workers in social assistance, 2006		
Industry segment	**Weekly**	**Hourly**
Total, private industry	$568	$16.76
Social assistance	$353	$11.76
Community food and housing, and emergency and other relief services	$422	$14.22
Individual and family services	$385	$12.79
Vocational rehabilitation services	$330	$11.05

Earnings in selected occupations in the social assistance, except child day care industry in May 2006 appear in **Table 17–12**.

As in most industries, professionals and managers commonly earn more than other workers, reflecting higher education levels, broader experience, and greater responsibility.

Benefits and Union Membership. Professional workers in this industry typically receive benefits, such as medical insurance and paid time off. However, those working in service occupations generally receive no benefits. About 12 percent of workers in the social assistance industry were union members or were covered by union contracts in 2006, about the same as workers throughout all industries.

ADDITIONAL INFORMATION

For information about careers in social work and voluntary credentials for social workers, contact:

- National Association of Social Workers, 750 First St. N.E., Suite 700, Washington, DC 20002-4241. http://www.socialworkers.org

For information on programs and careers in human services, contact:

- Council for Standards in Human Services Education, Harrisburg Area Community College, Human Services Program, One HACC Dr., Harrisburg, PA 17110-2999. http://www.cshse.org

Table
17–12

Median hourly earnings of the largest occupations in social assistance, except child day care, May 2006

Occupation	Individual and family services	Community food and housing and emergency and other relief services	Vocational rehabilitation services	All Industries
Social and community service managers	$22.83	$23.58	$22.62	$25.03
Mental health and substance abuse social workers	16.79	15.38	15.76	17.02
Child, family, and school social workers	15.71	14.29	14.61	18.02
Rehabilitation counselors	13.10	13.84	13.73	14.04
Social and human service assistants	11.78	11.67	10.83	12.30
Office clerks, general	10.48	10.33	10.29	11.40
Child care workers	9.32	9.65	9.10	8.48
Home health aides	9.27	8.51	9.41	9.34
Personal and home care aides	9.19	8.83	9.29	8.54
Janitors and cleaners, except maids and housekeeping cleaners	8.73	9.43	8.62	9.58

■ National Human Services Assembly 1319 F Street, N.W., Suite 402, Washington, DC 20004. http://www.nassembly.org

For information regarding jobs in nonprofit organizations and voluntary credential information, contact:

■ American Humanics, Inc. 1100 Walnut Ave, Suite 1900, Kansas City, MO 64106. http://www.humanics.org.

18

PSYCHOLOGY

Key Terms

- Clinical psychologist
- Health psychologist
- Neuropsychologist
- Geropsychologist
- Counseling psychologist
- Developmental psychologist
- Educational psychologist
- Engineering psychologist
- Personnel psychologist

- Experimental psychologist
- Industrial psychologist
- Psychometric psychologist
- Rehabilitation psychologist
- School psychologist
- Social psychologist
- Psychiatric or mental health technician
- Psychiatric aide

Psychologists

Psychologists study the human mind and human behavior. Psychology examines both normal and abnormal aspects of human behavior. It involves a scientific approach to gathering, quantifying, analyzing, and interpreting data on why people act as they do, and it provides insight into varied forms of human behavior and related mental and physical processes. Through the application of highly developed skills and knowledge, psychologists seek to identify, prevent, and solve various problems of human behavior.

As a health career, psychology is one of the allied professions devoted to mental health. Along with psychiatry, psychiatric nursing, and psychiatric social work, psychology contributes both to the prevention of mental illness and to its diagnosis and treatment. As distinguished from psychiatry, which is a branch of medicine, psychology is a nonmedical science. As distinguished from psychiatric social work, psychology looks first at the individual's reaction to his or her circumstances—family, job, and social relationships. The psychiatric social worker looks first at the individual's surrounding circumstances and relationships.

WORK DESCRIPTION

Psychologists study the behavior of individuals or groups to ascertain and understand the fundamental processes of human behavior. Some psychologists interview people and develop, administer, and score a variety of psychological tests. Others work in mental health and rehabilitation centers, hospitals, and private practice providing counseling and therapy to persons suffering emotional or adjustment problems. Since psychology is basically a science, the psychologist is often the most knowledgeable member among mental health team members regarding research. The science of psychology is one of the main sources of our increasing understanding of mental capacity and intelligence and of the effect of emotions on health. Psychological research contributes continuously to the improvement of diagnostic methods, and to the treatment and prevention of mental and emotional disorders. Psychologists also work with disabled persons, either individually or in groups, to diagnose behavioral problems and to help correct or compensate for these impairments.

A psychologist may also design, develop, and evaluate materials and procedures in order to resolve problems in educational and training programs. In addition, psychologists employ scientific techniques to deal with problems of motivation and morale in the work setting. Psychologists design and conduct experiments, and analyze the results in an effort to improve understanding of human and animal behavior.

Some psychologists engage in private practice; others work in colleges and universities, where they train graduate and undergraduate students and engage in basic research. Increasingly, they work as administrators of psychology programs in hospitals, clinics, and community health agencies. Many psychologists practice in federal, state, and local agencies, a variety of business and industrial organizations, and various branches of the armed forces.

The field of psychology offers a number of specializations that an individual can consider when planning a career. These include clinical psychology, counseling psychology, developmental psychology, educational psychology, engineering psychology, personnel psychology, experimental psychology, industrial psychology, psychometric psychology, rehabilitation psychology, and school and social psychology.

Clinical psychologists specialize in the assessment and treatment of persons with mental and emotional problems and illnesses. They apply experience and scientific knowledge of human behavior to diagnose and treat psychological problems ranging from the developmental crises of adolescence to extreme psychotic conditions. Working in hospitals, clinics, or similar medical institutions, clinical psychologists design and conduct research either alone or in conjunction with physicians or other social scientists. Although the emphasis may differ considerably from one position to another, all clinical psychologists apply scientific knowledge of human behavior to the care and treatment of the handicapped and the disturbed. Their purpose is to help the individual who is maladjusted learn new and better habits of behavior so as to find a more satisfactory way of living.

Clinical psychologists work directly with the patient, or client, to uncover everything that will help in understanding his or her difficulties. They also talk with the patient's family, friends, physicians, and teachers to round out this background. At times they consult with the psychiatrist, social worker, and others concerned with diagnosis and treatment.

Areas of specialization within clinical psychology include health psychology, neuropsychology, and geropsychology. *Health psychologists* promote good health through health maintenance counseling programs designed to help people achieve health-oriented goals, such as to stop smoking or lose weight. *Neuropsychologists* study the relationship between the brain and behavior. They often work in stroke and head injury programs. *Geropsychologists* deal with the special problems faced by the elderly. The emergence and subsequent growth of these specialties reflect the increasing participation of psychologists in providing direct services to special patient populations.

Counseling psychologists help normal or moderately maladjusted persons, either individually or in groups, to gain self-understanding, recognize problems, and develop methods of coping with their difficulties. Counseling psychologists pay particular attention to the role of education and work in a person's behavior and to the interaction between individuals and the environments in which they live. This type of counseling primarily emphasizes preventing or forestalling the onset of mental illness. Growing public awareness of mental health problems has highlighted the importance of and need for the services that counseling psychologists provide.

Developmental psychologists specialize in investigating the development of individuals from prenatal origins through old age. In studying the changes involved in mental, physical, emotional, and social growth, psychologists seek to determine the origins of human behavior and the reasons for human growth and decline. For example, psychologists study how an infant's behavior and feelings are related to biological growth of the body. Another example is the study of the influence of social learning and socialization on an infant's development into a socialized person.

Educational psychologists design, develop, and evaluate materials and procedures to resolve problems in educational and training programs. These psychologists analyze educational problems, develop instructional materials, determine the best conditions for instruction, and evaluate the effectiveness of educational programs. Educational psychologists are employed by school systems, the military, private research and development firms, and industrial concerns.

Engineering psychologists deal with the design and use of the systems and environments in which people live and work. Their main purpose is the development of efficient and acceptable interactions between individuals and the environments in which they function. These psychologists help to design equipment, work areas, and systems involving direct interaction of humans with machines. In addition, they develop the aids, training devices, and requirements necessary to train personnel to operate such systems successfully.

Personnel psychologists apply their professional knowledge and skills to the hiring, assignment, and promotion of employees in order to increase productivity and job satisfaction. These psychologists place great emphasis on data gathered from tests and interviews and apply the techniques of other psychological specialties, such as experimental, developmental, and psychometric, to normal work activities.

The *experimental psychologist* designs, conducts, and analyzes experiments to develop knowledge regarding human and animal behavior. Experimental psychology is a general term referring to the methods employed in studying behavioral processes. There are different types of experimental psychologists who are identified by their areas of specialization, such as comparative psychologists, learning psychologists, and physiological psychologists.

Industrial psychologists use scientific techniques to deal with problems of motivation and morale in the work setting. These psychologists study how work is organized and suggest improvements designed to increase quality, productivity, and worker satisfaction. They consult with all levels of management and present recommendations for developing better training programs and preretirement counseling services.

Psychometric psychologists directly measure human behavior, primarily through the use of tests. Typically well-trained in mathematics, statistics, and the use of computers, they design, develop, and validate intelligence, aptitude, and personality tests; analyze complex statistical data; and design various types of research investigations. In addition, they conduct pilot studies of newly developed materials and devise and apply procedures for measuring the psychological variables affecting human behavior.

Rehabilitation psychologists work with disabled persons, either individually or in groups, to assess the degree of disability and develop ways to correct or compensate for these impairments. The primary concern of these psychologists is the restoration of the patient's emotional, physical, social, and economic effectiveness.

School psychologists are concerned with developing effective programs for improving the intellectual, social, and emotional development of children in an educational system or school. They diagnose the needs of gifted, handicapped, and disturbed children and plan and carry out corrective programs to enable them to do schoolwork at their highest potential and to adjust to everyday pressures. To determine a child's needs, limitations, and potential, school psychologists often observe the child in the classroom and at play, study school records, consult with teachers and parents, and administer and interpret various tests. They advise school administrators and parent–teacher groups in matters involving psychological services within the school system and serve as consultants in education for children who are handicapped, mentally disturbed, or mentally retarded. School psychologists also engage in planning and developing special programs in the area of adult education.

Social psychologists study the effects of groups and individuals on the thoughts, feelings, attitudes, and behavior of the individual. They study, for example, the ways in which social attitudes develop and how members of families, neighborhoods, and communities influence each other.

Experimental or *research psychologists* work in university and private research centers and in business, nonprofit, and governmental organizations. They study the behavior of both human beings and animals such as rats, monkeys, and pigeons. Prominent areas of study in experimental and research psychology include motivation, thought, attention, learning and memory, sensory and perceptual processes, and the effects of substance abuse. Research and experimental psychologists also study genetic and neurological factors affecting behavior.

WORK ENVIRONMENT

A psychologist's specialty and place of employment determine his or her working conditions. Clinical, school, and counseling psychologists in private practice have their own offices and set their own hours. They often offer evening and weekend hours to accommodate their clients. Psychologists employed in hospitals, nursing homes, and other health facilities may work shifts including evenings and weekends, whereas those who work in schools and clinics generally work regular hours.

Psychologists employed as faculty by colleges and universities divide their time between teaching and research and may also have administrative responsibilities. Many have part-time consulting practices. Most psychologists in government and industry have well-structured schedules.

Increasingly, many psychologists work as part of a team and consult with other psychologists and various healthcare professionals. Many experience pressures due to deadlines, tight schedules, and overtime work. Their routines may be interrupted frequently. Travel is required to attend conferences or conduct research.

EMPLOYMENT OPPORTUNITIES

Psychologists held about 166,000 jobs in 2006. Educational institutions employed about 29 percent of psychologists in positions other than teaching, such as counseling, testing, research, and administration. About 21 percent were employed in health care, primarily in offices of mental health practitioners, hospitals, physicians' offices, and outpatient mental health and substance abuse centers. Government agencies at the state and local levels employed psychologists in correctional facilities, law enforcement, and other settings.

After several years of experience, some psychologists—usually those with doctoral degrees—enter private practice or set up private research or consulting firms. About 34 percent of psychologists were self-employed in 2006, compared with only 8 percent of all professional workers.

In addition to the previously mentioned jobs, many psychologists held faculty positions at colleges and universities and as high school psychology teachers.

EDUCATIONAL AND LEGAL REQUIREMENTS

A master's or doctoral degree, and a license, are required for most psychologists.

Education and Training. A doctoral degree usually is required for independent practice as a psychologist. Psychologists with a PhD or Doctor of Psychology (PsyD) qualify for a wide range of teaching, research, clinical, and counseling positions in universities, health care services, elementary and secondary schools, private industry, and government. Psychologists with a doctoral degree often work in clinical positions or in private practice, but they also sometimes teach, conduct research, or carry out administrative responsibilities.

A doctoral degree generally requires five to seven years of graduate study, culminating in a dissertation based on original research. Courses in quantitative research methods, which include the use of computer-based analysis, are an integral part of graduate study and are necessary to complete the dissertation. The PsyD degree may be based on practical work and examinations rather than a dissertation. In clinical, counseling, and school psychology, the requirements for the doctoral degree include an internship of at least one year.

A specialist degree or its equivalent is required in most states for an individual to work as a school psychologist, although a few states still credential school psychologists with master's degrees. A specialist (EdS) degree in school psychology requires a minimum of three years of full-time graduate study (at least 60 graduate semester hours) and a one-year full-time internship. In professional practice school psychologists address both the educational and the mental health components of students' development; as a consequence, their training includes coursework in both education and psychology.

People with a master's degree in psychology may work as *industrial-organizational psychologists*. They also may work as *psychological assistants* under the supervision of doctoral-level psychologists and may conduct research or psychological evaluations. A master's degree in psychology requires at least two years of full-time graduate study. Degree requirements usually include practical experience in an applied setting and a master's thesis based on an original research project.

Competition for admission to graduate psychology programs is keen. Some universities require applicants to have an undergraduate major in psychology. Others prefer only coursework in basic psychology with additional courses in statistics, mathematics, and the biological, physical, and social sciences.

A bachelor's degree in psychology qualifies a person to assist psychologists and other professionals in community mental health centers, vocational rehabilitation offices, and correctional programs. Bachelor's degree holders may also work as research or administrative assistants for psychologists. Some work as technicians in related fields, such as marketing research. Many find employment in other areas, such as sales, service, or business management.

In the federal government, candidates having at least 24 semester hours in psychology and one course in statistics qualify for entry-level positions. However, competition for these jobs is keen because this is one of the few ways in which one can work as a psychologist without an advanced degree.

The American Psychological Association (APA) presently accredits doctoral training programs in clinical, counseling, and school psychology, as well as institutions that provide internships for doctoral students in school, clinical, and counseling psychology. The National Association of School Psychologists, with the assistance of the National Council for Accreditation of Teacher Education, helps to approve advanced degree programs in school psychology.

Licensure. Psychologists in independent practice or those who offer any type of patient care—including clinical, counseling, and school psychologists—must meet certification or licensing requirements in all states and the District of Columbia. Licensing laws vary by state and by type of position, but require licensed or certified psychologists to limit their practice to areas in which they have developed professional competence through training and experience. Clinical and counseling psychologists usually need a doctorate in psychology, an approved internship, and one to two years of professional experience. In addition, all states require that applicants pass an examination. Most state licensing boards administer a standardized test, and many supplement that with additional oral or essay questions. Some states require continuing education for renewal of the license.

The National Association of School Psychologists (NASP) awards the Nationally Certified School Psychologist (NCSP) designation, which recognizes professional competency in school psychology at a national level. Currently, 29 states recognize the NCSP and allow those with the certification to transfer credentials from one state to another without taking a new certification exam. In states that recognize the NCSP, the requirements for certification or licensure and those for the NCSP often are the same or similar. Requirements for the NCSP include the completion of 60 graduate semester hours in school psychology; a 1,200-hour internship, 600 hours of which must be completed in a school setting; and a passing score on the National School Psychology Examination.

Other Qualifications. Aspiring psychologists who are interested in direct patient care must be emotionally stable, mature, and able to deal effectively with people. Sensitivity, compassion, good communication skills, and the ability to lead and inspire others are particularly important qualities for people wishing to do clinical work and counseling. Research psychologists should be able to do detailed work both independently and as part of a team. Patience and perseverance are vital qualities, because achieving results in the psychological treatment of patients or in research may take a long time.

Certification and Advancement. The American Board of Professional Psychology (ABPP) recognizes professional achievement by awarding specialty certification in 13 different areas. Candidates for ABPP certification need a doctorate in psychology, postdoctoral training in their specialty, several years of experience, professional endorsements, and successful completion of their specialty board examination. Psychologists can improve their advancement opportunities by earning an advanced degree and by participation in continuing education. Many psychologists opt to start their own practice after gaining experience working in the field.

EMPLOYMENT TRENDS

Faster-than-average employment growth is expected for psychologists. Job prospects should be best for people who have a doctoral degree from a leading university in an applied specialty, such as counseling or health, and people with a specialist or doctoral degree in school psychology. Master's degree holders in fields other than industrial-organizational psychology will face keen competition. Opportunities will be limited for bachelor's degree holders.

Employment Change. Employment of psychologists is expected to grow 15 percent from 2006 to 2016, faster than the average for all occupations. Employment will grow because of increased demand for psychological services in schools, hospitals, social service agencies, mental health centers, substance abuse treatment clinics, consulting firms, and private companies.

Employment growth will vary by specialty. Growing awareness of how students' mental health and behavioral problems, such as bullying, affect learning will increase demand for school psychologists to offer student counseling and mental health services.

The rise in healthcare costs associated with unhealthy lifestyles, such as smoking, alcoholism, and obesity, has made prevention and treatment more critical. An increase in the number of employee assistance programs, which help workers deal with personal problems, also should lead to employment growth for clinical and counseling specialties. Clinical and counseling psychologists also will be needed to help people deal with depression and other mental disorders, marriage and family problems, job stress, and addiction. The growing number of elderly will increase the demand for psychologists trained in geropsychology to help people deal with the mental and physical changes that occur as individuals grow older. There also will be increased need for psychologists to work with military veterans returning from armed conflicts.

Industrial-organizational psychologists also will be in demand to help to boost worker productivity and retention rates in a wide range of businesses. Industrial-organizational psychologists will help companies deal with issues such as workplace diversity and antidiscrimination policies. Companies also will use psychologists' expertise in survey design, analysis, and research to develop tools for marketing evaluation and statistical analysis.

Job Prospects. Job prospects should be the best for people who have a doctoral degree from a leading university in an applied specialty, such as counseling or health, and people with a specialty or doctoral degree in school psychology. Psychologists with extensive training in quantitative research methods and computer science may have a competitive edge over applicants without such a background.

Master's degree holders in fields other than industrial-organizational psychology will face keen competition for jobs because of the limited number of positions that require only a master's degree. Master's degree holders may find jobs as psychological assistants or counselors, providing mental health services under the direct supervision of a licensed psychologist. Still others may find jobs involving research and data collection and analysis in universities, government, or private companies.

Opportunities directly related to psychology will be limited for bachelor's degree holders. Some may find jobs as assistants in rehabilitation centers or other jobs involving data collection and analysis. Those who meet state certification requirements may become high school psychology teachers. **Table 18–1** shows some projection data provided by the Department of Labor.

Table 18–1	**Projections data from the National Employment Matrix**				
Occupational title	**Employment, 2006**	**Projected employment, 2016**	**Change, 2006–2016**		
			Number	**Percent**	
Psychologists	166,000	191,000	25,000	15	
Clinical, counseling, and school psychologists	152,000	176,000	24,000	16	
Industrial-organizational psychologists	1,900	2,400	400	21	
Psychologists, all other	12,000	13,000	900	8	

NOTE: Data in this table are rounded.

EARNINGS

Median annual earnings of wage and salary clinical, counseling, and school psychologists in May 2006 were $59,440. The middle 50 percent earned between $45,300 and $77,750. The lowest 10 percent earned less than $35,280, and the highest 10 percent earned more than $102,730. Median annual earnings in the industries employing the largest numbers of clinical, counseling, and school psychologists are shown in **Table 18–2.**

Table 18–2	*Median annual earnings in the industries employing the largest numbers of clinical, counseling, and school psychologists in May 2006*
Offices of mental health practitioners	$69,510
Elementary and secondary schools	$61,290
Local government	$58,770
Individual and family services	$50,780
Outpatient care centers	$50,310

Median annual earnings of wage-and-salary industrial-organizational psychologists in May 2006 were $86,420. The middle 50 percent earned between $66,310 and $115,000. The lowest 10 percent earned less than $48,380, and the highest 10 percent earned more than $139,620.

RELATED OCCUPATIONS

Psychologists work with people, developing relationships and comforting them. Other occupations with similar duties include counselors, social workers, clergy, sociologists, special education teachers, funeral directors, market and survey researchers, recreation workers, and managers and specialists in human resources, training, and labor relations. Psychologists also sometimes diagnose and treat problems, and assist patients in recovery. These duties are similar to those for physicians and surgeons, radiation therapists, audiologists, dentists, optometrists, and speech-language pathologists.

ADDITIONAL INFORMATION

For information on careers, educational requirements, financial assistance, and licensing in all fields of psychology, contact:

■ American Psychological Association, Center for Psychology Workforce Analysis and Research and Education Directorate, 750 1st St. N.E., Washington, DC 20002. http://www.apa.org/students

For information on careers, educational requirements, certification, and licensing of school psychologists, contact:

- National Association of School Psychologists, 4340 East West Hwy., Suite 402, Bethesda, MD 20814. http://www.nasponline.org

Information about state licensing requirements is available from:

- Association of State and Provincial Psychology Boards, P.O. Box 241245, Montgomery, AL 36124. http://www.asppb.org

Information about psychology specialty certifications is available from:

- American Board of Professional Psychology, Inc., 300 Drayton St., 3rd Floor, Savannah, GA 31401. http://www.abpp.org

RESPIRATORY CARE PRACTITIONERS

Key Terms

- Blood pH
- Lung capacity
- Arterial blood sample
- Chest physiotherapy
- Aerosol
- Oxygen/oxygen mixture

- Ventilator
- Committee on Accreditation for Respiratory Care (CoARC)
- Certified Respiratory Therapist Technician (CRT)
- Registered Respiratory Therapist (RRT)
- Cardiopulmonary diseases

Maintaining the Breath of Life

A person can live without water for a few days and without food for a few weeks, but if someone stops breathing for more than a few minutes, serious brain damage occurs. If oxygen is cut off for more than nine minutes, death usually results. *Respiratory therapists*, also known as *respiratory care personnel*, specialize in the evaluation, treatment, and care of patients with breathing disorders. Whenever the breath of life is at risk, the respiratory therapist is called upon to intervene. Respiratory therapists perform procedures crucial in maintaining the lives of seriously ill patients with breathing problems and assist in the treatment of patients with *cardiopulmonary* (heart and lung) diseases and disorders.

Respiratory Therapists

WORK DESCRIPTION

In this chapter the term *respiratory therapist* includes both respiratory therapists and respiratory therapy technicians.

Respiratory care therapists work to evaluate, treat, and care for patients with breathing disorders. They work under the direction of a physician.

Most respiratory therapists work with hospital patients in three distinct phases of care: diagnosis, treatment, and patient management. In the area of diagnosis, therapists test the capacity of the lungs and analyze the oxygen and carbon dioxide concentrations and potential of hydrogen (blood pH), a measure of the acidity or alkalinity level of the blood. To measure *lung capacity*, the therapist has the patient breathe into a tube connected to an instrument that measures the volume and flow of air during inhalation and exhalation. By comparing the reading with the norm for the patient's age, height, weight, and sex, the therapist can determine whether lung deficiencies exist.

To analyze oxygen, carbon dioxide, and pH levels, therapists need an *arterial blood sample*, for which they generally draw arterial blood. This procedure requires greater skill than is the case for routine tests, for which blood is drawn from a vein. Inserting a needle into a patient's artery and drawing blood must be done with great care; any slip can damage the artery and interrupt the flow of oxygen-rich blood to the tissues. Once the sample is drawn, it is placed in a gas analyzer, and the results are relayed to the physician.

Treatment of patients, such as premature infants whose lungs are not fully developed or elderly people whose lungs are diseased, is another important job duty. Treatment may range from giving temporary relief to patients with chronic asthma or emphysema to emergency care for heart failure, stroke, drowning, or shock. The three most common treatments, however, are chest physiotherapy, aerosol medication, and oxygen mixtures.

Chest physiotherapy is generally performed on patients who have undergone surgery. Anesthesia depresses respiration, so this treatment may be prescribed to help return the patient's lungs to their normal level of functioning and prevent the lungs from becoming congested. Chest physiotherapy also is used on patients suffering from lung diseases that cause increased amounts of sticky mucus to collect in the lungs. Chest physiotherapy helps remove mucus, making it easier for the patient to breathe. In chest physiotherapy, the patient is placed in a position to help drain mucus from the lungs. The therapist thumps and vibrates the patient's rib cage (percussion), after which the patient is instructed to cough. This procedure not only stimulates the lungs to expand, but also helps clear lungs of congestion. This process helps prevent respiratory illnesses that could complicate recovery.

Respiratory therapists also administer *aerosols*. Generally these formulations are liquid medications suspended in a gas that forms a mist the patient inhales. Therapists may either administer the medicine themselves or teach patients how to do so. In either case, the therapist must instruct the patient about how to inhale the aerosol properly. Improperly inhaled medicine will be ineffective.

Respiratory therapists use various kinds of equipment to administer oxygen and *oxygen mixtures*. In one case, a patient may need an increased concentration of oxygen. The therapist simply places an oxygen delivery device, such as a mask or a nasal cannula, on the patient and sets the oxygen flow at the level prescribed by the physician. In the case of a patient who cannot breathe on his or her own—someone who has undergone heart surgery, for example— the therapist would connect the patient to a *ventilator*, a machine that pumps air into the lungs. The therapist inserts a tube through the patient's mouth into the trachea, or windpipe; connects the tube to the ventilator; and sets the rate, volume, and oxygen concentration of the air entering the patient's lungs.

Monitoring patients who are using oxygen and ventilators occupies a good portion of the therapist's day. Patients and equipment must be checked regularly. If the patient appears to be having difficulty or if the oxygen, carbon dioxide, or pH level of the blood is unstable, the ventilator setting must be changed. The therapist alerts the doctor and adjusts the ventilator according to the physician's order. In addition, therapists continually check equipment to ensure that there are no mechanical complications and that the equipment is in working condition.

Providing respiratory care at home is a rapidly expanding area of practice. Respiratory therapists have long administered oxygen to patients in their homes. Increasingly, however, mechanical ventilators and other sophisticated life support systems are being used in the home. Therapists teach patients and their families how to use the equipment. Many of the people who receive home respiratory care will need it for the rest of their lives. They are taught how to operate complex equipment themselves, with several visits a month from respiratory therapists to inspect or clean the equipment and ensure its proper use.

Respiratory therapists often conduct rehabilitation classes, such as low-impact aerobic exercise classes, to help patients who suffer from chronic lung problems. They also conduct smoking cessation programs for hospital patients and others in the community who want to kick the tobacco habit. Other duties include keeping records of the cost of materials and charges to patients, and maintaining and making minor repairs to equipment.

Respiratory therapists are increasingly being asked to perform tasks that fall outside of their traditional role. They are moving into cardiopulmonary procedures such as electrocardiograms and stress testing, but also perform other tasks such as drawing blood samples from patients. Some therapists teach or supervise other respiratory therapy personnel.

WORK ENVIRONMENT

Respiratory therapists generally work between 35 and 40 hours per week. Because hospitals operate around the clock, therapists may work evenings, nights, or weekends. Respiratory therapists spend long periods standing and walking between patients' rooms. In an emergency, they work under a great deal of stress. Gases used by respiratory therapists are hazardous because they are used and stored under pressure. As with many health occupations, respiratory therapists who perform blood gas analysis run a risk of catching an infectious disease, such as AIDS, from accidental pricking of a needle. However, adherence to safety precautions and regular maintenance and testing of equipment minimize the risk of injury.

EMPLOYMENT OPPORTUNITIES

Respiratory therapists held about 122,000 jobs in 2006. About 79 percent of jobs were in hospitals, mainly in departments of respiratory care, anesthesiology, or pulmonary medicine. Most of the remaining jobs were in offices of physicians or other health practitioners, nursing care facilities, home health care services, or rental firms that supply respiratory equipment for home use. Holding a second job is relatively common for respiratory therapists. About 12 percent held another job, compared with 5 percent of workers in all occupations.

EDUCATIONAL AND LEGAL REQUIREMENTS

An associate degree is the minimum educational requirement, but a bachelor's or master's degree may be important for advancement. All states, except Alaska and Hawaii, require respiratory therapists to be licensed.

Education and Training. An associate degree is required to become a respiratory therapist. Training is offered at the postsecondary level by colleges and universities, medical schools, vocational-technical institutes, and the armed forces. Most programs award an associate or bachelor's degree and prepare graduates for jobs as advanced respiratory therapists. A limited number of associate degree programs lead to jobs as entry-level respiratory therapists. According to the *Commission on Accreditation of Allied Health Education Programs (CAAHEP)*, 45 entry-level and 334 advanced respiratory therapy programs were accredited in the United States in 2006.

Students in respiratory therapy programs study human anatomy and physiology, pathophysiology, chemistry, physics, microbiology, pharmacology, and mathematics. Other courses deal with therapeutic and diagnostic procedures and tests, equipment, patient assessment, cardiopulmonary resuscitation, the application of clinical practice guidelines, patient care outside of hospitals, cardiac and pulmonary rehabilitation, respiratory health promotion and disease prevention, as well as medical recordkeeping and reimbursement.

High school students interested in applying to respiratory therapy programs should take courses in health, biology, mathematics, chemistry, and physics. Respiratory care involves basic mathematical problem solving and an understanding of chemical and physical principles. For example, respiratory care workers must be able to compute dosages of medication and calculate gas concentrations.

Licensure and Certification. A license is required to practice as a respiratory therapist, except in Alaska and Hawaii. Also, most employers require respiratory therapists to maintain a cardiopulmonary resuscitation (CPR) certification.

Licensure is usually based, in large part, on meeting the requirements for certification from the *National Board for Respiratory Care (NBRC)*. The board offers the *Certified Respiratory Therapist (CRT)* credential to those who graduate from entry-level or advanced programs accredited by CAAHEP or the *Committee on Accreditation for Respiratory Care (CoARC)* and who also pass an exam.

The board also awards the *Registered Respiratory Therapist (RRT)* to CRTs who have graduated from advanced programs and pass two separate examinations. Supervisory positions and intensive-care specialties usually require the RRT.

Other Qualifications. Therapists should be sensitive to a patient's physical and psychological needs. Respiratory care practitioners must pay attention to detail, follow instructions, and work as part of a team. In addition, operating advanced equipment requires proficiency with computers.

Advancement. Respiratory therapists advance in clinical practice by moving from general care to the care of critically ill patients who have significant problems in other organ systems, such as the heart or kidneys. Respiratory therapists, especially those with a bachelor's or master's degree, also may advance to supervisory or managerial positions in a respiratory therapy department. Respiratory therapists in home health care and equipment rental firms may become branch managers. Some respiratory therapists advance by moving into teaching positions. Some others use the knowledge gained as a respiratory therapist to work in another industry, such as developing, marketing, or selling pharmaceuticals and medical devices.

EMPLOYMENT TRENDS

Faster-than-average employment growth is projected for respiratory therapists. Job opportunities should be very good, especially for respiratory therapists with cardiopulmonary care skills or experience working with infants.

Employment Change. Employment of respiratory therapists is expected to grow 19 percent from 2006 to 2016, faster than the average for all occupations. The increasing demand will come from substantial growth in the middle-aged and elderly population—a development that will increase the incidence of cardiopulmonary disease. Growth in demand also will result from the expanding role of respiratory therapists in case management, disease prevention, emergency care, and the early detection of pulmonary disorders.

Older Americans suffer most from respiratory ailments and cardiopulmonary diseases such as pneumonia, chronic bronchitis, emphysema, and heart disease. As their numbers increase, the need for respiratory therapists is expected to increase as well. In addition, advances in inhalable medications and in the treatment of lung transplant patients, heart attack and accident victims, and premature infants (many of whom are dependent on a ventilator during part of their treatment) will increase the demand for the services of respiratory care practitioners.

Job Prospects. Job opportunities are expected to be very good. The vast majority of job openings will continue to be in hospitals. However, a growing number of openings are expected to be outside of hospitals, especially in home health care services, offices of physicians or other health practitioners, consumer-goods rental firms, or in the employment services industry as a temporary worker in various settings. **Table 19–1** shows some projection data provided by the Department of Labor.

Table
19–1

Projections data from the National Employment Matrix

Occupational title	Employment, 2006	Projected employment, 2016	Change, 2006–2016	
			Number	Percent
All Respiratory therapists	122,000	145,000	23,000	19
Respiratory therapists	102,000	126,000	23,000	23
Respiratory therapy technicians	19,000	19,000	200	1

NOTE: Data in this table are rounded.

EARNINGS

Median annual earnings of wage-and-salary respiratory therapists were .$47,420 in May 2006. The middle 50 percent earned between $40,840 and $56,150. The lowest 10 percent earned less than $35,200, and the highest 10 percent earned more than $64,190.

Median annual earnings of wage-and-salary respiratory therapy technicians were $39,120 in May 2006. The middle 50 percent earned between $32,050 and $46,930. The lowest 10 percent earned less than $25,940, and the highest 10 percent earned more than $56,220.

ADDITIONAL INFORMATION

Information concerning a career in respiratory care is available from:

- American Association for Respiratory Care, 9425 N. MacArthur Blvd., Suite 100, Irving, TX 75063. http://www.aarc.org

For a list of accredited educational programs for respiratory care practitioners, contact either of the following organizations:

- Commission on Accreditation for Allied Health Education Programs, 1361 Park St., Clearwater, FL 33756. http://www.caahep.org

- Committee on Accreditation for Respiratory Care, 1248 Harwood Rd., Bedford, TX 76021.

Information on gaining credentials in respiratory care and a list of state licensing agencies can be obtained from:

- National Board for Respiratory Care, Inc., 18000 W. 105th St., Olathe, KS 66061. http://www.nbrc.org

PHYSICAL THERAPY

Key Terms

- Assistive devices
- Physical therapist
- Functional independence
- Passive exercise
- Documentation
- Research
- American Physical Therapy Association (APTA)

- Manual dexterity
- Rehabilitation
- Sports medicine
- Physical therapist assistant
- Physical therapist aide

Physical Therapy and Our Health

Physical therapy is a health profession whose primary purpose is the promotion of optimal human health and function through the application of scientific principles to prevent, identify, assess, correct, or alleviate acute or prolonged movement dysfunction. Physical therapy encompasses areas of specialized competence and includes the development of new principles and applications to effectively meet existing and emerging health needs. Physical therapists restore, maintain, and promote overall fitness and health. Their patients include accident victims and individuals with disabling conditions such as low back pain, arthritis, heart disease, fractures, head injuries, and cerebral palsy. Other professional activities in which physical therapists engage are research, education, consultation, and administration.

Possible therapeutic interventions include, but are not limited to, the use of therapeutic exercise with or without assistive devices, physical agents, electricity, manual procedures such as joint and soft tissue mobilization, neuromuscular reeducation, bronchopulmonary hygiene, and ambulation or gait training.

Physical therapists use tests and measurements to evaluate muscle strength, force, endurance, and tone; joint motion, mobility, and stability; reflexes and automatic reactions; movement skill and accuracy; sensations and perception; peripheral nerve integrity; locomotor skill, stability, and endurance; activities of daily living; cardiac, pulmonary, and vascular functions; fit, function, and comfort of prosthetic, orthotic, and other assistive devices; posture and body mechanics; limb length, circumference, and volume; thoracic excursion and breathing patterns; vital signs; photosensitivity; and home and work physical environments.

Physical Therapists

WORK DESCRIPTION

Physical therapists provide services that help restore function, improve mobility, relieve pain, and prevent or limit permanent physical disabilities. They restore, maintain, and promote overall fitness and health. Their patients include accident victims and individuals with disabling conditions such as low-back pain, arthritis, heart disease, fractures, head injuries, and cerebral palsy.

Therapists examine patients' medical histories and then test and measure the patients' strength, range of motion, balance and coordination, posture, muscle performance, respiration, and motor function. Next, physical therapists develop plans describing a treatment strategy and its anticipated outcome.

Treatment often includes exercise, especially for patients who have been immobilized or who lack flexibility, strength, or endurance. Physical therapists encourage patients to use their muscles to increase their flexibility and range of motion. More advanced exercises focus on improving strength, balance, coordination, and endurance. The goal is to improve how an individual functions at work and at home.

Physical therapists also use electrical stimulation, hot packs or cold compresses, and ultrasound to relieve pain and reduce swelling. They may use traction or deep-tissue massage to relieve pain and improve circulation and flexibility. Therapists also teach patients to use assistive and adaptive devices, such as crutches, prostheses, and wheelchairs. They also may show patients how to do exercises at home to expedite their recovery. As treatment continues, physical therapists document the patient's progress, conduct periodic examinations, and modify treatments when necessary.

Physical therapists often consult and practice with a variety of other professionals, such as physicians, dentists, nurses, educators, social workers, occupational therapists, speech-language pathologists, and audiologists.

Some physical therapists treat a wide range of ailments; others specialize in areas such as pediatrics, geriatrics, orthopedics, sports medicine, neurology, and cardiopulmonary physical therapy.

WORK ENVIRONMENT

Physical therapists practice in hospitals, clinics, and private offices that have specially equipped facilities. They also treat patients in hospital rooms, homes, or schools. These jobs can be physically demanding because therapists often have to stoop, kneel, crouch, lift, and stand for long periods. In addition, physical therapists move heavy equipment and lift patients or help them turn, stand, or walk.

In 2006, most full-time physical therapists worked a 40-hour week; some worked evenings and weekends to fit their patients' schedules. About one in five physical therapists worked part-time.

EMPLOYMENT OPPORTUNITIES

Physical therapists held about 173,000 jobs in 2006. The number of jobs is greater than the number of practicing physical therapists because some physical therapists hold two or more jobs. For example, some may work in a private practice, but also work part-time in another healthcare facility.

About six out of ten physical therapists worked in hospitals or in offices of other physical therapists. Additional jobs were in the home healthcare services industry, nursing care facilities, outpatient care centers, and offices of physicians. Some self-employed physical therapists in private practice saw individual patients and contracted to provide services in hospitals, rehabilitation centers, nursing care facilities, home healthcare agencies, adult day care programs, and schools. Physical therapists also teach in academic institutions and conduct research.

EDUCATIONAL AND LEGAL REQUIREMENTS

Physical therapists need a master's degree from an accredited physical therapy program and a state license, which requires passing scores on national and state examinations.

Education and Training. According to the American Physical Therapy Association, there were 209 accredited physical therapist education programs in 2007. Of the accredited programs, 43 offered master's degrees and 166 offered doctoral degrees. Only master's degree and doctoral degree programs are accredited, in accordance with the Commission on Accreditation in Physical Therapy Education. In the future, a doctoral degree might be the required entry-level degree. Master's degree programs typically last two years, and doctoral degree programs last three years.

Physical therapist education programs start with basic science courses such as biology, chemistry, and physics and then introduce specialized courses, including biomechanics, neuroanatomy, human growth and development, manifestations of disease, examination techniques, and therapeutic procedures. In addition to classroom and laboratory instruction, students receive supervised clinical experience.

Useful undergraduate courses for those planning to apply to a physical therapist education program include anatomy, biology, chemistry, social science, mathematics, and physics. Before granting admission, many programs require volunteer experience in the physical therapy department of a hospital or clinic. For high school students, volunteering with the school athletic trainer is a good way to gain experience.

Licensure. All states require physical therapists to pass national and state licensure exams before they can practice. They must also graduate from an accredited physical therapist education program.

Other Qualifications. Physical therapists should have strong interpersonal skills so that they can educate patients about their physical therapy treatments and communicate with patients' families. Physical therapists also should be compassionate and possess a desire to help patients.

Advancement. Physical therapists are expected to continue their professional development by participating in continuing education courses and workshops. In fact, a number of states require continuing education as a condition of maintaining licensure.

EMPLOYMENT TRENDS

Employment of physical therapists is expected to grow much faster than average. Job opportunities will be good, especially in acute hospital, rehabilitation, and orthopedic settings.

Employment Change. Employment of physical therapists is expected to grow 27 percent from 2006 to 2016, much faster than the average for all occupations. The impact of proposed federal legislation imposing limits on reimbursement for therapy services may adversely affect the short-term job outlook for physical therapists. However, the long-run demand for physical therapists should continue to rise as new treatments and techniques expand the scope of physical therapy practices. Moreover, demand will be spurred by the increasing numbers of individuals with disabilities or limited function.

The increasing elderly population will drive growth in the demand for physical therapy services. The elderly population is particularly vulnerable to chronic and debilitating conditions that require therapeutic services. Also, the baby-boom generation is entering the prime age for heart attacks and strokes, increasing the demand for cardiac and physical rehabilitation. And increasing numbers of children will need physical therapy as technological advances save the lives of a larger proportion of newborns with severe birth defects.

Future medical developments also should permit a higher percentage of trauma victims to survive, creating additional demand for rehabilitative care. In addition, growth may result from advances in medical technology that could permit the treatment of an increasing number of disabling conditions that were untreatable in the past.

Widespread interest in health promotion also should increase demand for physical therapy services. A growing number of employers are using physical therapists to evaluate worksites, develop exercise programs, and teach safe work habits to employees.

Job Prospects. Job opportunities will be good for licensed physical therapists in all settings. Job opportunities should be particularly good in acute hospital, rehabilitation, and orthopedic settings, where the elderly are most often treated. Physical therapists with specialized knowledge of particular types of treatment also will have excellent job prospects. **Table 20–1** shows some projection data provided by the Department of Labor.

Table 20–1

Projections data from the National Employment Matrix

Occupational title	Employment, 2006	Projected employment, 2016	Change, 2006–2016	
			Number	Percent
Physical therapists	173,000	220,000	47,000	27

NOTE: Data in this table are rounded.

EARNINGS

Median annual earnings of physical therapists were $66,200 in May 2006. The middle 50 percent earned between $55,030 and $78,080. The lowest 10 percent earned less than $46,510, and the highest 10 percent earned more than $94,810. Median annual earnings in the industries employing the largest numbers of physical therapists in May 2006 are shown in **Table 20–2**.

Table 20–2

Median annual earnings in the industries employing the largest numbers of physical therapists in May 2006

Home health care services	$70,920
Nursing care facilities	$68,650
General medical and surgical hospitals	$66,630
Offices of physicians	$65,900
Offices of physical, occupational and speech therapists, and audiologists	$65,150

RELATED OCCUPATIONS

Physical therapists rehabilitate people with physical disabilities. Others who work in the rehabilitation field include audiologists, chiropractors, occupational therapists, recreational therapists, rehabilitation counselors, respiratory therapists, and speech-language pathologists.

ADDITIONAL INFORMATION

Career information on physical therapy and a list of schools offering accredited programs can be obtained from:

■ The American Physical Therapy Association, 1111 North Fairfax St., Alexandria, VA 22314-1488. http://www.apta.org

Physical Therapist Assistants and Aides

WORK DESCRIPTION

Physical therapist assistants and aides help physical therapists to provide treatment that improves patient mobility, relieves pain, and prevents or lessens physical disabilities of patients. A physical therapist might ask an assistant to help patients exercise or learn to use crutches, for example, or an aide to gather and prepare therapy equipment. Patients include accident victims and individuals with disabling conditions such as lower-back pain, arthritis, heart disease, fractures, head injuries, and cerebral palsy.

Physical therapist assistants perform a variety of tasks. Under the direction and supervision of physical therapists, they provide part of a patient's treatment. This might involve exercises, massages, electrical stimulation, paraffin baths, hot and cold packs, traction, and ultrasound. Physical therapist assistants record the patient's responses to treatment and report the outcome of each treatment to the physical therapist.

Physical therapist aides help make therapy sessions productive, under the direct supervision of a physical therapist or physical therapist assistant. They usually are responsible for keeping the treatment area clean and organized and for preparing for each patient's therapy. When patients need assistance moving to or from a treatment area, aides push them in a wheelchair or provide them with a shoulder to lean on. Physical therapist aides are not licensed and do not perform the clinical tasks of a physical therapist assistant in states where licensure is required.

The duties of aides include some clerical tasks, such as ordering depleted supplies, answering the phone, and filling out insurance forms and other paperwork. The extent to which an aide or an assistant performs clerical tasks depends on the size and location of the facility.

WORK ENVIRONMENT

Physical therapist assistants and aides need a moderate degree of strength because of the physical exertion required in assisting patients with their treatment. In some cases, assistants and aides need to lift patients. Frequent kneeling, stooping, and standing for long periods also are part of the job.

The hours and days that physical therapist assistants and aides work vary with the facility. About 23 percent of all physical therapist assistants and aides work part-time. Many outpatient physical therapy offices and clinics keep evening and weekend hours to accommodate patients' personal schedules.

Employment Opportunities

Physical therapist assistants and aides held about 107,000 jobs in 2006. Physical therapist assistants held about 60,000 jobs; physical therapist aides, approximately 46,000. Both work with physical therapists in a variety of settings. About 71 percent of jobs were in offices of physical therapists or in hospitals. Others worked primarily in nursing care facilities, offices of physicians, home healthcare services, and outpatient care centers.

Educational and Legal Requirements

Most physical therapist aides are trained on the job, but most physical therapist assistants earn an associate degree from an accredited physical therapist assistant program. Some states require licensing for physical therapist assistants.

Education and Training. Employers typically require physical therapist aides to have a high school diploma. They are trained on the job, and most employers provide clinical on-the-job training.

In many states, physical therapist assistants are required by law to hold at least an associate degree. According to the American Physical Therapy Association, there were 233 accredited physical therapist assistant programs in the United States as of 2006. Accredited programs usually last two years, or four semesters, and culminate in an associate degree.

Programs are divided into academic study and hands-on clinical experience. Academic course work includes algebra, anatomy and physiology, biology, chemistry, and psychology. Clinical work includes certifications in CPR and other first aid and field experience in treatment centers. Both educators and prospective employers view clinical experience as essential to ensuring that students understand the responsibilities of a physical therapist assistant.

Licensure. Licensing is not required to practice as a physical therapist aide. However, some states require licensure or registration in order to work as a physical therapist assistant. States that require licensure stipulate specific educational and examination criteria. Additional requirements may include certification in cardiopulmonary resuscitation (CPR) and other first aid, and a minimum number of hours of clinical experience. Complete information on regulations can be obtained from state licensing boards.

Other Qualifications. Physical therapist assistants and aides should be well-organized, detail oriented, and caring. They usually have strong interpersonal skills and a desire to help people in need.

Advancement. Some physical therapist aides advance to become therapist assistants after gaining experience and, often, additional education. Sometimes, this education is required by law.

Some physical therapist assistants advance by specializing in a clinical area. They gain expertise in treating a certain type of patient, such as geriatric or pediatric, or a type of ailment, such as sports injuries. Many physical therapist assistants advance to administrative positions. These positions might include organizing all the assistants in a large physical therapy organization, or acting as the director for a specific department such as sports medicine. Other assistants go on to teach in an accredited physical therapist assistant academic program, lead health risk reduction classes for the elderly, or organize community activities related to fitness and risk reduction.

EMPLOYMENT TRENDS

Employment is expected to grow much faster than average because of increasing consumer demand for physical therapy services. Job prospects for physical therapist assistants are expected to be very good. Aides should experience keen competition for jobs.

Employment Change. Employment of physical therapist assistants and aides is expected to grow by 29 percent over the 2006 to 2016 decade, much faster than the average for all occupations. The impact of federal limits on Medicare and Medicaid reimbursement for therapy services may adversely affect the short-term job outlook for physical therapist assistants and aides. However, long-term demand for physical therapist assistants and aides will continue to rise, as the number of individuals with disabilities or limited function grows.

The increasing number of people who need therapy reflects, in part, the increasing elderly population. The elderly population is particularly vulnerable to chronic and debilitating conditions that require therapeutic services. These patients often need additional assistance in their treatment, making the roles of assistants and aides vital. In addition, the large baby-boom generation is entering the prime age for heart attacks and strokes, further increasing the demand for cardiac and physical rehabilitation. Moreover, future medical developments should permit an increased percentage of trauma victims to survive, creating added demand for therapy services.

Physical therapists are expected to increasingly use assistants to reduce the cost of physical therapy services. Once a patient is evaluated and a treatment plan is designed by the physical therapist, the physical therapist assistant can provide many parts of the treatment, as approved by the therapist.

Job Prospects. Opportunities for individuals interested in becoming physical therapist assistants are expected to be very good. Physical therapist aides may face keen competition from the large pool of qualified individuals. In addition to employment growth, job openings will result from the need to replace workers who leave the occupation permanently. Physical therapist assistants and aides with prior experience working in a physical therapy office or other healthcare setting will have the best job opportunities. **Table 20–3** shows some projection data provided by the Department of Labor.

EARNINGS

Median annual earnings of physical therapist assistants were $41,360 in May 2006. The middle 50 percent earned between $33,840 and $49,010. The lowest 10 percent earned less than $26,190, and the highest 10 percent earned more than $57,220. Median annual earnings in the industries employing the largest numbers of physical therapist assistants in May 2006 are included in **Table 20–4**.

Median annual earnings of physical therapist aides were $22,060 in May 2006. The middle 50 percent earned between $18,550 and $26,860. The lowest 10 percent earned less than

Table 20–3

Projections data from the National Employment Matrix

Occupational title	Employment, 2006	Projected employment, 2016	Change, 2006–2016	
			Number	Percent
Physical therapist assistants and aides	107,000	137,000	31,000	29
Physical therapist assistants	60,000	80,000	20,000	32
Physical therapist aides	46,000	58,000	11,000	24

NOTE: Data in this table are rounded.

Table 20–4

Median annual earnings in the industries employing the largest numbers of physical therapist assistants in May 2006

Home health care services	$46,390
Nursing care facilities	$44,460
Offices of physical, occupational and speech therapists, and audiologists	$40,780
General medical and surgical hospitals	$40,670
Offices of physicians	$39,290

$15,850, and the highest 10 percent earned more than $32,600. Median annual earnings in the industries employing the largest numbers of physical therapist aides in May 2006 are shown in **Table 20–5**.

RELATED OCCUPATIONS

Physical therapist assistants and aides work under the supervision of physical therapists. Other workers in the healthcare field who work under similar supervision include dental assistants; medical assistants; occupational therapist assistants and aides; pharmacy aides; pharmacy technicians; nursing, psychiatric, and home health aides; personal and home care aides; and social and human service assistants.

<table>

Table 20–5	Median annual earnings in the industries employing the largest numbers of physical therapist aides in May 2006	
Nursing care facilities		$24,170
Offices of physicians		$22,680
General medical and surgical hospitals		$22,680
Offices of physical, occupational and speech therapists, and audiologists		$21,230

</table>

ADDITIONAL INFORMATION

Career information on physical therapy and a list of schools offering accredited programs can be obtained from:

- The American Physical Therapy Association, 1111 North Fairfax St., Alexandria, VA 22314-1488. http://www.apta.org

OCCUPATIONAL THERAPY

Occupational Therapists

WORK DESCRIPTION

Occupational therapists treat people with mental, physical, developmental, or emotional disabilities. They employ a variety of techniques designed to help individuals develop or maintain daily living skills and to cope with the physical and emotional effects of disability. With support and direction from the therapist, patients learn (or relearn) many of the "ordinary" tasks that are performed every day at home, at work, at school, and in the community. The therapist's goal is to help clients establish a lifestyle that is as independent, productive, and satisfying as possible.

Like other health professionals, occupational therapists often work as members of a *multidisciplinary team* whose members may include a physician, nurse, physical therapist, psychologist, rehabilitation counselor, and social worker. Team members evaluate the patient in terms of their individual specialties and work together to develop goals that meet the patient's needs. During the course of treatment, team meetings are held to evaluate progress and to modify the treatment plan, if necessary.

Activities of various kinds can be used for treatment purposes. When working with children, for example, occupational therapists often use toys. For adults, therapy may include anything from activities that strengthen muscles to using a computer. While some treatments may give the appearance of recreation, all have a serious purpose. Working in the kitchen may produce a cake, but the skills practiced include memory, sequencing, coordination, and safety precautions, which are important for independent living at home. "Word find" games can help improve visual acuity and the ability to discern patterns. Specially designed computer programs help patients improve *cognitive skills*, including decision making, abstract reasoning, and problem solving, along with *perceptual skills*, such as peripheral vision and discrimination of letters, colors, and shapes. All of these treatments are designed to foster independence at home and at work.

During each therapy session, the therapist assesses the patient to determine treatment effectiveness and progress made toward meeting the treatment's goals. These assessments are then a basis for modifying goals and therapeutic procedures. A person with short-term memory loss, for instance, might be encouraged to make lists to aid recall. One with coordination problems might be given tasks to improve eye–hand coordination.

In addition to helping individuals strengthen basic motor functions and reasoning abilities, occupational therapists help them master daily living skills. Helping individuals with severe disabilities learn to cope with seemingly ordinary tasks such as getting dressed, using a bathroom, or driving a car requires sensitivity as well as skill. Disability may be recently acquired, such as a spinal cord injury resulting from a traffic accident, or a chronic condition present at birth, such as cerebral palsy. Therapists provide individuals with *adaptive equipment* such as wheelchairs, splints, and aids for eating and dressing. They may design and make special equipment and recommend changes in the home or work environment to facilitate functioning.

Computer-aided adaptive equipment offers the prospect of independence to some people with severe disabilities. Occupational therapists often work with rehabilitation engineers to develop such special equipment. Examples include microprocessing devices that permit individuals with paraplegia and quadriplegia to operate wheelchairs and household switches for appliances such as telephones, television sets, and radios. As such devices move out of the research and development stage, occupational therapists are involved in helping patients learn to use them.

An occupational therapist tends to work with a particular disability or age group. Approximately three out of five therapists work principally with persons who have physical disabilities; the rest work with those who have psychological, emotional, or developmental problems. A growing number of therapists are working in the wellness and health promotion areas. Often, the practice setting determines the age level and treatment needs of a therapist's patients. In home health care, for instance, a growing number of referrals involve older individuals with conditions such as arthritis, cardiac problems, and hip and other fractures.

The goals of occupational therapy in public schools focus not on treatment or rehabilitation, but on the resources that an individual child needs to participate effectively in the educational program. This may involve making an initial evaluation of a child's abilities and the implications for learning, recommending special therapeutic activities, consulting with parents and teachers, modifying classroom equipment or school facilities, and developing the functional, motor, and perceptual skills necessary for learning. Like teachers, these occupational therapists work regular school hours and participate in teachers' meetings and other activities.

Occupational therapists in mental health settings treat individuals with mental illness or emotional problems. Among the disorders and diseases often treated mainly as emotional disorders, occupational therapists encounter alcoholism, drug abuse, depression, eating disorders, and stress-related disorders. Therapists provide individual and group activities that simulate real-life experiences to help people learn to cope with the daily stresses of life and to manage their work and leisure more effectively. These activities include tasks that require planning and time-management skills, budgeting, shopping, meal preparation and homemaking, self-care, and using community resources such as public transportation and service agencies.

Keeping notes is an important part of an occupational therapist's job. Some of the records for which an occupational therapist may be responsible include an initial evaluation, progress notes, written reports to the physician, special internal staff notes, Medicare records, and discharge notes. Careful and complete documentation is required for reimbursement by insurance companies and Medicare.

Besides working with patients, occupational therapists may supervise student therapists, occupational therapy assistants, volunteers, and auxiliary nursing workers. Chief occupational therapists in a hospital may teach medical and nursing students the principles of occupational therapy. Many therapists supervise occupational therapy departments, coordinate patients' activities, or act as consultants to public health departments and mental health agencies. Some teach or conduct research in colleges and universities.

Work Environment

Although occupational therapists generally work a standard 40-hour week, they may occasionally have to work evenings or weekends. Their work environment varies according to the setting and available facilities. In a large rehabilitation center, for example, the therapist may work in a spacious room with a variety of equipment. In a nursing home, the therapist may work in a kitchen when using food preparation as therapy. Wherever they work and whatever equipment they use, they generally have adequate lighting and ventilation. The job can be physically tiring because therapists are on their feet much of the time. Those providing home health care may spend several hours a day driving from appointment to appointment. Therapists also face hazards such as back strain from lifting and moving patients and equipment.

Therapists are increasingly taking on supervisory roles. In an effort to curtail rising health-care costs, third-party payers are beginning to encourage occupational therapy assistants and aides to take more hands-on responsibility. Having assistants and aides work more closely with clients under the guidance of a therapist should reduce the cost of therapy. In 2006, more than a quarter of occupational therapists worked part-time.

EMPLOYMENT OPPORTUNITIES

Occupational therapists held about 99,000 jobs in 2006. About one in ten occupational therapists held more than one job. The largest number of jobs was in hospitals. Other major employers included offices of other health practitioners (including offices of other occupational therapists), public and private educational services, and nursing care facilities. Some occupational therapists were employed by home healthcare services, outpatient care centers, offices of physicians, individual and family services, community care facilities for the elderly, and government agencies.

A small number of occupational therapists were self-employed in private practice. These practitioners treated clients referred by other health professionals. They also provided contract or consulting services to nursing care facilities, schools, adult day care programs, and home healthcare agencies.

EDUCATIONAL AND LEGAL REQUIREMENTS

Occupational therapists must be licensed, requiring a master's degree in occupational therapy, six months of supervised fieldwork, and passing scores on national and state examinations.

Education and Training. A master's degree or higher in occupational therapy is the minimum requirement for entry into the field. In 2007, 124 master's degree programs offered entry-level education, 66 programs offered a combined bachelor's and master's degree, and five offered an entry-level doctoral degree. Most schools have full-time programs, although a growing number are offering weekend or part-time programs as well. Coursework in occupational therapy programs includes the physical, biological, and behavioral sciences, as well as applied occupational therapy theory and skills. Programs also require the completion of six months of supervised fieldwork.

People considering the profession of occupational therapy should take high school courses in biology, chemistry, physics, health, art, and the social sciences. College admissions offices also look favorably on paid or volunteer experience in the healthcare field. Relevant undergraduate majors include biology, psychology, sociology, anthropology, liberal arts, and anatomy.

Licensure. All 50 states, Puerto Rico, Guam, and the District of Columbia regulate the practice of occupational therapy. To obtain a license, applicants must graduate from an accredited educational program and pass a national certification examination. Those who pass the exam are awarded the title "Occupational Therapist Registered (OTR)." Some states have additional requirements for therapists who work in schools or early intervention programs. These requirements may include education-related classes, an education practice certificate, or early intervention certification.

Other Qualifications. Occupational therapists need patience and strong interpersonal skills to inspire trust and respect in their clients. Patience is necessary because many clients may not show rapid improvement. Ingenuity and imagination in adapting activities to individual needs are assets. Occupational therapists working in home healthcare services also must be able to adapt to a variety of settings.

Advancement. Occupational therapists are expected to continue their professional development by participating in continuing education courses and workshops. In fact, a number of states require continuing education as a condition of maintaining licensure.

Therapists are increasingly taking on supervisory roles. Because of rising healthcare costs, third-party payers are beginning to encourage occupational therapy assistants and aides to take more hands-on responsibility for clients. Occupational therapists can choose to advance their careers by taking on administrative duties and supervising assistants and aides.

Occupational therapists also can advance by specializing in a clinical area and gaining expertise in treating a particular type of patient or ailment. Therapists have specialized in gerontology, mental health, pediatrics, and physical rehabilitation. In addition, some occupational therapists choose to teach classes in accredited occupational therapy educational programs.

EMPLOYMENT TRENDS

Employment of occupational therapists is expected to grow much faster than the average for all occupations. Job opportunities should be good, especially for occupational therapists treating the elderly.

Employment Change. Employment of occupational therapists is expected to increase 23 percent between 2006 and 2016, much faster than the average for all occupations. The increasing elderly population will drive growth in the demand for occupational therapy services. In the short run, the impact of proposed federal legislation imposing limits on reimbursement for therapy services may adversely affect the job market for occupational therapists. However, over the long run, the demand for occupational therapists should continue to rise as a result of the increasing number of individuals with disabilities or limited function who require therapy services. The baby-boom generation's movement into middle age, a period when the incidence of heart attack and stroke increases, will spur demand for therapeutic services. Growth in the population of those 75 years and older—an age group that suffers from high incidences of disabling conditions—also will increase demand for therapeutic services. In addition, medical advances now enable more patients with critical problems to survive—patients who ultimately may need extensive therapy.

Hospitals will continue to employ a large number of occupational therapists to provide therapy services to acutely ill inpatients. Hospitals also will need occupational therapists to staff their outpatient rehabilitation programs.

Employment growth in schools will result from the expansion of the school-age population, the extension of services for disabled students, and an increasing prevalence of sensory disorders in children. Therapists will be needed to help children with disabilities prepare to enter special education programs.

Job Prospects. Job opportunities should be good for licensed occupational therapists in all settings, particularly in acute hospital, rehabilitation, and orthopedic settings because the elderly receive most of their treatment in these settings. Occupational therapists with specialized knowledge in a treatment area also will have increased job prospects. Driver rehabilitation and fall-prevention training for the elderly are emerging practice areas for occupational therapy. **Table 21–1** shows some projection data provided by the Department of Labor.

Table 21–1

Projections data from the National Employment Matrix

Occupational title	Employment, 2006	Projected employment, 2016	Change, 2006–2016	
			Number	Percent
Occupational therapists	99,000	122,000	23,000	23

NOTE: Data in this table are rounded.

EARNINGS

Median annual earnings of occupational therapists were $60,470 in May 2006. The middle 50 percent earned between $50,450 and $73,710. The lowest 10 percent earned less than $40,840, and the highest 10 percent earned more than $89,450. Median annual earnings in the industries employing the largest numbers of occupational therapists in May 2006 are shown in **Table 21–2**.

RELATED OCCUPATIONS

Occupational therapists use specialized knowledge to help individuals perform daily living skills and achieve maximum independence. Other workers performing similar duties include athletic trainers, audiologists, chiropractors, physical therapists, recreational therapists, rehabilitation counselors, respiratory therapists, and speech-language pathologists.

ADDITIONAL INFORMATION

For information on a career in occupational therapy and a list of accredited programs, contact:

- American Occupational Therapy Association, 4720 Montgomery Lane, Bethesda, MD 20824-1220. http://www.aota.org

Table 21–2	Median annual earnings in the industries employing the largest numbers of occupational therapists in May 2006	
Home health care services		$67,600
Nursing care facilities		$64,750
Offices of physical, occupational and speech therapists, and audiologists		$62,290
General medical and surgical hospitals		$61,610
Elementary and secondary schools		$54,260

Occupational Therapy Assistants and Aides

WORK DESCRIPTION

Occupational therapy assistants and aides work under the direction of occupational therapists to provide rehabilitative services to patients suffering from mental, physical, emotional, or developmental impairments. The ultimate goal is to improve clients' quality of life by helping them compensate for limitations. For example, occupational therapy assistants help injured workers reenter the labor force by helping them improve their motor skills; alternatively, they may help persons with learning disabilities increase their independence by teaching them to prepare meals or use public transportation.

Occupational therapy assistants help clients with the rehabilitative activities and exercises that are outlined in the treatment plan devised by the occupational therapist. The activities range from teaching the patient the proper method of moving from a bed into a wheelchair to the best way to stretch and limber the muscles of the hand. Assistants monitor the individual to ensure the client is performing the activities correctly and to provide encouragement. They also record their observations with regard to the patient's progress for use by the occupational therapist. If the treatment is not having the intended effect or if the client is not improving as expected, the treatment program may be altered to obtain better results. Assistants also document billing submitted to the patient's health insurance provider.

Occupational therapy aides typically prepare materials and assemble equipment used during treatment and are responsible for performing a range of clerical tasks. Their duties may include scheduling appointments, answering the telephone, restocking or ordering depleted supplies, and filling out insurance forms or other paperwork. Aides are not licensed, so by law they are not allowed to perform as wide a range of tasks as occupational therapy assistants do.

WORK ENVIRONMENT

Occupational therapy assistants and aides need to have a moderate degree of strength because of the physical exertion required to assist patients. For example, assistants and aides may need to lift patients. Constant kneeling, stooping, and standing for long periods also are part of the job.

The work schedules of occupational therapy assistants and aides vary by facility and with whether they are full or part-time. For example, many outpatient therapy offices and clinics have evening and weekend hours to accommodate patients' schedules.

EMPLOYMENT OPPORTUNITIES

Occupational therapy assistants and aides held about 33,000 jobs in 2006. Occupational therapy assistants held about 25,000 jobs, and occupational therapy aides held approximately 8,000. About 29 percent of jobs for assistants and aides were in hospitals, 23 percent were in offices of occupational therapists, and 21 percent were in nursing and residential care facilities. The rest were primarily in community care facilities for the elderly, home healthcare services, individual and family services, and state government agencies.

EDUCATIONAL AND LEGAL REQUIREMENTS

An associate degree or a certificate from an accredited community college or technical school is generally required to qualify for occupational therapy assistant jobs. In contrast, occupational therapy aides usually receive most of their training on the job.

Education and Training. There were 126 accredited occupational therapy assistant programs in 2007. The first year of study typically involves an introduction to health care, basic medical terminology, anatomy, and physiology. In the second year, courses are more rigorous and usually include occupational therapy courses in areas such as mental health, adult physical disabilities, gerontology, and pediatrics. Students also must complete 16 weeks of supervised fieldwork in a clinic or community setting.

Applicants to occupational therapy assistant programs can improve their chances of admission by taking high school courses in biology and health and by performing volunteer work in nursing care facilities, occupational or physical therapists' offices, or other healthcare settings.

Occupational therapy aides usually receive most of their training on the job. Qualified applicants must have a high school diploma, strong interpersonal skills, and a desire to help people in need. Applicants may increase their chances of getting a job by volunteering their services, thus displaying initiative and aptitude to the employer.

Licensure. In most states, occupational therapy assistants are regulated and must pass a national certification examination after they graduate. Those who pass the test are awarded the title "Certified Occupational Therapy Assistant."

Other Qualifications. Assistants and aides must be responsible, patient, and willing to take directions and work as part of a team. Furthermore, they should be caring and want to help people who are not able to help themselves.

Advancement. Occupational therapy assistants may advance into administration positions. They might organize all the assistants in a large occupational therapy department or act as the director for a specific department such as sports medicine. Some assistants go on to teach classes in accredited occupational therapy assistant academic programs or lead health risk reduction classes for the elderly.

EMPLOYMENT TRENDS

Employment is expected to grow much faster than average as demand for occupational therapy services rises and as occupational therapists increasingly use assistants and aides. Job prospects should be very good for occupational therapy assistants. Job seekers holding only a high school diploma might face keen competition for occupational therapy aide jobs.

Employment Change. Employment of occupational therapy assistants and aides is expected to grow 25 percent from 2006 to 2016, much faster than the average for all occupations. In the short run, the impact of proposed federal legislation imposing limits on reimbursement for therapy services may adversely affect the job market for occupational therapy assistants and aides. Over the long run, however, demand for both will continue to rise because of the increasing number of individuals with disabilities or limited function.

The growing elderly population is particularly vulnerable to chronic and debilitating conditions that require therapeutic services. These patients often need additional assistance in their treatment, making the role of assistants and aides vital. As the large baby-boom generation ages, it enters the prime age bracket for heart attacks and strokes, further increasing the demand for cardiac and physical rehabilitation. In addition, future medical developments should permit an increasing percentage of trauma victims to survive, creating added demand for therapy services. An increase of sensory disorders in children will also spur demand for occupational therapy services.

Occupational therapists are expected to increase their utilization of assistants and aides to reduce the cost of occupational therapy services. Once a patient is evaluated and a treatment plan is designed by the therapist, the occupational therapy assistant can provide many aspects of treatment, as prescribed by the therapist.

Job Prospects. Opportunities for individuals interested in becoming occupational therapy assistants are expected to be very good. In addition to employment growth, job openings will result from the need to replace occupational therapy assistants and aides who leave the occupation permanently between 2006 and 2016. Occupational therapy assistants and aides with prior experience working in an occupational therapy office or other healthcare setting will have the best job opportunities. However, individuals with only a high school diploma may face keen competition for occupational therapy aide jobs. **Table 21–3** shows some projection data provided by the Department of Labor.

EARNINGS

Median annual earnings of occupational therapy assistants were $42,060 in May 2006. The middle 50 percent earned between $34,130 and $50,230. The lowest 10 percent earned less than $26,050, and the highest 10 percent earned more than $58,270. Median annual earnings in the industries employing the largest numbers of occupational therapy assistants in May 2006 are included in **Table 21–4.**

Table 21–3

Projections data from the National Employment Matrix

Occupational title	Employment, 2006	Projected employment, 2016	Change, 2006–2016	
			Number	Percent
Occupational therapy assistants and aides	33,000	41,000	8,200	25
Occupational therapy assistants	25,000	31,000	6,400	25
Occupational therapy aides	8,200	10,000	1,800	22

NOTE: Data in this table are rounded.

Table 21–4

Median annual earnings in the industries employing the largest numbers of occupational therapist assistants in May 2006

Offices of physical, occupational and speech therapists, and audiologists	$45,130
Nursing care facilities	$43,280
General medical and surgical hospitals	$40,060

Median annual earnings of occupational therapy aides were $25,020 in May 2006. The middle 50 percent earned between $20,460 and $32,160. The lowest 10 percent earned less than $17,060, and the highest 10 percent earned more than $44,130. Median annual earnings in the industries employing the largest numbers of occupational therapy aides in May 2006 are shown in **Table 21–5**.

Table 21–5

Median annual earnings in the industries employing the largest numbers of occupational therapist aides in May 2006

Offices of physical, occupational and speech therapists, and audiologists	$26,960
General medical and surgical hospitals	$26,360
Nursing care facilities	$25,520

RELATED OCCUPATIONS

Occupational therapy assistants and aides work under the supervision and direction of occupational therapists. Other workers in the healthcare field who work under similar supervision include dental assistants; medical assistants; nursing, psychiatric, and home health aides; personal and home care aides; pharmacy aides; pharmacy technicians; and physical therapist assistants and aides.

ADDITIONAL INFORMATION

For information on a career in occupational therapy and a list of accredited programs, contact:

- American Occupational Therapy Association, 4720 Montgomery Lane, Bethesda, MD 20824-1220. http://www.aota.org

ADDITIONAL TECHNOLOGISTS AND TECHNICIANS

Key Terms

- Ambulatory monitoring
- Artifact
- Brain wave mapping
- Cardiology technologist
- Echocardiographer
- Electrocardiograph (EKG/ECG) technician
- Electroencephalography
- Electroneurodiagnostic technologist (EEG technologist)
- Evoked potential studies
- Gamma scintillation camera
- Holter monitoring

- Laboratory technicians: dental, medical and ophthalmic
- Neurology/neurophysiology
- Nuclear medicine
- Operating room
- Radionuclides
- Radiopharmaceuticals
- Sleep studies
- Stress testing
- Surgical technologist
- Vascular technologist

Cardiovascular Technologists and Technicians

WORK DESCRIPTIONS

Cardiovascular technologists and technicians assist physicians in diagnosing and treating cardiac (heart) and peripheral vascular (blood vessel) ailments.

Cardiovascular technologists and technicians schedule appointments, perform ultrasound or cardiovascular procedures, review doctors' interpretations and patient files, and monitor patients' heart rates. They also operate and maintain testing equipment, explain test procedures, and compare test results to a standard to identify problems. Other day-to-day activities vary significantly between specialties.

Cardiovascular technologists may specialize in any of three areas of practice: invasive cardiology, echocardiography, or vascular technology.

Invasive cardiology. Cardiovascular technologists specializing in invasive procedures are called *cardiology technologists.* They assist physicians with cardiac catheterization procedures in which a small tube, or catheter, is threaded through a patient's artery from a spot on the patient's groin to the heart. The procedure can determine whether a blockage exists in the blood vessels that supply the heart muscle. The procedure also can help to diagnose other problems. Part of the procedure may involve balloon angioplasty, which can be used to treat blockages of blood vessels or heart valves without the need for heart surgery. Cardiology technologists assist physicians as they insert a catheter with a balloon on the end to the point of the obstruction. Another procedure using the catheter is the electrophysiology test, which helps locate the specific areas of heart tissue that give rise to the abnormal electrical impulses that cause arrhythmias.

Technologists prepare patients for cardiac catheterization by first positioning them on an examining table and then shaving, cleaning, and administering anesthesia to the top of their leg near the groin. During the catheterization procedures, they monitor patients' blood pressure and heart rate with EKG equipment and notify the physician if something appears to be wrong. Technologists also may prepare and monitor patients during open-heart surgery, and during the insertion of pacemakers and stents that open up blockages in arteries to the heart and major blood vessels.

Noninvasive technology. Technologists who specialize in vascular technology or echocardiography perform noninvasive tests. Tests are called "noninvasive" if they do not require the insertion of probes or other instruments into the patient's body. For example, procedures such as Doppler ultrasound transmit high-frequency sound waves into areas of the patient's body and then process reflected echoes of the sound waves to form an image. Technologists view the ultrasound image on a screen and may record the image on videotape or photograph it for interpretation and diagnosis by a physician. As the technologist uses the instrument to perform scans and record images, technologists check the image on the screen for subtle differences between healthy and diseased areas, decide which images to include in the report to the physician, and judge whether the images are satisfactory for diagnostic purposes. They also explain the procedure to patients, record any additional medical history the patient relates, select appropriate equipment settings, and change the patient's position as necessary.

Vascular technology. Technicians who assist physicians in the diagnosis of disorders affecting the circulation are known as *vascular technologists* or *vascular sonographers*. Vascular technologists complete patients' medical history, evaluate pulses and assess blood flow in arteries and veins by listening to vascular flow sounds for abnormalities, and confirm that the appropriate vascular test has been ordered. Once confirmed, they perform a noninvasive procedure using ultrasound instruments to record vascular information such as vascular blood flow, blood pressure, oxygen saturation, cerebral circulation, peripheral circulation, and abdominal circulation. Many of these tests are performed during or immediately after surgery. Vascular technologists then provide a summary of findings to the physician to aid in patient diagnosis and management.

Echocardiography. This area of practice includes taking electrocardiograms (EKGs) and sonograms of the heart. Cardiovascular technicians who specialize in EKGs, stress testing, and those who perform *Holter monitor* procedures are known as cardiographic or *electrocardiograph (EKG) technicians.*

A basic EKG, which traces electrical impulses transmitted by the heart, requires technicians to attach electrodes to the patient's chest, arms, and legs, and then manipulate switches on an EKG machine to obtain a reading. An EKG is printed out for interpretation by the physician. This test is done before most kinds of surgery, or as part of a routine physical examination, especially on persons who have reached middle age or who have a history of cardiovascular problems.

Electrocardiograph technicians with advanced training perform Holter monitor and stress testing. For *Holter monitoring,* technicians place electrodes on the patient's chest and attach a portable EKG monitor to the patient's belt. Following 24 or more hours of normal activity by the patient, the technician removes a tape from the monitor and places it in a scanner. After checking the quality of the recorded impulses on an electronic screen, the technician usually prints the information from the tape for analysis by a physician. Physicians use the output from the scanner to diagnose heart ailments, such as heart rhythm abnormalities or problems with pacemakers.

For a treadmill stress test, EKG technicians document the patient's medical history, explain the procedure, connect the patient to an EKG monitor, and obtain a baseline reading and resting blood pressure. Next, they monitor the heart's performance while the patient is walking on a treadmill, gradually increasing the treadmill's speed to observe the effect of increased exertion. Like vascular technologists and cardiac sonographers, cardiographic technicians who perform EKG, Holter monitor, and stress tests are known as "noninvasive" technicians.

Technologists who use ultrasound to examine the heart chambers, valves, and vessels are referred to as *cardiac sonographers,* or *echocardiographers.* They use ultrasound instrumentation to create images called echocardiograms. An echocardiogram may be performed while the patient is either resting or physically active. Technologists may administer medication to physically active patients to assess their heart function. Cardiac sonographers also may assist physicians who perform transesophageal echocardiography, which involves placing a tube in the patient's esophagus to obtain ultrasound images.

WORK ENVIRONMENT

Cardiovascular technologists and technicians spend a lot of time walking and standing. Heavy lifting may be involved to move equipment or transfer patients. These workers wear heavy protective aprons while conducting some procedures. Those who work in catheterization laboratories may face stressful working conditions because they are in close contact with patients with serious heart ailments. For example, some patients may encounter complications that have life-or-death implications.

Some cardiovascular technologists and technicians may have the potential for radiation exposure, which is kept to a minimum by strict adherence to radiation safety guidelines. In addition, those who use sonography can be at an increased risk for musculoskeletal disorders such as carpel tunnel syndrome, neck and back strain, and eye strain. However, greater use of ergonomically correct equipment and an increasing awareness of hazards will continue to minimize such risks.

Technologists and technicians generally work a five-day, 40-hour week that may include weekends. Those in catheterization laboratories tend to work longer hours and may work evenings. They also may be on call during the night and on weekends.

EMPLOYMENT OPPORTUNITIES

Cardiovascular technologists and technicians held about 45,000 jobs in 2006. About three out of four jobs were in public and private hospitals, primarily in cardiology departments. Remaining jobs were mostly in offices of physicians, including cardiologists, or in medical and diagnostic laboratories, including diagnostic imaging centers.

EDUCATIONAL AND LEGAL REQUIREMENTS

An associate degree is the most common level of education completed by cardiovascular technologists and technicians. Certification, although not required in all cases, is available.

Education and Training. Although a few cardiovascular technologists, vascular technologists, and cardiac sonographers are currently trained on the job, most receive training in two- to four-year programs. The majority of technologists complete a two-year junior or community college program, but four-year programs are increasingly available. The first year is dedicated to core courses and is followed by a year of specialized instruction in either invasive, noninvasive cardiovascular, or noninvasive vascular technology. Those who are already qualified in an allied health profession need to complete only the year of specialized instruction.

The Joint Review Committee on Education in Cardiovascular Technology reviews education programs seeking accreditation. The *Commission on Accreditation of Allied Health Professionals (CAAHEP)* accredits these education programs; as of 2006, there were 31 programs accredited in cardiovascular technology in the United States. Similarly, students who want to study echocardiography or vascular sonography may also attend CAAHEP accredited programs in diagnostic medical sonography. In 2006, there were 147 diagnostic medical sonography programs accredited by CAAHEP. Those who attend these accredited programs are eligible to obtain professional certification.

Unlike most other cardiovascular technologists and technicians, most EKG technicians are trained on the job by an EKG supervisor or a cardiologist. On-the-job training usually lasts about 8 to 16 weeks. Most employers prefer to train people already in the healthcare field—nursing aides, for example. Some EKG technicians are students enrolled in two-year programs to become technologists, working part-time to gain experience and make contact with employers. One-year certification programs exist for basic EKGs, Holter monitoring, and stress testing.

Licensure and Certification. Some states require workers in this occupation to be licensed. For information on a particular state, contact that state's medical board. Certification is available from two organizations: *Cardiovascular Credentialing International (CCI)* and the *American Registry of Diagnostic Medical Sonographers* (ARDMS). The CCI offers four certifications—*Certified Cardiographic Technician (CCT)*, *Registered Cardiac Sonographer (RCS)*, *Registered Vascular Specialist (RVS)*, and *Registered Cardiovascular Invasive Specialist (RCIS)*. The ARDMS offers *Registered Diagnostic Cardiac Sonographer (RDCS)* and *Registered Vascular Technologist (RVT)* credentials. Some states require certification as part of licensure. In other states, certification is not required but many employers prefer it.

Other Qualifications. Cardiovascular technologists and technicians must be reliable, have mechanical aptitude, and be able to follow detailed instructions. A pleasant, relaxed manner for putting patients at ease is an asset. They must be articulate and well-spoken as they must communicate in technical detail with physicians and also explain procedures in a simple manner to patients.

Advancement. Technologists and technicians can advance to higher levels of the profession as many institutions structure the occupation in multiple levels, each having an increasing amount of responsibility. Technologists and technicians also can advance into supervisory or management positions. Other common possibilities include working in an educational setting or conducting laboratory work.

EMPLOYMENT TRENDS

Employment is expected to grow much faster than average; technologists and technicians trained to perform certain procedures will be in particular demand.

Employment Change. Employment of cardiovascular technologists and technicians is expected to increase by 26 percent through the year 2016, much faster than the average for all occupations. Growth will occur as the population ages, because older people have a higher incidence of heart disease and other complications of the heart and vascular system. Noninvasive procedures, such as ultrasound, are being performed more often as an alternative to more expensive and invasive procedures. Due to advances in medicine and greater public awareness, signs of vascular disease can be detected earlier, creating demand for cardiovascular technologists and technicians to perform various procedures.

Employment of vascular technologists and echocardiographers will grow as advances in vascular technology and sonography reduce the need for more costly and invasive procedures. Electrophysiology is also becoming a rapidly growing specialty. However, fewer EKG technicians will be needed, as hospitals train nursing aides and others to perform basic EKG procedures. Individuals trained in Holter monitoring and stress testing are expected to have more favorable job prospects than those who can perform only a basic EKG.

Medicaid has relaxed some of the rules governing reimbursement for vascular exams, which is resulting in vascular studies becoming a more routine practice. As a result of increased use of these procedures, individuals with training in vascular studies should have more favorable employment opportunities.

Job Prospects. Some additional job openings for cardiovascular technologists and technicians will arise from replacement needs as individuals transfer to other jobs or leave the labor force. Although growing awareness of musculoskeletal disorders has made prevention easier, some cardiovascular technologists and technicians have been forced to leave the occupation early because of these disorders.

It is not uncommon for cardiovascular technologists and technicians to move between the specialties within the occupation by obtaining certification in more than one specialty. **Table 22–1** shows some projection data provided by the Department of Labor.

Table 22–1	*Projections data from the National Employment Matrix*				
Occupational title	Employment, 2006	Projected employment, 2016	Change, 2006–2016		
			Number	Percent	
Cardiovascular technologists and technicians	45,000	57,000	12,000	26	

NOTE: Data in this table are rounded.

Median annual earnings of cardiovascular technologists and technicians were $42,300 in May 2006. The middle 50 percent earned between $29,900 and $55,670. The lowest 10 percent earned less than $23,670, and the highest 10 percent earned more than $67,410. Median annual earnings of cardiovascular technologists and technicians in 2006 were $41,960 in offices of physicians and $41,950 in general medical and surgical hospitals.

RELATED OCCUPATIONS

Cardiovascular technologists and technicians operate sophisticated equipment that helps physicians and other health practitioners to diagnose and treat patients. So do diagnostic medical sonographers, nuclear medicine technologists, radiation therapists, radiologic technologists and technicians, and respiratory therapists.

ADDITIONAL INFORMATION

For general information about a career in cardiovascular technology, contact:

■ Alliance of Cardiovascular Professionals, Thalia Landing Offices, Bldg. 2, 4356 Bonney Rd., Suite 103, Virginia Beach, VA 23452-1200. http://www.acp-online.org

For a list of accredited programs in cardiovascular technology, contact:

- Committee on Accreditation for Allied Health Education Programs, 1361 Park St, Clearwater, FL 33756. http://www.caahep.org

- Society for Vascular Ultrasound, 4601 Presidents Dr., Suite 260, Lanham, MD 20706-4381. http://www.svunet.org

For information on echocardiography, contact:

- American Society of Echocardiography, 1500 Sunday Dr., Suite 102, Raleigh, NC 27607. http://www.asecho.org

For information regarding registration and certification, contact:

- Cardiovascular Credentialing International, 1500 Sunday Dr., Suite 102, Raleigh, NC 27607. http://www.cci-online.org

- American Registry of Diagnostic Medical Sonographers, 51 Monroe St., Plaza East One, Rockville, MD 20850-2400. http://www.ardms.org

Nuclear Medicine Technologists

WORK DESCRIPTIONS

Diagnostic imaging embraces several procedures that aid in diagnosing ailments, the most familiar being the X-ray. In nuclear medicine, radionuclides—unstable atoms that emit radiation spontaneously—are used to diagnose and treat disease. Radionuclides are purified and compounded to form radiopharmaceuticals. Nuclear medicine technologists administer radiopharmaceuticals to patients and then monitor the characteristics and functions of tissues or organs in which the drugs localize. Abnormal areas show higher-than-expected or lower-than-expected concentrations of radioactivity. Nuclear medicine differs from other diagnostic imaging technologies because it determines the presence of disease on the basis of metabolic changes rather than changes in organ structure.

Nuclear medicine technologists operate cameras that detect and map the radioactive drug in a patient's body to create diagnostic images. After explaining test procedures to patients, technologists prepare a dosage of the radiopharmaceutical and administer it by mouth, injection, inhalation, or other means. They position patients and start a gamma scintillation camera, or "scanner," which creates images of the distribution of a radiopharmaceutical as it localizes in, and emits signals from, the patient's body. The images are produced on a computer screen or on film for a physician to interpret.

When preparing radiopharmaceuticals, technologists adhere to safety standards that keep the radiation exposure as low as possible to workers and patients. Technologists maintain patient records and document the amount and type of radionuclides that they receive, use, and discard.

WORK ENVIRONMENT

Physical stamina is important because nuclear medicine technologists are on their feet much of the day and may have to lift or turn disabled patients. In addition, technologists must operate complicated equipment that requires mechanical ability and manual dexterity.

Although the potential for radiation exposure exists in this field, it is minimized by the use of shielded syringes, gloves, and other protective devices and by adherence to strict radiation safety guidelines. The amount of radiation in a nuclear medicine procedure is comparable to that received during a diagnostic X-ray procedure. Technologists also wear badges that measure radiation levels. Because of safety programs, badge measurements rarely exceed established safety levels.

Nuclear medicine technologists generally work a 40-hour week, perhaps including evening or weekend hours, in departments that operate on an extended schedule. Opportunities for part-time and shift work also are available. In addition, technologists in hospitals may have on-call duty on a rotational basis, and those employed by mobile imaging services may be required to travel to several locations.

EMPLOYMENT OPPORTUNITIES

Nuclear medicine technologists held about 20,000 jobs in 2006. About 67 percent of all nuclear medicine technologists jobs were in hospitals—private and government. Most of the rest were in offices of physicians or in medical and diagnostic laboratories, including diagnostic imaging centers.

EDUCATIONAL AND LEGAL REQUIREMENTS

Nuclear medicine technology programs range in length from one to four years and lead to a certificate, an associate degree, or a bachelor's degree. Many employers and an increasing number of states require certification or licensure. Aspiring nuclear medicine technologists should check the requirements of the state in which they plan to work.

Education and Training. Completion of a nuclear medicine technology program takes one to four years and leads to a certificate, an associate degree, or a bachelor's degree. Generally, certificate programs are offered in hospitals, associate degree programs in community colleges, and bachelor's degree programs in four-year colleges and universities. Courses cover the physical sciences, biological effects of radiation exposure, radiation protection and procedures, the use of radiopharmaceuticals, imaging techniques, and computer applications.

One-year certificate programs are for health professionals who already possess an associate degree—especially radiologic technologists and diagnostic medical sonographers—but who wish to specialize in nuclear medicine. The programs also attract medical technologists, registered nurses, and others who wish to change fields or specialize.

The Joint Review Committee on Education Programs in Nuclear Medicine Technology accredits most formal training programs in nuclear medicine technology. In 2006, there were about 100 accredited programs in the continental United States and Puerto Rico.

Licensure and Certification. Educational requirements for nuclear medicine technologists vary from state to state, so it is important that aspiring technologists check the requirements of the state in which they plan to work. More than half of all states require certification or licensing of nuclear medicine technicians. Certification is available from the *American Registry of Radiologic Technologists (ARRT)* and from the *Nuclear Medicine Technology Certification Board (NMTCB)*. Although not required, some workers receive certification from both agencies. Nuclear medicine technologists must meet the minimum federal standards on the administration of radioactive drugs and the operation of radiation detection equipment.

The most common way to become eligible for certification by ARRT or NMTCB is to complete a training program recognized by those organizations. Other ways to become eligible are completing a bachelor's or associate degree in biological science or a related health field, such as registered nursing, or acquiring, under supervision, a certain number of hours of experience in nuclear medicine technology. ARRT and NMTCB have different requirements, but in all cases, one must pass a comprehensive exam to become certified.

In addition to the general certification requirements, certified technicians also must complete a certain number of continuing education hours. Continuing education is required primarily because of the frequent technological and innovative changes in the field of nuclear medicine. Typically, technologists must register annually with both the ARRT and the NMTCB.

Other Qualifications. Nuclear medicine technologists should have excellent communication skills, be detail-oriented, and have a desire to continue learning. Technologists must effectively interact with patients and their families and should be sensitive to patients' physical and psychological needs. Nuclear medicine technologists must be able to work independently as they usually have little direct supervision. Technologists also must be detailed-oriented and meticulous when performing procedures to assure that all regulations are being followed.

Advancement. Technologists may advance to supervisor, then to chief technologist, and to department administrator or director. Some technologists specialize in a clinical area, such as nuclear cardiology or computer analysis or leave patient care to take positions in research laboratories. Some become instructors in, or directors of, nuclear medicine technology programs, a step that usually requires a bachelor's or master's degree in the subject. Others leave the occupation to work as sales or training representatives for medical equipment and radiopharmaceutical manufacturing firms or as radiation safety officers in regulatory agencies or hospitals.

EMPLOYMENT TRENDS

Faster-than-average job growth will arise from an increase in the number of middle-aged and elderly persons, who are the primary users of diagnostic and treatment procedures. However, the number of job openings each year will be relatively low because the occupation is small.

Employment Change. Employment of nuclear medicine technologists is expected to increase by 15 percent from 2006 to 2016, faster than the average for all occupations. Growth will arise from technological advancement, the development of new nuclear medicine treatments, and an increase in the number of middle-aged and older persons, who are the primary users of diagnostic procedures, including nuclear medicine tests.

Technological innovations may increase the diagnostic uses of nuclear medicine. New nuclear medical imaging technologies, including *positron emission tomography (PET)* and *single photon emission computed tomography (SPECT)*, are expected to be used increasingly and to contribute further to employment growth. The wider use of nuclear medical imaging to observe metabolic and biochemical changes during neurology, cardiology, and oncology procedures also will spur demand for nuclear medicine technologists.

Nonetheless, cost considerations will affect the speed with which new applications of nuclear medicine grow. Some promising nuclear medicine procedures, such as positron emission tomography, are extremely costly, and hospitals contemplating these procedures will have to consider equipment costs, reimbursement policies, and the number of potential users.

Job Prospects. In spite of fast growth in nuclear medicine, the number of openings into the occupation each year will be relatively low because of the small size of the occupation. Technologists who have additional training in other diagnostic methods, such as radiologic technology or diagnostic medical sonography, will enjoy the best prospects. **Table 22-2** shows some projection data provided by the Department of Labor.

Table 22-2

Projections data from the National Employment Matrix				
Occupational title	Employment, 2006	Projected employment, 2016	Change, 2006–2016	
			Number	Percent
Nuclear medicine technologists	20,000	23,000	2,900	15

NOTE: Data in this table are rounded.

EARNINGS

Median annual earnings of nuclear medicine technologists were $62,300 in May 2006. The middle 50 percent earned between $53,530 and $72,410. The lowest 10 percent earned less than $46,490, and the highest 10 percent earned more than $82,310. Median annual earnings of nuclear medicine technologists in 2006 were $61,230 in general medical and surgical hospitals.

RELATED OCCUPATIONS

Nuclear medical technologists operate sophisticated equipment to help physicians and other health practitioners diagnose and treat patients. Cardiovascular technologists and technicians, clinical laboratory technologists and technicians, diagnostic medical sonographers, radiation therapists, radiologic technologists and technicians, and respiratory therapists perform similar functions.

ADDITIONAL INFORMATION

Additional information on a career as a nuclear medicine technologist is available from:

■ American Society of Radiologic Technologists, 15000 Central Ave. S.E., Albuquerque, NM 87123-3917. http://www.asrt.org

- American Registry of Radiologic Technologists, 1255 Northland Dr., St. Paul, MN 55120-1155. http://www.arrt.org

- Society of Nuclear Medicine Technologists, 1850 Samuel Morse Dr., Reston, VA 20190-5316. http://www.snm.org

For a list of accredited programs in nuclear medicine technology, contact:

- Joint Review Committee on Educational Programs in Nuclear Medicine Technology, 716 Black Point Rd., Polson, MT 59860. http://www.jrcnmt.org

Information on certification is available from:

- Nuclear Medicine Technology Certification Board, 2970 Clairmont Rd., Suite 935, Atlanta, GA 30329-4421. http://www.nmtcb.org

Surgical Technologists

WORK DESCRIPTIONS

Surgical technologists, also called scrubs and surgical or operating room technicians, assist in surgical operations under the supervision of surgeons, registered nurses, or other surgical personnel. Surgical technologists are members of operating room teams, which most commonly include surgeons, anesthesiologists, and circulating nurses.

Before an operation, surgical technologists help prepare the operating room by setting up surgical instruments and equipment, sterile drapes, and sterile solutions. They assemble both sterile and nonsterile equipment, as well as check and adjust it to ensure it is working properly. Technologists also get patients ready for surgery by washing, shaving, and disinfecting incision sites. They transport patients to the operating room, help position them on the operating table, and cover them with sterile surgical drapes. Technologists also observe patients' vital signs, check charts, and help the surgical team put on sterile gowns and gloves.

During surgery, technologists pass instruments and other sterile supplies to surgeons and surgeon assistants. They may hold retractors, cut sutures, and help count sponges, needles, supplies, and instruments. Surgical technologists help prepare, care for, and dispose of specimens taken for laboratory analysis and help apply dressings. Some operate sterilizers, lights, or suction machines, and help operate diagnostic equipment.

After an operation, surgical technologists may help transfer patients to the recovery room and clean and restock the operating room.

Certified surgical technologists with additional specialized education or training also may act as the surgical first assistant or circulator. The surgical first assistant, as defined by the American College of Surgeons (ACS), provides aid in exposure, hemostasis (controlling blood flow and stopping or preventing hemorrhage), and other technical functions under the surgeon's direction, to assist the surgeon in carrying out a safe operation. A circulating technologist is the "unsterile" member of the surgical team. The circulator interviews and prepares the patient prior to surgery; assists with anesthesia; obtains and opens packages from which the "sterile" team members remove sterile contents during the procedure; keeps a written account of the surgical procedure; and answers the surgeon's questions about the patient during the surgery.

Work Environment. Surgical technologists work in clean, well-lighted, cool environments. They must stand for long periods and remain alert during operations. At times, they may be exposed to communicable diseases and unpleasant sights, odors, and materials.

Most surgical technologists work a regular 40-hour week, although they may be on call or work nights, weekends, and holidays on a rotating basis.

EMPLOYMENT OPPORTUNITIES

Surgical technologists held about 86,000 jobs in 2006. About 70 percent of jobs for surgical technologists were in hospitals, mainly in operating and delivery rooms. Other jobs were in offices of physicians or dentists who perform outpatient surgery and in outpatient care centers, including ambulatory surgical centers. A few technologists, known as private scrubs, are employed directly by surgeons who maintain specialized surgical teams, such as those for liver transplants.

EDUCATIONAL AND LEGAL REQUIREMENTS

Training programs last 9 to 24 months and lead to a certificate, diploma, or associate degree. Professional certification can help in getting jobs and promotions.

Education and Training. Surgical technologists receive their training in formal programs offered by community and junior colleges, vocational schools, universities, hospitals, and the military. In 2006, the *Commission on Accreditation of Allied Health Education Programs (CAAHEP)* recognized more than 400 accredited training programs. Programs last from 9 to 24 months and lead to a certificate, diploma, or associate degree. High school graduation normally is required for admission. Recommended high school courses include health, biology, chemistry, and mathematics.

Surgical technologist training programs provide classroom education and supervised clinical experience. Students take courses in anatomy, physiology, microbiology, pharmacology, professional ethics, and medical terminology. Other topics covered include the care and safety of patients during surgery, sterile techniques, and surgical procedures. Students also learn to sterilize instruments; prevent and control infection; and handle special drugs, solutions, supplies, and equipment.

Certification and Other Qualifications. Most employers prefer to hire certified surgical technologists. Technologists may obtain voluntary professional certification from the *Liaison Council on Certification for the Surgical Technologist* by graduating from a CAAHEP-accredited program and passing a national certification examination. They may then use the *Certified Surgical Technologist (CST)* designation. Continuing education or reexamination is required to maintain certification, which must be renewed every four years.

Certification also may be obtained from the National Center for Competency Testing (NCCT). Candidates qualify for the exam by following one of three paths: they complete an accredited training program; undergo a two-year hospital on-the-job training program; or acquire seven years of experience working in the field. After passing the exam, individuals may use the designation *Tech in Surgery-Certified, TS-C (NCCT)*. This certification must be renewed every five years through either continuing education or reexamination.

Surgical technologists need manual dexterity sufficient to handle instruments quickly. They also must be conscientious, orderly, and emotionally stable to handle the demands of the operating room environment. Technologists must respond quickly and be familiar enough with operating room procedures to have instruments on hand for surgeons as needed. They are expected to keep abreast of new developments in the field.

Advancement. Technologists advance by specializing in a particular area of surgery, such as neurosurgery or open-heart surgery. They also may work as circulating technologists. With additional training, some technologists advance to surgical first assistant. Some surgical technologists manage central supply departments in hospitals, or take positions with insurance companies, sterile supply services, and operating equipment firms.

EMPLOYMENT TRENDS

Employment of surgical technologists is expected to grow much faster than the average for all occupations. Job opportunities will be best for technologists who are certified.

Employment Change. Employment of surgical technologists is expected to grow 24 percent between 2006 and 2016, much faster than the average for all occupations, as the volume of surgeries increases. The number of surgical procedures is expected to rise as the population grows and ages. Older people, including the baby boom generation, who generally require more surgical procedures, will account for a larger portion of the general population. In addition, technological advances, such as fiber optics and laser technology, will permit an increasing number of new surgical procedures to be performed and also will allow surgical technologists to assist with a greater number of procedures.

Hospitals will continue to be the primary employer of surgical technologists, although much faster employment growth is expected in offices of physicians and in outpatient care centers, including ambulatory surgical centers.

Job Prospects. Job opportunities will be best for technologists who are certified. **Table 22–3** shows some projection data provided by the Department of Labor.

Table 22–3

Projections data from the National Employment Matrix				
Occupational title	Employment, 2006	Projected employment, 2016	Change, 2006–2016	
			Number	Percent
Surgical technologists	86,000	107,000	21,000	24

NOTE: Data in this table are rounded.

EARNINGS

Median annual earnings of wage-and-salary surgical technologists were $36,080 in May 2006. The middle 50 percent earned between $30,300 and $43,560. The lowest 10 percent earned less than $25,490, and the highest 10 percent earned more than $51,140. Median annual earnings in the industries employing the largest numbers of surgical technologists is shown in **Table 22–4**.

Table 22–4	*Median annual earnings in the industries employing the largest numbers of surgical technologists in May 2006*
Offices of physicians	$37,300
Outpatient care centers	$37,280
General medical and surgical hospitals	$35,840
Offices of dentists	$34,160

Benefits provided by most employers include paid vacation and sick leave; health, medical, vision, dental, and life insurance; and retirement programs. A few employers also provide tuition reimbursement and child care benefits.

RELATED OCCUPATIONS

Other health occupations requiring approximately one year of training after high school include dental assistants, licensed practical and licensed vocational nurses, clinical laboratory technologists and technicians, and medical assistants.

ADDITIONAL INFORMATION

For additional information on a career as a surgical technologist and a list of CAAHEP-accredited programs, contact:

■ Association of Surgical Technologists, 6 West Dry Creek Circle, Suite 200, Littleton, CO 80120. http://www.ast.org

For information on becoming a Certified Surgical Technologist, contact:

■ Liaison Council on Certification for the Surgical Technologist, 6 West Dry Creek Circle, Suite 100, Littleton, CO 80120. http://www.lcc-st.org

For information on becoming a Tech in Surgery-Certified, contact:

■ National Center for Competency Testing, 7007 College Blvd., Suite 705, Overland Park, KS 66211.

Medical, Dental, and Ophthalmic Laboratory Technicians

WORK DESCRIPTIONS

When patients require a medical device to help them see clearly, chew and speak well, or walk better, their healthcare providers send requests for such devices to medical, dental, and ophthalmic laboratory technicians. These technicians produce a variety of implements to help patients.

Medical appliance technicians construct, fit, maintain, and repair braces, artificial limbs, joints, arch supports, and other surgical and medical appliances. They follow prescriptions or detailed instructions from podiatrists or orthotists, who request braces, supports, corrective shoes, or other devises. They also follow the instructions of prosthetists in constructing replacement limbs—arms, legs, hands, or feet—for patients who need them due to a birth defect, accident, or amputation. Other health professionals may also order medical appliances to be produced by medical appliance technicians. Medical appliance technicians who work with orthotic and prosthetic devices are called orthotic and prosthetic technicians. Other medical appliance technicians work with medical appliances that help correct other medical problems, such as aids to correct hearing loss.

Creating medical devices takes several steps. To make arch supports, for example, technicians first make a wax or plastic impression of the patient's foot. Then they bend and form a material so that it conforms to prescribed contours required to fabricate structural components. If a support is mainly required to correct the balance of a patient with legs of different lengths, a rigid material is used. If the support is primarily intended to protect those with arthritic or diabetic feet, a soft material is used. Supports and braces are polished with grinding and buffing wheels. Technicians may cover arch supports with felt to make them more comfortable.

For prostheses, technicians construct or receive a plaster cast of the patient's limb to use as a pattern. Then, they lay out parts and use precision measuring instruments to measure them. Technicians may use wood, plastic, metal, or other material for the parts of the artificial limb. Next, they carve, cut, or grind the material using hand or power tools. Then, they drill holes for rivets and glue, rivet, or weld the parts together. They are able to do very precise work using common tools. Next, technicians use grinding and buffing wheels to smooth and polish artificial limbs. Lastly, they may cover or pad the limbs with rubber, leather, felt, plastic, or another material. Also, technicians may mix pigments according to formulas to match the patient's skin color and apply the mixture to the artificial limb.

After fabrication, medical appliance technicians test devices for proper alignment, movement, and biomechanical stability using meters and alignment fixtures. They also may fit the appliance on the patient and adjust it as necessary. Over time the appliance will wear down, so technicians must repair and maintain the device. They also may service and repair the machinery used for the fabrication of orthotic and prosthetic devices.

Dental laboratory technicians fill prescriptions from dentists for crowns, bridges, dentures, and other dental prosthetics. First, dentists send a specification of the item to be manufactured, along with an impression or mold of the patient's mouth or teeth. With new technology, a technician may receive a digital impression rather than a physical mold. Then dental laboratory technicians, also called dental technicians, create a model of the patient's mouth by pouring plaster into the impression and allowing it to set. They place the model on an apparatus that mimics the bite and movement of the patient's jaw. The model serves as the basis of the prosthetic device. Technicians examine the model, noting the size and shape of the adjacent teeth, as well as gaps within the gum line. Based upon these observations and the dentist's specifications, technicians build and shape a wax tooth or teeth model, using small hand instruments called wax spatulas and wax carvers. The wax model is used to cast the metal framework for the prosthetic device.

After the wax tooth has been formed, dental technicians pour the cast and form the metal and, using small hand-held tools, prepare the surface to allow the metal and porcelain to bond. They then apply porcelain in layers, to arrive at the precise shape and color of a tooth. Technicians place the tooth in a porcelain furnace to bake the porcelain onto the metal framework, and then adjust the shape and color, with subsequent grinding and addition of porcelain to achieve a sealed finish. The final product is a nearly exact replica of the lost tooth or teeth.

In some dental laboratories, technicians perform all stages of the work, whereas in other labs, each technician works on only a few. Dental laboratory technicians can specialize in one of five areas: orthodontic appliances, crowns and bridges, complete dentures, partial dentures, or ceramics. Job titles can reflect specialization in these areas. For example, technicians who make porcelain and acrylic restorations are called *dental ceramists*.

Ophthalmic laboratory technicians—also known as manufacturing opticians, optical mechanics, or optical goods workers—make prescription eyeglass or contact lenses. Prescription lenses are curved in such a way that light is correctly focused onto the retina of the patient's eye, improving his or her vision. Some ophthalmic laboratory technicians manufacture lenses for other optical instruments, such as telescopes and binoculars. Ophthalmic laboratory technicians cut, grind, edge, and finish lenses according to specifications provided by dispensing opticians, optometrists, or ophthalmologists and may insert lenses into frames to produce finished glasses. Although some lenses still are produced by hand, technicians are increasingly using automated equipment to make lenses.

Ophthalmic laboratory technicians should not be confused with workers in other vision care occupations. Ophthalmologists and optometrists are "eye doctors" who examine eyes, diagnose and treat vision problems, and prescribe corrective lenses. Ophthalmologists are physicians who also perform eye surgery. Dispensing opticians, who also may do the work of ophthalmic laboratory technicians, help patients select frames and lenses, and adjust finished eyeglasses. (See chapter on physicians and surgeons, which includes ophthalmologists.)

Ophthalmic laboratory technicians read prescription specifications, select standard glass or plastic lens blanks, and then mark them to indicate where the curves specified on the prescription should be ground. They place the lens in the lens grinder, set the dials for the prescribed curvature, and start the machine. After a minute or so, the lens is ready to be "finished" by a machine that rotates it against a fine abrasive to grind it and smooth out rough edges. The lens is then placed in a polishing machine with an even finer abrasive, to polish it to a smooth, bright finish.

Next, the technician examines the lens through a lensometer, an instrument similar in shape to a microscope, to make sure that the degree and placement of the curve are correct. The technician then cuts the lenses and bevels the edges to fit the frame, dips each lens into dye if the prescription calls for tinted or coated lenses, polishes the edges, and assembles the lenses and frame parts into a finished pair of glasses.

In small laboratories, technicians usually handle every phase of the operation. In large ones, in which virtually every phase of the operation is automated, technicians may be responsible for operating computerized equipment. Technicians also inspect the final product for quality and accuracy.

WORK ENVIRONMENT

Medical, dental, and ophthalmic laboratory technicians generally work in clean, well-lighted, and well-ventilated laboratories. They have limited contact with the public. Salaried laboratory technicians usually work 40 hours a week, but some work part-time. At times, technicians wear goggles to protect their eyes, gloves to handle hot objects, or masks to avoid inhaling dust. They may spend a great deal of time standing.

Dental technicians usually have their own workbenches, which can be equipped with Bunsen burners, grinding and polishing equipment, and hand instruments, such as wax spatulas and wax carvers. Some dental technicians have computer-aided milling equipment to assist them with creating artificial teeth.

EMPLOYMENT OPPORTUNITIES

Medical, dental, and ophthalmic laboratory technicians held about 95,000 jobs in 2006. About 55 percent of salaried jobs were in medical equipment and supply manufacturing laboratories, which usually are small, privately owned businesses with fewer than five employees. However, some laboratories are large; a few employ more than 1,000 workers. **Table 22–5** shows employment by detailed occupation.

In addition to manufacturing laboratories, many medical appliance technicians worked in health and personal care stores, while others worked in public and private hospitals, professional and commercial equipment and supplies merchant wholesalers, or consumer goods rental centers. Some were self-employed.

Table 22–5

Employment by detailed occupation	
Dental laboratory technicians	53,000
Ophthalmic laboratory technicians	29,000
Medical appliance technicians	12,000

In addition to manufacturing laboratories, many dental laboratory technicians worked in offices of dentists. Some dental laboratory technicians open their own offices.

Most ophthalmic laboratory technician jobs, about 29 percent, were in medical equipment and supplies manufacturing laboratories, Another 29 percent of jobs were in health and personal care stores, such as optical goods stores that manufacture and sell prescription glasses and contact lenses. Some jobs were in offices of optometrists or ophthalmologists, while others were found at professional and commercial equipment and supplies merchant wholesalers. A few ophthalmic laboratory technicians worked in commercial and service industry machine manufacturing firms that produce lenses for other optical instruments, such as telescopes and binoculars.

EDUCATIONAL AND LEGAL REQUIREMENTS

Most medical, dental, and ophthalmic laboratory technicians learn their craft on the job; many employers, however, prefer to hire those with formal training.

Education and Training. High school students interested in becoming medical appliance technicians should take mathematics, metal and wood shop, and drafting. Medical appliance technicians usually begin as helpers and gradually learn new skills as they gain experience.

Formal training is also available. In 2006, there were four orthotic and prosthetic technician programs accredited by the *National Commission on Orthotic and Prosthetic Education (NCOPE)*. These programs offer either an associate degree or a one-year certificate for orthotic or prosthetic technicians. The programs instruct students on human anatomy and physiology, orthotic and prosthetic equipment and materials, and applied biomechanical principles to customize orthotics or prostheses. The programs also include clinical rotations to provide hands-on experience.

Dental laboratory technicians begin by learning simple tasks, such as pouring plaster into an impression, and progress to more complex procedures, such as making porcelain crowns and bridges. Becoming a fully trained technician requires an average of three to four years, depending upon the individual's aptitude and ambition, but it may take a few years more to become an accomplished technician. High school students interested in becoming dental laboratory technicians should take courses in art, metal and wood shop, drafting, and sciences. Courses in management and business may help those wishing to operate their own laboratories.

Training in dental laboratory technology also is available through community and junior colleges, vocational-technical institutes, and the armed forces. Formal training programs vary greatly both in length and in the level of skill they impart. In 2006, 20 programs in dental laboratory technology were accredited by the *Commission on Dental Accreditation* in conjunction with the *American Dental Association*. These programs provide classroom instruction in materials science, oral anatomy, fabrication procedures, ethics, and related subjects. In addition, each student is given supervised practical experience in a school or an associated dental laboratory. Accredited programs normally take two years to complete and lead to an associate degree. A few programs take about four years to complete and offer a bachelor's degree in dental technology. Graduates of two-year training programs need additional hands-on experience to become fully qualified.

Each dental laboratory owner operates in a different way, and classroom instruction does not necessarily expose students to techniques and procedures favored by individual laboratory owners. Students who have taken enough courses to learn the basics of the craft usually are considered good candidates for training, regardless of whether they have completed a formal program. Many employers will train someone without any classroom experience.

Ophthalmic laboratory technicians start on simple tasks if they are training to produce lenses by hand. They may begin with marking or blocking lenses for grinding; then progress to grinding, cutting, edging, and beveling lenses; and finally to assembling the eyeglasses. Depending on individual aptitude, it may take up to six months to become proficient in all phases of the work.

Employers filling trainee jobs prefer applicants who are high school graduates. Courses in science, mathematics, and computers are valuable; manual dexterity and the ability to do precision work are essential. Technicians using automated systems will find computer skills valuable.

A few ophthalmic laboratory technicians learn their trade in the armed forces or in the few programs in optical technology offered by vocational-technical institutes or trade schools. These programs have classes in optical theory, surfacing and lens finishing, and the reading and applying of prescriptions. Programs vary in length from six months to one year and award certificates or diplomas.

Other Qualifications. Dental technicians need a high degree of manual dexterity, good vision, and the ability to recognize very fine color shadings and variations in shape. An artistic aptitude for detailed and precise work also is important.

Certification and Advancement. Voluntary certification for orthotic and prosthetic technicians is available through the *American Board for Certification in Orthotics and Prosthetics (ABC).* Applicants are eligible for an exam after completing a program accredited by NCOPE, or obtaining two years of experience as a technician under the direct supervision of an ABC-certified practitioner. After successfully passing the appropriate exam, technicians receive the *Registered Orthotic Technician, Registered Prosthetic Technician,* or *Registered Prosthetic-Orthotic Technician* credential. Certification may help those orthotic and prosthetic technicians seeking to advance.

With additional formal education, medical appliance technicians who make orthotics and prostheses can advance to become orthotists or prosthetists, technicians who work with patients who need braces, artificial limbs, or related devices and help to determine the specifications for those devices.

In large dental laboratories, dental technicians may become supervisors or managers. Experienced technicians may teach or take jobs with dental suppliers in such areas as product development, marketing, and sales. Opening one's own laboratory is another, and more common, way to advance and earn more.

The *National Board for Certification,* an independent board established by the *National Association of Dental Laboratories,* offers certification in dental laboratory technology. Certification, which is voluntary except in three states, can be obtained in five specialty areas: crowns and bridges, ceramics, partial dentures, complete dentures, and orthodontic appliances. Certification may increase chances of advancement. Ophthalmic laboratory technicians can become supervisors and managers. Some become dispensing opticians, although further education or training generally is required in that occupation.

EMPLOYMENT TRENDS

Overall, slower-than-average growth is expected for employment of medical, dental, and ophthalmic laboratory technicians. However, job opportunities should be favorable because few people seek these positions.

Employment Change. Overall employment for these occupations is expected to grow 5 percent from 2006 to 2016, slower than the average for all occupations.

Employment of medical appliance technicians will grow at 9 percent, about as fast as the average for all occupations, because of the increasing prevalence of the two leading causes of limb loss—diabetes and cardiovascular disease. In addition, advances in technology may spur demand for prostheses that allow for greater movement.

Employment of dental laboratory technicians is expected to grow more slowly than average, at 4 percent. During the last few years, demand has arisen from an aging public that is growing increasingly interested in cosmetic prostheses. For example, many dental laboratories are filling orders for composite fillings that are the same shade of white as natural teeth to replace older, less attractive fillings. However, job growth for dental laboratory technicians will be limited. The overall dental health of the population has improved because of fluoridation of drinking water and greater emphasis on preventive dental care, which has reduced the incidence of dental cavities. As a result, full dentures will be less common, as most people will need only a bridge or crown.

Ophthalmic laboratory technicians are expected to experience employment growth of 7 percent, about as fast as the average for all occupations. Demographic trends make it likely that many more Americans will need vision care in the years ahead. Not only will the population grow, but also the proportion of middle-aged and older adults is projected to increase rapidly. Middle age is a time when many people use corrective lenses for the first time, and elderly persons usually require more vision care than others. However, the increasing use of automated machinery will temper job growth for ophthalmic laboratory technicians.

Job Prospects. Job opportunities for medical, dental, and ophthalmic laboratory technicians should be favorable, despite expected slower-than-average growth. Few people seek these jobs, reflecting the relatively limited public awareness and low starting wages. In addition to openings from job growth, many job openings also will arise from the need to replace technicians who transfer to other occupations or who leave the labor force. **Table 22–6** shows some projection data provided by the Department of Labor.

EARNINGS

Median hourly earnings of wage-and-salary medical appliance technicians were $14.99 in May 2006. The middle 50 percent earned between $11.34 and $19.65 an hour. The lowest 10 percent earned less than $8.93, and the highest 10 percent earned more than $27.00 an hour.

Median hourly earnings of wage-and-salary dental laboratory technicians were $15.67 in May 2006. The middle 50 percent earned between $11.61 and $20.57 an hour. The lowest 10 percent earned less than $9.16, and the highest 10 percent earned more than $26.13 an hour. In the two industries that employed the most dental laboratory technicians, medical equipment and supplies manufacturing and offices of dentists, median hourly earnings were $15.09 and $17.74, respectively.

Table
22–6

Projections data from the National Employment Matrix

Occupational title	Employment, 2006	Projected employment, 2016	Change, 2006–2016	
			Number	Percent
Medical, dental, and ophthalmic laboratory technicians	95,000	100,000	5,000	5
Dental laboratory technicians	53,000	55,000	2,000	4
Medical appliance technicians	12,000	13,000	1,200	9
Ophthalmic laboratory technicians	29,000	31,000	1,900	7

NOTE: Data in this table are rounded.

Median hourly earnings of wage-and-salary ophthalmic laboratory technicians were $12.24 in May 2006. The middle 50 percent earned between $9.86 and $15.82 an hour. The lowest 10 percent earned less than $8.38, and the highest 10 percent earned more than $19.98 an hour. Median hourly earnings were $11.63 in medical equipment and supplies manufacturing and $11.49 in health and personal care stores, the two industries that employ the most ophthalmic laboratory technicians.

RELATED OCCUPATIONS

Medical, dental, and ophthalmic laboratory technicians manufacture and work with the same devices that are used by dispensing opticians and orthotists and prosthetists. Other occupations that work with or manufacture goods using similar tools and skills are precision instrument and equipment repair, and textile, apparel, and furnishings occupations.

ADDITIONAL INFORMATION

For information on careers in orthotics and prosthetics, contact:

■ American Academy of Orthotists and Prosthetists, 526 King St., Suite 201, Alexandria, VA 22314. http://www.opcareers.org

For a list of accredited programs for orthotic and prosthetic technicians, contact:

■ National Commission on Orthotic and Prosthetic Education, 330 John Carlyle St., Suite 200, Alexandria, VA 22314. http://www.ncope.org

For information on requirements for certification of orthotic and prosthetic technicians, contact:

■ American Board for Certification in Orthotics and Prosthetics, 330 John Carlyle St., Suite 210, Alexandria, VA 22314. http://www.abcop.org

For a list of accredited programs in dental laboratory technology, contact:

■ Commission on Dental Accreditation, American Dental Association, 211 E. Chicago Ave., Chicago, IL 60611. http://www.ada.org

For information on requirements for certification of dental laboratory technicians, contact:

■ National Board for Certification in Dental Technology, 325 John Knox Rd., L103, Tallahassee, FL 32303. http://www.nbccert.org

For information on career opportunities in commercial dental laboratories, contact:

■ National Association of Dental Laboratories, 325 John Knox Rd., L103, Tallahassee, FL 32303. http://www.nadl.org

For information on an accredited program in ophthalmic laboratory technology, contact:

■ Commission on Opticianry Accreditation, P.O. Box 4342, Chapel Hill, NC 27515.

General information on grants and scholarships is available from individual schools. State employment service offices can provide information about job openings for medical, dental, and ophthalmic laboratory technicians.

ADDITIONAL HEALTH THERAPISTS, ASSISTANTS, AND AIDES

Key Terms

- Art therapy
- Corrective therapy
- Dance therapy
- Horticultural therapy

- Manual arts therapy
- Music therapy
- Recreational therapy

Health and Therapists

The objective of therapy is to help individuals with physical, mental, or social handicaps to regain their capacity for self-help and interdependence. To meet this goal, different kinds of therapists are employed, each with special knowledge and skills that can be used in rehabilitation. For example, art, dance, and music therapists bring both artistic and therapeutic skills to their work and try to improve the mental and physical well-being of their patients. Dance and art techniques are used as nonverbal means of communication, and, along with music, are often useful in helping patients resolve physical, emotional, and social problems. Horticultural therapists use gardening, an enjoyable and relaxing activity, for such purposes as training disabled or handicapped patients, evaluating the abilities of patients, or as a social activity for patients. Corrective therapists treat their patients by using medically prescribed exercises and activities. Physical therapists work with persons who are physically disabled by illness, accident, or birth defects. They use exercise and such treatments as heat, cold, and electricity to improve the patient's condition. (See Chapter 20.)

Occupational therapists help individuals with physical or emotional disabilities by teaching daily living skills or job skills. (See Chapter 21.) Manual arts therapists use industrial arts such as graphics or wood or metal working to rehabilitate their patients. Recreation therapists use sports, games, crafts, camping, and hobbies as part of the rehabilitation of ill, disabled, or handicapped persons. Athletic trainers care for and try to prevent injuries of individuals engaged in professional, amateur, and school athletics.

Persons whose limbs are lost or disabled through injury, disease, or birth defects require highly skilled and specialized services, provided by orthopedists and prosthetists. Orthopedists make and fit orthopedic braces, while prosthetists make and fit artificial limbs.

Speech pathologists and audiologists work with children and adults who have speech, language, or hearing impairments. Rehabilitation counselors help persons with physical, mental, or social problems return to or begin a normal life by obtaining satisfactory work.

Therapy and its related activities offer a broad spectrum of opportunities for career exploration by interested individuals; the following pages will explore in greater detail some of the specializations not described in previous chapters.

Recreational Therapists

WORK DESCRIPTIONS

Recreational therapists, also referred to as *therapeutic recreation specialists*, provide treatment services and recreation activities for individuals with disabilities or illnesses. Using a variety of techniques, including arts and crafts, animals, sports, games, dance and movement, drama, music, and community outings, therapists improve and maintain the physical, mental, and emotional well-being of their clients. Therapists help individuals reduce depression, stress, and anxiety; recover basic motor functioning and reasoning abilities; build confidence; and socialize effectively so that they can enjoy greater independence and reduce or eliminate the effects of their illness or disability. In addition, therapists help people with disabilities integrate into the community by teaching them how to use community resources and recreational activities. Recreational therapists are different from recreation workers, who organize recreational activities primarily for enjoyment.

In acute healthcare settings, such as hospitals and rehabilitation centers, recreational therapists treat and rehabilitate individuals with specific health conditions, usually in conjunction or collaboration with physicians, nurses, psychologists, social workers, and physical and occupational therapists. In long-term and residential care facilities, recreational therapists use leisure activities—especially structured group programs—to improve and maintain their clients' general health and well-being. They also may provide interventions to prevent the client from suffering further medical problems and complications.

Recreational therapists assess clients by gathering information from observations, medical records, standardized assessments, medical staff, clients' families, and clients themselves. Based on this information they develop and carry out therapeutic interventions consistent with the clients' needs and interests. For example, they may encourage clients who are isolated from others or who have limited social skills to play games with others, and they may teach right-handed people with right-side paralysis how to use their unaffected left side to throw a ball or swing a racket. Recreational therapists may instruct patients in relaxation techniques to reduce stress and tension, in stretching and limbering exercises, proper body mechanics for participation in recreational activities, pacing and energy conservation techniques, and team activities. As they work, therapists observe and document a patient's participation, reactions, and progress.

Community-based recreational therapists may work in park and recreation departments, special-education programs for school districts, or assisted-living, adult day care, and substance abuse rehabilitation centers. In these programs, therapists use interventions to develop specific skills, while providing opportunities for exercise, mental stimulation, creativity, and fun. Those few who work in schools help counselors, teachers, and parents address the special needs of students, including easing disabled students' transition into adult life.

WORK ENVIRONMENT

Recreational therapists provide services in special activity rooms, but also use offices to plan their activities and prepare documentation. When working with clients during community integration programs, they may travel locally to teach clients how to use public transportation and other public amenities, such as parks, playgrounds, swimming pools, restaurants, and theaters. Therapists often lift and carry equipment. Recreational therapists generally work a 40-hour week that may include some evenings, weekends, and holidays.

EMPLOYMENT OPPORTUNITIES

Recreational therapists held about 25,000 jobs in 2006. About 70 percent of these were in nursing and residential care facilities and hospitals. Other recreational therapists worked in state and local government agencies and in community care facilities for the elderly, including assisted-living facilities. The rest worked primarily in residential mental retardation, mental health, and substance abuse facilities; individual and family services; federal government agencies; educational services; and outpatient care centers. Only a small number of therapists were self-employed, generally contracting with long-term care facilities or community agencies to develop and oversee programs.

EDUCATIONAL AND LEGAL REQUIREMENTS

A bachelor's degree with a major or concentration in therapeutic recreation is the usual requirement for entry-level positions. Some states regulate recreational therapists, but requirements vary.

Education and Training. Most entry-level recreational therapists need a bachelor's degree in therapeutic recreation, or in recreation with a concentration in therapeutic recreation. People may qualify for paraprofessional positions with an associate degree in therapeutic recreation or another subject related to health care. An associate degree in recreational therapy; training in art, drama, or music therapy; or qualifying work experience may be sufficient for activity director positions in nursing homes.

Approximately 130 academic programs prepare students to become recreational therapists. Most offer bachelor's degrees, although some also offer associate, master's, or doctoral degrees. Therapeutic recreation programs include courses in assessment, treatment and program planning, intervention design, and evaluation. Students also study human anatomy, physiology, abnormal psychology, medical and psychiatric terminology, characteristics of illnesses and disabilities, professional ethics, and the use of assistive devices and technology.

Licensure. Some states regulate recreational therapists through licensure, registration, or regulation of titles. Requirements vary by state. In 2006, North Carolina, Utah, and New Hampshire required licensure to practice as a recreational therapist.

Certification and Other Qualifications. Although certification is usually voluntary, most employers prefer to hire candidates who are certified therapeutic recreation specialists. In 2006, about three out of four recreational therapists worked in a clinical setting, which often requires certification by the *National Council for Therapeutic Recreation Certification.* The council offers the *Certified Therapeutic Recreation Specialist* credential to candidates who have a bachelor's or graduate degree from an accredited educational institution, pass a written certification examination, and complete a supervised internship of at least 480 hours. Therapists must meet additional requirements to maintain certification. Therapists can also earn certifications in specific areas, such as art therapy and aquatic therapy.

Recreational therapists must be comfortable working with people who are ill or disabled. Therapists must be patient, tactful, and persuasive when working with people who have a variety of special needs. Ingenuity, a sense of humor, and imagination are needed to adapt activities to individual needs, and good physical coordination is necessary to demonstrate or participate in recreational activities.

Advancement. Therapists may advance to supervisory or administrative positions. Some teach, conduct research, or consult for health or social service agencies.

Employment Trends. Overall employment of recreational therapists is expected to grow more slowly than the average for all occupations. Competition for jobs is expected.

Employment Change. Employment of recreational therapists is expected to increase 4 percent from 2006 to 2016, slower than the average for all occupations. Employment of recreational therapists will grow to meet the therapy needs of the increasing number of older adults. In nursing care facilities—the largest industry employing recreational therapists—employment will grow slightly faster than the occupation as a whole as the number of older adults continues to grow. Fast employment growth is expected in the residential and outpatient settings that serve people who are physically disabled, cognitively disabled, elderly, or have mental illness or substance abuse problems. Employment is expected to decline in hospitals, however, as services shift to outpatient settings and employers emphasize cost containment.

Healthcare facilities will support a growing number of jobs in adult day care and outpatient settings offering short-term mental health and alcohol or drug abuse treatment services. Rehabilitation, home health care, and transitional programs will provide additional jobs.

Job Prospects. Recreational therapists will experience competition for jobs. Job opportunities should be best for people with a bachelor's degree in therapeutic recreation or in recreation with courses in therapeutic recreation. Opportunities also should be good for therapists who hold specialized certifications such as aquatic therapy, meditation, or crisis intervention. Recreational therapists might experience more competition for jobs in certain regions of the country. **Table 23–1** shows some projection data provided by the Department of Labor.

Table 23–1

Projections data from the National Employment Matrix				
Occupational title	Employment, 2006	Projected employment, 2016	Change, 2006–2016	
			Number	Percent
Recreational therapists	25,000	26,000	900	4

NOTE: Data in this table are rounded.

EARNINGS

Median annual earnings of recreational therapists were $34,990 in May 2006. The middle 50 percent earned between $26,780 and $44,850. The lowest 10 percent earned less than $20,880, and the highest 10 percent earned more than $55,530. Median annual earnings in the industries employing the largest numbers of recreational therapists in May 2006 are included in **Table 23–2**.

RELATED OCCUPATIONS

Recreational therapists primarily design activities to help people with disabilities lead more fulfilling and independent lives. Other workers who have similar jobs are occupational therapists, physical therapists, recreation workers, rehabilitation counselors, and special education teachers.

Table 23-2 *Median annual earnings in the industries employing the largest numbers of recreational therapists in May 2006*

General medical and surgical hospitals	$39,320
State government	$38,260
Psychiatric and substance abuse hospitals	$37,560
Nursing care facilities	$30,440
Community care facilities for the elderly	$28,980

ADDITIONAL INFORMATION

For information and materials on careers and academic programs in recreational therapy, contact:

■ American Therapeutic Recreation Association, 1414 Prince St., Suite 204, Alexandria, VA 22314-2853. http://www.atra-tr.org

■ National Therapeutic Recreation Society, 22377 Belmont Ridge Rd., Ashburn, VA 20148-4501. http://www.nrpa.org/content/default.aspx?documentid=530

Information on certification may be obtained from:

■ National Council for Therapeutic Recreation Certification, 7 Elmwood Dr., New City, NY 10956. http://www.nctrc.org

For information on licensure requirements, contact the appropriate recreational therapy regulatory agency for your state.

Behavioral Therapists

AN OVERVIEW

A behavioral therapist is a trained professional who uses common human behavioral modifications to improve the quality of life for a patient with a health problem. For example, a person may be depressed after surgery. Recovery may be better and faster if the patient is assisted by an art therapist. That is, the patient is assisted or encouraged to develop the enjoyment of painting, going to museums, visiting homes of famous artists and so on. Obviously the process of behavioral modification is much more complicated than, for example, going to a museum. Thus, there are therapists specializing in modifying a patient's behavior or attitude towards art, dance, horticulture, music and so on.

This chapter will discuss some of the most common or popular aspects of working as a behavioral therapist, but with the following premises in mind:

- Educational and legal requirements are highly variable because practically every state has its own. It is not possible to provide standard information.

The pay scale is also highly variable in both private and public sectors, varying from state to state, county to county, and city to city.

The same applies to employment trends.

As a result, there is not a single source in the federal government for an interested party to obtain reliable information. In view of this, there are two ways to obtain information and assistance:

- Employment bureaus, human resource departments, and similar units exist in the central government of each state. The easiest way to obtain relevant information is to use the state Web site to find specific data for each job category of behavioral therapy, for example, art therapists.

Practically every job category of behavior therapy is represented and promoted by its own nonprofit trade association. Most offer up-to-date employment information. The short list is provided below:

American Art Therapy Association, Inc.
5999 Stevenson Ave.
Alexandria, VA 22304
http://www.arttherapy.org/

American Dance Therapy Association (ADTA)
Suite 108
10632 Little Patuxent Parkway
Columbia, MD 21044
http://www.adta.org

The American Horticultural Therapy Association
201 East Main Street, Suite 1405
Lexington, KY 40507-2004
http://www.ahta.org/

American Kinesiology (Corrective) Therapy Association
118 College Drive, #5142
Hattiesburg, MS 39406
http://www.akta.org/

American Music Therapy Association, Inc.
8455 Colesville Road, Suite 1000
Silver Spring, MD 20910
http://www.musictherapy.org

National Coalition of Arts Therapy Associations
2000 Century Plz., Suite. 108
Columbia, MD 21044
http://www.nccata.org/
[Manual Art Therapy]

ART THERAPISTS

Expressing ideas and feelings through art and achieving some sense of well-being as a result is a very old concept. Pictures scratched or painted by primitive man have been found on cave walls, and many ancient tools and objects were designed to be not only useful but also artistically pleasing. Exactly what made the cave dwellers and their ancestors draw the pictures or design the objects is not known, but we can assume that they must have received some sort of emotional satisfaction from creating them. *Art therapy* is based on the use of art as a device for nonverbal expression and communication. Art therapy attempts to resolve the individual's emotional conflicts and encourages personal growth and self-understanding.

The most practical application of art therapy has been with those suffering from mental disorders, mental retardation, or other problems of social and psychological development, but innovative work has also been done on a variety of other problems. Art therapists confer with members of the medical health team to diagnose patients' problems. Combining art, education, and insight, art therapists assess their patients' problems, strengths, and weaknesses, and determine a course of treatment best suited to accomplish specific treatment goals. Art therapists plan art activities, maintain and distribute supplies and materials, provide art instruction, and observe and record the various interactions that occur during therapy sessions. Emphasis is not placed on the quality of the product, but rather on the well-being of the patient. Art therapists often work as members of teams of other professionals and coordinate their activities with those of other therapists.

Art therapists work with people of all ages who have various degrees of impairment. They may practice with individuals, groups, or families in clinical, educational, or rehabilitative settings, which include private psychiatric hospitals and clinics, community health centers, geriatric centers, drug and alcohol clinics, nursing homes, halfway houses, prisons, public and private schools, and institutions for the emotionally disturbed, learning disabled, brain damaged, deaf, blind, physically handicapped, and multiple disabled. Many art therapists who work in clinics also teach art therapy in colleges or universities, and may do research on some aspect of therapy. However, the primary involvement of most art therapists is with clients in some type of clinical setting.

Art therapists normally work a 40-hour week, although the hours and degree of responsibility vary with the setting. The facilities in which they work are usually fully equipped with art materials, tables, chairs, art desks, and storage areas; general working conditions are good.

CORRECTIVE THERAPISTS

Corrective therapy treats patients by applying medically prescribed physical exercises and activities to strengthen and coordinate body functions and prevent muscular deterioration caused by inactivity due to illness. *Corrective therapists* apply the principles, tools, techniques, and psychology of medically oriented physical education to help persons with physical and mental problems meet their treatment goals. Corrective therapists design or adjust equipment and devise exercises to meet the needs of patients. They instruct patients in proper exercise techniques and equipment usage to meet specified objectives such as walking, joint flexibility, endurance, strength, and emotional self-confidence and security. For the physically handicapped, the exercise routines are aimed at developing strength, dexterity, and muscle coordination. Therapists teach exercise routines to patients who use wheelchairs, instruct amputees or partially paralyzed patients how to walk and move around, and sometimes give driving lessons to handicapped persons using specially equipped automobiles. They also advise patients on the use of braces, artificial limbs, and other devices. For the emotionally ill or mentally retarded, therapists use exercises to relieve frustration or tension, or to bring about social involvement.

Corrective therapists also judge strength, endurance, and self-care ability to gauge the patient's recovery at successive stages. They participate in staff planning sessions and make hospital ward rounds as members of healthcare teams. They prepare progress reports on patients' responses to therapeutic treatment exercises and present findings orally or in writing at staff meetings and conferences. Therapists also counsel patients' family members on therapeutic matters.

Corrective therapy should not be confused with physical therapy. Physical therapists employ physical agents such as heat, water, and light in treatment routines, and perform tests to determine nerve, muscle, and skin condition and reaction. Corrective therapy is used mainly in the more advanced stages of rehabilitation where functional training is required.

Some corrective therapists choose areas of specialization. Corrective therapists who specialize in driver training are concerned with teaching handicapped persons safe driving methods, developing their remaining skills, and teaching them to use special driving devices. Seminars and workshops in driver training are required for this specialization, and therapists working in this area are primarily employed by the Veterans Administration. Corrective therapists who specialize in cardiac rehabilitation check patients' pulmonary function, establish work performance limits, and establish levels of progression to attain optimal fitness capabilities. Therapists receive specialized training in cardiopulmonary theory, methodology, and techniques and the use of specialized equipment. Some corrective therapists are beginning to specialize in therapeutic pool work in numerous hospital and health education sites. This specialization requires water safety certifications, such as those given by the Red Cross or YMCA/YWCA, and knowledge of the effects of water activities and effects of water on exercise performance.

Corrective therapists work in a variety of government, public, and private facilities, including hospitals, rehabilitation clinics, schools, colleges, nursing homes, special schools, recreation facilities, and camps for the handicapped. They work a 40-hour week, usually in an indoor setting, although outdoor recreation areas and pools are also used. A variety of physical demands are involved in being a corrective therapist, including demonstrating exercises and equipment use, lifting and balancing patients, and handling and adjusting therapeutic exercise equipment.

DANCE THERAPISTS

For centuries, dancing and related types of body movement have been recognized and used as a form of entertainment and as a way to ease tension and obtain other physical and emotional benefits. For many, this type of physical activity renews emotional well-being, encourages self-expression, and recharges energy drained by the frustrations of everyday living. For these reasons, dancing and body movement can be therapeutic activities. Dance therapy, used with individuals who have emotional and often physical impairments caused by injury, illness, or birth defects, has been developed by dance therapists and uses dance and body movement as a tool to further emotional and physical integration and well-being. Dance therapists take advantage of the expressive and communicative aspects of dance to help people resolve social, emotional, and physical disorders.

Dance therapists assess their clients' emotional and social behavior, movement capabilities, and general posture. They determine what types of movement experiences will best help clients develop an increased awareness of feelings and nonverbal behavior, a broader scope of interaction of mind and body, an improved body image, improved social relations, and relief from physical and emotional blocks. Working with individuals and groups, dance therapists plan and conduct movement sessions designed to achieve those goals and objectives. Dance therapists also participate in case conferences, staff meetings, community meetings, verbal therapy sessions, and other activities, depending on the setting in which they work. Some engage in research on movement behavior, teach or train others in educational or employment settings, or act as consultants to various agencies or organizations.

Dance therapy takes place in a wide variety of settings, but movement research is its only real area of specialization. The movement researcher observes, records, and analyzes nonverbal behavior in live settings, on videotape, or on film. In addition to the general knowledge and experience required of dance therapists, movement researchers must have completed advanced courses in movement observation and research methods.

Dance therapists work in a variety of mental health settings, including psychiatric hospitals, clinics, developmental centers, correctional facilities, special schools, substance abuse programs, and facilities for the aged. Registered dance therapists may also work in private practice or teach in educational facilities.

Hours and other working conditions vary, as do facilities. Some are modern and well equipped; others are older and sometimes quite sparse in terms of equipment and other elements that contribute to a pleasant work/therapy setting. Most aspects of dance therapy involve close physical contact with different types of patient groups as well as a good deal of physical activity. In all instances, strength, flexibility, stamina, and a strong desire to relate to and help others are necessary.

HORTICULTURE THERAPISTS

Horticultural therapy uses horticultural activities as the primary treatment method to bring about a beneficial change in an individual with a physical, mental, or social handicap. Horticulture therapists use gardening for a variety of purposes, such as to rehabilitate patients after illness or injury; train impaired, disabled, and handicapped persons; evaluate patients' disabilities and capabilities; and provide a social activity for physically and mentally impaired persons.

Horticulture therapists organize indoor or outdoor activities, usually in a group setting, for patients with different types of problems. They use plants and related materials to help hand-icapped individuals improve their emotional attitudes through a change in self-concept; their social skills through nonthreatening interactions with others; their physical skills through activities requiring both gross and fine-motor coordination; and their mental skills through planning, preparing, and caring for their plants. Horticulture therapists work closely with other staff members to design and conduct a program suited to the needs of the particular client. In some programs, particularly those related to vocational rehabilitation, the plants may be sold, and in this situation the therapist may also have some business responsibilities. In addition to working directly with patients, horticulture therapists often teach at local colleges or universities and conduct workshops and other training programs.

Most horticulture therapists work in public or private facilities for the handicapped, including convalescent homes, juvenile centers, schools and training centers for the mentally retarded, psychiatric hospitals, and general care hospitals. Horticulture therapists work closely with both people and plants, and the work setting is often a greenhouse or outside garden. Care of plants can be demanding, and the ability to move the hands easily and skillfully is very important. However, there are no physical requirements for the job, and handicapped individuals may, in fact, have the advantage of serving as role models for patients.

MANUAL ARTS THERAPISTS

Manual arts therapy uses mechanical, technical, and industrial activities that are voca-tionally significant to assist patients in their recovery and in maintaining, improving, or developing work skills. Under the direction of a physician, manual arts therapists develop a program of actual or simulated work situations, which help patients to prepare for an early return to their communities as well as to the world of work.

In rehabilitation, manual arts therapists apply clinical techniques for treating the physical or mental conditions of their patients, observe patient behavior, assist in patient adjustment to work situations, and evaluate manual abilities and work skills. The primary purpose is to engage patients in therapeutic activities that prove absorbing to them and help in their recov-ery, giving them a sense of confidence and achievement. These work activities also have a practical value because they serve to retrain patients in their own skills or trades or, where disability makes this reentry impossible, to help them explore and learn new work skills or avocational activities.

Manual arts therapists cooperate with other members of the patient's rehabilitation team to plan and organize work activities, while considering the patient's disabilities and capabilities. Manual arts therapy may be the only therapy prescribed for a patient, or it may be used in conjunction with other therapies in a combined treatment program. It may be prescribed at any stage in the hospitalization, depending on the patient's con-dition and rehabilitation goals.

Patients may explore various work activities offered in manual arts therapy, including wood working, metal working, electronics, printing and graphic arts, and sometimes agricul-ture. For example, a construction worker who has lost a leg in a fall may discover an interest in drawing and be taught technical drafting. A bedridden patient may learn basic electricity by using batteries and simple hookups and later advance to electronics. A patient in a wheelchair may explore jewelry or watch repair. A group of mental patients may help maintain hospital grounds. It is the job of the manual arts therapist to observe, evaluate, and guide patients in their work activities toward their rehabilitation goals.

Manual arts therapists prepare reports describing patients' emotional and social adjustment, physical performance, and work tolerance. The rehabilitation team uses these reports to judge the progress of patients and their ability to meet the physical and mental demands of their place in the community and in the world of work.

Most manual arts therapists are employed in hospitals and centers operated by the Veterans Administration, but they also work in sheltered workshops, mental health clinics, workers' compensation rehabilitation centers, and rehabilitation centers for the blind. The federal law that requires schooling for all handicapped children has opened a new field to manual arts therapy. Therapists normally work indoors from 8:00 a.m. to 4:30 p.m. five days a week, do little traveling, and generally have good working conditions. Because of the workshop setting, some noise and dust fumes are normally present, but these factors are usually controlled.

MUSIC THERAPISTS

Music therapy is an allied health profession in which music is used within a therapeutic relationship to address the physical, psychological, cognitive, and social needs of individuals.

Music has been a part of almost every culture and is recognized everywhere as having healing value. Much has been written about its effects, and it is often described as soothing, relaxing, exciting, moving, or in terms of some other emotional feeling it creates in the listener or performer. For each individual it serves a different purpose and, for some, many purposes. For those who are disabled, music may become part of medical treatment.

Music therapists understand music psychology and specialize in using music to accomplish treatment goals involving the restoration, maintenance, and improvement of mental and physical health. In its use with the mentally ill, music therapy may achieve changes in patients' behavior that will give them a new understanding of themselves and of the world around them. This new understanding can serve as a basis for improved mental health and more effective adjustment to normal living.

Often working as one member of a team that may include other therapists, psychiatrists, psychologists, social workers, and special educators, music therapists evaluate how a client might be helped through a music program. They determine what goals and objectives can probably be met and plan musical activities and experiences that are likely to meet them, on both an individual and a group basis. Music therapists treat patients of all ages, ranging from disturbed small children and adolescents to adults who suffer from mental illnesses of many types and various degrees of seriousness. The mentally retarded, those with cerebral palsy, individuals with physical impairments, and the blind make up a group that is second only to the mentally ill in the number receiving music therapy.

As members of the mental health team, music therapists devise programs to achieve aims prescribed by attending psychiatrists, and the treatment results are evaluated periodically. Music therapists may create programs of many kinds in an effort to gain and to hold the patient's interest. Much depends on the patient's potential for training; what would be possible for one would be inappropriate for another. Group singing is commonly used. Music appreciation and music education are appealing to others. Every effort is made to improve skills acquired in past years and to develop an interest that will give a new dimension to normal living.

Unlike most music programs, music therapy programs focus on the well-being of the client rather than a perfected musical product. Voice, as well as traditional and nontraditional instruments and music are used, and individual lessons are provided. In addition, instrumental and vocal music are often combined with body movements as a part of therapy.

Music therapists find employment in a variety of facilities throughout the country. They are usually employed in psychiatric hospitals, mental retardation centers, physical disability treatment and training institutions, day care centers, nursing homes, special education programs, community mental health centers, special service agencies, and other related facilities.

As in many therapy situations, music therapists work very closely with their clients and must be able to relate to them and their problems in a warm, professional manner. The work is not always a relaxing, pleasurable experience. The process of strengthening discipline and changing behavior can arouse temporary anxiety and negative attitudes. Music therapists must be able to deal with these problems when they arise and use tact and resourcefulness in solving them. They often must work in close cooperation with therapists in other disciplines when physical facilities are shared to plan and schedule activities. Standard work hours are usual, but music therapists may be called on from time to time to work evening hours and weekends.

Music therapists usually enter this career field for the stimulation of working with people in a therapy situation that involves music. There are rewards within the field itself, and there is always the possibility of being recognized for outstanding accomplishments or for having developed new and innovative methods.

Medical Assistants

WORK DESCRIPTIONS

Medical assistants perform administrative and clinical tasks to keep the offices of physicians, podiatrists, chiropractors, and other health practitioners running smoothly. They should not be confused with physician assistants, who examine, diagnose, and treat patients under the direct supervision of a physician. **(See chapter 13.)**

The duties of medical assistants vary from office to office, depending on the location and size of the practice and the practitioner's specialty. In small practices, medical assistants usually do many different kinds of tasks, handling both administrative and clinical duties and reporting directly to an office manager, physician, or other health practitioner. Those in large practices tend to specialize in a particular area, under the supervision of department administrators.

Medical assistants who perform administrative tasks have many duties. They update and file patients' medical records, fill out insurance forms, and arrange for hospital admissions and laboratory services. They also perform tasks less specific to medical settings, such as answering telephones; greeting patients; scheduling appointments; and handling correspondence, billing, and bookkeeping.

For clinical medical assistants, duties vary according to what is allowed by state law. Some common tasks include taking medical histories and recording vital signs, explaining treatment procedures to patients, preparing patients for examinations, and assisting physicians during examinations. Medical assistants collect and prepare laboratory specimens and sometimes perform basic laboratory tests on the premises, dispose of contaminated supplies, and sterilize medical instruments. They might instruct patients about medications and special diets, prepare and administer medications as directed by a physician, authorize drug refills as directed, telephone prescriptions to a pharmacy, draw blood, prepare patients for X-rays, take electrocardiograms, remove sutures, and change dressings. Medical assistants also may arrange examining room instruments and equipment, purchase and maintain supplies and equipment, and keep waiting and examining rooms neat and clean.

Ophthalmic medical assistants, optometric assistants, and *podiatric medical assistants* are examples of specialized medical assistants who have additional duties. Ophthalmic medical assistants help ophthalmologists provide eye care. They conduct diagnostic tests, measure and record vision, and test eye muscle function. They also show patients how to insert, remove, and care for contact lenses, and they apply eye dressings. Under the direction of the physician, ophthalmic medical assistants may administer eye medications. They also maintain optical and surgical instruments and may assist the ophthalmologist in surgery. Optometric assistants also help provide eye care, working with optometrists. They provide chair-side assistance, instruct patients about contact lens use and care, conduct preliminary tests on patients, and otherwise provide assistance while working directly with an optometrist. Podiatric medical assistants make castings of feet, expose and develop X-rays, and assist podiatrists in surgery.

Work Environment

Medical assistants work in well-lighted, clean environments. They constantly interact with other people and may have to handle several responsibilities at once. Most full-time medical assistants work a regular 40-hour week. However, many medical assistants work part-time, evenings, or weekends.

Employment Opportunities

Medical assistants held about 417,000 jobs in 2006. About 62 percent worked in offices of physicians; 12 percent worked in public and private hospitals, including inpatient and outpatient facilities; and 11 percent worked in offices of other health practitioners, such as chiropractors, optometrists, and podiatrists. Most of the remainder worked in other healthcare industries such as outpatient care centers and nursing and residential care facilities.

Educational and Legal Requirements

Some medical assistants are trained on the job, but many complete one-year or two-year programs.

Education and Training. Postsecondary medical assisting programs are offered in vocational-technical high schools, postsecondary vocational schools, and community and junior colleges. Programs usually last either one year and result in a certificate or diploma, or two years and result in an associate degree. Courses cover anatomy, physiology, and medical terminology, as well as typing, transcription, recordkeeping, accounting, and insurance processing. Students learn laboratory techniques, clinical and diagnostic procedures, pharmaceutical principles, the administration of medications, and first aid. They study office practices, patient relations, medical law, and ethics. There are various organizations that accredit medical assisting programs. Accredited programs often include an internship that provides practical experience in physicians' offices, hospitals, or other healthcare facilities.

Formal training in medical assisting, while generally preferred, is not always required. Some medical assistants are trained on the job, although this practice is less common than in the past. Applicants usually need a high school diploma or the equivalent. Recommended high school courses include mathematics, health, biology, typing, bookkeeping, computers, and office skills. Volunteer experience in the healthcare field also is helpful. Medical assistants who are trained on the job usually spend their first few months attending training sessions and working closely with more experienced workers. Some states allow medical assistants to perform more advanced procedures, such as giving injections, after passing a test or taking a course.

Certification and Other Qualifications. Employers prefer to hire experienced or certified workers. Although not required, certification indicates that a medical assistant meets certain standards of competence. The certification process varies. There are various associations—some listed among the sources of information below—that award certification credentials to medical assistants. A medical assistant may choose to become certified in a specialty, such as podiatry, optometry, or ophthalmology.

Medical assistants deal with the public; therefore, they must be neat, well groomed, and have a courteous, pleasant manner and they must be able to put patients at ease and explain physicians' instructions. They must respect the confidential nature of medical information. Clinical duties require a reasonable level of manual dexterity and visual acuity.

Advancement. Medical assistants may advance to other occupations through experience or additional training. For example, some may go on to teach medical assisting, and others pursue additional education to become nurses or other healthcare workers. Administrative medical assistants may advance to office manager, or qualify for a variety of administrative support occupations.

Employment Trends. Employment is projected to grow much faster than average, ranking medical assistants among the fastest growing occupations over the 2006 to 2016 decade. Job opportunities should be excellent, particularly for those with formal training or experience, and certification.

Employment Change. Employment of medical assistants is expected to grow 35 percent from 2006 to 2016, much faster than the average for all occupations. As the healthcare industry expands because of technological advances in medicine and the growth and aging of the population, an increased need for all healthcare workers will be felt. Increasing use of medical assistants in the rapidly growing healthcare industry will further stimulate job growth.

Helping to drive job growth is the increasing number of group practices, clinics, and other healthcare facilities that need a high proportion of support personnel, particularly medical assistants who can handle both administrative and clinical duties. In addition, medical assistants work primarily in outpatient settings, a rapidly growing sector of the healthcare industry.

Job Prospects. Job seekers who want to work as medical assistants should encounter excellent job prospects. Medical assistants are projected to account for a very large number of new jobs, and many other opportunities will come from the need to replace workers leaving the occupation. Those with formal training or experience—particularly those with certification—should have the best job opportunities. **Table 23–3** shows some projection data provided by the Department of Labor.

Table 23–3	Projections data from the National Employment Matrix				
Occupational title	**Employment, 2006**	**Projected employment, 2016**	**Change, 2006–2016**		
			Number	**Percent**	
Medical assistants	417,000	565,000	148,000	35	

NOTE: Data in this table are rounded.

EARNINGS

The earnings of medical assistants vary, depending on experience, skill level, and location. Median annual earnings of wage-and-salary medical assistants were $26,290 in May 2006. The middle 50 percent earned between $21,970 and $31,210. The lowest 10 percent earned less than $18,860, and the highest 10 percent earned more than $36,840. Median annual earnings in the industries employing the largest numbers of medical assistants in May 2006 are shown in **Table 23–4**.

Table 23–4	Median annual earnings in the industries employing the largest numbers of medical assistants in May 2006
General medical and surgical hospitals	$27,340
Outpatient care centers	$26,840
Offices of physicians	$26,620
Offices of chiropractors	$22,940
Offices of optometrists	$22,850

RELATED OCCUPATIONS

Medical assistants perform work similar to the tasks completed by other workers in medical support occupations. Administrative medical assistants do work similar to that of medical secretaries, medical transcriptionists, and medical records and health information technicians. Clinical medical assistants perform duties similar to those of dental assistants; dental hygienists; occupational therapist assistants and aides; pharmacy aides; licensed practical and licensed vocational nurses; surgical technologists; physical therapist assistants and aides; and nursing, psychiatric, and home health aides.

ADDITIONAL INFORMATION

Information about career opportunities and certification for medical assistants is available from:

- American Association of Medical Assistants, 20 North Wacker Dr., Suite 1575, Chicago, IL 60606. http://www.aama-ntl.org

- American Medical Technologists, 10700 West Higgins Rd., Suite 150, Rosemont, IL 60018. http://www.amt1.com

- National Healthcareer Association, 7 Ridgedale Ave., Suite 203, Cedar Knolls, NJ 07927.

Information about career opportunities, training programs, and certification for ophthalmic medical personnel is available from:

- Joint Commission on Allied Health Personnel in Ophthalmology, 2025 Woodlane Dr., St. Paul, MN 55125. http://www.jcahpo.org/newsite/index.htm

Information about career opportunities, training programs and certification for optometric assistants is available from:

- American Optometric Association, 243 N. Lindbergh Blvd., St. Louis, MO 63141. http://www.aoa.org

Information about certification for podiatric assistants is available from:

- American Society of Podiatric Medical Assistants, 2124 South Austin Blvd., Cicero, IL 60804. http://www.aspma.org

For lists of accredited educational programs in medical assisting, contact:

- Accrediting Bureau of Health Education Schools, 7777 Leesburg Pike, Suite 314 N, Falls Church, VA 22043. Internet: http://www.abhes.org

- Commission on Accreditation of Allied Health Education Programs, 1361 Park St., Clearwater, FL 33756. http://www.caahep.org

Nursing, Psychiatric, and Home Health Aides

WORK DESCRIPTIONS

Nursing and psychiatric aides help care for physically or mentally ill, injured, disabled, or infirm individuals in hospitals, nursing care facilities, and mental health settings. Home health aides have duties that are similar, but they work in patients' homes or residential care facilities. Nursing aides and home health aides are among the occupations commonly referred to as *direct care workers*, due to their role in working with patients who need long-term care. The specific care they give depends on their specialty.

Nursing aides are also known as nurse aides, nursing assistants, certified nursing assistants, geriatric aides, unlicensed assistive personnel, orderlies, or hospital attendants. They provide hands-on care and perform routine tasks under the supervision of nursing and medical staff. Specific tasks vary, but aides handle many aspects of a patient's care. They often help patients to eat, dress, and bathe. They also respond to calls for help, deliver messages, serve meals, make beds, and tidy up rooms. Aides sometimes are responsible for taking a patient's temperature, pulse rate, respiration rate, or blood pressure. They may help provide care to patients by assisting them in getting into and out of bed, helping them to walk, escorting them to operating and examining rooms, or providing skin care. Some aides help other medical staff by setting up equipment, storing and moving supplies, and assisting with some procedures. Aides also observe patients' physical, mental, and emotional states, and report any changes in them to the nursing or medical staff.

Nurse aides employed in nursing care facilities often are the principal caregivers, having far more contact with residents than do other members of the staff. Because some residents may stay in a nursing care facility for months or even years, aides develop ongoing relationships with them and interact with them in a positive, caring way.

Home health aides help elderly, convalescent, or disabled persons live in their own homes instead of in healthcare facilities. Under the direction of nursing or medical staff, they provide health-related services, such as administering oral medications. The last section in this chapter discusses information on personal and home care aides. Like nursing aides, home health aides may check patients' pulse rate, temperature, and respiration rate; help with simple prescribed exercises; and help patients to get in and out of bed, bathe, dress, and groom. Occasionally, aides change nonsterile dressings, give massages and provide skin care, or assist with braces and artificial limbs. Experienced home health aides, with training, also may assist with medical equipment such as ventilators, which help patients breathe. Most home health aides work with elderly or disabled persons who need more extensive care than family or friends can provide. Some help recently discharged hospital patients who have relatively short-term needs.

In home health agencies, a registered nurse, physical therapist, or social worker usually assigns specific duties to and supervises home health aides, who keep records of the services they perform and record each patient's condition and progress. The aides report changes in a patient's condition to the supervisor or case manager.

Psychiatric aides, also known as mental health assistants or psychiatric nursing assistants, care for mentally impaired or emotionally disturbed individuals. They work under the supervision of a team that may include psychiatrists, psychologists, psychiatric nurses, social workers, and therapists. Psychiatric aides help patients dress, bathe, groom, and eat, but they also socialize with them and lead them in educational and recreational activities. Psychiatric aides may play card games or other games with patients, watch television with them, or participate in group activities, such as playing sports or going on field trips. They observe patients and report any physical or behavioral signs that might be important for the professional staff to know. They accompany patients to and from therapy and treatment. As a result of such close contact with patients, psychiatric aides can have a great deal of influence on their outlook and treatment.

WORK ENVIRONMENT

Work as a nursing, home health, or psychiatric aide can be physically demanding. Aides spend many hours standing and walking, and they often confront heavy workloads. Aides must guard against back injury because they may have to move patients into and out of bed or help them to stand or walk. It is important for them to be trained in and to follow the proper procedures for lifting and moving patients. Aides also may face hazards from minor infections and major diseases, such as hepatitis, but can avoid infections by following proper procedures.

Aides also perform tasks that some may consider unpleasant, such as emptying bedpans and changing soiled bed linens. The patients they care for may be disoriented, irritable, or uncooperative. Psychiatric aides must be prepared to care for patients whose illness may cause violent behavior. Although their work can be emotionally demanding, many aides gain satisfaction from assisting those in need.

Home health aides may go to the same patient's home for months or even years. However, most aides work with a number of different patients, each job lasting a few hours, days, or weeks. Home health aides often visit multiple patients on the same day.

Home health aides generally work alone, with periodic visits from their supervisor. They receive detailed instructions explaining when to visit patients and what services to perform. Aides are individually responsible for getting to patients' homes, and they may spend a good portion of the working day traveling from one patient to another. Mechanical lifting devices available in institutional settings are not as frequently available in patients' homes; consequently, home health aides must take extra care to avoid injuries resulting from overexertion when they assist patients.

Most full-time aides work about 40 hours per week, but because patients need care 24 hours a day, some aides work evenings, nights, weekends, and holidays. In 2006, 23 percent of aides worked part-time compared with 15 percent of all workers.

EMPLOYMENT OPPORTUNITIES

Nursing, psychiatric, and home health aides held about 2.3 million jobs in 2006. Nursing aides held the most jobs—approximately 1.4 million. Home health aides held roughly 787,000 jobs, and psychiatric aides held about 62,000 jobs. About 52 percent of nursing aides worked in nursing and residential care facilities and another 29 percent worked in hospitals. Home health aides were mainly employed by home healthcare services, nursing and residential care facilities, and social assistance agencies. About 47 percent of all psychiatric aides worked in hospitals, primarily in psychiatric and substance abuse hospitals, although some also worked in the psychiatric units of general medical and surgical hospitals. Others were employed in state government agencies; residential mental retardation, mental health, and substance abuse facilities, as well as nursing and residential care facilities.

EDUCATIONAL AND LEGAL REQUIREMENTS

In many cases, a high school diploma or its equivalent is necessary to obtain a job as a nursing or psychiatric aide. However, a high school diploma generally is not required for a job as a home health aide. Specific qualifications vary by occupation, state laws, and work setting. Advancement opportunities for aides are limited.

Education and Training. Nursing and psychiatric aide training is offered in high schools, vocational-technical centers, some nursing care facilities, and some community colleges. Courses cover body mechanics, nutrition, anatomy and physiology, infection control, communication skills, and resident rights. Personal care skills, such as how to help patients bathe, eat, and groom, also are taught. Hospital employers may require previous experience as a nursing aide or home health aide. Some states also require psychiatric aides to complete a formal training program. However, most psychiatric aides learn their skills on the job from experienced co-workers.

Home health aides are generally not required to have a high school diploma. They usually are trained on the job by registered nurses, licensed practical nurses, or experienced aides. Clients themselves may prefer that tasks are done a particular way, and may suggest changes or procedures to the home health aide. A competency evaluation may be required to ensure the aide can perform the required tasks.

Some employers provide classroom instruction for newly hired aides, while others rely exclusively on informal on-the-job instruction by a licensed nurse or an experienced aide. Such training may last from several days to a few months. Aides also may attend lectures, workshops, and in-service training.

Licensure and Certification. The federal government has guidelines for home health aides whose employers receive reimbursement from Medicare. Federal law requires home health aides to pass a competency test covering a wide range of areas. A home health aide may receive training before taking the competency test. In addition, the *National Association for Home Care and Hospice* offers voluntary certification for home health aides. Some states also require aides to be licensed.

Similar federal requirements exist for nurse aides who work in nursing care facilities. These aides must complete a minimum of 75 hours of state-approved training and pass a competency evaluation. Aides who complete the program are known as Certified Nurse Assistants (CNAs) and are placed on the state registry of nurse aides.

Other Qualifications. Aides must be in good health. A physical examination, including state-regulated tests such as those for tuberculosis, may be required. A criminal background check also is usually required for employment.

Applicants should be tactful, patient, understanding, emotionally stable, and dependable and should have a desire to help people. They also should be able to work as part of a team, have good communication skills, and be willing to perform repetitive, routine tasks. Home health aides should be honest and discreet because they work in private homes. They also will need access to a car or public transportation to reach patients' homes.

Advancement. Opportunities for advancement within these occupations are limited. Aides generally need additional formal training or education to enter other health occupations. The most common healthcare occupations for former aides are licensed practical nurse, registered nurse, and medical assistant.

For some individuals, these occupations serve as entry-level jobs. For example, some high school and college students gain experience working in these occupations while attending school. In addition, experience as an aide can help individuals decide whether to pursue a career in health care.

EMPLOYMENT TRENDS

Excellent job opportunities for nursing, psychiatric, and home health aides will arise from a combination of rapid employment growth and the need to replace the many workers who leave the occupation each year.

Employment Change. Overall employment of nursing, psychiatric, and home health aides is projected to grow 28 percent between 2006 and 2016, much faster than the average for all occupations. However, growth will vary according to the individual occupations. Home health aides are expected to gain jobs faster than other aides as a result of growing demand for home services from an aging population and efforts to contain costs by moving patients out of hospitals and nursing care facilities as quickly as possible. Consumer preference for care in the home and improvements in medical technologies for in-home treatment also will contribute to much-faster-than-average employment growth for home health aides.

Nursing aide employment will not grow as fast as home health aide employment, largely because nursing aides are concentrated in relatively slower-growing industries. Employment of nursing aides is expected to grow faster than the average for all occupations through 2016, in response to the long-term care needs of an increasing elderly population. Financial pressures on hospitals to discharge patients as soon as possible should boost admissions to nursing care facilities. As a result, job openings will be more numerous in nursing and residential care facilities than in hospitals. Modern medical technology also will drive demand for nursing aides because, as the technology saves and extends more lives, it increases the need for long-term care provided by aides.

Little or no change is expected in employment of psychiatric aides—the smallest of the three occupations. Most psychiatric aides currently work in hospitals, but the industries most likely to see growth will be residential facilities for people with developmental disabilities, mental illness, and substance abuse problems. The long-term trend toward treating psychiatric patients outside of hospitals continues because it is more cost effective and allows patients to live more independent lives. Demand for psychiatric aides in residential facilities will rise in response to the increase in the number of older persons, many of whom will require mental health services. Growing demand for these workers also rests on an increasing number of mentally disabled adults who were formerly cared for by their elderly parents and who will continue to need care. Job growth also could be affected by changes in government funding of programs for the mentally ill.

Job Prospects. High replacement needs for nursing, psychiatric, and home health aides reflect modest entry requirements, low pay, high physical and emotional demands, and limited opportunities for advancement within the occupation. For these same reasons, the number of people looking to enter the occupation will be limited. Many aides leave the occupation to attend training programs for other healthcare occupations. Therefore, people who are interested in, and suited for, this work should have excellent job opportunities. **Table 23–5** shows some projection data provided by the Department of Labor.

Table 23–5

Projections data from the National Employment Matrix				
Occupational title	**Employment, 2006**	**Projected employment, 2016**	**Change, 2006–2016**	
			Number	**Percent**
Nursing, psychiatric, and home health aides	2,296,000	2,944,000	647,000	28
Home health aides	787,000	1,171,000	384,000	49
Nursing aides, orderlies, and attendants	1,447,000	1,711,000	264,000	18
Psychiatric aides	62,000	62,000	0	0

NOTE: Data in this table are rounded.

EARNINGS

Median hourly earnings of nursing aides, orderlies, and attendants were $10.67 in May 2006. The middle 50 percent earned between $9.09 and $12.80 an hour. The lowest 10 percent earned less than $7.78, and the highest 10 percent earned more than $14.99 an hour. Median hourly earnings in the industries employing the largest numbers of nursing aides, orderlies, and attendants in May 2006 is shown in **Table 23–6**.

Nursing and psychiatric aides in hospitals generally receive at least one week of paid vacation after one year of service. Paid holidays and sick leave, hospital and medical benefits, extra pay for late-shift work, and pension plans also are available to many hospital employees and to some nursing care facility employees.

Median hourly earnings of home health aides were $9.34 in May 2006. The middle 50 percent earned between $7.99 and $10.90 an hour. The lowest 10 percent earned less than $7.06, and the highest 10 percent earned more than $13.00 an hour. Median hourly earnings in the industries employing the largest numbers of home health aides in May 2006 is shown in **Table 23–7**.

Home health aides receive slight pay increases with experience and added responsibility. Usually, they are paid only for the time worked in the home, not for travel time between jobs, and must pay for their travel costs from their earnings. Most employers hire only on-call hourly workers and provide no benefits.

Table 23–6

Median hourly earnings in the industries employing the largest numbers of nursing aides, orderlies, and attendants in May 2006	
Local government	$12.15
Employment services	$11.47
General medical and surgical hospitals	$11.06
Nursing care facilities	$10.37
Community care facilities for the elderly	$10.07

Table 23–7

Median hourly earnings in the industries employing the largest numbers of home health aides in May 2006	
Nursing care facilities	$9.76
Residential mental retardation facilities	$9.34
Services for the elderly and persons with disabilities	$9.26
Home health care services	$9.14
Community care facilities for the elderly	$8.87

Median hourly earnings of psychiatric aides were $11.49 in May 2006. The middle 50 percent earned between $9.20 and $14.46 an hour. The lowest 10 percent earned less than $7.75, and the highest 10 percent earned more than $17.32 an hour. Median hourly earnings in the industries employing the largest numbers of psychiatric aides in May 2006 is included in **Table 23–8**.

RELATED OCCUPATIONS

Nursing, psychiatric, and home health aides help people who need routine care or treatment. So do child care workers, licensed practical and licensed vocational nurses, medical assistants, occupational therapist assistants and aides, personal and home care aides, physical therapist assistants and aides, radiation therapists, and registered nurses. Social and human service assistants, who sometimes work with mental health patients, do work similar to that of psychiatric aides.

Table 23–8	*Median hourly earnings in the industries employing the largest numbers of psychiatric aides in May 2006*	
State government		$13.27
General medical and surgical hospitals		$12.31
Psychiatric and substance abuse hospitals		$11.76
Residential mental health and substance abuse facilities		$9.65
Residential mental retardation facilities		$8.80

ADDITIONAL INFORMATION

Information about employment opportunities may be obtained from local hospitals, nursing care facilities, home healthcare agencies, psychiatric facilities, state boards of nursing, and local offices of the state employment service.

Information on licensing requirements for nursing and home health aides, and lists of state-approved nursing aide programs are available from state departments of public health, departments of occupational licensing, boards of nursing, and home care associations.

For more information on training and requirements for home health aides, contact:

- National Association for Home Care and Hospice, 228 7th St. S.E., Washington, DC 20003. http://www.nahc.org

For more information on the home healthcare industry, contact:

- Visiting Nurse Associations of America, 8403 Colesville Rd., Suite 1550, Silver Spring, MD 20910-6374. http://www.vnaa.org

For more information on the healthcare workforce, contact:

- The Center for the Health Professions, 3333 California St., San Francisco, CA 94118. http://www.futurehealth.ucsf.edu

HEALTH RELATED PROFESSIONS

Objectives

Objectives listed below are for all chapters in Part III. After studying these chapters the student should be able to:

1. Describe the responsibilities and work of each profession.

2. Classify the specialties in each profession.

3. Discuss the environment in which the work takes place.

4. Identify any adjunct personnel who assist the professionals with their work.

5. Compare and contrast the following factors among the professions: educational requirements, employment trends, opportunities for advancement, salary potential, and career ladders.

6. Identify other professionals who do similar tasks or have similar responsibilities.

7. Discuss the advantages of the national organizations to which professionals belong.

8. Explain the concept and functions of interdisciplinary teams.

CLINICAL LABORATORY TECHNOLOGY

Key Terms

- Clinical laboratory (medical) technologist
- Centrifuge
- Calibration
- Clinical chemistry
- Blood bank technology
- Cytotechnology
- Hematology

- Histology
- Microbiology
- Immunology
- Clinical laboratory (medical) technician
- Histology technician
- Cytotechnologist
- Nuclear medicine technologist

The Laboratory Team

The practice of modern medicine would be impossible without the tests performed in the clinical laboratory. A medical team of pathologists, specialists, technologists, and technicians works together to determine the presence, extent, or absence of disease and to provide data to evaluate the effectiveness of treatment.

Physicians order laboratory work for a wide variety of reasons: Test results may be used to establish values against which future measurements can be compared; to monitor treatment, as with tests for drug levels in the blood that can indicate whether a patient is adhering to a prescribed drug regimen; to reassure patients that a disease is absent or under control; or to assess the status of a patient's health, as with cholesterol measurements.

Although physicians depend heavily on laboratory results, they do not ordinarily perform the tests themselves. This job falls to clinical laboratory personnel. Clinical laboratory testing plays a crucial role in the detection, diagnosis, and treatment of disease. *Clinical laboratory technologists* and *technicians*, also known as *medical technologists* and *technicians*, perform most of these tests.

Clinical Laboratory (Medical) Technologists and Technicians

WORK DESCRIPTION

Changes in body fluids, tissues, and cells are often a sign that something is wrong. Clinical laboratory testing plays a crucial role in the detection and diagnosis of disease. Clinical laboratory and medical technologists perform laboratory testing in conjunction with pathologists (physicians who diagnose the cause and nature of disease) and other physicians or scientists who specialize in clinical chemistry, microbiology, or the other biological sciences. Medical technologists develop data on the blood, tissues, and fluids in the human body by using a variety of precision instruments.

Many clinical laboratories are highly automated, and job duties reflect this fact. Using computerized instruments that perform a number of tests simultaneously, as well as microscopes, centrifuges, and other kinds of sophisticated laboratory equipment, these workers perform tests, verify the results, and relay them to the patient's physician.

Depending on the worker's level of skill, he or she may run routine tests or perform complex analyses that require a number of steps to arrive at the information needed by the physician. The types of tests that clinical laboratory personnel perform and the amount of responsibility they assume vary by employment setting, but depend to a large extent on the kind of educational preparation they have. Laboratory procedures require an array of complex precision instruments and a variety of automated and electronic equipment, but men and women interested in helping others are the foundation of a successful laboratory. Laboratory technologists and technicians must be accurate and reliable, have an interest in science, and be able to recognize the responsibility they bear for human lives.

Clinical laboratory and medical technologists hold a bachelor's degree in medical technology or in one of the life sciences, or they have a combination of formal training and work experience. They perform complicated chemical, biologic, hematologic, immunologic, microscopic, and bacteriologic tests. These may include chemical tests to determine blood cholesterol level, blood glucose, or microscopic examinations of blood and other substances to detect the presence of diseases such as leukemia. Technologists microscopically examine other body constituents; make cultures of body fluid or tissue samples to determine the presence of bacteria, fungi, parasites, or other microorganisms; and analyze samples for chemical content or reaction. They also type and cross-match blood samples for transfusions.

The exact procedure followed depends on the test being performed. Most blood chemistry tests, for example, are highly automated. The technologist or technician calibrates an instrument known as a chemical analyzer, loads it with the specimens to be tested, selects the appropriate test code, and monitors the instrument to make sure it does not malfunction. When the results are ready, the technologist verifies them for accuracy and sends them out or reports them to the attending physician. If a test requires the identification of cell types, such as in leukemia, the procedures are very different. In addition to identifying the cells on a stained blood film or from bone marrow, special stains may be required, cell markers performed, and chromosome studies completed.

Technologists in small laboratories perform many types of tests, while those in large laboratories usually specialize in one type of test. Among the areas in which they can specialize are *clinical chemistry* (the chemical analysis of body fluids), *blood bank technology* (the collection and preparation of blood products for transfusion), *cytotechnology* (the study of human body cells), *hematology* (the study of blood cells), *histology* (the study of human tissue), *microbiology* (the study of bacteria and other microorganisms), and *immunology* (the study of the human immune system).

Most medical technologists perform tests ordered by physicians for their patients. Others conduct research, develop laboratory techniques, teach, or assume laboratory management and administrative duties. Some technologists work as independent consultants, advising physicians on how to set up and operate office laboratories. Still others work in product development and sales.

Clinical laboratory and medical laboratory technicians generally have an associate degree from a community or junior college, or a diploma or certificate from a trade or technical school. They are mid-level laboratory supervisors. They perform a wide range of routine tests and laboratory procedures. Technicians may prepare specimens and operate automatic analyzers, for example, or they may perform manual tests following detailed instructions. Like technologists, they may work in several different areas of the clinical laboratory or specialize in just one.

Histology technicians cut and stain tissue specimens for microscopic examination by pathologists and phlebotomists and draw and test blood. They usually work under the supervision of medical technologists or laboratory managers.

Work Environment

Hours and other working conditions vary according to the size and type of employment setting. In large hospitals or in commercial laboratories that operate continuously, workers are hired specifically for the day, evening, or night shift. Weekend or holiday work may be required because these laboratories operate 365 days a year. Some smaller laboratories also operate 24 hours a day. Laboratory personnel in small facilities are likely to work on rotating rather than regular shifts; they may work the evening or weekend shift one week, and the day shift the following week. In some facilities, laboratory personnel are required to be on call (available in case of emergency) several nights a week.

Clinical laboratory personnel are trained to work with infectious specimens. It is of the utmost importance that they handle specimens properly to ensure that neither staff nor other test specimens become contaminated by disease-causing organisms. When they follow proper methods of control and sterilization, few hazards of infection exist.

Laboratories generally are well lighted and clean. At times, unpleasant odors may be present.

Laboratory workers may spend much time on their feet. Their work can create emotional, as well as physical stress because patient treatment options often depend on quick and accurate analysis of laboratory specimens.

EMPLOYMENT OPPORTUNITIES

Clinical laboratory technologists and technicians held about 319,000 jobs in 2006. More than half of jobs were in hospitals. Most of the remaining jobs were in offices of physicians and in medical and diagnostic laboratories. A small proportion was in educational services and in all other ambulatory healthcare services.

EDUCATIONAL AND LEGAL REQUIREMENTS

Working as a clinical laboratory technologist generally requires a bachelor's degree in medical technology or in one of the life sciences; clinical laboratory technicians usually need an associate degree or a certificate.

Education and Training. The usual requirement for an entry-level position as a clinical laboratory technologist is a bachelor's degree with a major in medical technology or one of the life sciences; however, it is possible to qualify for some jobs with a combination of education and on-the-job and specialized training. Universities and hospitals offer medical technology programs.

Bachelor's degree programs in medical technology include courses in chemistry, biological sciences, microbiology, mathematics, and statistics, as well as specialized courses devoted to knowledge and skills used in the clinical laboratory. Many programs also offer or require courses in management, business, and computer applications. The Clinical Laboratory Improvement Act requires technologists who perform highly complex tests to have at least an associate degree.

Medical and clinical laboratory technicians generally have either an associate degree from a community or junior college or a certificate from a hospital, a vocational or technical school, or the armed forces. A few technicians learn their skills on the job.

The *National Accrediting Agency for Clinical Laboratory Sciences (NAACLS)* fully accredits about 470 programs for medical and clinical laboratory technologists, medical and clinical laboratory technicians, histotechnologists and histotechnicians, cytogenetic technologists, and diagnostic molecular scientists. NAACLS also approves about 60 programs in phlebotomy and clinical assisting. Other nationally recognized agencies that accredit specific areas for clinical laboratory workers include the *Commission on Accreditation of Allied Health Education Programs* and the *Accrediting Bureau of Health Education Schools.*

Licensure. Some states require laboratory personnel to be licensed or registered. Licensure of technologists often requires a bachelor's degree and the passing of an exam, but requirements vary by state and specialty. Information on licensure is available from state departments of health or boards of occupational licensing.

Certification and Other Qualifications. Many employers prefer applicants who are certified by a recognized professional association. Associations offering certification include the Board of Registry of the American Society for Clinical Pathology, the American Medical Technologists, the National Credentialing Agency for Laboratory Personnel, and the Board of Registry of the American Association of Bioanalysts. These agencies have different requirements for certification and different organizational sponsors.

In addition to certification, employers seek clinical laboratory personnel with good analytical judgment and the ability to work under pressure. Technologists in particular are expected to be good at problem solving. Close attention to detail is also essential for laboratory personnel because small differences or changes in test substances or numerical readouts can be crucial to a diagnosis. Manual dexterity and normal color vision are highly desirable, and with the widespread use of automated laboratory equipment, computer skills are important.

Advancement. Technicians can advance and become technologists through additional education and experience. Technologists may advance to supervisory positions in laboratory work or may become chief medical or clinical laboratory technologists or laboratory managers in hospitals. Manufacturers of home diagnostic testing kits and laboratory equipment and supplies also seek experienced technologists to work in product development, marketing, and sales.

Professional certification and a graduate degree in medical technology, one of the biological sciences, chemistry, management, or education usually speeds advancement. A doctorate usually is needed to become a laboratory director. Federal regulation requires directors of moderately complex laboratories to have either a master's degree or a bachelor's degree, combined with the appropriate amount of training and experience.

EMPLOYMENT TRENDS

Rapid job growth and excellent job opportunities are expected. Most jobs will continue to be in hospitals, but employment will grow faster in other settings.

Employment Change. Employment of clinical laboratory workers is expected to grow 14 percent between 2006 and 2016, faster than the average for all occupations. The volume of laboratory tests continues to increase with both population growth and the development of new types of tests.

Technological advances will continue to have opposing effects on employment. On the one hand, new, increasingly powerful diagnostic tests will encourage additional testing and spur employment. On the other, research and development efforts targeted at simplifying routine testing procedures may enhance the ability of nonlaboratory personnel—physicians and patients in particular—to perform tests now conducted in laboratories.

Although hospitals are expected to remain the major employer of clinical laboratory workers, employment is expected to grow faster in medical and diagnostic laboratories, offices of physicians, and all other ambulatory healthcare services.

Job Prospects. Job opportunities are expected to be excellent because the number of job openings is expected to continue to exceed the number of job seekers. Although significant, job growth will not be the only source of opportunities. As in most occupations, many additional openings will result from the need to replace workers who transfer to other occupations, retire, or leave the workforce for other reasons.

EARNINGS

Median annual wage-and-salary earnings of medical and clinical laboratory technologists were $49,700 in May 2006. The middle 50 percent earned between $41,680 and $58,560. The lowest 10 percent earned less than $34,660, and the highest 10 percent earned more than $69,260. Median annual earnings in the industries employing the largest numbers of medical and clinical laboratory technologists are shown in **Table 24–1**.

Table 24–1	*Median annual earnings in the industries employing the largest numbers of medical and clinical laboratory technologists in May 2006*
Federal government	$57,360
Medical and diagnostic laboratories	$50,740
General medical and surgical hospitals	$49,930
Offices of physicians	$45,420
Colleges, universities, and professional schools	$45,080

Median annual wage-and-salary earnings of medical and clinical laboratory technicians were $32,840 in May 2006. The middle 50 percent earned between $26,430 and $41,020. The lowest 10 percent earned less than $21,830, and the highest 10 percent earned more than $50,250. Median annual earnings in the industries employing the largest numbers of medical and clinical laboratory technicians can be seen in **Table 24–2**.

RELATED OCCUPATIONS

Clinical laboratory technologists and technicians analyze body fluids, tissue, and other substances, using a variety of tests. Similar or related procedures are performed by chemists and material scientists, science technicians, and veterinary technologists and technicians.

Table 24–2

Median annual earnings in the industries employing the largest numbers of medical and clinical laboratory technicians in May 2006

General medical and surgical hospitals	$34,200
Colleges, universities, and professional schools	$33,440
Offices of physicians	$31,330
Medical and diagnostic laboratories	$30,240
Other ambulatory healthcare services	$29,560

ADDITIONAL INFORMATION

For a list of accredited and approved educational programs for clinical laboratory personnel, contact:

- National Accrediting Agency for Clinical Laboratory Sciences, 8410 W. Bryn Mawr Ave., Suite 670, Chicago, IL 60631. http://www.naacls.org

Information on certification is available from:

- American Association of Bioanalysts, Board of Registry, 906 Olive St., Suite 1200, St. Louis, MO 63101. http://www.aab.org

- American Medical Technologists, 10700 Higgins Rd., Suite 150, Rosemont, IL 60018. http://www.amt1.com

- American Society for Clinical Pathology, 33 West Monroe Street, Suite 1600, Chicago, IL 60603. http://www.ascp.org

- National Credentialing Agency for Laboratory Personnel, P.O. Box 15945, Lenexa, KS 66285. http://www.nca-info.org

Additional career information is available from:

- American Association of Blood Banks, 8101 Glenbrook Rd., Bethesda, MD 20814. http://www.aabb.org

- American Society for Clinical Laboratory Science, 6701 Democracy Blvd., Suite 300, Bethesda, MD 20817. http://www.ascls.org

- American Society for Cytopathology, 400 West 9th St., Suite 201, Wilmington, DE 19801. http://www.cytopathology.org

- Clinical Laboratory Management Association, 989 Old Eagle School Rd., Suite 815, Wayne, PA 19087. http://www.clma.org

HEALTH INFORMATION PERSONNEL

Key Terms

- Health information personnel
- Diagnosis and treatment plan
- Symptoms and response
- Documentation
- Insurance claims
- Medicare reimbursement
- Assessments
- Health information administrator

- Statistics
- Health information technician
- Code
- Diagnosis-related groupings (DRGs)
- Tumor registrar
- Accredited record technician (ART)
- Medical transcriptionist
- Medical (health science) librarian

Providing and Preserving Essential Information

Providing and preserving information of ethical, scientific, and legal value to the appropriate professional personnel is one of the most valuable aspects of health care. Managing an information system that meets medical, administrative, ethical, and legal requirements involves the teamwork of administrators, technicians, transcriptionists, and medical librarians, collectively known as health information personnel.

Just as schools and colleges keep transcripts of grades and employers maintain personnel records, doctors and hospitals set up a permanent file for every patient they treat. This file is known as the patient's medical record or chart. It includes the patient's medical history, results of physical examinations, results of X-ray and laboratory tests, diagnoses, treatment plans, doctors' orders and notes, and nurses' notes.

The medical record is the centerpiece of the health information system because it contains the entire history of each patient who receives health care. This medical record—a permanent document of the history and progress of one person's illness or injury—preserves information of medical, scientific, legal, and planning value. It is compiled from observations and findings recorded by the patient's physician and other professional members of the medical team. The entries and reports noted in it originate from various points in the hospital, clinic, nursing home, health center, or other healthcare facility. Through a network of communications systems, they are entered in the individual patient's record. This vital medical profile constitutes each patient's unique medical history.

The medical record shows what the patient's symptoms were, what tests were ordered, and how the patient responded to treatment. Although accurate and orderly records are essential for clinical purposes, medical records have other important uses as well. They provide background and documentation for insurance claims and Medicare reimbursement, legal actions, professional review of treatment and medications prescribed, and training of health professions personnel. Medical records are used for research and planning purposes. They provide data for clinical studies, evaluations of the benefits and costs of various medical and surgical procedures, and assessments of community health needs.

Health Information Administrators

WORK DESCRIPTION

Health information administrators direct and control the activities of the medical record department. They train and supervise the medical record staff, and develop systems for documenting, storing, and retrieving medical information. Information administrators compile statistics required by federal and state agencies, assist the medical staff in evaluations of patient care or research studies, and sometimes testify in court about medical records and procedures of recordkeeping.

Health information managers are responsible for the maintenance and security of all patient records. Recent regulations enacted by the federal government require that all healthcare providers maintain secure electronic patient records. As a result, health information managers must keep up with current computer and software technology and with legislative requirements. In addition, as patient data become more frequently used for quality management and in medical research, health information managers ensure that databases are complete, accurate, and available only to authorized personnel.

Increasingly, medical record administrators are viewed as key members of the management team, and they work closely with the finance department to monitor hospital-spending patterns. As part of the management team, health administrators establish and implement policies, objectives, and procedures for their department; evaluate personnel and work performance; develop reports and budgets; coordinate activities with other managers, and work closely with physicians.

WORK ENVIRONMENT

Most health information administrators work in pleasant and comfortable offices, but they may work long hours if they are called in to help solve unexpected problems. Those who work at computers for prolonged periods may experience muscle pain and eyestrain.

EMPLOYMENT OPPORTUNITIES

Employment of medical and health services managers is expected to grow 16 percent from 2006 to 2016, faster than the average for all occupations.

Managers will be needed to oversee the computerization of patient records and to ensure their security as required by law. Additional demand for managers will stem from the need to recruit workers and increase employee retention, to comply with changing regulations, and to implement new technology. Hospitals will continue to employ the majority of medical and health services managers; however, the number of new jobs created in hospitals is expected to increase at a slower rate than in many other industries because of the growing use of clinics and other outpatient care sites. Employment will grow fastest in practitioners' offices, home healthcare agencies and consulting firms.

EDUCATIONAL AND LEGAL REQUIREMENTS

The minimum educational program for a *registered record administrator* is a bachelor's degree in health information or medical record administration. In 2007, there were forty-two accredited bachelor's degree programs and three master's degree programs in health information management according to the *Commission on Accreditation for Health Informatics and Information Management Education*. Health information managers who hold a bachelor's degree or postbaccalaureate from an approved program and who pass an exam, can earn certification as a *Registered Health Information Administrator* from the *American Health Information Management Association*. The preprofessional curriculum includes studies in the humanities and behavioral, biological, and physical sciences. The professional curriculum covers medical terminology, medical care organizations, disease classifications, organization, supervision, healthcare statistics, and principles of law, as well as advanced data processing.

EARNINGS

Earnings of health information administrators vary by type and size of the facility as well as by the level of education and responsibility. Salaries also vary according to geographic region. According to the latest statistics available in 2006, mean annual earnings for health information administrators were $75,126 for those with a baccalaureate degree.

RELATED OCCUPATIONS

Health information administrators receive training and experience in both health sciences and management. Other occupations and services requiring knowledge of both fields include hospital and nursing home administrators, public health directors, health agency directors, clinical laboratory workers, nursing services, physical therapists, rehabilitation services, radiology, respiratory therapists, and outpatient services administrators.

ADDITIONAL INFORMATION

Information on careers in health information management may be obtained from:

- American Health Information Management Association, 233 N. Michigan Avenue, 21st Floor, Chicago, IL 60601-5800. http://www.ahima.org

Health Information Technicians

WORK DESCRIPTION

Every time a patient receives health care, a record is maintained of the observations, medical or surgical interventions, and treatment outcomes. This record includes information that the patient provides concerning his or her symptoms and medical history, the results of examinations, results of X-rays and laboratory tests, diagnoses, and treatment plans. Medical record and health information technicians organize and evaluate these records for completeness and accuracy.

Technicians assemble patients' health information, making sure that patients' initial medical charts are complete. They also ensure that all forms are completed, properly identified, authenticated, and all necessary information placed on file in the computer. They regularly communicate with physicians and other healthcare professionals to clarify diagnoses or to obtain additional information.

Technicians regularly use computer programs to tabulate and analyze data in order to improve patient care, contain costs, and provide documentation for use in legal actions or research studies.

Some medical record and health information technicians specialize in coding patients' medical information for insurance purposes. These technicians assign a code to each diagnosis and procedure, relying on their knowledge of disease processes. Technicians then use classification systems software to assign the patient to one of several hundred "diagnosis-related groups," or DRGs. The DRG determines the amount for which Medicare or other insurance programs using the DRG system will reimburse the hospital if the patient is covered. In addition to the DRG system, coders use other coding systems, such as those required for ambulatory settings, physician offices, or long-term care.

Health information technicians' duties vary according to the size of the facility. In large to medium facilities, technicians may specialize in one aspect of health information, or supervise health information clerks and transcribers while a health information administrator manages the department. In small facilities, an accredited health information technician sometimes manages the department.

Work Environment

Medical records personnel generally work a standard 40-hour week. Some overtime may be required. In hospitals where medical record departments are open 18 to 24 hours a day, seven days a week, medical record personnel work on day, evening, and night shifts. Part-time work is generally available.

This is one of the few health occupations in which there is little or no physical contact with patients. The work environment is usually pleasant and comfortable, but some aspects of the job can be stressful. The utmost accuracy is essential, which demands concentration and close attention to detail. The emphasis on accuracy can cause fatigue and mental strain. Medical record technicians who work at video display terminals for prolonged periods may experience eyestrain and musculoskeletal pain.

Employment Opportunities

Medical records and health information technicians held about 170,000 jobs in 2006. About two out of five jobs were in hospitals. The rest were mostly in offices of physicians, nursing care facilities, outpatient care centers, and home healthcare services. Insurance firms that deal in health matters employ a small number of health information technicians to tabulate and analyze health information. Public health departments also employ technicians to supervise data collection from healthcare institutions and to assist in research.

Employment Opportunities

Employment of medical record and health information technicians is expected to increase by 18 percent through 2016—faster than the average for all occupations—because of rapid growth in the number of medical tests, treatments, and procedures that will be increasingly scrutinized by health insurance companies, regulators, courts, and consumers. In addition, technicians will be needed to enter patient information into computer databases to comply with federal legislation mandating the use of electronic medical records.

Educational and Legal Requirements

Medical record and health information technicians entering the field usually have a two-year associate degree from a community or junior college. Associate degree coursework includes classes in medical terminology and diseases, anatomy and physiology, legal aspects of medical record, coding and abstraction of data, statistics, databases, quality assurance methods, and computer training as well as general education. High school students can improve their chances of acceptance into a health information education program by taking courses in biology, chemistry, health, and especially computer training.

Many employers favor technicians who have become *Registered Health Information Technicians (RHIT)*. Registered Health Information Technicians must pass a written examination offered by the *American Health Information Management Association (AHIMA)*. To take the examination, a person must graduate from a two-year associate degree program accredited by the *Commission on Accreditation for Health Informatics and Information Management Education (CAHIIM)*. Technicians trained in non-CAHIIM-accredited programs or trained on the job are not eligible to take the examination. In 2007, there were about 245 CAHIIM accredited programs in Health Informatics and Information Management Education.

Experienced health information technicians usually advance in one of two ways—by specializing or by managing. Many senior health information technicians specialize in coding—particularly Medicare coding—or in tumor registry. Technicians who specialize in coding may also obtain voluntary certification.

In large health information departments, experienced technicians may advance to section supervisor, overseeing the work of coding, correspondence, or discharge sections. Senior technicians with RHIT credentials may become director or assistant director of a health information department in a small facility. In large institutions, however, the director is typically a health information administrator, with a bachelor's degree in health information administration.

EMPLOYMENT TRENDS

New jobs are expected in offices of physicians because of increasing demand for detailed records, especially in large group practices. New jobs also are expected in home healthcare services, outpatient care centers, and nursing and residential care facilities. Although employment growth in hospitals will not keep pace with growth in other healthcare industries, many new jobs will, nevertheless, be created. Cancer registrars should experience job growth. As the population continues to age, the incidence of cancer may increase.

EARNINGS

According to the latest information, median annual earnings of health information technicians were $28,030. The middle 50 percent earned between $22,420 and $35,990 per year. The lowest 10 percent earned less than $19,060 and the highest 10 percent earned more than $45,260 per year. Median annual earnings in the industries employing the largest number of health information technicians is shown in **Table 25–1**.

Table 25–1	*Median annual earnings in the industries employing the largest number of health information technicians*
General medical and surgical hospitals	$29,400
Nursing care facilities	$28,410
Outpatient care centers	$26,680
Offices of physicians	$24,170

RELATED OCCUPATIONS

Health information technicians need strong clinical background knowledge to analyze the contents of medical records. Other occupations that require knowledge of medical terminology, anatomy, and physiology, but do not interact directly with patients, are medical secretaries, transcriptionists, writers, and illustrators.

ADDITIONAL INFORMATION

Information on careers in medical record and health information technology, including a list of accredited programs, is available from:

■ American Health Information Management Association, 233 N. Michigan Ave., 21st Floor, Chicago, IL 60601-5800. http://www.ahima.org

Medical Transcriptionists

WORK DESCRIPTION

Medical transcriptionists translate and edit recorded dictation by physicians and other healthcare providers regarding patient assessment and treatment. They use headsets and transcribing machines to listen to recordings made by physicians and other healthcare professionals. These workers transcribe a variety of medical reports about emergency room visits, diagnostic imaging studies, operations, chart reviews, and final summaries.

To understand and accurately transcribe dictated reports into a format that is clear and comprehensible for the reader, the medical transcriptionist must understand the language of medicine, anatomy and physiology, diagnostic procedures, and treatment. They also must be able to translate medical jargon and abbreviations into their expanded forms. After reviewing and editing for grammar and clarity, the medical transcriptionist transcribes the dictated reports and returns them in either printed or electronic form to the dictating physician or care provider for review and signature, or correction. These reports eventually become a part of the patient's permanent file.

WORK ENVIRONMENT

The majority of medical transcriptionists are employed in comfortable settings. They usually work in hospitals, doctors' offices, or medical transcription services. An increasing number of court reporters and medical transcriptionists work from home-based offices as subcontractors for law firms, hospitals, and transcription services.

The work presents few hazards. Sitting in the same position for long periods can be tiring, however, and workers can suffer wrist, back, neck, or eye problems due to strain, and risk incurring repetitive motion injuries such as carpal tunnel syndrome. The pressure to be both accurate and fast also can prove stressful.

Most medical transcriptionists work a standard 40-hour week, although about one in four works part-time. A substantial number of medical transcriptionists are self-employed, which may allow for irregular working hours.

EMPLOYMENT OPPORTUNITIES

Employment of medical transcriptionists is projected to grow 14 percent from 2006 to 2016, faster than the average for all occupations. A growing and aging population will spur demand for medical transcription services because older age groups receive proportionately greater numbers of medical tests, treatments, and procedures requiring documentation. The continuing need for electronic documentation that can be shared easily among providers, third-party payers, regulators, consumers, and health information system will sustain a high level of demand for transcription services. Growing numbers of medical transcriptionists will be needed to amend patients' records, edit documents produced by speech recognition systems, and identify discrepancies in medical reports.

Outsourcing of transcription work overseas and advancements in speech recognition technology are not expected to reduce the need for well-trained medical transcriptionists within the United States. Outsourcing transcription work abroad—to countries such as India, Pakistan, Philippines, and the Caribbean—has grown more popular as transmitting confidential health information over the Internet has become more secure; however, the demand for overseas transcription services is expected only to supplement the demand for well-trained domestic medical transcriptionists. In addition, reports transcribed by overseas medical transcription services usually require editing for accuracy by domestic medical transcriptionists before they meet U.S. quality standards.

Speech recognition technology allows physicians and other health professionals to dictate medical reports into a computerized program that converts speech to text. In spite of advancements in this technology, speech recognition software has been slow to grasp and analyze the human voice and the English language, and the medical vernacular with all its diversity. As a result, there will continue to be a need for skilled medical transcriptionists to identify and appropriately edit the inevitable errors created by speech recognition systems, and to create a final document.

Job opportunities should be best for those who earn an associate degree or certification from the American Association for Medical Transcription.

EDUCATION AND LEGAL REQUIREMENTS

Employers prefer to hire transcriptionists who have completed postsecondary training in medical transcription offered by many vocational schools, community colleges, and distance-learning programs.

Completion of a two-year associate degree or one-year certificate program—including coursework in anatomy, medical terminology, legal issues relating to healthcare documentation, and English grammar and punctuation—is highly recommended, but not always required. Many of these programs include supervised on-the-job experience. Some transcriptionists, especially those already familiar with medical terminology from previous experience as a nurse or medical secretary, become proficient through refresher courses and training.

Formal accreditation is not required for medical transcription programs. However, the Approval Committee for Certificate Programs (AACP)—established by the *Association for Healthcare Documentation Integrity (AHDI)* and the *American Health Information Management Association*—offers voluntary accreditation for medical transcription programs. Although voluntary, completion of an ACCP approved program may be required for transcriptionists seeking certification.

The AHDI awards two voluntary designations, the *Registered Medical Transcriptionist (RMT)* and the *Certified Medical Transcriptionist (CMT)*. Medical transcriptionists who are recent graduates of medical transcription educational programs, or have fewer than two years experience in acute care, may become a registered RMT. The RMT credential is awarded upon successfully passing the AHDI level 1 registered medical transcription exam. The CMT designation requires at least two years of acute care experience working in multiple specialty surgery areas using different format, report, and dictation types. Candidates also must earn a passing score on a certification examination. Because medicine is constantly evolving, medical transcriptionists are encouraged to update their skills regularly. RMTs and CMTs must earn continuing education credits every three years to be recertified. As in many other fields, certification is recognized as a sign of competence.

For those seeking work as medical transcriptionists, understanding medical terminology is essential. Good English grammar and punctuation skills are required, as well as familiarity with personal computers and word processing software. Good listening skills are also necessary, because some doctors and health care professionals speak English as a second language.

EARNINGS

The most recent data show that medical transcriptionists had median hourly earnings of $14.40. The middle 50 percent earned between $12.17 and $17.06. The lowest 10 percent earned less than $10.22, and the highest 10 percent earned more than $20.15. Median hourly earnings in the industries employing the largest numbers of medical transcriptionists is detailed in **Table 25–2**.

Table 25–2	Median hourly earnings in the industries employing the largest numbers of medical transcriptionists	
	Medical and diagnostic laboratories	$15.68
	General medical and surgical hospitals	$14.62
	Business support services	$14.34
	Outpatient care centers	$14.31
	Office of physicians	$14.00

Compensation methods for medical transcriptionists vary. Some are paid based on the number of hours worked or on the number of lines transcribed. Others receive a base pay per hour with incentives for extra production. Large hospitals and healthcare organizations usually prefer to pay for the time an employee works. Independent contractors and employees of transcription services usually receive production-based pay.

RELATED OCCUPATIONS

A number of other workers type, record information, and process paperwork. Among these are administrative assistants, bookkeepers, receptionists, secretaries, and human resource clerks. Medical secretaries may also transcribe as part of their job. Other workers who provide medical support include medical assistants and medical record technicians.

ADDITIONAL INFORMATION

For information on a career as a medical transcriptionist, contact:

- Association for Healthcare Documentation Integrity, 4230 Kierman Avenue, Suite 130, Modesto, CA 95356. http://www.ahdionline.org

Medical Librarians

WORK DESCRIPTION

Medical, or health science, librarians provide essential services to professional staff and personnel in medicine, dentistry, nursing, pharmacy, the allied health professions, and other related technologies. Because health and related fields are growing rapidly, professional staff need quick and efficient access to large volumes of information and materials to keep abreast of developments, new procedures and techniques, and other relevant data. Relevant information and materials are used in education and training programs, in exchange-of-information activities among different health professions, and in biomedical research. Health science librarians make this information available to those who need it, utilizing knowledge of both library science and health science in their work.

Depending on the size of the facility where they work, health science librarians may take charge of an entire library or be assigned to specific functions. They select and order books, journals, and other materials, and classify and catalog acquisitions to allow their easy retrieval. Other duties include preparing guides to reference materials, compiling bibliographies, and selecting and acquiring films and other audiovisual materials.

Readers and researchers frequently call on the specialized skills of the librarian to track down information on a particular subject. The material may be bound in obscure documents or scattered in many places, requiring detective work to locate it. If the document is in another language, the librarian may be called on to obtain a translation. Frequently, the librarian is asked to compile a bibliography or to provide a comprehensive review or summary on a particular subject.

Aside from assisting patrons in person, the medical librarian also responds to mail, e-mail, and phone inquiries. Success in handling these inquiries depends largely on the librarian's skill. Librarians may have only very general knowledge of medicine, but they must know how and where to locate all types of information on short notice.

In hospitals, services offered by the medical library may depend on whether the hospital conducts research and training, or on the categories of illness treated there. Some hospitals have separate medical, nursing, and patient libraries. Increasingly, however, these collections are grouped together under the direction of one chief librarian, with assistants in charge of the separate services.

The medical librarian also plays an important role in the hospital's rehabilitation services. In addition, librarians serving patients provide book cart services, develop programs of interest for ambulatory patients, and visit new patients to learn about their reading interests.

WORK ENVIRONMENT

In addition to hospitals, medical librarians work in schools of medicine, nursing, dentistry, and pharmacy; research institutes; pharmaceutical and related industries; health departments; professional societies; and voluntary health agencies. Medical libraries are found in numerous locations throughout the country but tend to be concentrated in or near population centers. Individual size and working conditions vary greatly from library to library. For instance, hospital libraries may range from a staff size of one to slightly fewer than 100. In ill-equipped offices, librarians may risk eyestrain, backache, and carpal tunnel syndrome. Nevertheless, surroundings are usually pleasant and free of hazards or unusual environmental working conditions.

EMPLOYMENT OPPORTUNITIES

Employment of librarians is expected to grow by 4 percent between 2006 and 2016, slower than the average for all occupations. Growth in the number of librarians will be limited by government budget constraints and the increasing use of electronic resources. Both will result in the hiring of fewer librarians and the replacement of librarians with less costly library technicians and assistants. As electronic resources become more common and patrons and support staff become more familiar with their use, fewer librarians are needed to maintain and assist users with these resources. In addition, many libraries are equipped for users to access library resources directly from their homes or offices through library Web sites. Some users bypass librarians altogether and conduct research on their own. Librarians will still be needed, however, to manage staff, help users define their research needs and develop database search techniques, address complicated reference requests, and choose appropriate materials.

Over the next decade, jobs for medical librarians outside traditional settings will grow fastest. These settings include private industry, nonprofit organizations, and consulting firms. Examples of jobs in industry for medical librarians include the biotechnology, insurance, pharmaceutical, publishing, and medical equipment industries.

Many companies are turning to librarians because of their research and organizational skills and their knowledge of computer databases and library automation systems. Librarians also are hired by organizations to organize information on the Internet. Librarians working in these settings may be classified as systems analysts, database specialists and trainers, webmasters or web developers, or local area network (LAN) coordinators.

Most recently, medical and other librarians held about 158,000 jobs. Most were in school and academic libraries; others were in public and special libraries. A small number of librarians worked for hospitals and religious organizations. Others worked for governments. Entrepreneurial librarians sometimes start their own consulting practices, acting as freelance librarians or information brokers and providing services to other libraries, businesses, or government agencies. Projected slower-than-average employment growth through 2008 will result in fewer job openings for librarians. Replacement needs will account for more job openings over the next decade, as more than two out of three librarians are aged 45 or older, which will result in many job openings as these librarians retire. Slower than average employment growth, coupled with an increasing number of graduates with master's degrees in library science (MLS), will result in more applicants competing for fewer jobs. Applicants for librarian jobs in large cities or suburban areas will face competition, while those willing to work in rural areas should have better job prospects.

Educational and Legal Requirements

An MLS degree is necessary for librarian positions in most public, academic, and special libraries and in some school libraries. The federal government requires an MLS or the equivalent in education and experience. Many colleges and universities offer MLS programs, but employers often prefer graduates of the approximately 50 schools accredited by the American Library Association. Most MLS programs require a bachelor's degree; any liberal arts major is appropriate preparation for such graduate work.

Most MLS programs take one year to complete, but some take two. A typical graduate program includes courses in the foundations of library and information science, including the history of books and printing, intellectual freedom and censorship, and the role of libraries and information in society. Other basic courses cover material selection and processing, the organization of information, reference tools and strategies, and user services. Courses are adapted to educate librarians in using such new resources as online reference systems, Internet search methods, and automated circulation systems. Computer-related coursework is an increasingly important component of an MLS degree.

An MLS degree provides general preparation for library work, but some individuals specialize in one particular area. The minimum qualifications for librarians specializing in medicine are as follows:

- A master's of library and information science from an American Library Association–accredited school

- Strong oral and written communication skills

- Strong interpersonal skills

- Strong computer skills

Librarians participate in continuing training once they are on the job to keep abreast of new information systems brought about by changing technology. Most MLS schools offer courses in Health Sciences Information, which is recommended for those interested in becoming a medical librarian.

Earnings

Salaries of librarians vary according to the individual's qualifications and the type, size, and location of the library. Librarians with primarily administrative duties often have greater earnings. Median annual earnings of librarians were $49,060 in May 2006. The middle 50 percent earned between $39,250 and $60,800. The lowest 10 percent earned less than $30,930 and the highest 10 percent earned more than $74,670 per year.

The Medical Library Association reports that the average starting salary was $40,832 in 2005. The overall average salary for medical librarians in 2005 was $57,982. Library directors can earn up to $158,000.

RELATED OCCUPATIONS

Librarians play an important role in the transfer of knowledge and ideas by providing people with access to the information they need and want. Jobs requiring similar analytical, organizational, and communication skills include physicians, nurses, health educators, allied healthcare professionals, administrators, and information technology programmers and specialists.

ADDITIONAL INFORMATION

Information on librarianship, including information on scholarships or loans, is available from the American Library Association. Consult its Web site for a listing of accredited library education programs.

- American Library Association, Office for Human Resource Development and Recruitment, 50 East Huron St., Chicago, IL 60611. http://www.ala.org

For information on employment opportunities as a health science librarian, scholarship information, credentialing information, and a list of MLA-accredited schools offering programs in health sciences librarianship, contact:

- Medical Library Association, 65 East Wacker Place, Suite 1900, Chicago, IL 60601-7246. http://www.mlanet.org

HEALTH SERVICES ADMINISTRATION

Key Terms

- Programs
- Budgets
- Health services (generalist, clinical)
- Review
- Organization and coordination
- Executive
- Chief executive officer (CEO)
- Negotiation

- Leadership
- Financial viability
- Associate administrator
- Assistant administrator
- Marketing
- Strategic planning
- Governing board
- Policies
- Philosophy

The Need for Professional Management

Effective management of healthcare organizations and of the considerable resources at their disposal requires competent managers. Like their counterparts in any organization, health services managers are responsible for facilities, services, programs, staff budgets, and relations with other organizations.

The term "health services manager" encompasses individuals who plan, direct, coordinate, and supervise the delivery of health care. Health services managers may be either generalists or specialists. Generalists manage or help to manage an entire facility or system, whereas specialists are in charge of specific clinical departments or services.

The job of managing a healthcare facility increases in complexity as advances in medical technology multiply and dozens of specialty health professions continue to emerge. These developments, together with significant changes in consumer expectations, business practices, and healthcare financing result in a growing need for competent professional health services managers.

In line with their training and/or experience in a specific clinical area, clinical managers have more specific responsibilities than generalist managers. For example, directors of physical therapy are experienced physical therapists, and most health information and medical record administrators have a bachelor's degree in health information or medical record administration. These managers establish and implement policies, objectives, and procedures for their departments; evaluate personnel and work performance; develop reports and budgets; and coordinate activities with other managers.

Another aspect of professional management is the need to address the extensive oversight and scrutiny to which health facilities are subject. Both past performance and future plans are subject to review by a variety of groups and organizations, including consumer groups, government agencies, professional oversight bodies, insurance companies and other third-party payers, business coalitions, and even the courts. Preparing for inspection visits by observers from regulatory bodies and submitting appropriate records and documentation can be time consuming as well as technically demanding.

Health Services Managers

WORK DESCRIPTION

Health services manager is an inclusive term for individuals in many different positions who plan, organize, and coordinate the delivery of health care. Hospitals provide more than half of all jobs in this field. Other employers of health services managers include medical group practices; outpatient clinics; HMOs; nursing homes; hospices; home health agencies; rehabilitation, community mental health, emergency care, and diagnostic imaging centers; and offices of doctors, dentists, and other health practitioners.

Three functional levels of administration are found in hospitals and other large facilities—executive, internal management, and specialized staff. The chief executive officer (CEO) provides overall management direction, but also is concerned with community outreach, planning, policy making, response to government agencies and regulations, and negotiation. The CEO often speaks before civic groups, promotes public participation in health programs, and coordinates the hospital or facility's activities with those of government or community agencies. Institutional planning is an increasingly important responsibility of chief administrators, who continually must assess the need for services, personnel, facilities, and equipment, and periodically recommend changes such as shutting down a maternity ward or opening an outpatient clinic. Chief administrators need leadership ability as well as technical skills to respond effectively to community requirements for health care, while at the same time satisfying demand for financial viability, cost containment, and public and professional accountability. Within a single institution, such as a community hospital, the healthcare administrator is directly accountable to a board of trustees made up of community leaders who are voted onto the board to determine broad policies and objectives for the hospital.

Day-to-day management, particularly in large facilities, may be the responsibility of one or more associate or assistant administrators, who work with service unit managers and staff specialists. Depending on the size of the facility, associate or assistant administrators may be responsible for budget and finance; human resources, including personnel administration, education, and in-service training; information management; and direction of the medical, nursing, ancillary services, housekeeping, physical plant, and other operating departments. As the healthcare system becomes more specialized, skills in financial management, marketing, strategic planning, systems analysis, and labor relations will be needed as well.

Hospital and nursing home administration differ in important respects. Hospitals are complex organizations, housing as many as 30 highly specialized departments, including admissions, surgery, clinical laboratory, therapy, emergency medicine, nursing, physical plant, medical records, accounting, and so on. The hospital administrator works with the governing board in establishing general policies and operating philosophy and provides direction to the department heads and the assistant administrators (or vice presidents), who implement those policies. The hospital administrator coordinates the activities of the assistant administrators and department heads to ensure that the hospital runs efficiently, provides high-quality medical care, and recovers adequate revenue to remain solvent or profitable. Administrators represent the hospital to the community and the state. Nationally, they participate in professional associations such as the American Hospital Association, the American Public Health Association, and the Association of Mental Health Administrators.

Nursing home administrators need many of the same management skills as hospital administrators. Administrative staffs in nursing homes, however, are typically much smaller than those in hospitals. Nursing home administrators often have only one or two assistant administrators, and sometimes none. As a result, nursing home administrators are involved in day-to-day management decisions much more often than hospital administrators in all but the smallest hospitals. Nursing home administrators wear various hats—personnel director, director of finance, director of facilities, and admissions director, for example. They analyze data and then make daily management decisions in all of these areas. In addition, because many nursing home residents stay for months or even years, administrators must try to create an environment that nourishes residents' psychological, social, and spiritual well-being, as well as tends to their healthcare needs.

In the growing field of group practice management, administrators and managers need to be able to work effectively with the physicians who own the practice. Specific job duties vary according to the size of the practice. While an office manager handles the business side in very small medical groups, leaving policy decisions to the physicians themselves, larger groups generally employ a full-time administrator to provide advice on business strategies and coordinate the day-to-day management of the practice.

A group of 10 or 15 physicians might employ a single administrator to oversee personnel matters, billing and collection, budgeting, planning, equipment outlays, advertising, and patient flow, whereas a practice of 40 or 50 physicians would require a chief administrator and several assistants, each responsible for a different area of management. In addition to providing overall management direction, the chief administrator of a group practice is responsible for ensuring that the practice maintains or strengthens its competitive position. This is no small task, given the rapidly changing nature of the healthcare environment. Ensuring competitiveness might entail market research to analyze the services the practice currently offers and those it might offer, negotiating contracts with hospitals or other healthcare providers to gain access to specialized facilities and equipment, or entering into joint ventures for the purchase of an expensive piece of medical equipment, such as a magnetic resonance imager.

Managers in HMOs perform all the functions of administrators and managers in large medical group practices, plus one additional function—administering what amounts to an insurance company. HMO subscribers pay an annual fee that covers almost all of their care. HMO managers must establish a comprehensive medical benefits package with enrollment fees low enough to attract adequate enrollments but high enough to operate successfully. In addition, they may work more in the areas of community outreach and preventive care than do managers of a group practice. The size of the administrative staff in HMOs varies according to the size and type of HMO. Some health services managers oversee the activities of health systems that may encompass a number of inpatient and outpatient facilities and offer a wide range of patient services.

WORK ENVIRONMENT

Health services managers often work long hours. Facilities such as nursing homes and hospitals operate around the clock, and administrators and managers may be called at all hours to deal with emergencies. The job also may include travel to attend meetings or to inspect healthcare facilities.

EMPLOYMENT OPPORTUNITIES

Medical and health services managers held about 262,000 jobs in 2006. About 37 percent worked in hospitals, and another 22 percent worked in offices of physicians or in nursing and residential care facilities. Most of the remainder worked in home healthcare services, federal government healthcare facilities, outpatient care centers, insurance companies, and community care facilities for the elderly.

EDUCATIONAL AND LEGAL REQUIREMENTS

Health services managers must be familiar with management principles and practices. A master's degree in health services administration, long-term care administration, health sciences, public health, public administration, or business administration is the standard credential for most generalist positions in this field. However, a bachelor's degree is adequate for some entry-level positions in smaller facilities and for some entry-level positions at the departmental level within healthcare organizations. In addition, physicians' offices and some other facilities may accept on-the-job experience as a substitute for formal education.

For clinical department heads, a degree and work experience in the appropriate field may be sufficient for entry, but a master's degree in health services administration or a related field may be required to advance. For example, nursing services administrators are usually chosen from among supervisory registered nurses who have administrative abilities and a graduate degree in nursing or health services administration.

Bachelor's, master's, and doctoral degree programs in health administration are offered by colleges, universities, and schools of public health, medicine, allied health, public administration, and business administration. In 2006, 73 schools had accredited programs leading to a master's degree in health services administration, according to the Accrediting Commission on Education for Health Services Administration.

Some graduate programs seek out students with undergraduate degrees in business or health administration; others prefer students with a liberal arts or health profession background. Candidates with previous work experience in health care may also have an advantage. Competition for entry into these graduate programs is keen, and applicants need above-average grades to gain admission.

Graduate degree programs usually last between two and three years. They may include as much as one year of supervised administrative experience and coursework in hospital organization and management, marketing, accounting and budgeting, human resource administration, strategic planning, health economics, and health information systems. Some programs allow students to specialize in one type of facility—hospitals, nursing homes, mental health facilities, HMOs, or medical groups, for example. Other programs encourage a generalist approach to health administration education.

Recent graduates with master's degrees in health services administration may start as department managers or in staff positions. The level of the starting position varies with the experience of the applicant and the size of the organization. Hospitals and other health facilities offer postgraduate residencies and fellowships, which are usually staff positions. Graduates from master's degree programs also take jobs in HMOs, large group medical practices, clinics, mental health facilities, multifacility nursing home corporations, and consulting firms.

Graduates with bachelor's degrees in health administration usually begin as administrative assistants or assistant department heads in larger hospitals, or as department heads or assistant administrators in small hospitals or nursing homes.

All states and the District of Columbia require nursing home administrators to have a bachelor's degree, pass a licensing examination, complete a state-approved training program, and pursue continuing education. A license is not required in other areas of health services management.

Health services managers are often responsible for millions of dollars in facilities and equipment and hundreds of employees. In order to make effective decisions, they need to be open to different opinions and good at analyzing contradictory information. They must understand finance and information systems and be able to interpret data. Motivating others to implement their decisions requires strong leadership abilities. Tact, diplomacy, flexibility, and communication skills are essential, because health services managers spend most of their time interacting with others.

Health services managers advance by moving into more responsible and higher-paying positions, such as assistant or associate administrator, or by moving to larger facilities.

EMPLOYMENT TRENDS

Employment of medical and health services managers is expected to grow 16 percent between 2006 and 2016, faster than the average for all occupations. The healthcare industry will continue to expand and diversify, requiring managers who can help ensure smooth business operations. Job opportunities will be good, especially for applicants with work experience in the healthcare field and strong business management skills. Medical and health services managers with experience in large hospital facilities will enjoy an advantage in the job market, as hospitals become larger and more complex.

As insurance companies and Medicare demand higher levels of accountability, medical and health services managers will be needed in all healthcare settings to improve quality and efficiency of health care while controlling costs, hospitals will continue to be the largest employers of medical and health services managers over the 2006 to 2016 decade. However, the number of new jobs created is expected to increase at a slower rate in hospitals than in many other industries because of the increasing use of clinics and other outpatient care sites.

Employment will grow fastest in practitioners' offices and in home healthcare agencies. Demand in medical group practice management will grow as medical group practices become larger and more complex. Medical and health services managers also will be sought by healthcare management companies that provide management services to hospitals and other organizations, including to specific departments such as emergency, information management, managed care contract negotiations, and physician recruiting.

EARNINGS

According to the latest data, median annual earnings of medical and health services managers were $73,340. The middle 50 percent earned between $57,240 and $94,780 per year. The lowest 10 percent earned less than $45,050 and the highest 10 percent earned more than $127,830 per year. Median annual earnings in the industries employing the largest number of medical and health services managers is shown in **Table 26–1**.

Earnings of health services managers vary by type and size of the facility as well as by level of responsibility. For example, the Medical Group Management Association reported the following median salaries in 2006 for administrators by group practice size:

Table 26–1	*Median annual earnings in the industries employing the largest number of medical and health service managers*	
General medical and surgical hospitals		$78,660
Outpatient care centers		$67,920
Offices of physicians		$67,540
Nursing care facilities		$66,730
Home health care services		$66,720

- Fewer than seven physicians, $72,875
- Seven to 25 physicians, $95,766
- More than 26 physicians, $132,955

According to a survey conducted by *Modern Healthcare* magazine,[1] median annual compensation in 2001 for managers of the following clinical departments was as follows:

- Respiratory therapy, $76,800
- Radiology, $93,500
- Laboratory services, $88,000
- Physical therapy, $81,000
- Rehabilitation services, $94,400
- Nursing services, $102,800
- Pharmacy, $113,200

Salaries also varied according to size of facility and geographic region.

RELATED OCCUPATIONS

Health services managers have training or experience in both health care and management. Other occupations requiring knowledge of both fields are public health directors, social welfare administrators, directors of voluntary health agencies and health professional associations, and underwriters in health insurance companies.

ADDITIONAL INFORMATION

General information about health administration is available from:

■ American College of Healthcare Executives, One North Franklin St., Suite 1700, Chicago, IL 60606. http://www.ache.org

Information about undergraduate and graduate academic programs in this field is available from:

■ Association of University Programs in Health Administration, 2000 14th Street North, Suite 780, Arlington, VA 22201. http://www.aupha.org

For a list of accredited graduate programs in health services administration, contact:

■ Commission on Accreditation of Health Care Management Educators. 2000 14th Street North, Suite 780, Arlington, VA 22201. http://www.cahme.org

For information about career opportunities in long-term care administration, contact:

■ American College of Health Care Administrators, 12100 Sunset Hills Road, Suite 130, Reston, VA 20190. www.achca.org.

For information about career opportunities in medical group practices and ambulatory care management, contact:

■ Medical Group Management Association, 104 Inverness Terrace East, Englewood, CO 80112. http://www.mgma.com

For information about healthcare office managers, contact:

■ Professional Association of Health Care Office Managers, 4700 W. Lake Ave., Glenview, IL 60025. http://www.pahcom.com

Reference

1.   *Modern Health Care*, The Labor Scene, June 18, 2001.

FEDERAL AND STATE HEALTH REGULATORS

Key Terms

- Federal and state health regulators
- City, county, district, state, and federal laws
- Interpretation and enforcement
- Environmental health control
- Environmental hazards
- Consumer safety inspectors and officers
- Inspection
- Occupational Safety and Health Administration (OSHA) inspectors

- Investigations
- Environmental health inspectors (sanitarians)
- Food inspectors
- National Oceanic and Atmospheric Administration
- U.S. Department of Agriculture's Food Safety and Inspection Service (FSIS)
- U.S. Food and Drug Administration (FDA)

Government Health and Safety Officers

Federal and state health regulators are responsible for controlling, preserving, or improving environmental conditions so that community health, safety, comfort, and well-being are maintained. City, county, district, state, federal, and other laws regulate sanitary standards for food and water supplies; garbage, waste, and sewage disposal; as well as housing maintenance. Health and safety officers interpret and enforce these laws. Within the field of environmental health control, they regulate hazardous substances and their disposal, and monitor water and air quality. New sanitary problems are created as the population increases and as more people move into the cities and suburbs of expanding metropolitan areas. With technical training and experience, regulators are equipped to recognize and anticipate environmental hazards. Their responsibilities entail calling these problems to the attention of local and other relevant governments, community leaders, civic groups, and the general public. They also recommend changes for solving the problems.

WORK DESCRIPTION

Federal and state regulators, usually referred to as inspectors and compliance officers, help to keep workplaces safe, food healthy, and the environment clean. They also ensure that workers' rights are recognized in a variety of settings. They enforce rules on matters as diverse as health, safety, food quality, licensing, and finance. As the following occupations demonstrate, their duties vary widely, depending on their area of responsibility and level of experience.

Consumer safety inspectors and officers inspect food, feeds, pesticides, weights and measures, biological products, cosmetics, drugs, medical equipment, and radiation-emitting products. Working individually or in teams under a senior inspector, they check on firms that use, produce, handle, store, or market the products that they regulate. They ensure that standards are maintained and respond to consumer complaints by questioning employees, vendors, and others to obtain evidence. Inspectors look for inaccurate product labeling, inaccurate scales, and decomposition or chemical/bacteriological contamination that could result in a product becoming harmful to health. After completing their inspection, inspectors discuss their observations with plant managers or business owners to point out areas where corrective measures are needed. They write reports of their findings and compile evidence for use in court if legal action is required.

Occupational Safety and Health Administration (OSHA) inspectors serve the Department of Labor as expert consultants on the application of safety principles, practices, and techniques in the workplace. They conduct fact-finding investigations of workplaces to determine the existence of specific safety hazards. They may be assigned to conduct safety inspections and investigations, using any supplies, sampling and measuring devices, or other technical equipment required to complete their work. These inspectors attempt to prevent accidents by using their knowledge of engineering safety codes and standards, and they may order the suspension of activities that pose threats to workers.

Environmental health inspectors, also called sanitarians, work primarily for governments. The U.S. Food and Drug Administration is responsible for the safety of both domestic and imported foods. Inspectors analyze substances to identify contamination or the presence of disease, and investigate sources of contamination to ensure that food, water, and air meet government standards. They certify the purity of food and beverages produced in dairies and processing plants or served in restaurants, hospitals, and other institutions. Inspectors may find pollution sources through collection and analysis of air, water, or waste samples. When they determine the nature and cause of pollution, they initiate action to stop it and force the firm or individual responsible for the pollutants to pay for their removal.

Food inspectors ensure that products are fit for human consumption in accordance with federal laws governing the wholesomeness and purity of meat, poultry, and egg products. The Food Safety and Inspection Service (FSIS) of the U.S. Department of Agriculture is the governmental agency responsible for meat, poultry, and egg products. Its food inspectors visually examine livestock or poultry prior to slaughter, and conduct post-mortem inspections to determine that the resulting food product is not contaminated and that sanitation procedures are maintained. Food processing inspectors specialize in processed meat and poultry products, and all other ingredients contained in the final products, including frozen dinners, canned goods, and cured and smoked products. They have the authority to shut a plant down if they encounter a problem that they are unable to resolve.

WORK ENVIRONMENT

Inspection and compliance officers work with many different people and in a variety of environments. Their jobs often involve considerable fieldwork, and some inspectors travel frequently. When traveling, they are generally furnished with an automobile or are reimbursed for their travel expenses.

Inspectors may experience unpleasant, stressful, and dangerous working conditions. For example, federal food inspectors work in highly mechanized plant environments near operating machinery with moving parts, or with poultry or livestock in confined areas in extreme temperatures and on slippery floors. Their duties often require working with sharp knives, moderate lifting, and walking or standing for long periods. Many inspectors work long and often irregular hours. In addition, they may find themselves in adversarial roles when the organization or individual being inspected objects to the inspection process or its consequences.

EMPLOYMENT OPPORTUNITIES

Most recently, inspectors and compliance officers held about 176,000 jobs. State governments employed 30 percent, the federal government—chiefly the Departments of Defense, Labor, Treasury, and Agriculture—employed 31 percent, and local governments employed 19 percent of these workers. The remaining 20 percent were employed throughout the private sector in educational institutions, hospitals, insurance companies, and manufacturing firms.

A wide range of agencies employs inspectors and compliance officers who work for the federal government. Some consumer safety inspectors, for example, work for the U.S. Food and Drug Administration, but the majority work for state governments. The U.S. Department of Agriculture employs most food inspectors and agricultural commodity graders. Other food inspectors are employed by the National Oceanic and Atmospheric Administration within the Department of Commerce and are responsible for the safety of fish and fish products.

Many health inspectors work for state and local governments. Compliance inspectors are employed primarily by the Departments of Treasury and Labor on the federal level, but some work for state and local governments. The Department of Defense employs the majority of quality assurance inspectors. The Environmental Protection Agency employs inspectors to verify compliance with pollution control and other laws. The U.S. Department of Labor and many state governments employ safety and health inspectors, equal opportunity officers, and mine safety and health inspectors. The U.S. Department of the Interior employs park rangers.

Average growth in employment of inspectors and compliance officers is expected through 2006, reflecting the trend of balancing the continuing public demand for a safe environment and quality products against the desire for smaller government and fewer regulations. Additional job openings will arise from the need to replace workers who transfer to other occupations, retire, or leave the labor force for other reasons. In private industry, employment growth will reflect industry growth and the continuing self-enforcement of government and company regulations and policies, particularly among franchise operations in various industries.

Employment of inspectors and compliance officers is seldom affected by general economic fluctuations. Federal, state, and local governments, which employ four-fifths of all inspectors, provide considerable job security.

EDUCATIONAL AND LEGAL REQUIREMENTS

Because of the diversity of the functions they perform, qualifications for inspector and compliance officer jobs vary widely. Requirements include a combination of education, experience, and passing scores on written examinations. Many employers, including the federal government, require college degrees for some positions. Experience in the area being investigated is also a prerequisite for many positions.

Environmental health inspectors or sanitarians, familiar to many health facility personnel, provide one example of the educational and other qualifications needed for work as an inspection and compliance officer. Entry level environmental health inspectors may have completed a full four-year course of study that meets all of the requirements for a bachelor's degree, and that included or was supplemented by at least 30 semester hours in a science or any combination of sciences directly related to environmental health—for example, sanitary science, public health, chemistry, microbiology, or any appropriate agricultural, biological, or physical science. Alternately, sanitarians may have four years of specialized experience in inspectional, investigational, technical support, or other work that provided a fundamental understanding of environmental health principles, methods, and techniques equivalent to that which would have been gained through a four-year college curriculum or some combination of education and experience as described above. Most environmental scientists need a master's degree in environmental science or a related science, such as a life science or chemistry, for jobs in the government. In most states, they are licensed by examining boards.

Personal qualifications that mark the true professional in any discipline may be applicable in this occupation as well. These characteristics include the ability to work effectively with people, a commitment to service, and true concern for public health and well-being. Prospective inspectors also should have a strong interest in science.

All inspectors and compliance officers are trained in the applicable laws or inspection procedures through some combination of classroom and on-the-job training. In general, people who want to enter this occupation should be responsible and like detailed work. Inspectors and compliance officers should be able to communicate well.

Federal government inspectors and compliance officers whose job performance is satisfactory can advance up their particular career ladder to a specified full-performance level. For positions above this level, usually supervisory positions, advancement is competitive and based on agency needs and individual merit. Advancement opportunities in state and local governments and the private sector are often similar to those found in the federal government.

EARNINGS

According to the latest information, the median annual salary of inspectors and compliance officers (other than construction inspectors) was $54,920. The middle half earned between $41,800 and $70,230. The lowest 10 percent earned less than $32,230 while the highest 10 percent earned more than $83,720. Inspectors and compliance officers employed by local governments had earnings of $52,110; those who worked for state governments earned a median annual salary of $49,690; and those in the federal government earned $68,890.

In the federal government, the annual starting salaries for inspectors varied from $28,862 to $53,438 in 2006, depending on geographic location and the nature of the inspection or compliance activity. Beginning salaries were slightly higher in selected areas where the prevailing local pay level was higher. Average salaries for selected inspectors and compliance officers in the federal government in nonsupervisory, supervisory, and managerial positions in early 2006 are shown in **Table 27–1**.

Most inspectors and compliance officers work for federal, state, and local governments or in large private firms, most of which generally offer more generous benefits than do smaller firms.

Table 27–1

Average salaries for selected inspectors and compliance officers in the federal government in nonsupervisory, supervisory, and managerial positions in early 2006

Environmental protection specialists	$68, 280
Safety and occupational health managers	$59,270
Agricultural commodity graders	$44,141
Consumer safety inspectors	$40,779
Food inspectors	$39,864

RELATED OCCUPATIONS

Inspectors and compliance officers ensure that laws and regulations are obeyed. Others who enforce laws and regulations include construction and building inspectors; fire marshals; federal, state, and local law enforcement professionals; correctional officers; fish and game wardens; aviation safety inspectors; equal opportunity specialists; mine safety and health inspectors; park rangers; and securities compliance examiners.

ADDITIONAL INFORMATION

Information on obtaining a job with the federal government is available from the Office of Personnel Management through a telephone-based system. Consult a telephone directory under U.S. Government for a local number or call (703) 724-1850 or (978) 461-8404 (TDD). Information is also available on the Internet at http://www.usajobs.opm.gov.

Information regarding jobs in federal, state, and local governments, as well as in private industry, is available from each state's employment service.

Environmental Health Technicians and Aides

A growing need exists for environmental health technicians and aides. Correspondingly, greater recognition exists that these paraprofessionals need a career ladder to advance to first-degree professional (bachelor's degree in science) and to postgraduate levels should they desire. Accredited community colleges, therefore, frequently offer a two-year associate of science degree, which includes the necessary general education courses, and which allows students to transfer to a four-year college or university to complete their training. Students interested in pursuing a course of study to become an environmental health technician or aide should contact local community or junior colleges for specifics.

28 HEALTH EDUCATION

Key Terms

- Special education
- Physical and mental disabilities
- Emotional disturbance
- Cultural difference
- Mental and intellectual gifts and talents
- Health educator
- Health education programs

- Educational therapist
- Orientation and mobility instructor
- Rehabilitation teacher
- School health educator
- Teachers of those who are blind or have visual impairment
- Itinerant program

Health Educators in Specialized Settings

The health field offers a variety of career opportunities to persons interested in education—community health education, school health education, educational therapy, and special education. These professions and specialties within them are detailed in this chapter.

Health education is an expanding field that emphasizes the importance of preventive health care. As professionals, health educators use educational skills and a sound knowledge of public health to educate the public about health and disease and what can be done to maintain good health, prevent disease, or secure treatment.

While the health educator concentrates on the nonschool community, school health educators are concerned with the school environment. Their main concerns are classroom teaching and the factors that influence the knowledge, behavior, attitudes, and practices that affect the health of students.

Educational therapy is another career area of major importance in the health field. Educational therapists work with individuals who live with emotional disturbance, or physical, geriatric, or other disability, in a variety of health and educational facilities. Educational therapists combine both educational and therapeutic approaches in treating individuals of all ages with learning disabilities or learning problems. Examples of learning disability are attention deficit disorder, poor social skills, poor organizational or study skills, language processing problems or visual processing problems. Career opportunities are also available for teachers in special education. Special education teachers work with pupils who have physical disabilities, emotional disturbances, mental retardation, or specific mental and intellectual gifts and talents. They also work with pupils experiencing cultural differences. These types of pupils are found in school systems, institutions, hospitals, or rehabilitation centers, and, because of their unusual or extraordinary traits, they need the services that only special education can provide.

A significant branch of the health education field presents challenging career opportunities for work with individuals who are blind or have visual impairments. Professionals in this work provide essential services to persons with these conditions, enabling them to function successfully in a sighted world. The different types of specialists who work with those who are blind or have visual impairment include orientation and mobility instructors, rehabilitation teachers, and other specially trained teachers.

Health Educators

WORK DESCRIPTION

The basic function of health educators is to provide people with the facts about health, the causes of disease, and methods of prevention so they will act for their own well-being and that of their families. The basic goals and duties of health educators are the same, but their jobs vary greatly depending on the type of organization in which they work. Most health educators work in medical care settings, colleges and universities, schools, public health departments, nonprofit organizations, and private business.

Within medical care facilities, health educators tend to work one-on-one with patients and their families. Their goal in this setting is to educate individual patients on their diagnosis and how that may change or affect their lifestyle. This often includes explaining necessary procedures or surgeries, as well as how patients will need to change their lifestyles in order to manage their illness or return to full health. This may include directing patients to outside resources that may be useful in their transition, such as support groups, home health agencies, or social services. Health educators often work closely with physicians, nurses, and other staff to create educational programs or materials, such as brochures, Web sites, and classes. In some cases, health educators train hospital staff how to interact better with patients.

Health educators in colleges and universities work primarily with the student population. Generally, they create programs on health topics that affect young adults, like sexual activity, smoking, and nutrition. They may need to alter their teaching methods to attract audiences to their events. For example, they might show a popular movie and follow it with a discussion, or hold programs in dormitories or cafeterias. They may teach courses for credit or give lectures on health-related topics. Often they train students to lead their own programs as peer educators.

Health educators in schools are typically found in secondary schools, where they generally teach health class. They develop lesson plans that are relevant and age appropriate to their students. They may need to cover sensitive topics, like sexually transmitted diseases, alcohol, and drugs. They may be required to teach other subjects, such as science or physical education. Some develop the health education curriculum for the school or the entire school district.

Health educators working in public health are employed primarily by state and local departments of public health and, therefore, administer state-mandated programs. They often serve as members of statewide councils or national committees on topics like aging. As part of this work, they inform other professionals of changes to health policy. They work closely with nonprofit organizations to help them obtain the resources, such as grants, that they may need to continue serving the community.

Health educators in nonprofit organizations strive to get information out to the public on various health problems and make people aware of the community resources available to help them. While some organizations target a particular audience, others educate the community regarding one particular disease or health issue. Health educators in this setting, therefore, may be limited in the topics they cover or the population they serve. Work in this setting may include creating printed materials for distribution to the community, often while organizing lectures, health screenings, and other activities intended to increase awareness.

In private industry, health educators create programs to educate employees of an entire firm or organization. They organize programs that fit into workers' schedules by arranging lunchtime speakers or daylong health screenings so that workers may attend when it is most convenient. Educators in this setting must align their work with the overall goals of their employers. For example, a health educator working for a medical supply company may hold a program related to the company's newest product.

Health educators attempt to prevent illnesses by informing and educating individuals and communities about health-related topics. They assess the needs of their audience, which includes determining which topics to cover and how best to present the information. For example, they may hold programs on self-examinations for breast cancer detection to women who are at higher risk, or may teach classes on the effects of binge drinking to college students. Health educators must take the cultural norms of their audience into account. Programs targeted at the elderly may need to be drastically different from those aimed at college students.

After assessing their audiences' needs, health educators must decide how to meet those needs. They have many options to choose from when putting together programs. Health educators may organize a lecture, class, demonstration, or health screening; or they may create a video, pamphlet or brochure. Often, planning a program requires working with others on a team or committee within a given organization. Health educators also must consider the goals and objectives of their employers when planning a program. For example, many nonprofit organizations educate the public about a single disease or health issue, such as cardiovascular disease and, therefore, limit their programs to topics related to that disease or issue.

After planning their effort, health educators move on to implementing their proposed plan. They may obtain funding by applying for grants, writing curricula for classes, or creating written materials that would be made available to the public. In addition, implementing their programs may require dealing with basic logistics problems, such as finding speakers or locations for the planned event.

Generally, after a program is presented, health educators evaluate its success. This could include tracking the absentee rate of employees from work and students from school, surveying participants on their opinions about the program, or other methods of collecting evidence that suggests whether the programs were effective. Through evaluation, health educators can improve plans for the future by learning from mistakes and capitalizing on strengths.

Although programming is a large part of their job, health educators also serve as a resource on health topics. They may locate services, reference material, and other resources useful to the community they serve, and refer individuals or groups to appropriate organizations or medical professionals.

Health educators may work through a wide variety of intermediaries in the community—teachers, club leaders, health officers, public health nurses, trade-union program directors, scout leaders, and community group leaders. In this way, health educators can reach a much larger audience than they would otherwise. These various intermediaries have a personal relationship with those being educated and are therefore likely to have a significant influence on them.

Health educators also work with the mass media, including newspapers, magazines, radio and television programs, trade newspapers, and organizational newsletters. They prepare or direct the preparation of appropriate articles, features, and photographs for use by the media, or work directly with writers, editors, or program directors. As a result, the influence of community health educators is extended to vast audiences that could not be reached otherwise. Contact with the public through the media is admittedly less desirable than personal contact. However, in health education, as in other educational efforts, many methods are used to complement and reinforce each other for a cumulative effect.

Educators have recognized that it is not enough just to point out the hazards of one practice or the advantages of another. There are many obstacles to perception and appropriate action, including emotional resistance, language barriers, or psychological blocks. Whatever the obstacles are, it is the job of the health educator to identify them and devise methods to overcome or sidestep them. Otherwise, health education will be ineffective or will not take place, because health education is meant to be more than information—it is meant to motivate effective action. To overcome resistance, health educators use various techniques of investigation—interviews, surveys, and community studies—together with insights gained from psychology, sociology, and anthropology. A basic tenet of health educators is that the individuals they are educating should be the ones to make final decisions about health practices. Nevertheless, educators accept responsibility for providing access to all sources of necessary information so that individuals can relate desirable health practices to their personal goals, aspirations, and values.

Health educators thus serve as psychological stage setters, stimulating people in the community to recognize health problems of which they may be unaware and to work for their solution. Such problems might be pollution of the environment, chronic disease, overpopulation, drug abuse, or any of hundreds of ills that plague today's society. Health educators know that constructive group action can often accomplish wonders. Even more important, when people work together to solve a problem of common concern, they are more likely to arrive at a solution that will work.

When a particular community interest group is ready to act, the health educator helps its members set up effective relationships with other interested groups in the community—schools, churches, health agencies, welfare organizations, and labor unions. Perhaps the health educator will assist in organizing a conference, planning a neighborhood cleanup campaign, or developing a television series dramatizing poor health conditions in farm labor camps. Whatever the duties they may take on in any particular case, the aim of the educator is always to encourage more effective individual and group action designed to maintain and improve the health of people throughout the community.

Sometimes the obstacles to health promoting action lie not with the community, but with the people providing health services. Clinic hours may be arranged more for the convenience of the professionals working there than for the public. Clinic staff may be curt and impersonal in their treatment of the people they serve. Advice may be given in technical terms rather than in language that lay people can easily understand. In these cases, the health educator can play an important role by helping other health personnel plan and deliver health care in ways that the community can and will utilize. Community health educators also often have the task of educating legislators and other policy makers in the importance of considering consumer interests while planning and funding health programs.

With major changes taking place in the delivery of health care at local, regional, and national levels, participation of health educators in planning groups is increasingly in demand. By seeking the involvement of all interested persons, health educators work toward the solution of a particular problem through a variety of avenues. They help to define common goals and to stimulate and guide discussion to assist various groups in reaching their own decisions and determining how they will implement them. Whether helping a ghetto neighborhood plan its own health center, or helping representatives from state agencies agree on needed regional medical facilities, the health educator helps people to help themselves by bringing needs and resources together to create new partnerships for health.

Frequently, improving health care involves training for health workers who must keep abreast of new knowledge in their own professional disciplines through continuing education; for young people entering a new health career; for neighborhood health aides who will help to improve health communications among the poor; and for ethnic group members and citizen volunteers who are ready to assume community leadership. Here again, the health educator can contribute to better health by helping to develop training programs, by suggesting creative methods, and even by training the trainers themselves to be better teachers.

EDUCATIONAL AND LEGAL REQUIREMENTS

Entry-level health educator positions generally require a bachelor's degree in health education, but some employers prefer a bachelor's degree and some related experience gained through an internship or volunteer work. A master's degree may be required for some positions and is usually required for advancement. In addition, some employers may require candidates to be *Certified Health Education Specialists*.

Undergraduate programs teach students the theories of health education and help them develop the skills necessary to implement health education programs. Courses in psychology, human development, and a foreign language are helpful, and experience gained through an internship or other volunteer opportunities can make graduates more appealing to employers.

A graduate degree is usually required to advance to jobs such as executive director, supervisor, or senior health educator. Work in these positions may require more time on planning and evaluating programs than on their implementation, and may require supervising other health educators who implement the programs. Health educators at this level may also work with other administrators of related programs.

Graduate health education programs are often offered under titles such as community health education, school health education, or health promotion, and lead to a Master of Arts, Master of Science, Master of Education, or a Master of Public Health degree. Many students pursue their master's in health education after majoring or working in another related field, such as nursing or psychology. A master's degree is required for most health educator positions in public health. Doctoral degrees are also offered in public health education. Many persons with doctoral degrees in this specialty will continue to be needed to meet the growing demand for research and evaluation skills in health education and for teaching in institutions of higher learning.

Health educators may choose to become a *Certified Health Education Specialist*, a credential offered by the National Commission of Health Education Credentialing, Inc. The certification is awarded after successful completion of an examination in the basic areas of responsibility for a health educator. In addition, to maintain certification, health educators must complete 75 hours of approved continuing education courses or seminars over a five-year period. Some employers may require and pay for educators to take continuing education courses to keep their skills up-to-date.

Like workers in many other health occupations, community health educators should enjoy people and work well with them. They must be able to play a variety of roles successfully and adjust to the demands of different situations. At times, these educators work behind the scenes to help others start and carry out projects in the public interest. Sometimes they need to help people caught in conflict understand one another's point of view, while they maintain the trust and goodwill of all parties concerned. At other times, educators must be people's advocates until the people come forward to speak for themselves.

School Health Educators

WORK DESCRIPTION

School health educators help children and young people develop the knowledge, attitudes, and skills they need to live healthfully and safely. They cooperate closely in this task with the school's physician and nurse, as well as with the school's other teachers and service personnel. Usually, they also participate in community health activities as representatives of the school health education program.

Health education has a place all the way from nursery school and kindergarten through high school and on into college because it deals with day-to-day living. It is health education when five-year-olds learn to eat new foods, and when high school seniors make a field survey of the health services available in their community.

Depending on the school system and on the school grades covered, health courses may include such subject matter as family life education, first aid, safety education, choice and use of health services and products, nutrition, personal hygiene, air and water pollution, alcohol and drug abuse, and community health. Health courses include the principles of mental health and good human relations, as well as marriage and family life. Comprehensive health education curricula include sex education where allowed; in some states, it is required.

School health educators may have even broader responsibilities as health coordinators. School health coordinators may work in a single school or in an entire school system; they furnish leadership in developing and maintaining an adequate, well-balanced health program and helping all groups interested in the health of schoolchildren work together effectively.

EDUCATIONAL AND LEGAL REQUIREMENTS

The school health educator needs four years of college education leading to a bachelor's degree, with a background in the biological, behavioral, and social sciences and health education. Increasingly, a master's degree is required.

The school health educator must meet the regular certification standards for teachers in the state. Generally, these call for 15 to 20 credits in professional courses in a school of education. These courses usually include educational philosophy, the techniques of teaching, child growth and development, and educational psychology. A period of internship may also be required. These standards vary from state to state, and the student is advised to check desired locations for requirements.

For the school health educator, the advanced degree is usually in the field of health education. A doctoral degree is often required for college teaching jobs. The school health educator should have an aptitude for scientific and social studies. In general, personal qualifications for this educational specialist are similar to those for the successful teacher in any field. It is important to like working with children and young people and to have patience, a sense of humor, good judgment, and emotional stability.

EMPLOYMENT OPPORTUNITIES

Employment of health educators is expected to grow much faster than the average for all occupations. Job prospects for health educators with bachelor's degrees will be favorable, but better for those who have acquired experience through internships or volunteer jobs. According to the American School Health Association, moderate increases are expected in the demand for school health educators. This expectation is based primarily on greater public interest in health programs, as well as on increases in federal funds available for health education programs.

EMPLOYMENT TRENDS IN HEALTH EDUCATION

The rising cost of health care has increased the need for health educators. Health educators are employed by insurance companies, employers and governments in an attempt to curb costs. One of the more cost effective ways is to employ health educators to teach people how to live healthy lives and avoid costly treatments for illnesses. Awareness of the number of illnesses, such as lung cancer, HIV, heart disease, and skin cancer that may be avoided with lifestyle changes has increased. In addition, many illnesses, such as breast and testicular cancer are best treated with early detection. The need to provide the public with this information will result in state and local governments, hospitals, and businesses employing a growing number of health educators.

The emphasis on health education has been coupled with a growing demand for qualified health educators. In the past, it was thought that anyone could do the job of a health educator and the duties were often given to nurses or other healthcare professionals. However, in recent years, employers have recognized that those trained specifically in health education are better qualified to perform those duties. Therefore, demand for health professionals with a background specifically in health education has increased. Demand for health educators will increase in most industries, but their employment may decrease in secondary schools. Many schools, facing budget cuts, ask teachers trained in other fields, such as science or physical education, to teach the subject of health education.

EARNINGS

Salaries for health educators will vary depending on the work setting. Those in school-affiliated roles receive salaries and benefits on the same scale as other teachers in their school system. Health educators working in industry and government usually receive higher salaries, commensurate with their education and experience. Those in college teaching receive the same range of pay as other teachers. Those in consultant roles usually set their own fees, based on their location and other factors.

Median annual earnings of health educators were $41,330 in May 2006; the middle 50 percent earned between $31,300 and $56,580. The lowest 10 percent earned less than $24,750, and the highest 10 percent earned more than $72,500. Median annual earnings in the industries employing the largest numbers of health educators in May 2006 are shown in **Table 28–1.**

Table 28–1	**Median annual earnings in the industries employing the largest numbers of health educators in May 2006**
General medical and surgical hospitals	$40,890
State government	$33,100
Local government	$32,420
Outpatient care centers	$27,530
Individual and family services	$25,760

Educational Therapists

WORK DESCRIPTION

Educational therapy is designed to meet the needs of the individual patient through instruction in prescribed subjects, and it provides treatment and rehabilitation measures to assist in restoring patients to their fullest mental and physical capacities.

Educational therapy is part of a prescribed medical treatment program for patients with physical disabilities, emotional disturbance, or senility, or those who are acutely and/or chronically ill. It is used mainly with patients who, because of their disability, are withdrawn, depressed, or agitated, or who feel detached from normal life and reality. As the name implies, educational therapy is a form of teaching. However, the purpose is not so much to give knowledge, as it is to stimulate interest, confidence, and self-esteem; to overcome abnormal moods and emotions; and to restore a sense of connection with the world and other people.

As a member of the rehabilitation team, the educational therapist evaluates the patient's learning ability and retention of previous learning experiences, interests, needs, and goals. Using this information, the therapist devises a treatment plan that fits into the patient's total rehabilitation program. The therapist then starts group or individual training in elementary, secondary, commercial, or vocational subjects to meet the needs and goals of the patient. Subject areas include English, chemistry, biology, mathematics, typing, shorthand, painting, bookkeeping, driver education, basic living skills, and preparation for obtaining a high school equivalency diploma. The educational therapist adapts course content and teaching methods to the patient's particular disability and individual needs.

Educational therapists may administer tests and send results to school authorities or state departments of education for grading and certification of the patient's education level. They also report to the rehabilitation team on patients' emotional reactions to and progress in individual and group situations. Educational therapists also refer patients to community education services such as colleges, universities, and credit-by-exam programs.

WORK ENVIRONMENT

Many educational therapists work in Veterans Administration (VA) facilities such as hospitals, centers, domiciliaries, and regional offices. They are also employed in private and state schools, federal prisons, the Job Corps, and adult learning centers. Therapists work under the direction of doctors in VA facilities, but usually without them in other types of facilities. Educational therapists usually work from 8:00 a.m. to 4:30 p.m., five days a week. Their work setting is often unstructured, and therapists are often allowed to organize and conduct patient therapy independently, under the direction of the chief therapist. Clinics are often small, with a staff of three to five therapists who work closely with patients on a one-to-one basis. There are no unusual physical demands in this work, and therapists who have visual impairments, are partly or almost completely paralyzed, or use prosthetic devices can be successful if they have adapted to their disabilities.

EDUCATIONAL AND LEGAL REQUIREMENTS

Certain personal qualities are essential for success in educational therapy. Among these are sensitivity to underlying moods and emotions, strong motivation to help people with disabilities overcome their difficulties, and the ability to "reach" and communicate with troubled people. Before deciding on this field, a student should gain some volunteer experience in a community or institutional healthcare setting, with exposure to health and other rehabilitation problems.

After completing high school, a student interested in a career in educational therapy must enroll in a four-year Bachelor of Arts or Bachelor of Sciences degree program. The degree must be in elementary or secondary education or child development with courses in educational assessment, learning theory, learning disabilities, and principles of educational therapy. Typical coursework includes subjects such as psychology, working with people with emotional disturbance and physical disabilities, and the psychology of disability. In addition to a college degree, two to seven months of clinical training are required, either as in-service training or at a training center affiliated with a professional school. While in clinical training, the student observes patient treatments, attends patient conferences, and receives training in all areas of educational therapy. The student works with patients under the guidance of therapists in various specialties and is evaluated for job performance, completion of clinical projects, and successful completion of a final examination. Several training institutions also offer postgraduate programs for qualified educational therapists.

Professional membership in the Association of Educational Therapists (AET) is open to educational therapists who have a master's degree or have met the course requirements, are engaged in educational therapy, have met the direct service delivery minimum of 1,500 hours and have completed their Board Certified Educational Therapist (BCET) Supervised Hours. To become a *Board Certified Educational Therapist*, AET members must meet the following additional requirements to sit for the certification exam: master's degree, one-year membership in AET at the Professional level and 1000 hours of professional practice.

EMPLOYMENT OPPORTUNITIES

Employment prospects for educational therapists are expected to continue to be favorable. This expectation is based on the current nationwide expansion of rehabilitation facilities and the growing recognition of the importance of educational therapy. In addition, as life expectancy increases, there should be a greater need for therapists in programs for the aging. Disabilities resulting from military service or those caused by daily stress and poor living conditions should create a number of jobs for educational therapists. Qualified therapists can advance to supervisory positions; promotions are generally based on work experience and completion of advanced education courses.

Orientation and Mobility Instructors for People Who Are Blind or Have Visual Impairments

WORK DESCRIPTION

Orientation and mobility instructors are specialists who teach people with blindness or visual impairments to move about effectively, efficiently, and safely in familiar and unfamiliar environments. They work with people of differing ages and abilities, from young children to adults who have recently lost their sight. They also may work with persons who have multiple disabilities. Their objective is to help these individuals adjust personally and achieve maximum independence through specialized training. Orientation and mobility instructors evaluate their clients to determine their level of adjustment, degree of motivation, and the extent and safety of their indoor and outdoor mobility. Based on this information, they plan and provide individualized programs for instruction.

Most instructors work on a one-to-one basis and assist clients in making the maximum use of their remaining senses, primarily auditory (sound) and tactile (touch). They train clients to orient themselves to physical surroundings and use a variety of actual or simulated travel situations to develop the clients' ability to travel alone, with or without a cane.

Orientation and mobility instructors evaluate and prepare progress reports on each of their clients and work closely with other professionals such as physicians and social workers, as well as volunteers and families of clients. They work with others to develop community resources within their area of expertise and attend various professional seminars, workshops, and conferences to keep abreast of the latest methods, techniques, and travel aids.

WORK ENVIRONMENT

Orientation and mobility instructors are employed in residential and public schools, rehabilitation centers, and public and private community-based agencies, hospitals, nursing homes, and homes of clients. Working conditions for instructors vary from one facility to another. They normally can expect to work a 40-hour week, with hours from 8:00 a.m. to 4:30 p.m., and occasionally are required to work at a specific location. Instructors may sometimes accompany their clients to recreational activities and social gatherings.

EDUCATIONAL AND LEGAL REQUIREMENTS

Persons considering a career in this area must enjoy working with people and have the capacity to learn from, as well as teach clients. This work requires instructors to work closely with other professionals as part of a rehabilitation team, as well as with families, friends, and colleagues of clients. Orientation and mobility instructors should possess mature judgment, emotional and social maturity, adaptability, resourcefulness, and leadership potential.

The basic educational requirement for this work is a bachelor's degree, although a master's degree is preferable. If the bachelor's degree is not in the specific field and a higher degree is being sought, it is preferred that the bachelor's degree be in one of the behavioral sciences. Programs consist of combined academic and clinical training; upon completion of the training, graduates are required to serve an internship. In addition, students entering this field must have no less than 20/40 visual acuity in the better eye with best possible correction and minimum of 140-degree continuous field measured together.

The Academy for Certification of Vision Rehabilitation and Education Professionals provides certification for orientation and mobility instructors who meet specified education and experience standards. However, there are no nationwide uniform legal requirements for licensing, certification, or registration that serve as standards for employment. State or local licensing agencies should be contacted to determine relevant current standards.

EMPLOYMENT OPPORTUNITIES

Employment prospects for qualified orientation and mobility instructors are quite favorable, and available openings far exceed the number of graduates entering the labor market each year.

Orientation and mobility instructors can advance to supervisory, managerial, and administrative positions in this field. Generally, advancement is based on work experience and expertise, and the completion of advanced education courses.

Rehabilitation Teachers

WORK DESCRIPTION

Rehabilitation teachers are specialists who provide instruction and guidance to individuals who are blind or those who have visual impairments. They develop plans of instruction that enable their clients to carry out daily activities, develop independence, and achieve satisfactory ways of living. Rehabilitation teachers work with individuals or small groups in the home setting, as well as in healthcare facilities, such as rehabilitation centers, hospitals, nursing homes, retirement homes, or community centers. They must have a broad knowledge of many subjects, and some teachers may specialize in a particular skill. For example, they help those who are newly blind or congenitally blind develop communications skills by providing instruction in the use of Braille, large print, recorded materials, low-vision aids, and telephones. In addition, they teach nonverbal communication skills, such as facial expressions, hand movements, and head nods for use in communication with sighted persons.

Rehabilitation teachers provide instruction in personal and home management skills for normal living. These skills include personal hygiene and grooming, table etiquette, cooking, budget preparation, childcare, and minor home repairs. These teachers also help clients obtain specially designed equipment, such as Braille clocks and watches, sewing aids, and various types of appliances.

Each client with whom the rehabilitation teacher works is unique. Beyond the obvious fact that they are adults with visual impairments, the most common attribute of clients is that they are individuals with their own needs and desires, levels of functioning, and goals. These differences must be noted and respected by the rehabilitation teacher, whose role is to help the client reach the level of functioning he or she wishes, rather than make the client fit a preconceived image.

EDUCATIONAL AND LEGAL REQUIREMENTS

Students considering this career area can expect to spend four to six years in preparation after completing high school. The minimum educational standard for entry into this field is a bachelor's degree from an accredited college; however, a master's degree in this specialization is preferable in most cases.

The Academy for Certification of Vision Rehabilitation and Education Professionals certifies rehabilitation teachers who meet specified education and experience requirements. However, there are no national legal standards concerning licensure, registration, certification, or continuing education. State or local licensing agencies should be contacted to obtain information specific to a particular locale.

EMPLOYMENT OPPORTUNITIES

The need for qualified rehabilitation teachers is growing due to increases throughout the country in the number of persons experiencing blindness or visual impairment, particularly among senior citizens. Each of these individuals will need the professional, specialized services that only a rehabilitation teacher can provide.

Qualified rehabilitation teachers can advance to supervisory or administrative positions in health agencies, or to teaching positions in colleges or universities. Generally, advancement in this field is governed by experience, skill level, and the completion of advanced education programs.

Teachers for People Who Are Blind or Have Visual Impairments

WORK DESCRIPTION

Teachers trained to teach students who are blind or have visual impairments provide specialized educational services to children in residential, public, or private schools. Residential schools are those in which children live and attend regular classes with other children who are also blind. Teachers in these schools usually concentrate their efforts on teaching a single subject, such as history or mathematics, but they may also be called on to give special education courses.

Resource programs differ from residential schools and programs by allowing students to attend regular public school classes. In these programs, a central location is provided for use by participating students from several school districts. Here resource teachers provide instruction in special skills, such as Braille or the use of recording devices. In addition, the teachers make certain that the students' assignments are up-to-date and that each student has required lessons in Braille, large type, or recorded form. Besides working directly with their students, resource teachers coordinate their efforts with classroom teachers, school psychologists, and parents to ensure that educational objectives are being met.

An itinerant program is the third type of program employing teachers for students with blindness or visual impairments. In itinerant programs, teachers travel from school to school and meet with students on a regularly scheduled basis. In this way, students are able to attend classes at their regular neighborhood school and receive special instruction there, without needing to travel to a central school district location. Teachers in itinerant programs also act as consultants on special education to classroom teachers, parents, and school officials. It is important to note that teachers specializing in instruction of those with blindness or visual impairments, regardless of the type of program in which they work, may be called on to teach a wide range of regular school subjects along with special education courses.

EDUCATIONAL AND LEGAL REQUIREMENTS

Students considering this career area can expect to spend from four to six years in preparation after completing high school. The educational minimum for entry into this work is a bachelor's degree from an accredited college; however, a master's degree is preferred in most cases.

The Academy for Certification of Vision Rehabilitation and Education Professionals certifies teachers who meet specified education and experience requirements. In addition, these teachers must be certified or licensed by the department of education in the state in which they work. Because these requirements vary throughout the country, students considering this career should contact their local superintendent of schools or state department of education to obtain specific information.

EMPLOYMENT OPPORTUNITIES

Employment prospects in this career area are favorable. As greater numbers of children with visual impairments require specialized education services, the demand for qualified teachers is expected to grow. Increasing need also exists for services to the elderly who develop vision problems as part of the aging process. There are currently 10 million Americans with visual impairments. The majority, 6.5 million, are 55 years and older; and the number of older adults with vision loss or impairment is expected to double by 2030. The elderly often do not receive the assistance needed to maintain independence with loss of vision. Should they wish to do so, qualified teachers in this specialty can advance to supervisory and administrative positions or teach at the college level. Advancement is usually based on experience, skill level, and the completion of advanced education courses.

RELATED OCCUPATIONS

Health education is a profession that bridges the gap between health information and health practices. It also seeks to encourage the responsibility of individuals for their own health and to work toward the national goal of optimal health for all. Other members of the healthcare team who engage in similar work include dietitians, nurses, physicians, physical therapists, occupational therapists, vocational rehabilitation counselors, and other related health professionals.

ADDITIONAL INFORMATION

For further information, contact:

- Association of Schools of Public Health, 1011 15th St. N.W., Suite 910, Washington, DC 20005. http://www.asph.org

- American School Health Association, 7263 State Route 43, P.O. Box 708, Kent, OH 44240. http://www.ashaweb.org

- U.S. Department of Health and Human Services, HRSA, Bureau of Health Professions, 5600 Fishers Ln., Room 805, Rockville, MD 20857. http://www.hrsa.gov/

- Association of Educational Therapists, 11300 W. Olympic Bend, Suite 600, Los Angeles, CA 90064. http://www.aetonline.org/

- American Foundation for the Blind, 11 Penn Plaza, Suite 300, New York, NY 10001. http://www.afb.org/

- Commission on Rehabilitation Counselor Certification, 300 N. Martengale Road, Suite 460, Schaumburg, IL 60173. http://www.crccertification.com/

- Academy of Certification of Vision Rehabilitation and Education Professionals, 3333 N. Campbell Avenue, Suite 11, Tucson, AZ 85719. http://www.acvrep.org/

- American Counseling Association, 5999 Stevenson Ave., Alexandria, VA 22304. http://www.counseling.org/

- National Rehabilitation Association, 633 S. Washington Street, Alexandria, VA 22314-4119. http://www.nationalrehab.org/

VETERINARY MEDICINE

Key Terms

- Animal and human health
- Standards for pure food from animal sources
- Livestock health
- Veterinarian
- Transmissible diseases
- Space research
- Marine research
- Companion animal medicine
- Food animal veterinarian
- Research
- Food safety inspections
- Physician/veterinarian teams
- Regulatory medicine
- Public health
- Toxicology
- Animal technician
- Groomer
- Groom
- Veterinary assistant
- Keeper

Veterinary Medicine

Veterinary medicine is one of the oldest healing arts and involves both animal and human health. One of its main functions is the control of diseases transmissible from animals to humans, and the discovery of new knowledge in comparative medicine.

Veterinary medicine has come to the rescue of a disappearing food supply. Doctors of veterinary medicine (DVM's) monitor the food supply. They guard the health of all domestic protein-producing animals, and set and enforce standards for pure food from animal sources. Safeguarding our food supply by ensuring livestock health and wholesomeness is one of veterinary medicine's most important functions. Through this work the whole population is served directly.

Veterinarians

WORK DESCRIPTION

Veterinarians care for the health of pets, livestock, and animals in zoos, racetracks, and laboratories. Some veterinarians use their skills to protect humans against diseases carried by animals and conduct clinical research on human and animal health problems. Others work in basic research, broadening our knowledge of animals and medical science, and in applied research, developing new ways to use knowledge.

Most veterinarians diagnose animal health problems; vaccinate against diseases, such as distemper and rabies; medicate animals suffering from infections or illnesses; treat and dress wounds; set fractures; perform surgery; and advise owners about animal feeding, behavior, and breeding.

According to the American Medical Veterinary Association, more than 70 percent of veterinarians who work in private medical practices predominately, or exclusively, treat small animals. Small-animal practitioners usually care for companion animals, such as dogs and cats, but also treat birds, reptiles, rabbits, ferrets, and other animals that can be kept as pets. About one-fourth of all veterinarians work in mixed animal practices, where they see pigs, goats, cattle, sheep, and some wild animals in addition to companion animals.

A small number of veterinarians in private practice work exclusively with large animals, mostly horses or cattle; some also care for various kinds of food animals. These veterinarians usually drive to farms or ranches to provide veterinary services for herds or individual animals. Much of this work involves preventive care to maintain the health of the animals. These veterinarians test for and vaccinate against diseases, and consult with farm or ranch owners and managers regarding animal production, feeding, and housing issues. They also treat and dress wounds, set fractures, and perform surgery, including cesarean sections on birthing animals. Other veterinarians care for zoo, aquarium, or laboratory animals. Veterinarians of all types euthanize animals when necessary.

Veterinarians who treat animals use medical equipment such as stethoscopes, surgical instruments, and diagnostic equipment, including radiographic and ultrasound equipment. Veterinarians working in research use a full range of sophisticated laboratory equipment.

Veterinarians contribute to human as well as animal health. A number of veterinarians work with physicians and scientists as they research ways to prevent and treat various human health problems. For example, veterinarians contributed greatly in conquering malaria and yellow fever, solved the mystery of botulism, produced an anticoagulant used to treat some people with heart disease, and defined and developed surgical techniques for humans, such as hip and knee joint replacements, and limb and organ transplants. Today, some determine the effects of drug therapies, antibiotics, or new surgical techniques by testing them on animals.

Some veterinarians are involved in food safety and inspection. Veterinarians who are livestock inspectors, for example, check animals for transmissible diseases, such as E. coli, advise owners on the treatment of their animals, and may quarantine animals. Veterinarians who are meat, poultry, or egg product inspectors examine slaughtering and processing plants, check live animals and carcasses for disease, and enforce government regulations regarding food purity and sanitation. More veterinarians are finding opportunities in food security as they ensure that the nation has abundant and safe food supplies. Veterinarians involved in food security often work along the nation's borders as animal and plant health inspectors, where they examine imports and exports of animal products to prevent disease here and in foreign countries. Many of these workers are employed by the Department of Homeland Security or the Department of Agriculture's Animal and Plant Health Inspection Service division.

WORK ENVIRONMENT

Veterinarians in private or clinical practice often work long hours in a noisy indoor environment. Sometimes they have to deal with emotional or demanding pet owners. When working with animals that are frightened or in pain, veterinarians risk being bitten, kicked, or scratched.

Veterinarians in large-animal practice spend time driving between their office and farms or ranches. They work outdoors in all kinds of weather, and may have to treat animals or perform surgery under unsanitary conditions.

Veterinarians working in nonclinical areas, such as public health and research, experience working conditions similar to those of other professionals in those lines of work. These veterinarians enjoy clean, well-lit offices or laboratories, and spend much of their time dealing with people rather than animals.

Veterinarians often work long hours. Those in group practices may take turns being on call for evening, night, or weekend work; solo practitioners may work extended and weekend hours, responding to emergencies or squeezing in unexpected appointments.

EMPLOYMENT OPPORTUNITIES

Veterinarians held about 62,000 jobs in 2006. According to the American Veterinary Medical Association, about three out of four veterinarians were employed in a solo or group practice. Most others were salaried employees of another veterinary practice. Data from the U.S. Bureau of Labor Statistics show that the federal government employed about 1,400 civilian veterinarians, chiefly in the U.S. Departments of Agriculture, Health and Human Services, and, increasingly, Homeland Security. Other employers of veterinarians are state and local governments, colleges of veterinary medicine, medical schools, research laboratories, animal food companies, and pharmaceutical companies. A few veterinarians work for zoos, but most veterinarians caring for zoo animals are private practitioners who contract with the zoos to provide services, usually on a part-time basis.

In addition, many veterinarians hold veterinary faculty positions in colleges and universities and are classified as teachers.

EDUCATIONAL AND LEGAL REQUIREMENTS

Veterinarians must obtain a Doctor of Veterinary Medicine degree and a state license. Keen competition exists for admission to veterinary school.

Education and Training. Prospective veterinarians must graduate with a Doctor of Veterinary Medicine (DVM or VMD) degree from a four-year program at an accredited college of veterinary medicine. There are 28 colleges in 26 states that meet accreditation standards set by the Council on Education of the American Veterinary Medical Association (AVMA).

The prerequisites for admission to veterinary programs vary. Many programs do not require a bachelor's degree for entrance, but all require a significant number of credit hours—ranging from 45 to 90 semester hours—at the undergraduate level. However, most of the students admitted have completed an undergraduate program and earned a bachelor's degree. Applicants without a degree face a difficult task gaining admittance.

Preveterinary courses should emphasize the sciences. Veterinary medical colleges typically require applicants to have taken classes in organic and inorganic chemistry, physics, biochemistry, general biology, animal biology, animal nutrition, genetics, vertebrate embryology, cellular biology, microbiology, zoology, and systemic physiology. Some programs require calculus; some require only statistics, college algebra, and trigonometry, or pre-calculus. Most veterinary medical colleges also require some courses in English or literature, other humanities, and the social sciences. Increasingly, courses in general business management and career development have become a standard part of the curriculum to teach new graduates how to effectively run a practice.

In addition to satisfying preveterinary course requirements, applicants must submit test scores from the Graduate Record Examination (GRE), the Veterinary College Admission Test (VCAT), or the Medical College Admission Test (MCAT), depending on the preference of the college to which they are applying. Currently, 22 schools require the GRE, four require the VCAT, and two accept the MCAT.

There is keen competition for admission to veterinary school. The number of accredited veterinary colleges has remained largely the same since 1983, but the number of applicants has risen significantly. Only about one in three applicants was accepted in 2005.

New graduates with a Doctor of Veterinary Medicine degree may begin to practice veterinary medicine once they receive their license, but many new graduates choose to enter a one-year internship. Interns receive a modest salary, but often find that their internship experience leads to better paying opportunities later, relative to the opportunities of other veterinarians. Veterinarians who then seek board certification also must complete a three- to four-year residency program that provides intensive training in one of the 20 AVMA-recognized veterinary specialties, which include internal medicine, oncology, pathology, dentistry, nutrition, radiology, surgery, dermatology, anesthesiology, neurology, cardiology, ophthalmology, preventive medicine, and exotic small-animal medicine.

Licensure. All states and the District of Columbia require that veterinarians be licensed before they can practice. The only exemptions are for veterinarians working for some federal agencies and some state governments. Licensing is controlled by the states and is not strictly uniform, although all states require the successful completion of the DVM degree—or equivalent education—and a passing grade on a national board examination, the North American Veterinary Licensing Exam. This eight-hour examination consists of 360 multiple-choice questions covering all aspects of veterinary medicine, as well as visual materials designed to test diagnostic skills.

The Educational Commission for Foreign Veterinary Graduates grants certification to individuals trained outside the United States who demonstrate that they meet specified requirements for English language and clinical proficiency. This certification fulfills the educational requirement for licensure in all states.

Most states also require candidates to pass a state jurisprudence examination covering state laws and regulations. Some states do additional testing on clinical competency as well. There are few reciprocal agreements between states, veterinarians who wish to practice in a different state usually must first pass that state's examinations.

Other Qualifications. When deciding whom to admit, some veterinary medical colleges place heavy consideration on a candidate's veterinary and animal experience. Formal experience, such as work with veterinarians or scientists in clinics, agribusiness, research, or some area of health science, is particularly advantageous. Less formal experience, such as working with animals on a farm, ranch, stable or animal shelter, also can be helpful. Students must demonstrate ambition and an eagerness to work with animals.

Prospective veterinarians must have good manual dexterity. They should have an affinity for animals and the ability to get along with their owners, especially pet owners, who usually have strong bonds with their pets. Veterinarians who intend to go into private practice should possess excellent communication and business skills, because they will need to manage their practice and employees successfully and to promote, market, and sell their services.

Advancement. Most veterinarians begin as employees in established group practices. Despite the substantial financial investment in equipment, office space, and staff, many veterinarians with experience eventually set up their own practice or purchase an established one.

Newly trained veterinarians can become federal government meat and poultry inspectors, disease-control workers, animal welfare and safety workers, epidemiologists, research assistants, or commissioned officers in the U.S. Public Health Service or various branches of the armed forces. A state license may be required.

Nearly all states have continuing education requirements for licensed veterinarians. Requirements differ by state and may involve attending a class or otherwise demonstrating knowledge of recent medical and veterinary advances.

EMPLOYMENT TRENDS

Employment is expected to increase much faster than average. Excellent job opportunities are expected.

Employment Change. Employment of veterinarians is expected to increase 35 percent over the 2006 to 2016 decade, much faster than the average for all occupations. Veterinarians usually practice in animal hospitals or clinics and care primarily for companion animals. Recent trends indicate particularly strong interest in cats as pets. Faster growth of the cat population is expected to increase the demand for feline medicine and veterinary services, while demand for veterinary care for dogs should continue to grow at a more modest pace.

Many pet owners are relatively affluent and consider their pets a member of the family. These owners are becoming more aware of the availability of advanced care and are more willing to pay for intensive veterinary care than owners in the past. Furthermore, the number of pet owners purchasing pet insurance is rising, increasing the likelihood that considerable money will be spent on veterinary care.

More pet owners also will take advantage of nontraditional veterinary services, such as cancer treatment and preventive dental care. Modern veterinary services have caught up to human medicine; certain procedures, such as hip replacement, kidney transplants, and blood transfusions, which were once only available for humans, are now available for animals.

Continued support for public health, food and animal safety, national disease control programs, and biomedical research on human health problems will contribute to the demand for veterinarians, although the number of positions in these areas is limited. Homeland security also may provide opportunities for veterinarians involved in efforts to maintain abundant food supplies and minimize animal diseases in the United States and in foreign countries.

Job Prospects. Excellent job opportunities are expected because there are only 28 accredited schools of veterinary medicine in the United States, resulting in a limited number of graduates—about 2,700—each year. The limited number of veterinary schools, however, also means that applicants face keen competition for admission.

New graduates continue to be attracted to companion-animal medicine because they prefer to deal with pets and to live and work near heavily populated areas, where most pet owners live. Employment opportunities are good in cities and suburbs, but even better in rural areas because fewer veterinarians compete to work there.

Beginning veterinarians may take positions requiring evening or weekend work to accommodate the extended hours of operation that many practices are offering. Some veterinarians take salaried positions in retail stores offering veterinary services. Self-employed veterinarians usually have to work hard and long to build a sufficient client base.

The number of jobs for large-animal veterinarians is likely to grow more slowly than jobs for companion-animal veterinarians. Nevertheless, job prospects should be better for veterinarians who specialize in farm animals because of lower earnings in the farm-animal specialty and because many veterinarians do not want to work in rural or isolated areas.

Veterinarians with training in food safety and security, animal health and welfare, and public health and epidemiology should have the best opportunities for a career in the federal government. **Table 29–1** shows some projection data provided by the Department of Labor.

EARNINGS

Median annual earnings of veterinarians were $71,990 in May 2006. The middle 50 percent earned between $56,450 and $94,880. The lowest 10 percent earned less than $43,530, and the highest 10 percent earned more than $133,150. The average annual salary for veterinarians in the federal government was $84,335 in 2007. According to a survey by the

Table 29–1	Projections data from the National Employment Matrix				
Occupational title	Employment, 2006	Projected employment, 2016	**Change, 2006–2016**		
			Number	Percent	
Veterinarians	62,000	84,000	22,000	35	

NOTE: Data in this table are rounded.

American Veterinary Medical Association, average starting salaries of veterinary medical college graduates in 2006 varied by type of practice are indicated in **Table 29–2**.

Table 29–2	Average starting salaries of veterinary medical college graduates in 2006 by type of practice
Large animals, exclusively	$61,029
Small animals, predominantly	$57,117
Small animals, exclusively	$56,241
Private clinical practice	$55,031
Large animals, predominantly	$53,397
Mixed animals	$52,254
Equine (horses)	$40,130

RELATED OCCUPATIONS

Veterinarians prevent, diagnose, and treat diseases, disorders, and injuries in animals. Those who do similar work for humans include chiropractors, dentists, optometrists, physicians and surgeons, and podiatrists. Veterinarians have extensive training in physical and life sciences, and some do scientific and medical research, as do biological scientists and medical scientists.

Animal care and service workers and veterinary technologists and technicians also work extensively with animals. Like veterinarians, they must have patience and feel comfortable with animals. However, the level of training required for these occupations is substantially less than that needed by veterinarians.

ADDITIONAL INFORMATION

For additional information on careers in veterinary medicine, a list of U.S. schools and colleges of veterinary medicine, and accreditation policies, send a letter-size, self-addressed, stamped envelope to:

- American Veterinary Medical Association, 1931 N. Meacham Rd., Suite 100, Schaumburg, IL 60173. http://www.avma.org

For information on veterinary education, contact:

- Association of American Veterinary Medical Colleges, 1101 Vermont Ave. N.W., Suite 301, Washington, DC 20005. http://www.aavmc.org

For information on scholarships, grants, and loans, contact the financial aid officer at veterinary schools of interest.

For information on veterinarians working in zoos, see the *Occupational Outlook Quarterly* article "Wild jobs with wildlife," online at http://www.bls.gov/opub/ooq/2001/spring/art01.pdf.

Information on obtaining a veterinary position with the federal government is available from the Office of Personnel Management through USAJOBS, the federal government's official employment information system. This resource for locating and applying for job opportunities can be accessed through the Internet at http://www.usajobs.opm.gov or through an interactive voice response telephone system available from the Web site. These numbers are not toll-free, and charges may result.

For advice on how to find and apply for federal jobs, see the *Occupational Outlook Quarterly* article "How to get a job in the Federal Government," online at http://www.bls.gov/opub/ooq/2004/summer/art01.pdf.

Veterinary Technologists and Technicians

WORK DESCRIPTION

Owners of pets and other animals today expect state-of-the-art veterinary care. To provide this service, veterinarians use the skills of veterinary technologists and technicians, who perform many of the same duties for a veterinarian that a nurse would for a physician, including routine laboratory and clinical procedures. Although specific job duties vary by employer, there often is little difference between the tasks carried out by technicians and by technologists, despite some differences in formal education and training. As a result, most workers in this occupation are called technicians.

Veterinary technologists and technicians typically conduct clinical work in a private practice under the supervision of a licensed veterinarian. They often perform various medical tests, as well as treat and diagnose medical conditions and diseases in animals. For example, they may perform laboratory tests such as urinalysis and blood counts, assist with dental prophylaxis, prepare tissue samples, take blood samples, or assist veterinarians in a variety of tests and analyses for which they often use various items of medical equipment, such as test tubes and diagnostic equipment. While most of these duties are performed in a laboratory setting, many are not. For example, some veterinary technicians obtain and record patients' case histories, expose and develop X-rays, and provide specialized nursing care. In addition, experienced veterinary technicians may discuss a pet's condition with its owners and train new clinic personnel. Veterinary technologists and technicians assisting small-animal practitioners usually care for companion animals, such as cats and dogs, but can perform a variety of duties with mice, rats, sheep, pigs, cattle, monkeys, birds, fish, and frogs. Very few veterinary technologists work in mixed animal practices where they care for both small companion animals and larger, nondomestic animals.

Besides working in private clinics and animal hospitals, veterinary technologists and technicians may work in research facilities, where they administer medications orally or topically; prepare samples for laboratory examination; and record information on an animal's genealogy, diet, weight, medications, food intake, and clinical signs of pain and distress. Some may sterilize laboratory and surgical equipment, as well as provide routine postoperative care. At research facilities, veterinary technologists typically work under the guidance of veterinarians or physicians. Some veterinary technologists vaccinate newly admitted animals and occasionally may have to euthanize seriously ill, severely injured, or unwanted animals.

While the goal of most veterinary technologists and technicians is to promote animal health, some contribute to human health as well. Veterinary technologists occasionally assist veterinarians in implementing research projects as they work with other scientists in medically related fields such as gene therapy and cloning. Some find opportunities in biomedical research, wildlife medicine, the military, livestock management, or pharmaceutical sales.

WORK ENVIRONMENT

People who love animals get satisfaction from working with and helping them. However, some of the work may be unpleasant, physically and emotionally demanding, and sometimes dangerous. At times, veterinary technicians must clean cages and lift, hold, or restrain animals, risking exposure to bites or scratches. These workers must take precautions when treating animals with germicides or insecticides. The work setting can be noisy.

Veterinary technologists and technicians who witness abused animals or who euthanize unwanted, aged, or hopelessly injured animals may experience emotional stress. Those working for humane societies and animal shelters often deal with the public, some of whom might react with hostility to any implication that the owners are neglecting or abusing their pets. Such workers must maintain a calm and professional demeanor while they enforce the laws regarding animal care.

In some animal hospitals, research facilities, and animal shelters, a veterinary technician is on duty 24 hours a day, which means that some may work night shifts. Most full-time veterinary technologists and technicians work about 40 hours a week, although some work 50 or more hours a week.

EMPLOYMENT

Veterinary technologists and technicians held about 71,000 jobs in 2006. About 91 percent worked in veterinary services. The remainder worked in boarding kennels, animal shelters, stables, grooming salons, zoos, state and private educational institutions, and local, state, and federal agencies.

EDUCATIONAL AND LEGAL REQUIREMENTS

There are primarily two levels of education and training for entry to this occupation: a two-year program for veterinary technicians and a four-year program for veterinary technologists.

Education and Training. Most entry-level veterinary technicians have a two-year associate degree from an American Veterinary Medical Association (AVMA)-accredited community college program in veterinary technology in which courses are taught in clinical and laboratory settings using live animals. About 16 colleges offer veterinary technology programs that are longer and that culminate in a four-year bachelor's degree in veterinary technology. These four-year colleges, in addition to some vocational schools, also offer two-year programs in laboratory animal science. Several schools offer distance learning.

In 2006, 131 veterinary technology programs in 44 states were accredited by the American Veterinary Medical Association (AVMA). Graduation from an AVMA-accredited veterinary technology program allows students to take the credentialing exam in any state in the country.

Persons interested in careers as veterinary technologists and technicians should take as many high school science, biology, and math courses as possible. Science courses taken beyond high school, in an associate or bachelor's degree program, should emphasize practical skills in a clinical or laboratory setting.

Technologists and technicians usually begin work as trainees in routine positions under the direct supervision of a veterinarian. Entry-level workers whose training or educational background encompasses extensive hands-on experience with a variety of laboratory equipment, including diagnostic and medical equipment, usually require a shorter period of on-the-job training.

Licensure and Certification. Each state regulates veterinary technicians and technologists differently; however, all states require them to pass a credentialing exam following coursework. Passing the state exam assures the public that the technician or technologist has sufficient knowledge to work in a veterinary clinic or hospital. Candidates are tested for competency through an examination that includes oral, written, and practical portions and that is regulated by the State Board of Veterinary Examiners or the appropriate state agency. Depending on the state, candidates may become registered, licensed, or certified. Most states, however, use the National Veterinary Technician (NVT) exam. Prospects usually can have their passing scores transferred from one state to another, so long as both states use the same exam.

Employers recommend American Association for Laboratory Animal Science (AALAS) certification for those seeking employment in a research facility. AALAS offers certification for three levels of technician competence, with a focus on three principal areas—animal husbandry, facility management, and animal health and welfare. Those who wish to become certified must satisfy a combination of education and experience requirements prior to taking the AALAS examination. Work experience must be directly related to the maintenance, health, and well-being of laboratory animals and must be gained in a laboratory animal facility as defined by AALAS. Candidates who meet the necessary criteria can begin pursuing the desired certification on the basis of their qualifications. The lowest level of certification is *Assistant Laboratory Animal Technician (ALAT)*, the second level is *Laboratory Animal Technician (LAT)*, and the highest level of certification is *Laboratory Animal Technologist (LATG)*.

The AALAS examination consists of multiple-choice questions and is longer and more difficult for higher levels of certification, ranging from two hours and 120 multiple choice questions for the ALAT to three hours and 180 multiple choice questions for the LATG.

Other Qualifications. Communication skills become very important as veterinary technologists and technicians deal with pet owners, which they often do. In addition, technologists and technicians should be able to work well with others, because teamwork alongside veterinarians is common. Organizational ability and the ability to pay attention to detail also are important.

Advancement. As they gain experience, technologists and technicians take on more responsibility and carry out more assignments under only general veterinary supervision. Some eventually may become supervisors.

Employment Trends

Excellent job opportunities will stem from the need to replace veterinary technologists and technicians who leave the occupation and from the limited output of qualified veterinary technicians from two-year programs, which are not expected to meet the demand over the 2006 to 2016 period. Employment is expected to grow much faster than average.

Employment Change. Employment of veterinary technologists and technicians is expected to grow 41 percent over the 2006 to 2016 projection period, which is much faster than the average for all occupations. Pet owners are becoming more affluent and more willing to pay for advanced veterinary care because many of them consider their pet to be part of the family. This growing affluence and view of pets will continue to increase the demand for veterinary care. The vast majority of veterinary technicians work at private clinical practices under the supervision of veterinarians. As the number of veterinarians grows to meet the demand for veterinary care, so will the number of veterinary technicians needed to assist them.

The number of pet owners who take advantage of veterinary services for their pets—currently about six in ten—is expected to grow over the projection period, increasing employment opportunities. The availability of advanced veterinary services, such as preventive dental care and surgical procedures, also will provide opportunities for workers specializing in these advanced procedures as they will be needed to assist licensed veterinarians who perform them. The rapidly growing number of cats kept as companion pets is expected to boost the demand for feline medicine and services. Further demand for these workers will stem from the desire to replace veterinary assistants with more highly skilled technicians and technologists in animal clinics and hospitals, shelters, boarding kennels, and humane societies.

Biomedical facilities, diagnostic laboratories, wildlife facilities, humane societies, animal control facilities, drug or food manufacturing companies, and food safety inspection facilities will provide additional jobs for veterinary technologists and technicians. Keen competition, however, is expected for veterinary technologist and technician jobs in zoos and aquariums, due to anticipated slow growth in facility capacity, low turnover among workers, a limited number of positions, and the fact that the work in zoos and aquariums attracts many applicants.

Job Prospects. Excellent job opportunities are expected because of the relatively few veterinary technology graduates each year. The number of two-year programs has recently grown to 131, but due to small class sizes, fewer than 3,000 graduates are anticipated each year, which is not expected to meet demand. Additionally, many veterinary technicians remain in the field for only seven to eight years, so the need to replace workers who leave the occupation each year also will produce many job opportunities.

Employment of veterinary technicians and technologists is relatively stable during periods of economic recession. Layoffs are less likely to occur among veterinary technologists and technicians than in some other occupations because animals will continue to require medical care. **Table 29–3** shows some projection data provided by the Department of Labor.

Table 29–3

Projections data from the National Employment Matrix

Occupational title	Employment, 2006	Projected employment, 2016	Change, 2006–2016	
			Number	Percent
Veterinary technologists and technicians	71,000	100,000	29,000	41

NOTE: Data in this table are rounded.

EARNINGS

Median hourly earnings of veterinary technologists and technicians were $12.88 in May 2006. The middle 50 percent earned between $10.44 and $15.77. The bottom 10 percent earned less than $8.79, and the top 10 percent earned more than $18.68.

RELATED OCCUPATIONS

Others who work extensively with animals include animal care and service workers, veterinary assistants, and laboratory animal caretakers. Like veterinary technologists and technicians, workers in these related occupations must have patience and feel comfortable with animals. However, the level of training required for these occupations is less than that needed by veterinary technologists and technicians. Veterinarians, who need much more formal education, also work extensively with animals, preventing, diagnosing, and treating their diseases, disorders, and injuries.

ADDITIONAL INFORMATION

For information on certification as a laboratory animal technician or technologist, contact:

■ American Association for Laboratory Animal Science, 9190 Crestwyn Hills Dr., Memphis, TN 38125. http://www.aalas.org

Animal Care and Service Workers

WORK DESCRIPTION

Many people like animals, but as pet owners can attest, taking care of them is hard work. Animal care and service workers—who include animal caretakers and animal trainers—train, feed, water, groom, bathe, and exercise animals. They also clean, disinfect, and repair their cages. They play with the animals, provide companionship, and observe behavioral changes that could indicate illness or injury. Boarding kennels, pet stores, animal shelters, veterinary hospitals and clinics, stables, laboratories, aquariums, natural aquatic habitats, and zoological parks all house animals and employ animal care and service workers. Job titles and duties vary by employment setting.

Kennel attendants care for pets while their owners are working or traveling out of town. Beginning attendants perform basic tasks, such as cleaning cages and dog runs, filling food and water dishes, and exercising animals. Experienced attendants may provide basic animal health care, as well as bathe animals, trim nails, and attend to other grooming needs. Attendants who work in kennels also may sell pet food and supplies, assist in obedience training, help with breeding, or prepare animals for shipping.

Groomers are animal caretakers who specialize in grooming or maintaining a pet's appearance. Most groom dogs and a few groom cats. Some groomers work in kennels, veterinary clinics, animal shelters, or pet-supply stores. Others operate their own grooming business, typically at a salon, or increasingly, by making house calls. Such mobile services are growing rapidly as they offer convenience for pet owners, flexibility of schedules for groomers, and minimal trauma for pets resulting from their being in unfamiliar surroundings. Groomers clean and sanitize equipment to prevent the spread of disease, maintain grooming equipment, and maintain a clean and safe environment for the animals. Groomers also schedule appointments, discuss pets' grooming needs with clients, and collect information on the pet's disposition and its veterinary care. Groomers often are the first to notice a medical problem, such as an ear or skin infection that requires veterinary attention.

Grooming the pet involves several steps: an initial brush-out is followed by a first clipping of hair or fur using electric clippers, combs, and grooming shears; the groomer then cuts the nails, cleans the ears, bathes, and blow-dries the animal, and ends with a final clipping and styling.

Animal caretakers in animal shelters perform a variety of duties and work with a wide variety of animals. In addition to attending to the basic needs of the animals, caretakers at shelters also must keep records of the animals received and discharged and any tests or treatments done. Some vaccinate newly admitted animals under the direction of a veterinarian or veterinary technician, and euthanize (painlessly put to death) seriously ill, severely injured, or unwanted animals. Animal caretakers in animal shelters also interact with the public, answering telephone inquiries, screening applicants for animal adoption, or educating visitors on neutering and other animal health issues.

Grooms, or caretakers, care for horses in stables. They saddle and unsaddle horses, give them rubdowns, and walk them to cool them off after a ride. They also feed, groom, and exercise the horses; clean out stalls and replenish bedding; polish saddles; clean and organize the tack (harness, saddle, and bridle) room; and store supplies and feed. Experienced grooms may help train horses.

In zoos, animal care and service workers, called *keepers*, prepare the diets and clean the enclosures of animals, and sometimes assist in raising them when they are very young. They watch for any signs of illness or injury, monitor eating patterns or any changes in behavior, and record their observations. Keepers also may answer questions and ensure that the visiting public behaves responsibly toward the exhibited animals. Depending on the zoo, keepers may be assigned to work with a broad group of animals such as mammals, birds, or reptiles, or they may work with a limited collection of animals such as primates, large cats, or small mammals.

Animal trainers train animals for riding, security, performance, obedience, or assisting people with disabilities. Animal trainers do this by accustoming the animal to human voice and contact, and by conditioning the animal to respond to commands. The three most commonly trained animals are dogs, horses, and marine mammals, including dolphins. Trainers use several techniques to help them train animals. One technique, known as a bridge, is a stimulus used by a trainer to communicate the precise moment an animal does something correctly. When the animal responds correctly, the trainer gives positive reinforcement in a variety of ways: food, toys, play, rubdowns, or speaking the word "good." Animal training takes place in small steps and often takes months and even years of repetition. During the conditioning process, trainers provide animals with mental stimulation, physical exercise, and husbandry care. A relatively new form of training teaches animals to cooperate with workers giving medical care. Animals learn "veterinary" behaviors, such as allowing and even cooperating with the collection of blood samples; physical, X-ray, ultrasonic, and dental exams; physical therapy; and the administration of medicines and replacement fluids.

Training also can be a good tool for facilitating the relocation of animals from one habitat to another, easing, for example, the process of loading horses onto trailers. Trainers often work in competitions or shows, such as circuses or marine parks, aquariums, animal shelters, dog kennels and salons, or horse farms. Trainers in shows work to display the talent and ability of an animal, such as a dolphin, through interactive programs to educate and entertain the public.

In addition to their hands-on work with the animals, trainers often oversee other aspects of animal care, such as preparing feed and providing a safe and clean environment and habitat.

WORK ENVIRONMENT

People who love animals get satisfaction from working with and helping them. However, some of the work may be unpleasant, physically and emotionally demanding, and sometimes dangerous. Most animal caretakers and service workers have to clean animal cages and lift, hold, or restrain animals, risking exposure to bites or scratches. Their work often involves kneeling, crawling, repeated bending, and lifting heavy supplies like bales of hay or bags of feed. Animal caretakers must take precautions when treating animals with germicides or insecticides. They may work outdoors in all kinds of weather, and the work setting can be noisy. Caretakers of show and sports animals travel to competitions.

Animal caretakers and service workers experience the same emotional distress as veterinary technologists and technicians in dealing with the public in issues such as abused animals, owners' feelings or attitudes. Such workers must maintain a calm and professional demeanor while helping to enforce the laws regarding animal care. Also see discussion under technologists and technicians.

Animal care and service workers often work irregular hours. Most animals are fed every day, so caretakers often work weekend and holiday shifts. Some zoo animals skip one meal a week to mimic their lives in the wild. In some animal hospitals, research facilities, and animal shelters, an attendant is on duty 24 hours a day, which means night shifts.

EMPLOYMENT OPPORTUNITIES

Animal caretakers and service workers held 200,000 jobs in 2006. Over three out of four worked as animal caretakers in settings other than farms; the remainder worked as animal trainers. Nonfarm animal caretakers often worked in boarding kennels, animal shelters, stables, grooming shops, pet stores, animal hospitals, and veterinary offices. A significant number of caretakers worked for animal humane societies, racing stables, dog and horse racetrack operations, zoos, theme parks, circuses, and other amusement and recreation services.

Employment of animal trainers is concentrated in animal services that specialize in training and in commercial sports, where they train racehorses and dogs. In 2006, about 57 percent of animal trainers were self-employed.

EDUCATIONAL AND LEGAL REQUIREMENTS

On-the-job training is the most common way animal caretakers and service workers learn their work; however, employers generally prefer to hire people who have experience with animals. Some preparatory programs are available for specific types of caretakers, such as groomers.

Education and Training. Animal trainers often need a high school diploma or GED equivalent. Some animal training jobs may require a bachelor's degree and additional skills. For example, marine mammal trainers usually need a bachelor's degree in biology, marine biology, animal science, psychology, or a related field. An animal health technician degree also may qualify trainers for some jobs.

Most equine trainers learn their trade by working as a groom at a stable. Some study at an accredited private training school. Because large animals are involved, most horse-training jobs have minimum weight requirements for candidates.

Many dog trainers attend workshops and courses at community colleges and vocational schools. Topics include basic study of canines, learning theory of animals, teaching obedience cues, problem solving methods, and safety. Many also offer business training.

Many zoos require their caretakers to have a bachelor's degree in biology, animal science, or a related field. Most require experience with animals, preferably as a volunteer or paid keeper in a zoo.

Most pet groomers learn their trade by completing an informal apprenticeship, usually lasting six to ten weeks, under the guidance of an experienced groomer. Prospective groomers also may attend one of the fifty-two state-licensed grooming schools throughout the country, with programs varying in length from two to eighteen weeks. Beginning groomers often start by taking on one duty, such as bathing and drying the pet. They eventually assume responsibility for the entire grooming process, from the initial brush-out to the final clipping.

Animal caretakers in animal shelters are not required to have any specialized training, but training programs and workshops are available through the Humane Society of the United States, the American Humane Association, and the National Animal Control Association. Workshop topics include cruelty investigations, appropriate methods of euthanasia for shelter animals, proper guidelines for capturing animals, techniques for preventing problems with wildlife, and dealing with the public.

Beginning animal caretakers in kennels learn on the job and usually start by cleaning cages and feeding and watering animals.

Certification and Other Qualifications. Certifications are available in many animal service occupations. For dog trainers, certification by a professional association or one of the hundreds of private vocational or state-approved trade schools can be advantageous. The National Dog Groomers Association of America offers certification for master status as a groomer. The American Boarding Kennels Association offers a three-stage, home-study program for individuals interested in pet care. Those who complete the third stage and pass oral and written examinations become Certified Kennel Operators (CKO).

All animal caretakers and service workers need patience, sensitivity, and problem solving ability. They also need tact and communication skills. This is particularly true for those in shelters, who often deal with individuals who abandon their pets. The ability to handle emotional people is vital for workers at shelters.

Animal trainers especially need problem-solving skills and experience in animal obedience. Successful marine mammal trainers should also have good public speaking skills as seminars and presentations are a large part of the job. Usually four to five trainers work with a group of animals at one time, therefore, each trainer should be able to work as part of a team. Marine mammal trainers must also be good swimmers; certification in SCUBA (Self-contained Underwater Breathing Apparatus) is a plus.

Advancement. With experience and additional training, caretakers in animal shelters may become adoption coordinators, animal control officers, emergency rescue drivers, assistant shelter managers, or shelter directors. Pet groomers who work in large retail establishments or kennels may, with experience, move into supervisory or managerial positions. Experienced groomers often choose to open their own salons. Advancement for kennel caretakers takes the form of promotion to kennel supervisor, assistant manager, and manager; those with enough capital and experience may open up their own kennels. Zookeepers may advance to senior keeper, assistant head keeper, head keeper, and assistant curator, but very few openings occur, especially for the higher-level positions.

EMPLOYMENT TRENDS

Because many workers leave this occupation each year, there will be good job opportunities for most positions. Faster-than-average employment growth also will add to job openings, in addition to replacement needs.

Employment Change. Employment of animal care and service workers is expected to grow 19 percent over the 2006 to 2016 decade, faster than the average for all occupations. The companion pet population, which drives employment of animal caretakers in kennels, grooming shops, animal shelters, and veterinary clinics and hospitals, is expected to increase. Pet owners—including a large number of baby boomers, whose disposable income is expected to increase as they age—are expected to increasingly purchase grooming services, daily and overnight boarding services, training services, and veterinary services, resulting in more jobs for animal care and service workers. As more pet owners consider their pets part of the family, demand for luxury animal services and the willingness to spend greater amounts of money on pets should continue to grow. Demand for marine mammal trainers, on the other hand, should grow slowly.

Demand for animal care and service workers in animal shelters is expected to grow as communities increasingly recognize the connection between animal abuse and abuse toward humans, and continue to commit private funds to animal shelters, many of which work hand-in-hand with social service agencies and law enforcement teams.

Job Prospects. Due to employment growth and the need to replace workers who leave the occupation, job opportunities for most positions should be good. The need to replace workers leaving the field will create the overwhelming majority of job openings. Many animal caretaker jobs require little or no training and have flexible work schedules, making them suitable for people seeking a first, temporary, or part-time job. The outlook for caretakers in zoos and aquariums, however, is not favorable due to slow job growth and keen competition for the few positions available.

Prospective mammal trainers will face keen competition as the number of applicants greatly exceeds the number of available positions. Prospective horse trainers should anticipate an equally challenging labor market as the number of entry-level positions is limited. Dog trainers, however, should experience conditions that are more favorable. Opportunities for dog trainers should be best in large metropolitan areas.

Job opportunities for animal care and service workers may vary from year to year because the strength of the economy affects demand for these workers. Pet owners tend to spend more on animal services when the economy is strong. **Table 29–4** shows some projection data provided by the Department of Labor.

Table 29–4

Occupational title	Employment, 2006	Projected employment, 2016	Change, 2006–2016	
			Number	**Percent**
Animal care and service workers	200,000	238,000	39,000	19
Animal trainers	43,000	53,000	9,800	23
Nonfarm animal caretakers	157,000	185,000	29,000	18

Projections data from the National Employment Matrix

NOTE: Data in this table are rounded.

EARNINGS

Earnings are relatively low. Median hourly earnings of nonfarm animal caretakers were $8.72 in May 2006. The middle 50 percent earned between $7.50 and $10.95. The bottom 10 percent earned less than $6.56, and the top 10 percent earned more than $14.64. Median hourly earnings in the industries employing the largest numbers of nonfarm animal caretakers in May 2006 are shown in **Table 29–5**.

Table 29–5	*Median hourly earnings in the industries employing the largest numbers of nonfarm animal caretakers in May 2006*
Spectator sports	$9.38
Other personal services	$8.78
Social advocacy organizations	$8.31
Other professional, scientific, and technical services	$8.23
Veterinary services	$8.23
Other miscellaneous store retailers	$8.22

Median hourly earnings of animal trainers were $12.65 in May 2006. The middle 50 percent earned between $9.11 and $17.39. The lowest 10 percent earned less than $7.66, and the top 10 percent earned more than $22.42.

RELATED OCCUPATIONS

Others who work extensively with animals include farmers, ranchers, and agricultural managers; agricultural workers; veterinarians; veterinary technologists, technicians, and assistants; and biological scientists.

ADDITIONAL INFORMATION

For career information and information on training, certification, and earnings of the related occupation of animal control officer, contact:

■ National Animal Control Association, P.O. Box 1480851, Kansas City, MO 64148-0851. http://www.nacanet.org

For information on becoming an advanced pet care technician at a kennel, contact:

■ American Boarding Kennels Association, 1702 East Pikes Peak Ave., Colorado Springs, CO 80909. http://www.abka.com/abka

For general information on pet grooming careers, including certification information, contact:

■ National Dog Groomers Association of America, P.O. Box 101, Clark, PA 16113. http://www.nationaldoggroomers.com

NON-CLINICAL AND HEALTH-RELATED PROFESSIONS

Key Terms

- Biological photographer
- Ophthalmic photography
- Photomicrography
- Cinematography
- Dental photography

- Autopsy/specimen photography
- Medical and scientific illustrators
- Medical, science, and technical writers
- Medical secretary

Health Professions Not Involved in Clinical Care of a Patient

The general public has a strong interest in health, medicine, and science and desires to learn more about them. People want to understand what is happening and how new developments will affect their lives and careers. Advanced communication technology has made delivery of this knowledge possible; the publishing and broadcast media provide both oral and written materials in these fields.

In addition, public and private organizations and agencies have a professional interest in keeping the public informed. They know that people who are informed about current developments and discoveries in health and medicine show more initiative in getting medical, dental, or preventive care for their families and themselves. These agencies and organizations also want to keep the public interested and involved in starting and supporting adequate healthcare facilities in the form of community hospitals, clinics, and mobile screening units.

In addition to the general public, other more specialized groups seek health information. These individuals include the various health professionals who require authoritative information to keep abreast of developments in their fields. There are many career opportunities in health information and communications; the following pages discuss the qualifications and duties of biological photographers, medical writers, science writers, technical writers, and medical illustrators.

Another important part of health information and communications is maintaining medical records and data for various health facilities. Typically, a health facility employs a staff consisting of a medical record administrator, medical record technician, medical transcriptionist, and other clerical personnel to handle all facets of medical information. They prepare medical reports; organize, analyze, and preserve the medical information of patients; and develop a variety of statistical reports. Maintaining this flow of health information is an extremely important function, because it is used in evaluating patient care, diagnosing and treating illness, and planning healthcare activities. Careers involving medical records and data are discussed in another chapter on health information personnel.

Library services in the health field occupy an important place in health information and communication activities. Year after year, a vast store of knowledge accumulates in many branches of medicine, in medical research, and in scientific research related to medicine. This knowledge is recorded in periodicals, textbooks, monographs, and other publications. These publications, coming from every part of the world, are collected in the medical library, where they are made available to health professionals.

Doctors, nurses, dentists, pharmacists, therapists of various kinds, technicians, and those studying for these health professions may come to the library for texts or monographs on a subject of special interest. They may search the journals for background material or for research reports on the latest developments in their fields. The medical and scientific journals are also used by research scientists and research students; these are the main sources of information on what has been done and what is currently being done in their fields.

Libraries are maintained by almost all hospitals, schools, research institutions, and pharmaceutical houses, and by many other health organizations. They vary in size and function, but all serve to maintain information needed by their staffs, students, patients, or other interested persons. This is discussed in another chapter in the book.

Biological Photographers

WORK DESCRIPTION

Biological photographers are scientific professionals responsible for the production of still and motion pictures of subjects for the health professions and natural sciences. These specialists apply a complete range of photographic skills creatively to complete a variety of assignments. Their role in health information and communications is very important. They prepare and produce motion pictures, videotapes, prints, and transparencies to document and record a broad spectrum of subjects and events used for education, patient records, and research, and as illustrations in publications. Photography is used to document the absence, presence, extent, and progress of a patient's disease or injury, and still or motion pictures are used to record and study surgical procedures. Furthermore, photographs of specimens can be magnified to serve as records or to illustrate medical conditions for use in classrooms, courtrooms, or research laboratories. Biological photographers also participate in the planning, coordination, production, and dissemination of educational programs encompassing both visual and auditory media, and they are key personnel in any project in which recording of diagnosis, treatment, special technology, or any other aspect of health care is critical.

A *biological photographer* can specialize in one of several areas. *Ophthalmic photography*, for example, involves the use of specialized equipment and techniques to photograph disorders and injuries of the eye; *photomicrography* involves photographs taken through a microscope; and *cinematography* is the production of motion pictures. Other specializations include *dental photography*, which records dental techniques and procedures, and *autopsy/specimen photography*, in which postmortem or surgical specimens are documented.

Biological photographers are employed by many public and private hospitals; universities; medical schools; federal health organizations; research institutions; dental, veterinary, or natural science facilities; and some private medical and pharmaceutical suppliers. For the most part, they work regular hours, within normal hospital, office, or laboratory environments, and are not normally required to travel extensively. Occasionally, the physical conditions under which a biological photographer works change quite dramatically. For instance, he or she may spend some time working in close contact with patients, doctors, and staff members, along with some time in isolation working in the darkroom. Biological photographers may also come in contact with harmful chemicals, strong odors, and contagious diseases when carrying out assignments. The biological photographer must, therefore, have the ability to adapt to a wide range of tasks and environmental conditions in addition to being skilled and creative in this profession.

EDUCATIONAL AND LEGAL REQUIREMENTS

There are several ways to prepare for a career in biological photography. A number of colleges and universities offer full four-year programs leading to a bachelor's degree in this field.

Other educational institutions provide training in two-year programs and grant a certificate or associate degree. One of the accrediting agencies for these training programs is the Biological Photographic Association. Many individuals acquire skills in this work by successfully completing on-the-job or apprenticeship training programs, which may last up to two to three years.

Certification in this field is not mandatory, but those seeking certification can obtain the requirements through the Board of Registry of the BioCommunication Association. The prerequisites for certification are two years of satisfactory employment or training in an accredited school, plus successful completion of a three-part examination. Many employers determine general requisites before making final education or training arrangements for their employees.

EMPLOYMENT OPPORTUNITIES

Growth in biological photography is quite rapid and is closely related to the entire healthcare industry, the growth of medical education, and the increased documentation requirements of government and independent agencies. Because photography occupies an increasingly significant place in scientific and medical research and education, opportunities are expected to be favorable for these specialized skills.

Advancement opportunities in this field, as in many other health career areas, depend on the individual system worked out by the employer. Government agencies usually have career ladders with several steps, each of which represents an advancement opportunity. Private industry and education may have other opportunities. The biological photographer typically advances from photographic technician through photographer positions to department or service head. Possibilities also include general health facility administration or related positions in education for individuals with advanced degrees or experience.

ADDITIONAL INFORMATION

For further information, contact:

BioCommunication Association
Nancy Hurtgen
220 Southwind Lane
Hillsborough, NC 27278
www.BCA.org

Medical Illustrators

WORK DESCRIPTION

Medical and scientific illustrators combine artistic skills with knowledge of the biological sciences. Medical illustrators draw illustrations of human anatomy and surgical procedures. Scientific illustrators draw illustrations of animals and plants. This artwork is used in medical and scientific publications and in audiovisual presentations for teaching purposes. Medical illustrators also work for lawyers, producing exhibits for court cases and doctors.

Medical illustrators can best be described as paramedical artists who illustrate medical or biological subjects, using many types of visual presentations. Historically, detailed and complicated drawings of life systems were done by artists because drawings were the only means available to capture and communicate the essence of scientific subjects. At one time, the illustrator's work was limited to drawings and charts for medical journals, textbooks, monographs, and similar publications. Later, additional technical training became necessary as a variety of graphic arts techniques began to be used to illustrate surgical procedures, anatomical and pathological specimens, clinical disorders, and microorganisms.

The health professions depend on the illustrator to produce visual presentations for their own use and for the public. Scientific illustrations are now widely used in general magazines, professional journals, textbooks, exhibits, and pamphlets. Medical education relies heavily on the work of medical illustrators, and with recent advancements in instructional technology, using specially prepared audiovisual materials for teaching in medical and health sciences, the medical illustrator's role of visual interpretation has expanded into a variety of new applications. For the most part, medical illustrators are employed by or do freelance work for hospitals, clinics, medical schools, public and private research institutes, large pharmaceutical firms, and medical publishing houses. Regardless of where medical illustrators are employed, their final illustrations must present information clearly and aesthetically.

Today's medical illustrators have broadened their scope and use drawings, models, photography, exhibits, and television to record facts and progress in many health fields, and they work with physicians, research scientists, educators, and authors. Illustrators tend to specialize along lines required by the employer. For example, a medical book publishing company may need illustrators with special photographic or illustration skills; a museum may require an illustrator with a strong background in medical sculpture. Illustrators may also work with specialists in subjects such as anatomy, pathology, embryology, and ophthalmology.

EDUCATIONAL REQUIREMENTS

Students intending to become medical illustrators should be science minded, with the scientist's capacity for accurate observation, and they must have the ability to visualize imaginatively and persevere. Medical illustrating is not a career for everyone interested in art. High school studies should include biology, other science courses, foreign languages, and courses in design. Students should evidence interest in various graphic art forms—still life drawing in particular—and maintain a portfolio demonstrating ability in several media. Programs of education for medical illustrators require six to seven years of college-level study beyond the high school level.

ADDITIONAL INFORMATION

For information on careers in medical illustration, contact:

The Association of Medical Illustrators
810 East 10th Street
Lawrence, KS 66044
www.medical-illustrators.org

Commission on Accreditation of
Allied Health Education Programs
1361 Park Street
Clearwater, FL 33756
www.caahep.org

Writers: Medical, Science, and Technical

Individuals with good communications skills, a basic knowledge of life sciences, and an interest in health care or in medical research and development are finding career opportunities as medical writers in the mass media, the medical press, industry, hospitals, medical schools, and other settings. Technological, clinical, and sociological changes in the field of medicine and health are occurring at an unprecedented rate. As a result, both healthcare professionals and the general public represent vast audiences for medical news, information, and instructional material at virtually all levels of sophistication and in all media.

WORK DESCRIPTION

In response to the public's keen interest in medicine and health, many newspapers, magazines, radio stations, and television stations employ trained journalists who function as science writers and specialize in interpreting scientific and technical developments for the general public. Their job is to acquaint the public with what is happening in the field of medicine: new treatments for cancer or heart disease, improved surgical techniques, research gains for the mentally ill, and changing concepts of health care. Like other science writers in the mass media, medical writers not only report, but also interpret. Unlike sports writers, whose audience is already familiar with the subject, writers in the health field must explain new and complex developments in nontechnical terms that can be readily understood by a lay audience. Moreover, because of the critical nature of the subject, medical writers must be meticulously accurate and objective in presenting facts. The physicians, scientists, and health administrators to whom medical journalists look for information will hesitate to talk freely unless they know the writers are competent and trustworthy. Similarly, the confidence of the public depends on the writers' caution and integrity. Because these writers deal with experts from every branch of medicine and related disciplines, they must have at least a speaking acquaintance with the health sciences. Medical writers might interview neurosurgeons one day, pharmacologists the next, and biomedical engineers the next. They ask pertinent questions, weigh the value of the answers, and obtain additional supporting evidence. Finally, they present the information in such a way that it will not be misunderstood.

Other medical writers with training or experience in journalism—or in its "sister" discipline, public relations—are employed by hospitals, clinics, medical schools, voluntary health agencies, and medical societies as health information specialists. These communicators are responsible for keeping the public as well as their organization's personnel, clients, and supporters informed about the achievements, programs, and concerns of the organization. To generate and sustain good public relations, health information specialists may develop informational brochures, plan exhibits, publish "in-house" newsletters and magazines, and arrange for media coverage. To accomplish these tasks, health information specialists must have working knowledge of almost every medium of communication.

Medical writers sometimes function as technical writers specializing in reporting and writing about scientific and technical developments, primarily for users. In industry, and to a lesser extent in nonprofit medical research laboratories, there is growing demand for individuals who have a basic knowledge of electronics, biochemistry, or other technical subjects, as well as good communication skills and an interest in medicine and health. Developers and manufacturers of sophisticated diagnostic and treatment devices such as electrocardiographs, computerized imaging systems, heart-lung machines, and hemodialysis equipment employ medical writers in a variety of capacities. As in other settings, scientists, engineers, and health professionals working in industry rarely have the proficiency and time to meet all needs for scientific and technical information—hence the demand for medical communicators who can digest complex source material and write clearly and accurately for diverse audiences. Medical writers may produce promotional literature for health professionals and administrators or educational information for patients. Like other technical writers, they may prepare instruction manuals for operating and maintenance technicians, proposals, or reports for scientists and engineers, for management, or for a company's stockholders. With the increasing application of computers in medicine, some medical writers are now involved in development of software. To become familiar with their subject, these writers may study technical books, journals, working papers, and mathematical data; interview scientific personnel; or tour laboratories, hospitals, and field stations. Often they simply work with the "raw material" provided by scientists, engineers, and health professionals.

Medical writers may find similar career opportunities in the pharmaceutical industry, which invests great amounts of money in research and development of new drugs and new applications for existing drugs. Pharmaceutical companies have an ongoing need for individuals who can assist in documenting and reporting new discoveries and in promoting product lines. Pharmaceutical writers may prepare abstracts of journal articles, package inserts (descriptions of a drug's actions, indications, contraindications, and side effects), or reports of research findings. They may write market research reports or articles for in-house periodicals. Those with a creative bent may produce sales brochures, advertising copy, or other promotional material; scripts for educational films or closed-circuit broadcasts; or exhibits to be displayed at medical conferences. Like their counterparts in the medical equipment industry, pharmaceutical writers use all possible sources to become familiar with their subject.

Medical writers are employed by government agencies, companies that publish newspapers and magazines for health professionals, advertising agencies, film and art studios, and book publishing companies.

Within most settings there are opportunities for communicators at all levels of experience and expertise—and, quite often, for freelancers, who are hired for specific assignments as the need arises. Responsibilities in the field of medical writing span a wide range. At one end of the spectrum are such critical but relatively simple tasks as editing others' writing to ensure grammatical correctness and clarity of presentation, checking the accuracy of references, or proofreading. At the other end is such challenging and sophisticated work as writing books on medical subjects for lay persons, directing a corporate publications department, or designing and managing a new periodical.

WORK ENVIRONMENT

In general, medical writers work in comfortable and well-lighted surroundings. They usually work a 40-hour week but may be called on to put in additional hours to meet publication deadlines.

EDUCATIONAL REQUIREMENTS

Medical writing is not a well-defined profession with a prescribed course of training and a standardized licensing or certification procedure. On the contrary, it is a field characterized by its practitioners' diversity of background, expertise, and professional responsibilities and activities. On-the-job training is the most common.

Medical research reports, textbooks, and other highly technical materials are often written by physicians, allied health professionals, or scientists. The great majority of medical writers do not have advanced training in a healthcare discipline.

While there are no uniform standards for entry into the field, a bachelor's degree from a four-year college is generally considered a minimum requirement. To develop the background and skills essential to a medical writing career, students should take as many courses as possible in the life sciences and in English composition, journalism, or related discipline. In addition, a few basic courses in electronics, electrical and mechanical engineering, or in basic physics can be useful. Although graduate education is not a formal requirement, more and more medical writing jobs are going to individuals with advanced degrees in scientific, medical, or communication specialties.

Perhaps more important than a specific educational background are personal characteristics such as the ability to think clearly and precisely, to pay close attention to detail, to handle the English language with ease, and to deal comfortably with a variety of people.

It is interesting to point out that most medical or science writers in the printed news media learn their skills via "on-the-job" training. Most start out as a reporter.

EMPLOYMENT OPPORTUNITIES

Employment prospects in this field are favorable. Opportunities for qualified medical writers tend to grow in direct proportion to accumulation of new data from basic research and clinical studies, increasing sophistication of both experimental and clinical technology, growing use of audiovisual teaching techniques, increasing numbers of medical conferences and workshops, growth of medical specialty journals and news publications for health professionals, need for more frequent updating of medical textbooks, greater use of computers in medicine, creation of new abstracting and indexing services, and mounting public interest in health-related information and issues. In this era of increasingly complex diagnostic techniques, constant therapeutic discoveries, growing interest in prevention of disease and disability, and enormous expenditures on healthcare services and products, the need for well-trained and informed medical writers has never been greater. However, because many people are interested in this type of career, there may be heavy competition for jobs, especially in the mass media. Individuals considering a career in medical writing should carefully evaluate the labor market in the area in which they intend to work.

As in most professions, the skills helpful for entry may not be sufficient for advancement. For example, a recent college graduate with a major in biology, a minor in English, and perhaps some typing ability may find employment as an editorial assistant in a research laboratory or in a medical publishing house. To advance to a position such as director of communications for a research laboratory or series development editor for a medical publisher, the individual would have to acquire additional knowledge of medicine, become expert in many facets of communication, and develop whatever other skills may be required in a particular setting or particular medium. Skills necessary for advancement may be acquired through continuing education, practical experience, or both. In general, those who advance in this field are avid readers, careful researchers, meticulously accurate writers, flexible stylists who can adapt to the requirements of various media, and disciplined and dedicated workers who recognize the importance of deadlines.

ADDITIONAL INFORMATION

For further information, contact:

American Medical Writers Association
40 West Gude Drive, Suite 101
Rockville, MD 20850-1192
www.amwa.org

National Association of Science Writers
P.O. Box 890
Hedgesville, WV 25427
www.nasw.org

Medical Secretaries

WORK DESCRIPTION AND ENVIRONMENT

Medical secretaries work in private medical offices, hospitals, clinics, group practices, and other health facilities. Their responsibilities are limited to administrative and clerical duties, and they are not trained to assist physicians with clinical or laboratory tasks. Medical secretaries are primarily responsible for the orderly, efficient operation of the office. Typical duties include keeping individual medical records, taking simple medical histories, filling out insurance forms, and billing patients for medical services. They also schedule appointments for patients, arrange for patients to be hospitalized, handle telephone inquiries, and act as receptionists for incoming patients. Medical secretaries take dictation and type correspondence, reports, and manuscripts. They may also do bookkeeping, prepare financial records, and handle credit and collections for their employers.

Medical secretaries generally work in pleasant surroundings in modern medical offices. Their work is often performed under pressure and requires patience and tact at all times in dealing with patients.

EDUCATIONAL AND LEGAL REQUIREMENTS

Persons considering this career should be high school graduates or the equivalent, preferably with courses in English, biology, and typing. They should be familiar with or gain knowledge of computer word processing, spreadsheets, and database programs. A sound knowledge of spelling, punctuation, grammar, and vocabulary is also important. One- or two-year programs in secretarial science, with a medical option, are given by accredited vocational schools and junior or community colleges. Graduates of one-year programs receive certificates, those in two-year programs are awarded the Associate in Applied Science degree. While postsecondary education is not required for all beginning jobs in this field, it may be helpful in gaining initial employment and for job advancement.

In some cases, persons with secretarial experience in other fields prepare for this career by taking medical terminology and related courses as part of a continuing education program.

EMPLOYMENT OPPORTUNITIES

Employment prospects for qualified medical secretaries are expected to be quite favorable. This outlook is based on increased public demand for health services; the expansion of medical facilities, HMOs, and group medical practices; and broader insurance coverage by government-sponsored and private health insurance plans. Qualified medical secretaries can advance to such positions as administrative assistant or office manager.

SALARIES FOR HEALTH PROFESSIONS

Profession	Salaries
Animal care and service worker	$7 – $15/hour
Cardiovascular technologist and technician	$24,000 – $68,000/year
Clinical laboratory technologist and technician	$35,000 – $70,000/year
Dental assistant	$10 – $20/hour
Dental hygienist	$20 – $45/hour
Dental laboratory technician	$9 – $27/hour
Dentist	$130,000 – $200,000/year
Dietetic technician	$16,000 – $30,000/year
Dietitian	$30,000 – $70,000/year
Emergency medical technician (paramedic)	$17,000 – $45,000/year
Healthcare worker	$30,590 – $50,500/year
Health information administrator	$55,676 – $75,600/year
Health information technician	$28,030 – $35,000/year

Profession	Salaries
Health educator	$31,300 – $56,580/year
Health services manager	$57,240 – $94,780/year
Home health aide	$7 – $15/hour
Human service worker	$21,360 – $30,600/year
Inspector/compliance officer	$41,800 – $70,230/year
Medical assistant	$18,000 – $37,000/year
Medical laboratory technician	$9 – $27/hour
Medical librarian	$40,560 – $75,230/year
Nuclear medicine technologist	$46,000 – $82,000/year
Nurse, practical	$26,000 – $51,000/year
Nurse, registered	$40,000 – $70,000/year
Nursing aides	$7 – $15/hour
Nursing home administrator	$78,750 – $97,890/year
Occupational therapist	$40,000 – $90,000/year
Occupational therapy assistant/aide	$26,000 – $58.000/year
Ophthalmic laboratory technician	$9 – $27/hour
Optician, dispensing	$20,000 – $50,000/year
Optometrist	$85,000 – $150,000/year
Pharmacist	$68,000 – $120,000/year
Pharmacy technician	$10 – $20/hour
Physical therapist	$46,000 – $95,000/year
Physical therapy assistant aide	$26,000 – $57,000/year
Physician assistant	$45,000 – $110,000/year
Physician	$150,000 – $350,000/year
Practical nurse	$26,000 – $51,000/year
Psychiatric aide	$7 – $15/hour

Profession	Salaries
Psychologist	$35,000 – $103,000/year
Radiation therapist	$55,000 – $93,000/year
Radiology technologist and technician	$33,000 – $69,000/year
Recreational therapist	$20,000 – $56,000/year
Registered nurse	$40,000 – $70,000/year
Respiratory technician	$21,000 – $30,000/year
Respiratory therapist	$25,000 – $57,999/year
Social worker	$25,000 – $59,000/year
Social and human service assistant	$16,000 – $41,000/year
Social assistance except child day care	$9 – $25/hour
Sonographer, diagnostic, medical	$40,000 – $77,000/year
Speech-language pathologist	$38,000 – $95,000/year
Speech-language audiologist	$38,000 – $90,000/year
Surgical technician	$26,000 – $51,000/year
Veterinarian	$43,000 – $134,000/year
Veterinarian technologist and technician	$9 –$19/hour

NOTES

Most data are from Occupational Outlook Handbook 2007–2008, U.S. Department of Labor Statistics.

Only salaries of major health professions are shown. Space limitation does not permit the listing of all health and health-related jobs.

Earnings vary with education, experience, level of responsibility, performance, industry, amount of unionization, geographic area, specialized services rendered, and whether the practitioner is self-employed or part-time.

No attempt is made to show variance by specialties.

Salaries shown are income averages and change rapidly as time progresses.

For details, updating and data on unlisted health professions, consult the section on "additional information" under each chapter. Use the resources and Internet Web sites where applicable.

Sources of Career Information

This appendix is provided for student use from the *Occupational Outlook Handbook*, 2008–2009 edition. Listed below are several places to begin collecting information on careers and job opportunities.

Personal Contacts

The people close to you—your family and friends—can be extremely helpful in providing career information. They may be able to answer your questions directly or put you in touch with someone else who can. Networking can lead to meeting someone who can answer your questions about a specific career or company, and who can provide inside information and other helpful hints. It is an effective way to learn the type of training necessary for a certain position, the way in which someone in that position entered the field, the prospects for advancement, and aspects of the work that the person likes and dislikes.

Public Libraries, Career Centers, and Guidance Offices

These institutions maintain a great deal of up-to-date material. To begin your library search, look in the computerized catalog listings under "vocations" or "careers," and then under specific types of work. Check the library's periodicals section, where trade and professional magazines and journals about specific occupations and industries are kept. Become familiar with the concerns and activities of potential employers by skimming their annual reports and other public documents. Occupational information from audiovisual materials, computerized information systems, or the Internet can be valuable. Don't forget the librarians; they can be a great resource and can save you valuable time by directing you to relevant information.

Check your school's career centers for resources such as individual counseling and testing, guest speakers, field trips, books, career magazines, and career days.

Always assess career guidance materials carefully. The information should be current and objective. Beware of materials that seem to glamorize the occupation, overstate the earnings, or exaggerate the demand for workers.

Counselors

Counselors are professionals trained to help you discover your strengths and weaknesses, evaluate your goals and values, and help you determine what you would like in a career. Counselors will not tell you what to do, but they may administer interest inventories and aptitude tests, interpret the results, and help you explore various options. They may also discuss local job markets and the entry requirements and costs of schools, colleges, or training programs.

Counselors are found in:

- High school guidance offices

- College career planning and placement offices

- Placement offices in private vocational or technical schools and institutions

- Vocational rehabilitation agencies

- Counseling services offered by community organizations

- Private counseling agencies and private practices

- State employment service offices

Before employing the services of a private counselor or agency, you may want to seek recommendations and check the agency or counselor's credentials. The International Association of Counseling Services (IACS) accredits counseling services throughout the country. To receive a listing of accredited services for your region, send a self-addressed, stamped, business-size envelope to:

- International Association of Counseling Services (IACS), 101 South Whiting St., Suite 211, Alexandria, VA 22304. Phone: (703) 823-9840.
  Internet: http://www.iacsinc.org

The Directory of Accredited Centers, an IACS publication providing employment counseling and other assistance, may be available in your library or school career counseling center. A list of certified career counselors by city or state is available from:

- National Board for Certified Counselors, 3 Terrace Way, Suite D, Greensboro, NC 27403-3660. Phone: (336) 547-0607. Internet: http://www.nbcc.org/

Internet Networks and Resources

The growth of online listings has made countless resources instantly available at any time. Most companies, professional societies, academic institutions, and government agencies maintain Internet sites that highlight the organizations' latest information and activities.

Listings may include information such as government documents, schedules of events, and job openings. Listings for academic institutions often provide links to career counseling and placement services through career resource centers, as well as information on financing your education. Colleges and universities also offer online guides to campus facilities and admission requirements and procedures.

The career information that is available through the Internet matches much of the information that is available through libraries, career centers, and guidance offices. No single network or resource will contain all desired information, however, so be prepared to search in many places. As in a library search, search various lists by field or discipline, or by using keywords.

Career sites can be an excellent place to obtain information about job opportunities. They provide a forum for employers to list job openings and for individuals to post their résumés. Some Internet sites also provide an opportunity to research a particular industry or company.

America's Job Bank (AJB), administered by the U.S. Department of Labor, lists as many as 1 million job openings on any given day. These job openings are compiled by state employment service offices throughout the nation.

Information about health related careers is available from the American Medical Association Web site:

- American Medical Association, 515 N. State Street, Chicago, IL 60610. Phone: 1-800-621-8335. Internet: http://www.ama-assn.org/ama/pub/category /13087.html

High growth careers are listed on a government Web site as a collaborative effort between the U.S. Department of Labor and the U.S. Department of Education. The site is designed to provide information on high growth, in-demand occupations along with the skills and education needed to attain those jobs. Toll-Free Help Line, 1-877-US-2JOBS (1-877-872-5627) or TTY 1-877-889-5627. Internet: http://www.CareerVoyages.gov

Professional Societies, Trade Associations, Labor Unions, Business Firms, and Educational Institutions

These organizations provide a variety of free or inexpensive career material. Many of these groups are listed in the Additional Information section of the Handbook. Some are described below. For information on occupations not covered in the Handbook, consult directories in your library's reference section to find the names of potential sources. You might start with *The Guide to American Directories* or *The Directory of Directories*. Another useful resource is *The*

Encyclopedia of Associations, an annual publication listing trade associations, professional societies, labor unions, and fraternal and patriotic organizations.

The National Technical Information Service Audiovisual Center, a central source for audiovisual material produced by the U.S. government, sells material on jobs and careers. For a catalog, contact:

- ■ NTIS/NAC Audiovisual Center, U.S. Department of Commerce, 5285 Port Royal Road, Springfield, VA 22161. Phone: 800-553-6847. Internet: http://www.ntis.gov

Federal Government

Information on employment with the federal government is available from the Office of Personnel Management. Consult your telephone directory under U.S. Government for a local number or call (703) 724-1850 or (978) 461-8404 (TDD). The Information Center of the Web site http://www.USAjobs.opm.gov/infocenter includes a career interest center with links for specific groups such as veterans.

Organizations for Specific Groups

The organizations listed below provide information on career planning, training, or job opportunities prepared for specific groups. Consult directories in your library's reference center or a career guidance office for information on additional organizations associated with specific groups.

DISABLED WORKERS

Counseling, training, and placement services for those with disabilities is available from:

- ■ National Business and Disability Council, 201 I.U. Willets Rd., Albertson, NY 11507. Phone: (516) 465-1516. Internet: http://www.business-disability.com

BLIND WORKERS

Information on the free national reference and referral service for the blind can be obtained by contacting:

- ■ National Federation of the Blind, Employment and Rehabilitation,1800 Johnson St., Baltimore, MD 21230. Phone: (410) 659-9314. Internet: http://www.nfb.org

OLDER WORKERS

- ■ Senior Community Service Employment Program (SCSEP), c/o National Council on the Aging, 1901 L St. N.W., 4th Floor, Washington, DC 20036. Phone: (202) 479-1200. Internet: http://www.ncoa.org

- ■ National Caucus and Center on Black Aged, Inc., 1220 L St. N.W., Suite 800, Washington, DC 20005. Phone: (202) 637-8400. Internet: http://www.ncba-aged.org

■ Asociación Nacional pro Personas Mayores (National Association for Hispanic Elderly), 234 East Colorado Blvd., Suite 300, Pasadena, CA 91101. Phone: (626) 564-1988. Internet: http://www.anppm.org

VETERANS

Contact the nearest regional office of the U.S. Department of Labor Veterans' Employment and Training Service or:

■ Veterans' Employment and Training Service (VETS), 200 Constitution Ave. N.W., Room S-1325, Washington, DC 20210. Phone: (202) 693-4701. Internet: http://www.dol.gov/vets/

WOMEN

■ Department of Labor, Women's Bureau, 200 Constitution Ave. N.W., Washington, DC 20210. Phone: 800-827-5335. Internet: http://www.dol.gov/wb/

■ Wider Opportunities for Women, 1001 Connecticut Avenue N.W., Suite 930, Washington, DC 20036. Phone: (202) 464-1596. Internet: http://ww.wowonline.org

Federal laws, executive orders, and selected federal grant programs bar discrimination in employment based on race, color, religion, sex, national origin, age, and disability. Information on how to file a charge of discrimination is available from U.S. Equal Employment Opportunity Commission offices around the country. Their addresses and telephone numbers are listed in telephone directories under U.S. Government, EEOC.

How to Create an Effective Résumé

All information in this appendix has been modified from *Training Manual and Supplements*, Transition Assistance Program, U.S. Department of Labor Veterans' Employment and Training Service, September 2007, available at www.dol.gov.

This discussion offers examples of résumé preparation. The final version of any individual résumé will depend on the job seeker's career plans and choices.

Purpose of a Résumé

- Marketing tool—sells YOU!
- Summarizes how your skills and abilities can contribute to the work of a company or other employer
- Helps you land a job interview
- Serves as an employer screening tool

To write the most effective résumé, you need to determine the career field that interests you and research the following:

- The career field you would like to pursue
- Where the jobs are and who is hiring
- What qualifications and credentials you need to attain
- How best to market your qualifications

Résumé Formats

The four major résumé formats to choose from are:

- Chronological
- Functional
- Combination
- Targeted

CHRONOLOGICAL FORMAT

- Focuses on your work history with most recent position first
- Allows potential employers to follow your career history and career progression easily

Figure C–1 provides a sample *Chronological Résumé*.

Ben Turner
2345 Brook Avenue, Englewood, CO 12345
(123) 456-7890
ben.turner@email.com

OBJECTIVE: Seeking a position as an armed security guard for Pinkerton Services

SUMMARY OF QUALIFICATIONS

Active U.S. government security clearance

Bilingual—fluent in both English and Spanish

Superior performance award for past four years in security management

Able to make difficult decisions in stressful situations

EXPERIENCE

19XX–20XX **Security Specialist** U.S. Marine Corps

Supervised $100 million of highly sensitive equipment—efforts led to zero loss in a 3-year period.

Implemented new system security plan that led to increased lockdown protection for brig personnel.

Provided leadership, instruction, and supervision of 25 personnel—efforts resulted in a 30% decrease in staff turnover and a 10% increase in promotions.

Expertly managed investigative reports—recognized as NCO of the Quarter for efficiency and accuracy of written instructions and documents.

Proven ability to communicate effectively in diverse environments—efficiently managed a diverse workforce and inmate population resulting in a 10% decrease in inmate violence.

19XX–19XX **Warehouse Supervisor** Micro Chemical, Inc., Denver, CO

Supervised a crew of 15 in daily operations, including evaluation and discipline—efforts led to a company-record promotion rate for staff and a 10% decrease in staff turnover.

Monitored complex cataloging and ordering systems, implemented a fast-track procurement system for office supplies resulting in a 20% decrease in supply turn-around.

Helped develop and implement an effective security system—efforts led to $24K savings annually by reducing pilferage and damage.

Proficient at using Windows Vista, Microsoft Office, and PeopleSoft Databases.

19XX–19XX **Security Guard** Mayfield Malls, Denver, CO

Coordinated work assignments, evaluated performance, and disciplined a four-member security team—recognized as "Security Supervisor of the Quarter" for boosting morale and encouraging an innovative and safe working environment.

Investigated security and safety violations and wrote detailed incident reports—led to Mayfield Mall being recognized as the "Safest Shopping Facility in the Mountain States."

Helped diffuse conflicts in a public environment with regard to everyone's safety—consistently recognized through customer feedback for excellent customer relations.

EDUCATION

U.S. Marine Corps Specialized Training: Explosives, Firearms, Leadership, Diversity, Communication
Metro State College 42 Semester Units in Administration of Justice, Denver, CO

FUNCTIONAL FORMAT

- Focuses on your skills and experience. Skills are grouped into functional areas
- Used most often when changing careers or to address employment gaps

Figure C–2 provides a sample *Functional Résumé*.

Ben Turner
2345 Brook Avenue, Englewood, CO 12345
(123) 456-7890
ben.turner@email.com

OBJECTIVE: Seeking a position as an armed security guard for Pinkerton Services

SUMMARY OF QUALIFICATIONS

Active U.S. government security clearance
Bilingual—fluent in both English and Spanish
Superior performance award for past four years in security management
Able to make difficult decisions in stressful situations

EXPERIENCE

Security

- Supervised $100 million of highly sensitive equipment—efforts led to zero loss in a 3-year period.
- Implemented new system security plan that led to increased lockdown protection for brig personnel.
- Monitored restricted personnel in a correctional facility ensuring they remained in detention.

- Helped develop and implement an effective security system—efforts led to $24K savings annually by reducing pilferage and damage.

Investigation

- Investigated security and safety violations and wrote detailed incident reports—led to Mayfield Mall being recognized as the "Safest Shopping Facility in the Mountain States."
- Expertly managed investigative reports—recognized as NCO of the Quarter for efficiency and accuracy of written instructions and documents.

Communication

- Proven ability to communicate effectively in diverse environments—efficiently managed a diverse workforce and inmate population resulting in a 10% decrease in inmate violence.
- Helped diffuse conflicts in a public environment with regard to everyone's safety—consistently recognized through customer feedback for excellent customer relations.
- Proficient at using Windows Vista, Microsoft Office, and PeopleSoft Databases.

Supervision

- Provided leadership, instruction, and supervision of 25 personnel—efforts resulted in a 30% decrease in staff turnover and a 10% increase in promotions.
- Supervised a crew of 15 in daily operations, including evaluation and discipline—efforts led to a company-record promotion rate for staff and a 10% decrease in staff turnover.

EMPLOYMENT HISTORY

Security Specialist U.S. Marine Corps

Warehouse Supervisor Micro Chemical, Inc. Denver, CO

Security Guard Mayfield Malls Denver, CO

EDUCATION

U.S. Marine Corps Specialized Training: Explosives, Firearms, Leadership, Diversity, and Communication

Metro State College 42 Semester units in Administration of Justice, Denver, CO

COMBINATION FORMAT

- Combines the Chronological and Functional Résumé formats
- Highlights skills while providing the chronological work history that some employers prefer

Figure C–3 provides a sample *Combination Résumé*

Ben Turner
2345 Brook Avenue, Englewood, CO 12345
(123) 456-7890
ben.turner@email.com

OBJECTIVE: Seeking a position as an armed security guard for Pinkerton Services

SUMMARY OF QUALIFICATIONS

- Active U.S. government security clearance
- Bilingual—fluent in both English and Spanish
- Superior performance award for past four years in security management
- Able to make difficult decisions in stressful situations

EXPERIENCE

Security

- Supervised $100 million of highly sensitive equipment—efforts led to zero loss in a 3-year period.
- Implemented new system security plan that led to increased lockdown protection for brig personnel.
- Monitored restricted personnel in a correctional facility ensuring they remained in detention.
- Helped develop and implement an effective security system—efforts led to $24K savings annually by reducing pilferage and damage.

Investigation

- Investigated security and safety violations and wrote detailed incident reports—led to Mayfield Mall being recognized as the "Safest Shopping Facility in the Mountain States."
- Expertly managed investigative reports—recognized as NCO of the Quarter for efficiency and accuracy of written instructions and documents.

Communication

- Proven ability to communicate effectively in diverse environments—efficiently managed a diverse workforce and inmate population resulting in a 10% decrease in inmate violence.
- Helped diffuse conflicts in a public environment with regard to everyone's safety—consistently recognized through customer feedback for excellent customer relations.
- Proficient at using Windows Vista, Microsoft Office, and PeopleSoft Databases.

Supervision

- Provided leadership, instruction, and supervision of 25 personnel—efforts resulted in a 30% decrease in staff turnover and a 10% increase in promotions.
- Supervised a crew of 15 in daily operations, including evaluation and discipline—efforts led to a company-record promotion rate for staff and a 10% decrease in staff turnover.

EMPLOYMENT HISTORY

- 19XX–20XX Security Specialist, U.S. Marine Corps
- 19XX–19XX Warehouseman Supervisor, Micro Chemical, Inc., Denver, CO
- 19XX–19XX Security Guard, Mayfield Malls, Denver, CO

EDUCATION

- **U.S. Marine Corps** Specialized Training: Explosives, Firearms, Leadership, Diversity, and Communication
- **Metro State College** 42 Semester units in Administration of Justice Denver, CO

TARGETED FORMAT

- Customized to a specific job

- Written specifically to the employer's needs

The résumé's Objective Statement is important and must refer specifically to the position sought. The résumé will then be directed to the appropriate company personnel.

There are other more specialized résumé formats, but they will not be discussed here.

RÉSUMÉ COMPARISON

One can evaluate the appropriateness of each of the four types of résumé formats by studying the comparison chart in **Figure C–4**.

Only a few of the many aspects of preparing a suitable résumé are discussed here. For more details, major reference sources are:

- The original U.S. Department of Labor document mentioned at the beginning of this appendix.

- The career development centers located in most educational institutions, including high schools, colleges, and universities.

- Public library resources devoted to jobs and careers.

Resume Comparison Chart

Resume Format	Advantages	Disadvantages	Best Used By
Chronological	• Widely used format • Logical flow, easy to read • Showcases growth in skills and responsibility • Easy to prepare	• Emphasizes gaps in employment • Not suitable if you have no work history • Highlights frequent job changes • Emphasizes employment but not skill development • Emphasizes lack of related experience and career changes	• Individuals with steady work record
Functional	• Emphasizes skills rather than employment • Organizes a variety of experience (paid and unpaid work, other activities) • Disguises gaps in work record or a series of short-term jobs	• Viewed with suspicion by employers due to lack of information about specific employers and dates	• Individuals who have developed skills from other than documented employment and who may be changing careers • Individuals with no previous employment • Individuals with gaps in employment • Frequent job changers
Combination	• Highlights most relevant skills and accomplishments • De-emphasizes employment history in less relevant jobs • Combines skills developed in a variety of jobs or other activities • Minimizes drawbacks such as employment gaps and absence of directly related experience	• Confusing if not well organized • De-emphasizes job tasks, responsibilities • Requires more effort and creativity to prepare	• Career changers or those in transition • Individuals reentering the job market after some absence • Individuals who have grown in skills and responsibility • Individuals pursuing the same or similar work as they have had in the past
Targeted (should be used in all resumes)	• Personalized to company/position • Shows research • More impressive to employer • Written specifically to employer's needs	• Time consuming to prepare • Confusing if not well organized • Should be revised for each employer	• Everyone—because any of the other formats can be made into a targeted resume

REFERENCES

Adams JM. Health care becomes city cause: San Francisco plan covers the uninsured. *Chicago Tribune*, September 19, 2007.

AMA Health Policy Group, Division of Socioeconomic Policy Development. *Expanding health insurance: The AMA proposal for reform.* http://www.ama-assn.org/ama/pub /category/7834.html

Barr DA, Lee PR, Benjamin, AE. Health care and health policy in a changing world. In: Wallace HG, Green G, Jaros K, eds. *Health and Welfare for Families in the 21st Century*, 2nd ed. Sudbury, MA: Jones and Bartlett; 2003.

Bernstein AB, Hing E, Moss AJ, Allen KF, Siller AB, Tiggle RB. *Health Care in America: Trends in Utilization.* Hyattsville, MD: National Center for Health Statistics; 2003.

Buerhaus PI, Potter V, Staiger DO, French J, Auerbach DI. *The Future of the Nursing Workforce in the United States: Data, Trends and Implications.* Sudbury, MA: Jones and Bartlett; 2009.

Bureau of Labor Statistics. *Occupational Outlook Handbook 2008–2009.* Washington, DC: U.S. Dept. of Labor; 2007.

Caldwell LB. *Guide to Careers in the Health Professions.* New York: Princeton Review; 2001.

Centers for Disease Control and Prevention and the Merck Company. *The State of Aging and Health in America 2007.* Whitehouse Station, NJ: The Merck Company Foundation; 2007.

Centers for Medicare and Medicaid Services. *Medicare and You 2007.* Baltimore, MD: U.S. Dept. of Health and Human Services, CMS Publication no. 10050. http://www.medicare.gov/

Centers for Policy and Research. *Innovations in Chronic Care. A New Generation of Initiatives to Improve America's Health.* Washington, DC: America's Health Insurance Plans; 2007.

Clark MJ. *Community Health Nursing: Advocacy for Population Health*, 5th ed. Upper Saddle River, NJ: Prentice-Hall, Inc.; 2007.

Cohen RA, Martinez ME. *Health insurance coverage: Early release of estimates from the National Health Interview Survey, January–June 2007*. December 2007. http://www.cdc.gov/nchs/nhis.htm

Committee on Crossing the Quality Chasm: Adaptation to Mental Health and Addictive Disorders. *Improving the Quality of Health Care for Mental and Substance-Abuse Conditions.* Washington, DC: National Academy of Science; 2006.

Committee on Quality of Health Care in America. Institute of Medicine. *Crossing the Quality Chasm: A New Health System for the 21st Century.* Washington, DC: National Academy of Science; 2001.

Damp D. *Health Care Job Explosion: High Growth Health Care Careers and Job Locator,* 4th ed. McKees Rocks, PA: Bookhaven Press, LLC; 2006.

Decker FH, Gruhu P, Matthews-Martin L, Dollard KJ, Ticker AU, Bizette L. 2002 AHCA Survey of Nursing: Staff vacancy and Turnover in Nursing Homes. Washington DC: American Health Care Association; 2003.

DeNavas-Walt C, Proctor B, Smith J. *Income, Poverty, and Health Insurance Coverage in the United States: 2006.* Washington, DC: U.S. Census Bureau, Current Population Reports; 2007.

Drake KA. *The Medical Transcription Career Handbook.* Upper Saddle River, NJ: Prentice Hall; 1999.

Drucker PF. *Management Challenges for the 21st Century.* New York: Harper Business Collins; 1999.

The Economic Security of Older Women and Men in the United States. Briefing Paper, November 2007. Washington, DC: Institute for Women Policy Research. http://www.iwpr.org/pdf/BPD480.pdf

Favreault MM. Women and Social Security. *Older Americans' Economic Security No. 7,* Washington, DC: The Urban Institute; 2005. http://www.urban.org/

Federal Interagency Forum on Aging-Related Statistics. Health care utilization. In: *Older Americans Update 2006: Key Indicators of Well-Being.* Hyattsville, MD: National Center for Health Statistics; 2006. http://www.agingstats.gov/

Field S. *Career Opportunities in Health Care (Career Opportunities Series),* 3rd ed. New York, Checkmark Books; 2007.

Gauwitz DF, Bayt PT. *Administering Medications: Pharmacology for Health Careers.* New York: McGraw Hill; 2000.

Goldstein D, Groen PJ, Ponkshe S, Wine M. *Medical Informatics 20/20: Quality and Electronic Health Records through Collaboration, Open Solutions, and Innovation.* Sudbury, MA: Jones and Bartlett; 2007.

Harrington C, Estes CL, eds. *Health Care and Reform in the U.S. Health Care Delivery System,* 3rd ed. Sudbury, MA: Jones and Bartlett; 2008.

He W, Sengupta M, Velkoff VA, DeBarros KA. *65+ in the United States: 2005.* Washington, DC: U.S. Census Bureau, Current Population Reports.

Health Care Coalition for the Uninsured. http://www.healthcarefortheininsured.org/. Accessed January 26, 2008.

Health Professions Education Directory, 2000–2002, 27th ed. Chicago: American Medical Association; 2000.

Health, United States, 2006. With Chartbook on Trends in the Health of Americans. Hyattsville, MD: National Center for Health Statistics; 2006.

Health, United States, 2007. With Chartbook on Trends in the Health of Americans. Executive Summary and Highlights 2007-1232. Hyattsville, MD: National Center for Health Statistics; 2007.

Healthy People (http://www.healthypeople.gov/). This is a website created by the U.S. Department of Health and Human Services and is devoted entirely to the health of the nation. It is the source for the serial publication (Healthy People 2000, 2010, and develping 2020).*Healthy People 2000 Final Review.* Hyattsville, MD: National Center for Health Statistics; 2001.

Healthy People 2010. 2nd ed. With Understanding and Improving Health and Objectives for Improving Health. 2 vols. Washington, DC: U.S. Dept. of Health and Human Services; 2000.

Indian Health service (http://www.ihs.gov/). This is a website created by the U.S. Department of Health and Human Services and is devoted entirely to the health of American Indians.

Institute of Medicine. 20/20 Vision: Health in the 21st Century. Washington, DC: National Academy Press; 1996.

Johnson RW, Toohey D, Wiener JM. *Meeting the Long-Term Care Needs of the Baby Boomers: How Changing Families Will Affect Paid Helpers and Institutions.* Washington, DC: The Urban Institute; 2007.

Kaiser Family Foundation. *Women's Health Insurance Coverage. Fact Sheet.* Kaiser Family Foundation; 2007.

Kongstvedt PR. *Essentials of Managed Health Care,* 5th ed. Sudbury, MA: Jones and Bartlett; 2007.

Komisar HL, Thompson LS. *National Spending for Long-Term Care. Fact Sheet.* The Georgetown University Long-Term Care Financing Project Washington, DC: Georgetown University; 2007.

Lee PR, Estes CL. *The Nation's Health,* 7th ed. Sudbury, MA: Jones and Bartlett; 2003.

Longest BB. *Health Policy Making in the United States,* 3rd ed. Chicago: Health Administration Press; 2002.

McCutcheon M, Phillips M. *Exploring Health Careers,* 3rd ed. Clifton Park, NY: Cengage Delmar Learning; 2006.

Milstead JA. *Health Policy and Politics: A Nurse's Guide.* Sudbury, MA: Jones and Bartlett; 2008.

Miniño AM, Heron MP, Smith BL. *Deaths: Preliminary Data for 2004. National Vital Statistics Reports Vol. 54, No.19.* Hyattsville, MD: National Center for Health Statistics; 2006.

Mumford CJ. *The Medical Job Interview: Secrets for Success*, 2nd ed. Malden, MA: Wiley-Blackwell Sciences; 2005.

National Commission for Quality Long-Term Care. *From Isolation to Integration: Recommendations to Improve Quality in Long-Term Care* Washington, DC: National Commission for Quality Long-Term Care, 2007. Final report.

National Health Services Corps (http://nhsc.bhpr.hrsa.gov/). This is a website created by the U.S. Department of Health and Human Services and is devoted entirely to information on professionals, providing health services for the American people.

National Institute on Aging, *Growing Older in America: The Health & Retirement Study*. Bethesda, MD: National Institutes of Health, U.S. Dept. of Health and Human Services; 2007, NIH Publication No. 07-5757.

Physician Supply and Demand: Projections to 2020. Washington, DC: Bureau of Health Professions, Health Resources and Services Administration, U.S. Dept. of Health and Human Services; 2006.

Reagan P, Brookins-Fisher J. *Community Health in the 21st Century*, 2nd ed. San Francisco: Benjamin/Cummings Publishing; 2002.

Robinson K. Trends in health status and health care use among older women. *Aging Trends No. 7*. Hyattsville, MD: National Center for Health Statistics; 2007.

Ryder T. *Health Professionals Abroad: A Directory of Worldwide Opportunities*, 2nd ed. Lawrenceville, NJ: Peterson's: a Nelnet Company; 2000.

Scott RW. *Guide for the New Health Care Professional*. Sudbury, MA: Jones and Bartlett; 2007.

Stone, RI, Weiner JM. *Who will care for us? Addressing Long-Term Care Workforce Crisis*. Washington DC: The Urban Institute; 2001.

Swanson-Anderson LL, Malaski CK. *Occupational Therapy as a Career: An Introduction to the Field and a Structured Method for Observation*. Philadelphia, PA: F. A. Davis; 1999.

The Uninsured: A Primer. Key Facts About Americans Without Health Insurance. Washington DC: The Kaiser Family Foundation; 2007.

Thomson Delmar Learning. *Health Care Career Exploration* (CD-ROM). Clifton Park, NY: CENCAGE Delmar Learning; 2004.

Trends Affecting Hospital and Health Systems: Trendwatch Chartbook 2007. Chicago: American Hospital Association; 2007. http://www.aha.org/aha/trendwatch/chartbook/2007/07 chartbooktoc.ppt

Weiner JA, Freiman MP, Brown D. *Nursing Home Quality. Twenty Years After the Omnibus Budget Reconciliation Act of 1987*. Menlo Park, CA: The Henry J. Kaiser Family Foundation; 2007.

Wischnitzer S. *Health-Care Careers for the 21st century: A Career Guidance Manual, Job Description Overview, and Training Program Directory in One!* Indianapolis, IN: Jist Works; 2000.

Wolfe JR. *The Coming Health Crisis: Who Will Pay for Care for the Aged in the Twenty-First Century?* Chicago, IL: University of Chicago Press; 1993.

Wyman JR. *Safety and the Security Professional: A Guide to Occupational Safety and Health Strategies*. United Kingdom: Butterworth-Heinemann; 2000.

INDEX

Note: Italicized numbers indicate tables or figures.